ROUTLEDGE LIBRARY EDITIONS:
COLD WAR SECURITY STUDIES

Volume 52

SOVIET NATIONALITIES IN STRATEGIC PERSPECTIVE

SOVIET NATIONALITIES IN STRATEGIC PERSPECTIVE

Edited by
S. ENDERS WIMBUSH

LONDON AND NEW YORK

First published in 1985 by Croom Helm Ltd

This edition first published in 2021
by Routledge
2 Park Square, Milton Park, Abingdon, Oxon OX14 4RN

and by Routledge
52 Vanderbilt Avenue, New York, NY 10017

Routledge is an imprint of the Taylor & Francis Group, an informa business

© 1985 S. Enders Wimbush

All rights reserved. No part of this book may be reprinted or reproduced or utilised in any form or by any electronic, mechanical, or other means, now known or hereafter invented, including photocopying and recording, or in any information storage or retrieval system, without permission in writing from the publishers.

Trademark notice: Product or corporate names may be trademarks or registered trademarks, and are used only for identification and explanation without intent to infringe.

British Library Cataloguing in Publication Data
A catalogue record for this book is available from the British Library

ISBN: 978-0-367-56630-2 (Set)
ISBN: 978-1-00-312438-2 (Set) (ebk)
ISBN: 978-0-367-61783-7 (Volume 52) (hbk)
ISBN: 978-1-00-310654-8 (Volume 52) (ebk)

Publisher's Note
The publisher has gone to great lengths to ensure the quality of this reprint but points out that some imperfections in the original copies may be apparent.

Disclaimer
The publisher has made every effort to trace copyright holders and would welcome correspondence from those they have been unable to trace.

SOVIET nationalities in STRATEGIC perspective

Edited by
S. ENDERS WIMBUSH

CROOM HELM
London & Sydney

©1985 S. Enders Wimbush
Croom Helm Ltd, Provident House, Burrell Row,
Beckenham, Kent BR3 1AT

Croom Helm Australia Pty Ltd, Suite 4, 6th Floor,
64-76 Kippax Street, Surry Hills, NSW 2010, Australia

British Library Cataloguing in Publication Data

Soviet nationalities in strategic perspective.
   1. Ethnology—Political aspects—Soviet Union
   I. Wimbush, S. Enders
   947'.004   DK33

ISBN 0-7099-2794-0

Printed and bound in Great Britain

CONTENTS

Acknowledgments	vii
Foreword	ix
Contributors	xix
Introduction: The Ethnic Costs of Empire	xxi
The Spectre and Implications of Internal Nationalist Dissent: Historical and Functional Comparisons *Paul B. Henze*	1
Muslim National Minorities in Revolution and Civil War *Chantal Lemercier-Quelquejay*	36
Soviet Nationalities Under Attack: The World War II Experience *Alexander R. Alexiev*	61
Empire, Nationalities, Borders: Soviet Assets and Liabilities *Daniel C. Matuszewski*	75
Nationality Dynamics in Sino-Soviet Relations *Hans Bräker*	101
Poland and the Soviet West *Roman Solchanyk*	158
Institutional Religion and Nationality in the Soviet Union *Bohdan R. Bociurkiw*	181
Soviet Muslims and the Muslim World *Alexandre Bennigsen*	207
Nationalities in the Soviet Armed Forces *S. Enders Wimbush*	227
Index	249

ACKNOWLEDGMENTS

I wish to thank Nadia Diuk, who, despite many other professional commitments and personal responsibilities, assisted in the preparation of many parts of this volume. I also wish to thank Caroline E. Gray for preparing the manuscripts and for general technical assistance.

FOREWORD

Albert Wohlstetter

The Soviet empire — even more than the Tsarist empire before it — includes, but has not dissolved and absorbed, many diverse nationalities. These persistently distinct nationalities, as disturbances in the empire from time to time continue to suggest, would prefer to be free of Great Russian and Soviet rule. In fact, *Soviet* rule continues to be challenged by some extraordinarily brave *Russian* dissenters. One of them, Vladimir Bukovsky, suggests laconically that there are 275 million political prisoners in the Soviet Union, including perhaps the jailers. For, as George Kennan observed in his 1947 essay on 'The Sources of Soviet Conduct':

> "The 'organs of suppression', in which the Soviet leaders had sought security from rival forces, became in large measure the masters of those whom they were designed to serve."

The 'organs of suppression' have developed so routine an efficiency that they need less frequent and less overtly bloody application. They inspire caution and self-restraint among all but the indomitable few like Sakharov, Solzhenitsyn, and Bukovsky; and, among the chief jailers, succession problems have been made less lethal to the losers.

However, the keepers of Soviet power have, in essentials, disappointed Kennan's hope that, 'in ten or 15 years' after the time of writing, they would either tolerate a steady relaxation of their grip on their subjects, a 'gradual mellowing'; or that the empire would suffer a 'breakup'. If they have wanted the first they have not been able to manage it. They have no desire for the second. As a result, the U.S.S.R. and its satellites have the brittle stability of an explosive mixture in a strong container capped under high pressure.

For two-thirds of a century Soviet rulers have succeeded in containing enormous internal pressures by an unprecedentedly elaborate apparatus of repression designed to make collective dissent unfeasible and individual dissent hopeless. They also feel threatened by the very existence of states outside their boundaries that offer the visible

Foreword

possibility of freedom for their citizens. This threat has nothing to do with any desire on the part of the democracies to intervene in the Soviet Union; or to roll back the boundaries of the Soviet Union; or to give the various nationalities who came under Tsarist and then Soviet control the right to choose their government; or even to roll back the control over territory the Soviets acquired starting with their collaboration with Nazi Germany in 1939. The threat exists in spite of the democracies' recurrent attempts to offer subsidized loans to finance Western investment in the East, to expand East-West trade, and to establish cultural exchanges and other communications with the Communist world. In fact, in a clear sense these attempts by the democracies to foster peaceful exchanges with the Soviets exacerbate the problem the Soviets have in containing the desires of their subject peoples to achieve the freedoms and prosperity available in the democracies.

The West persists in misunderstanding this. The experience of the American sociologist, David Riesman, principal author of the famous work, *The Lonely Crowd*, and a keen observer of the social character of American democracy, illustrates the misunderstanding vividly. Early in the 1950s he related a parable suggesting that the West would do better if, instead of preparing to defend itself by military means that inevitably would seem threatening to the paranoid Russians, it waged a 'Nylon War' against the Warsaw Pact: an all out bombardment of the Soviet Union with nylon hose, packs of cigarettes, yo-yos, wrist watches, and other products of the abundance of the free enterprise system. This show of warmth, the fable suggested, would be much more successful in allaying Soviet fears, reducing tensions, and achieving peace than the blasts of chill wind so characteristic of the Cold War. It was a modern version of the old fable of the victory of the Sun over the Wind in a contest to induce a stubborn man to unbutton and shed his heavy coat.

A decade after this gentle fantasy was proposed, it became obvious that the West had been conducting a nylon war all along; and that the leaders of the Eastern Bloc could not stand exposing their subjects to all that seductive warmth. They buttoned up more tightly. They had no intention of permitting those rays of warmth to continue unobstructed. East Germans, who had had more access to Western consumer goods and technology than other members of the Bloc, nonetheless wanted more. They flocked into West Germany to get not only the products of the free market that were visible just over the border, but freedom itself. To dam this rising tide of emigration, which reached 15,000 a

Foreword

week in August 1961, the Soviets supported the Communist rulers of East Germany in building the infamous Wall. They erected the Wall, of course, not to keep West Berliners from moving permanently to East Berlin, but to limit face-to-face communications of the West with the East and to prevent East Germans from getting out. It clearly violated the Quadripartite Agreement for governing Berlin. It was deplored by many in the West but was challenged by none. Among the many who welcomed the Wall, ironically, was the author of the Nylon War.

In short, the internal problem of keeping in all the subjects who want to get out, or who want to separate themselves from Soviet rule and choose another form of rule in their own homeland, is exacerbated by the fact that people who live in freedom outside the Soviet empire have no desire to come under Soviet rule even if their governments are perfectly willing to coexist with the Soviet Empire. Their very existence with more freedom and prosperity than Soviet subjects constitutes a persistent danger to the Soviet regime.

Westerners tend to see detente as a way of working out a less tense and more durable coexistence between East and West. Soviet leaders see it as a temporary convenience (enabling them, among other things, to benefit from Western technology) without diminishing their desire to make coexistence itself only temporary. In fact, the Soviet leaders see detente as one way of changing the correlation of forces in their favor with the long-term expectation of expanding their control over territory at the expense of the West. In this connection a relative improvement in their military technology figures with a special importance. But they are acutely aware that détente, by multiplying contacts with the West, as it did in Poland in the 1970s, can increase their problems in keeping the lid shut tight on their own empire. And they therefore keep these contacts under strict control. 'Basket III' of the 1975 Helsinki Accords was supposed to open communications between the populations of the East and the West in return for formal recognition of the Soviet Bloc's expanded western frontier. The Bloc never seriously implemented its part of the bargain.

Western leaders, during the detente, hoped that aid and increased communications with the West might lead the Soviets to soften the harshness of their rule, and incidentally lead the Poles and other dissident ethnic groups to reconcile themselves to living in a more 'organic' relationship with the Soviet Union. That term was employed by Dr. Kissinger's aide, Helmut Sonnenfeldt, when he advanced the famous 'Sonnenfeldt Doctrine' to describe a relation involving self-discipline

Foreword

in the satellite populations to replace any explicit threat or use of Soviet force in preserving the relation between ruler and ruled. ('Digested' seems to be the word for the organic process he had in mind.) However the nationalities resist being digested; and it is not easy for Soviet rulers to relax their hold on the many diverse nationalities that make up an already large and increasing minority of their empire. To do so would threaten their total authority over the Great Russians who still make up the majority.

The internal pressures which the elaborate Soviet apparatus keep under tight control in peacetime are more likely to explode in wartime when that apparatus is under strain from dealing with the problem of controlling Soviet soldiers and civilians who are in contact with the external enemies the Soviets may be invading. The prospect of such explosions inside the Soviet Union might deter Soviet expansion. Opponents of a strong defense in the democracies often use that as an argument suggesting that the Soviets are extremely unlikely ever to start a war. They discount any Soviet 'threat' and make their doubts explicit by always using the word 'threat' in quotation marks. In general, however, they are mum on how they would exploit internal dissidence, or whether they would do so at all, if the Soviet Union did start a war. The Soviet leaders are unlikely to be much deterred or distracted by the prospect of wartime dissidence unless they believed that the West is willing and prepared to encourage and support such dissidence as part of its strategy for fighting back.

The record of the democracies in supporting those who want to be free of Communist rule is not reassuring. Six months after Hitler had attacked his partner in the Stalin-Hitler Non-Aggression Pact, Stalin was fighting for his life and desperately needed Western help. Though the British had immediately offered him assistance, he insisted that they also recognize the incorporation into the Soviet Union of the Baltic States, the parts of Finland and Rumania which he had seized in 1940, and the eastern half of Poland he had acquired in 1939 while Hitler was invading the western half. Even though Britain had entered the war as the result of the invasion of Poland, the British Foreign Secretary favored this recognition. Churchill, in August 1941 had joined President Roosevelt in affirming the high-minded principles of the Atlantic Charter: 'the right of all peoples to choose the form of government in which they will live' and more particularly the restoring of 'sovereign rights and self-government ... to those who had been forcibly deprived of them.' He sharply rejected Anthony Eden's suggestion. He reaffirmed the British government's adherence to the

Foreword

principles of the Atlantic Charter and, indicating that he did not regard the Charter simply as a propaganda exercise, he said 'that these principles must become especially active whenever any question of transferring territory is raised':

> We have never recognized the 1941 frontiers of Russia except *de facto*. They were acquired by acts of aggression in shameful collusion with Hitler. The transfer of peoples of the Baltic States to Soviet Russia against their will would be contrary to all the principles for which we are fighting this war and would dishonour our Cause.

Nonetheless, Eden persisted in regarding this concession to Stalin as 'a test of sincerity' of British and American desire to work with the Soviets during and after the war. (Western leaders seem always pathetically eager to prove their sincerity to the Soviets who always apparently only await a sign of Western good faith.) Saddest of all, Churchill himself, two months later in February 1942, was persuaded. He urged Roosevelt to construe the Atlantic Charter broadly enough to permit the Soviets to keep the territory they had acquired in the period of their collaboration with Hitler; and Roosevelt with some reluctance agreed in all essentials.

That was not the end of the West's conceding to the Communist powers their dominance over populations who want to be free of such domination. At the end of World War II the British sent back several million Soviet subjects, who had been forced into labor by the Nazis, or were prisoners of war or refugees. Many were destined for the gulags; some attempted suicide to escape them. The United States again agreed with the British. We did nothing to support the East Berliners when they rebelled in 1953. We may have encouraged the Hungarians before their revolt in 1956, but did nothing to impede the brutal suppression of that rebellion and their attempt to achieve independence and neutrality between the blocs; we lobbied against any action by the United Nations and even abstained from supporting and so killed a motion tabled by Britain, France, Taiwan and Australia to continue the debate on Hungary in the Security Council. We sent no bulldozers to knock down the Wall in 1961.

Today, we hesitate to talk about, or even to think about, taking advantage of internal dissidence in the Soviet Union in wartime even after a million Soviet soldiers may have crossed into NATO territory. We fear that such a response to a Soviet invasion, exploiting and

Foreword

encouraging resistance as we did against the Nazis during World War II, would be misinterpreted, or, if that is not too far-fetched given the West's ignominious history, at the least misrepresented as a plan to roll back Soviet rule in time of peace. Yet such resistance might be of critical strategic importance during a war — as the French Resistance was in holding down German reinforcements at the time of the Allied landings in Normandy. We may be sure that the Soviet disinformation agencies would misrepresent any Western thinking on this subject in just the way we fear. But Soviet disinformation might be redundant. Liberal opinion in the democracies is extremely timorous on this subject.

NATO, since the early 1960s, has tended to define 'the defensive' character of the alliance as if, unlike the Western Alliance in World War II, it excluded counter-attacking on the ground. And as if NATO expected to maintain the Sonnenfeldt Doctrine throughout World War III. The Federal Republic, for example, has continued to regard as a cardinal part of NATO policy a 'Forward Defense'. But West German defense ministers since Uwe von Hassel in the early 1960s, have cautiously redefined the word 'forward'. To be sure, they continue to want to avoid falling back, lest they find themselves out of Germany. But they are extremely circumspect about the prospect of *moving* ahead. They stopped using the word *'vorwaerts'*, which is associated with a forward march and talked only of *'vorne verteidegung'* — that is a defense *facing* forward.

Western declaratory policy has for years comprised many paradoxes and revealing absurdities. Political elites in NATO on both sides of the Atlantic are willing to contemplate American (and French and British) threats to annihilate tens or even hundreds of millions of bystanders of many nationalities in the Soviet empire. Yet they find it hard to contemplate responding to a Soviet invasion of Western Europe with a political-military strategy offering dissident subjects of the Soviet empire the freedom to choose their government. Such a strategy would have to be backed by a willingness to counter-attack on the ground. That willingness (not to say concrete contingency planning) seems hardly thinkable today in NATO for fear that the Soviets might get wind of it and distort it. They would describe that entirely reasonable and useful contingent response to a Soviet invasion of the West as if it were a fixed Western plan to conduct an unprovoked invasion of the Soviet Union.

The Soviets exhibit no reciprocal restraint. They are busily engaged in efforts to destabilize the Western democracies and Third World countries wherever they see an opportunity to increase their influence and to advance their ambitions eventually to expand their control over territory. They have stirred up disorder and terrorism, or used spontaneously generated terror and chaos, especially in the unstable countries bordering their southern flank. These countries have a particular strategic interest to both the East and the West.

As Daniel Matuszewski in his chapter in this volume stresses, the geopolitical stakes for the West as well as the East in these countries today exceed the substantial prizes which were the subject of the 'great game' played by the Russians and the British in the 19th century for the control of southwest Asia. Control of oil is now the key additional prize. And oil is not merely a critical wartime material, but, since the beginning of the 1960s, an essential for the peacetime economies of all the major Western powers. Moreover, in spite of the changes in the conditions for supply and demand for oil during the last dozen years — the expansion of alternative energy supplies and especially the more efficient use of energy induced by increased oil prices — oil will continue to be critical to Western economies into the next century. And by the 1990s virtually all remaining low cost oil reserves will be located in the Persian Gulf.

Iran stands in the way of Soviet access to the Persian Gulf. And Turkey, allied with the West and lying on the immediate flank of the optimal Soviet invasion routes to the Gulf, would threaten such a Soviet invasion. It was to be expected, then, that the Soviets would be deeply engaged in manoeuvers to exploit the chaos in Iran; and in the massive assault on the stability of Turkey which had reached the level of nearly one terrorist murder per hour before the military stepped in to restore the elementary conditions of public safety and begin the restoration of a viable democracy. The Soviets have continued to stir up trouble in the strategic provinces of Eastern Turkey; more recently with increasing intensity among the Kurds who live there. They have used Soviet Armenians to increase their support among the Armenian diaspora, and supported the Armenian Secret Army for the Liberation of Armenia (ASALA), which in turn calls for the 'liberation' of the six 'Armenian' provinces in Eastern Turkey and their union with 'free' Armenia — that is, the Armenian S.S.R. ASALA has operated in Western countries all over the world, assassinating Turkish foreign services officers and members of their families. Turkey's Western allies have, for the most part, been extremely lax in pursuing and punishing Armenian terrorists. This has helped drive a wedge between Turkey and its allies and thus served the broader Soviet purpose of weakening the

Foreword

cohesion of the Western defensive alliance.

The Soviets, as several of the authors in this volume indicate, have great resources for using members of their various nationalities all along their borders from the Baltic through central Asia to create a favorable image of the Soviet Union and to weaken the influence of the West. They are particularly skilful in disturbing the tranquility of neighboring countries and ultimately in challenging their ability to defend and govern themselves. They do this during peacetime. If they were to invade NATO, it is even more obvious that they would use every internal division among and within NATO countries to weaken resistance to their aggression. The democracies should focus more attention on the dangers presented by the Soviets' adroit use of ethnic minorities in the West. But they should also consider the wartime opportunities presented to the West by the persistent resistance of these groups to being absorbed by their Soviet rulers.

The Soviet threat to the West has not only grown, it has spread. Their interior lines of communication as a land power, which we've always talked about, used to be largely potential rather than real. Their instruments for movement were always quite limited. But with the growth in recent years of their ability to project power, these lines of communication are now very real. They now have long-range Backfire bombers armed with supersonic air-to-surface missiles, fighters of increasingly extended range and high performance, seven powerful airborne divisions, and a large military airlift capable of transporting them quickly to widely separated points near the Soviet periphery which are critical for the West. They can move their forces much more rapidly to various critical points near their periphery than the United States, which has lost much of its access to airspace and airbases, can now move forces to counter them.

From the standpoint of discouraging Soviet aggression and defending the West, it would be important to convert the advantage of the interior lines of communication, which the Soviets currently enjoy, to the disadvantages they might face, if they invade the West, of having to fight a war on several fronts; and having to be concerned about a potential instability or actual resistance in the rear of each of several of these fronts.

When the Nazis, a most repulsive and racist totalitarian power, invaded the Soviet Union, they made at least a minimal effort, for example by organizing a Georgian Brigade and the like, to get the support of Soviet nationalities yearning to be free of Soviet rule. If the Nazis, who regarded Slavs as subhuman (and other Soviet nationalities as

Foreword

even less than that) succeeded in attracting substantial support, then the democracies, resisting an invasion by a totalitarian power, should be able to do better. At a minimum, they can promise to fulfill, rather than betray, the desire of the populations who want to be free of subjection. That would be an appropriate part of a less apocalyptic strategy than the one that has preoccupied the West for the last twenty years. Such a promise could be a more powerful deterrent to Soviet aggression than empty threats to kill innocent Soviet bystanders in tens or hundreds of millions while at the same time assuring the destruction of the West.

In the development of such a realistic political and military strategy, this fascinating and authoritative book will be a rich resource.

CONTRIBUTORS

ALEXANDER R. ALEXIEV is a Senior Researcher in the Political Science Department of the Rand Corporation, Santa Monica, California.

ALEXANDRE BENNIGSEN is Professor Emeritus at the École des Hautes Études en Sciences Sociales, Paris.

BOHDAN R. BOCIURKIW is Professor of Political Science at Carleton University, Ottawa.

HANS BRÄKER is Deputy Director of the Bundesinstitut für Ostwissenschaftliche und internationale Studien, Cologne, and Professor of International Politics at the University of Trier.

PAUL B. HENZE is Vice President of Foreign Area Research, Inc., and a consultant to the Rand Corporation, Washington, D.C.

CHANTAL LEMERCIER-QUELQUEJAY is Maitre Assistant at the École des Hautes Études en Sciences Sociales, Paris.

DANIEL C. MATUSZEWSKI is Deputy Director of International Research and Exchanges Board, New York.

ROMAN SOLCHANYK is a Senior Research Analyst at Radio Liberty, Munich.

S. ENDERS WIMBUSH is Director of the Society for Central Asian Studies at Oxford, England, and President of Foreign Area Research, Inc.

ALBERT WOHLSTETTER is Director of Research of Pan Heuristics and President of the European American Institute for Security Research.

INTRODUCTION: The Ethnic Costs of Empire

S. Enders Wimbush

A common theme pervades the essays in this collection: The nationality problem in the USSR is one of and perhaps the most important long-term problem the Soviet leadership must resolve if it is to maintain the stability and continuity of its far-flung empire. Nationality issues affect and occasionally dominate many of the critical domestic and foreign policy questions all Soviet leaders have had to face in the past and will continue to face in the future. Nationality dynamics within the Soviet Union itself are accelerating, making this a more urgent consideration for both Soviet leaders and Western observers than it was only a decade ago. Moreover, nationality trends in the empire's immediate periphery have conduced to make the relationship between Soviet domestic nationality concerns and Soviet foreign policy clearer. In short, the Soviet nationality problem both affects and is affected by its strategic environment. This small volume is a tentative and admittedly incomplete attempt to examine this environment and the forces at work within it. It is hoped that, in addition to providing timely information and analysis to those who have begun to think about the issues herein for the first time or who are rekindling a rather more longstanding interest, these essays will heighten public awareness generally of how multi-nationalism in the Soviet Union contributes to the cost of empire, as well as stimulate professional discussion and debate on these and the larger spectrum of related issues.

The Soviet Union is an empire in the classical sense that it covers a territory of considerable extent embracing a vast diversity of ethnically dissimilar peoples who are ruled by a single sovereign authority, Russia. In this case, imperial rule is channelled through a unique political control mechanism, the Communist Party of the Soviet Union. Soviet authorities reject the charge that theirs is an 'empire', claiming instead that the non-Russian peoples of the USSR came together with the Russians by mutual agreement and that all now constitute a 'federation'. Of course, historical facts make nonsense of these claims, as Soviet scholars know better than most. In any event, the claims lose much of their meaning in the face of the total control of all regions of the USSR by the Communist Party, which is a Russian creation and which continues to exercise its prerogatives as a result of the Russian-dominated security apparati and military forces that give the Party its power and authority. It stretches even the most liberal interpretation of political science theory to suggest that the Soviet multi-ethnic state is held together by some form of recognizable political concensus, that the Soviet people are not ruled but rather share in the act of governing. While it certainly is the case that in the Russian and non-Russian regions alike local questions routinely are addressed and acted upon locally, the right of the Communist Party to intervene whenever and however Russian authorities choose is absolute, and those individuals and groups brash enough to challenge this ultimate authority do so at considerable personal or corporate risk. Non-Russian nations which seek to leave the Soviet state are guilty of a counter-revolutionary act, as Lenin himself made explicit, despite the lip-service paid to the minorities' right to secede and past constitutional guarantees to this effect. Any consideration of the Soviet nationality issue logically should start from this point: Soviet non-Russians and their territories are integral parts of perhaps the most tightly controlled empire the world has known. Their importance to the physical and ideological integrity of the Soviet state is, in Soviet eyes, a given.

The ethnic diversity of the Soviet empire is indeed enormous. The 1979 Soviet census listed 104 distinct nationalities of whom twenty-two are 'foreign', such as Germans, Poles, Koreans, and Greeks: that is, ethnic groups whose nominal national homeland is beyond Soviet borders. Fifty other nationalities with vernacular or written languages mostly belonging to the Christian Orthodox tradition have no or a very weak cultural background of their own; it is unlikely that these will be able to resist assimilation by Russians over the long-term. Finally, there are twenty-four Muslim nations, Armenians, Georgians, and Balts (Lithuanians, Latvians, and Estonians), who can be described as 'historical nations' with traditions, cultures, and religions of their own. It would be difficult for the Russians to assimilate these nations under any conditions. Ukrainians and Jews, who fall midway between the last two categories, have had a mixed experience resisting Russification.

All multi-ethnic states are subject to divisive tensions and strains that are the natural consequence of the interaction of peoples of diverse backgrounds within a definite territory and political system. The Soviet Union, despite the claims of its leaders to have largely

Introduction: The Ethnic Costs of Empire

overcome these inherent problems through liberal applications of scientific Leninism, cannot escape comparison with the experience of other multi-ethnic states. Within this broader comparative context, the authors of these essays seek to assess the assets and liabilities that accrue to the Soviet state as a result of its multi-ethnic character. While most of the contributors explicitly or implicitly argue that liabilities currently appear to outweigh assets and that this trend is accelerating, one would be negligent to ignore that multi-nationalism gives the Soviet Union unique strategic and tactical opportunities that more ethnically homogeneous states frequently lack. For example, as Alexandre Bennigsen notes in his chapter on 'Soviet Muslims and the Muslim World', Soviet objectives and diplomacy in the Muslim world at times have been advanced in various ways by the timely, controlled involvement of the USSR's own Muslim representatives. Daniel C. Matuszewski, prefacing his discussion of cross-border ethnic dynamics, wisely cautions that while there are many ethnically divisive trends visible in domestic Soviet policy and practice and as a result of heightened pressure from abroad, Soviet authorities have nonetheless been fairly successful at coopting some non-Russian elites to play critical roles on behalf of the larger Soviet state. And it is undeniable, as Matuszewski points out, that many non-Russians now have an economic, political, or social stake in the existing Soviet system: commitments that at face value suggest that Russian efforts to subdue nationalist dissent and to excise the more extreme anti-Russian feelings from the historical memory, if not of entire national groups at least of pivotal individuals among them, have been moderately fruitful. However, it is clear from the frequent Soviet media campaigns against nationalism within the Soviet Union, by the continuous propaganda whose aim is the deracination of historical, largely ethnic identities of Soviet nationalities in favour of a non-national 'new Soviet-man', by the stringent measures adopted by Soviet authorities to limit minority access to information or contacts that might throw Soviet official explanations and claims about the nature of the Soviet multi-ethnic policy in doubt, and by the tactical positioning of Russians as control and regulatory agents — such as KGB heads and Communist Party second secretaries — in most of the Union republics, that Soviet leaders are themselves less than confident about the extent and effect of native cooptation. Their skepticism is probably well justified, for if the recent history of national independence initiatives elsewhere in the world indicates anything it is this: that those who play by the rules of the game do not necessarily accept those rules as permanent or inviolable. "Abstract gratitude for political power and economic improvements is a short-lived emotion among former colonial peoples", observes Paul B. Henze. "Nothing we know about the non-Russian peoples of the Soviet Empire provides any basis for believing their reactions are different from those of the rest of mankind."

Henze examines the question of identity formation among Soviet nationalities and the way the Soviet communist authorities have attempted to guide and channel it. Comparing Soviet attempts to similar ethnic processes in the United States and the Ottoman Empire, he notes the stark differences between those policies and practices which have proved so successful at promoting ethnic integration in the US and those in use in the USSR, many of which appear to be promoting not integration but its opposite.

All political systems require outlets and channels for accommodating and dissipating dissent. Multi-ethnic states everywhere require special mechanisms for this task, due to the formidable mobilizing power and emotional appeal of nationalism. Where national identity merges or overlaps with religious identity, as it does among many Soviet peoples, organised religious practice can serve as a safety valve for social pressures and strains that might otherwise be expressed as nationalism. Thus it is seemingly paradoxical that organised religion in the Soviet Union not only is condemned for ideological reasons but is openly persecuted as a potential political danger as well. Bohdan Bociurkiw examines the unique inter-relationship between religion and nationality in the USSR and its implications for Soviet policy.

Does the scarcity of ethnic safety valves in the Soviet Union mean that the Ukrainians (or Uzbeks, or any other minority nationality) will revolt? This question, unfortunately, has enjoyed too much popularity among many who are interested in the long-term strategic viability of the Soviet state. The answer is: Yes, they will ... and ... No, they won't. They certainly will under some conditions, such as those which preceded the German invasion of the Ukraine in World War II, which became specifically meaningful in the context of opportunities for political action the invasion offered, as Alexander R. Alexiev points out in his chapter, 'Soviet Nationalities Under Attack'. Similarly, there is abundant evidence that revolts among Soviet Muslims were widespread in Central Asia and the Caucasus during the 1918-1945 period, events that are analysed by Chantal Lemercier-Quelquejay. But there have been many occasions when one might have expected revolts that did not occur. The problem with the "Will they revolt?" question is that it is almost impossible to study, and because of the complex and unique interaction of factors and events that stimulate revolts in each case

Introduction: The Ethnic Costs of Empire

prediction becomes simple guesswork. Under conditions similar to the German invasion Ukrainians might again revolt; then again, they might not. On the other hand, they might revolt for reasons that seem considerably less urgent than the opportunities offered by Russian weakness in war — food shortages, or the destruction of a cherished national monument, for example. The threshold at which both incentives and opportunities to revolt can be found and the amount of pure, perhaps irrational spontaneity that goes into it, except in the most obvious instances, is usually ambiguous and very seldom susceptible to 'scientific' analysis. In short, neither we nor the Soviets, who presumably have more information about the psychology of their colonial peoples than Western analysts, are apt to be able to predict the timing of ethnic unrest or understand the constellation of real and imaginery forces that touch it off.

This is not to say that the USSR will not burst apart at its ethnic seams someday (or slowly implode) or that we should pay no attention to this possibility. Indeed, Soviet authorities indicate clearly by their choice of particular policies that they are aware of the possibility of serious ethnic unrest. As I attempt to explain in my chapter, 'Nationalities in the Soviet Armed Forces', for example, stationing patterns for non-Russian troops are such as to ensure that most of them serve nowhere near their own ethnic territories, where they might be able to lend armed support to any local uprising; and internal security troops, whose responsibility it is to manage local disruptions of all kinds, including ethnic disturbances, routinely are composed of troops who are foreign, often hostile, to the peoples of the regions in which they are billeted. Like the Soviet leadership, we should be alert to the possibility of unchecked ethnic unrest in the USSR and examine its local and regional implications. Multi-ethnicity is an ongoing cost of empire, and for the political accountant ethnic unrest is an inflated cost at any given time.

Another ethnic cost of empire is the potential deterrent effect on political and military opportunities caused by borders which split ethnic groups between the USSR and an adjoining state or, in some cases, among several states. Matuszewski demonstrates that this is a problem along the entirety of Soviet land borders from Central Asia to the Baltic. For example, Soviet reluctance to become militarily involved in Poland may have a lot to do with the Soviet perception of the political spillover and nationalist contagion such an involvement could cause in the Soviet Baltic and Ukrainian regions; Roman Solchanyk describes the potential for spillover from Poland in his chapter.

S. Enders Wimbush

During the Russian Empire and throughout the Soviet period the volatile North Caucasians have served as a brake on Russian designs on Turkey and Iran (see the chapter by Lemercier-Quelquejay). Hans Bräker recounts the Soviet manipulation of shared border nationalities in the Sino-Soviet conflict, noting that at least in this case the fact of shared minorities has until recently provided the Soviets with a unique offensive capability to meddle in the domestic politics of the People's Republic of China. While this possibility does exist, the Soviets have been reluctant to use it systematically. In fact, Soviet policy on its southern flank since the early 1920s is characterised by its avoidance of contact between Soviet borderland minorities and those of similar ethnic and religious backgrounds on the other side. Recently it has been argued widely in the popular press that the Soviet invasion of Afghanistan in December 1979 was intended to eliminate the real and potential infection to Soviet Central Asians from militant Afghan Muslims. There is very little evidence to substantiate this claim, however. Indeed, on the face of it, it is contradictory. The invasion and its after effects appear to have fed the infection in Soviet Central Asia, as might have been expected, not eliminated it. The Soviet invasion of Afghanistan was probably undertaken for other strategic reasons and opportunities associated with the collapse of the Shah in Iran and the resulting American weakness in the region generally.

Several authors draw our attention to rapid demographic shifts which could give rise to a variety of new ethnic costs of empire. Russians long ago lost their demographic dynamism; Soviet Asian peoples, especially Soviet Muslims, have just discovered theirs. Between the last two censuses, for example, Soviet Muslim nationalities managed collectively an impressive annual increase of nearly 2.5 percent compared to less than one percent for the USSR as a whole and only 0.7 percent for Russians. Turkic Uzbeks and Iranian Tajiks showed the greatest vitality with annual increases of 3.43 percent and 3.45 percent respectively. During the 1970-1979 period, the annual growth of the Muslim peoples climbed to 2.74 times the national growth rate compared to only 2.4 times the national growth rate in the last intercensal period (1959-1970). Other Soviet minorities are less dynamic in this regard, the Balts in fact registering the lowest growth rates in the entire empire.

We can already see some of the costs that result from this change, in the military for example. Others, such as heightened regional competition for scarce investment resources, will probably become more evident over time. Of course large empires have in the past been directed

Introduction: The Ethnic Costs of Empire

by peoples who themselves did not constitute a majority in them. Russians now probably make up less than fifty percent of the Soviet population, but it will be a long time before any single other nationality or logical combination of several is numerically strong enough to challenge Russia's dominant position. Still, demographic change of this rapidity in the Soviet Muslim regions — which has created a combined Muslim nationality population of about 50 million today and which could reach 60-80 million by the year 2000 — must be a real concern to the Soviet leadership, especially in light of the tumultuous events in the larger Muslim world just across the Soviet border.

One could easily slide into believing that the costs of empire that result from Soviet multi-nationalism are borne *in abstracto* by the Communist Party. To be sure, the multi-ethnic empire offers Soviet leaders some minor political assets while simultaneously saddling them with some serious political liabilities. But the costs of empire as they are understood here are in fact borne by people, and no people in the USSR is more likely to see itself as the bearer of the major proportion of these costs than the Russians themselves. The Russians, too, are part of the nationality spectrum of the Soviet state, indeed the largest nationality of all, and no treatment of the ethnic costs of empire could be complete without an assessment of the real and perceived cost to the Russian nation. In recent years, Russian nationalism has been the subject of several books and many articles in the West, which is why it is not treated in depth in this short study. Russian nationalism today has many strains, ranging from what one might describe as 'liberal nationalism' to outright racism. Importantly, nearly all Russian nationalists address the costs of an enormous multi-ethnic empire to the Russian nation. Some argue for a genuine confederation of equal peoples, some for letting the minorities go altogether while consolidating the historic Slavic lands into a new political and spiritual entity, and still others for whipping the minorities into line through sheer brute strength and exploiting their economies and their resources for the benefit of Mother Russia. In this sense, Russian nationalism is itself a cost of empire; its *raison d'être* is derived in no small measure from real or imagined ethnic costs elsewhere.

The Soviet communist leadership has shown great flexibility in the past in harnessing Russian nationalism for its own causes and it may be able to do so again if the moment is propitious and the need great enough; alternatively it may be able to suppress Russian nationalism indefinitely, although this is a remote possibility. Is Russian nationalism the cost of empire for which the Communist Party has only limited ideological collateral, which, ultimately, will bring the Soviet empire down? "Only a foolhardy historian could rate this empire as a strong

S. Enders Wimbush

prospect for survival into the 21st century without basic change", writes Henze. "Is it too late for change from above without disruptive consequences?" The recent rapid succession of one feeble old man after another — Brezhnev, Andropov, Chernenko — to lead the Communist Party of the Soviet Union and, hence, the Soviet state inspires little confidence in the likelihood of 'change from above'. Therefore, we should not be surprised to see the ethnic costs of empire accumulate and even rise.

THE SPECTRE AND IMPLICATIONS OF INTERNAL NATIONALIST DISSENT:
Historical and Functional Comparisons

Paul B. Henze

The Soviet Union is a special kind of multi-ethnic state. To gain some measure of the unique problems its multi-ethnic character poses for it, it will be instructive to compare the Soviet Union to two other large, complex states encompassing a broad variety of nationalities: the United States and the Ottoman Empire. The fact that the United States, like the Soviet Union, is still very much alive and evolving while the Ottoman Empire has passed irretrievably into history does not undermine the validity of the comparisons. For most of their history, the Ottoman and Russian empires were rivals and often enemies. There is some parallelism in their history. Both suffered degradation and collapse, but the Russian Empire, at the very moment when it seemed to be falling apart, was reconstituted and restored as the Soviet Union while only the core of the Ottoman Empire survived to become a conventional national state.

The Soviet Union was long alleged to be a new and different kind of political entity — neither a continuation of the Russian Empire nor, indeed, an empire at all, but a higher order of polity than had previously evolved in the world, the natural result of the working of the laws of scientific socialism as elucidated by Marx and Lenin. This claim has long been dismissed as a self-serving myth in the world at large. In the Soviet Union itself the myth has lost most of its original vitality, but it continues to receive lip service and is exploited by different elements in the population for their own purposes.

Americans do not look upon their state as multi-ethnic, though there can be no question about the multi-ethnic character of American society. The American tradition regards government as a sub-element of society which need not — and should not — concern itself with the full range of interactions which national existence generates. The concept of minimalist government has eroded, especially in the 20th century, as the scope of governmental impact on American life has rapidly broadened, but the idea of government as arbiter of all social or economic issues, or as the instrument for establishing the norms by

Paul B. Henze

which the society gauges its own performance, arouses deep antagonism in the American *psyche* and leads to periodic surges of effort to reduce the size and scope of the central government, such as we are experiencing in the 1980's.

Pervasive governmental intervention in society was widely accepted as the natural order of things in the Russian Empire. From its inception, this notion was even more consciously and firmly built into the Soviet system. Forms of passive dissent that were tolerated by the tsars have been unacceptable to Soviet leaders.

Confronting some of the same challenges the Russian Empire faced, the Ottoman Empire often found different ways of dealing with them. In the end it can be said to have been less successful, because it lost its capacity to survive or regenerate itself. This may have had less to do with basic political dynamism than with economic momentum and the role of leaders at crucial junctures.

Interesting as these questions are, I will not attempt to explore them deeply in this essay. Here I wish to concentrate comparisons on differing attitudes toward ethnicity, the way in which these are reflected in state structure and governmental processes and the implications of these attitudes and practices for the evolution of society. Let us begin by examining the United States from this perspective.

The Melting Pot

The United States is still commonly called an Anglo-Saxon country. In terms of governmental derivation, language and culture such a designation is not incorrect, though evolution over 200 years of independent American history has been toward continuous dilution of the Anglo-Saxon heritage. Even at the time of the founding of the republic, though predominant, it was by no means universal. Other ethnic strains — both in terms of blood and culture — were important from the beginning: Dutch, German, French, African, even American Indian. From its earliest years the United States was organized on the melting pot principle, though the concept was not consciously articulated until well into the 19th century.

As new territories were added, more inhabitants of Spanish, French and Indian origin were added. More Germans and Scandinavians and Irish came. Southern and Eastern Europeans began to pour in as the country entered its second century and soon sizable groups of more distant and different ethnic origin joined the stream: Chinese, Japanese,

The Spectre and Implications of Internal Nationalist Dissent

Greeks, Armenians, Russian Jews, Ukrainians, Arabs. Religious distinctions sometimes outweighed linguistic and ethnic factors as criteria for group identification. Pragmatism rather than theory or dogma was the key to absorption of this enormous immigrant flow. People were free to cling to old ways, original languages, distinctive foods, dress, morals and habits if they wished, but there was never serious doubt about assimilation to the predominant features of American culture as the norm and goal: English as the national language, common observance of democratic laws and pluralistic principles in economic and social life.

American society was always open and with little social stratification, no inherited status and great economic and geographic mobility. No serious consideration was given in the United States to setting up separate territories for different ethnic or religious groups, though in both urban and rural areas people sometimes gathered into tight and occasionally exclusive territorial enclaves. No comprehensive legal recognition of corporate separateness on ethnic or religious grounds — analogous to the Ottoman *millet* system — took root in America, though all new ethnic groups were free to organize for cultural, religious, limited economic and even political-pressure purposes in the framework of the principles of pluralism that applied to everyone in American society. Since the United States offered space and economic opportunities for all, exclusiveness seldom led to controversy of serious dimensions or persisted beyond a generation or two. With the growth of new generations the natural tendency was toward adjustment and assimilation. Religion has often remained — stronger among some groups than others — as the longest-surviving badge of ethnic identification. During the mid- to late-20th century, absorption of large groups of often exotic new arrivals into American society — Koreans, Filipinos, Indians from Asia, Cubans, Vietnamese and ever more varied kinds of Africans and Latin Americans — has proceeded with astonishing smoothness and rapidity. The same principles that developed in the 19th century have continued to operate.[1]

The only large groups in respect to which there have been some deviations from the American historical norm are 'Blacks' and 'Hispanics'. While these are easy to describe in a general sense, in specific situations definitions of who is Black or Hispanic have been flexible, sometimes controversial and have often reflected a good deal of political expediency. Both political opportunism and idealism as well as several kinds of humanitarian impulse have generated 'affirmative action' to benefit these groups and resulted in an incipient tendency toward granting them separate corporate status in the U.S. population. Efforts to give their languages — Spanish and 'Black English' — special recognition go against the mainstream of American political and social evolution as well as constitutional tradition. The pendulum has already begun to swing back on these issues.[2] It is doubtful that any principle of legalization of permanent minority language rights, let alone recognition of ethnic groups as corporate entities distinct from the rest of the population, can survive determined legal challenge. There has always been a strong undercurrent of feeling among Americans that their government should not attempt to engineer such matters. The momentum of American social and economic development is almost certain to continue to ensure primacy of English as the national language and the principle of equality before the law for all citizens.

On the other hand, interest in ethnic food and fashions, and preoccupation with cultural and historical origins — 'roots' — have grown steadily as affluence has spread, but none of these phenomena appears to be leading to fragmentation of American society or producing hardened ethnic attitudes. Quite the opposite. In all the large and more basic features of American life the trends continue toward assimilation and adaptation to the mainstream, for Alaskan Eskimos as well as for descendents of the English colonists who arrived on the Mayflower. These processes are occurring at a much more rapid rate in the late 20th century than they did in the 19th. Exposure to media, especially television, speeds up language learning. American society has always been highly mobile, but both geographic and social mobility have increased in recent decades.

Institutions such as the military services have always played a major role — now greater than ever — in 'processing' both immigrant and native-born minorities into the mainstream of American life. The general thrust of the American educational system has always been in this same direction. Nevertheless, the prime factor which has worked against the development of social or political ethnic particularism and prevented ethnic tensions from becoming a disruptive factor in American life has been the economic dynamism of the country. A continually expanding economy providing more goods and services for everyone and a never-ending variety of new opportunities for individual enterprise and initiative creates an atmosphere where ethnic affiliations, as such, are more often than not automatically perceived as illogical as organizing principles in society or government. Grievances that take ethnic form are mitigated by flexible economic and political processes. It will be important to keep these observations in mind when we examine how the Soviet system is working.

The Spectre and Implications of Internal Nationalist Dissent

Ethnic preoccupations — even tendencies toward renewal of ethnic values and cohesiveness — tend, therefore, to operate constructively in American life. There is no reason to believe that the future is going to bring radical discontinuities. Hispanics may well replace Blacks as the largest officially identified minority, but Cubans and Mexicans are unlikely to produce permanent enclaves in American society which will function on a radically different basis from the mainstream. Puerto Ricans and southwestern Hispanics have not. The Asian element in the American population may expand as rapidly as the Hispanic, but among these immigrants too the dominant momentum is in the direction of adaptation and assimilation, not separation.

At most levels of American life the trend toward greater ethnic intermixing is becoming more pronounced. Homogeneity in the armed forces, fair employment practices in government and industry, fair housing laws are producing amalgamations of people in workplaces, institutions and neighbourhoods who represent not only what are conventionally considered different ethnic groups, but different 'races' (whatever that term may really mean): Orientals, South Asians, Africans, Near Eastern peoples and 'Hispanics' whose ancestors are more likely to have lived in pre-Columbian America than in Spain. In a single ride on the Washington Metro any evening of the week, one is likely to encounter faces that would be common in Bangkok, Karachi, Kabul or Qom, as well as others characteristic of the Mayan highlands of Guatemala or the Ethiopian plateau. All these people are, or are becoming, Americans. They and the society are both gaining as a result.

'Interracial' marriages have been increasing for decades and are no longer predominantly the result of soldiers bringing warbrides from Korea or Vietnam. Already there are millions of Americans whose ancestry is so 'racially' mixed that it is impossible to classify them in conventional terms. A majority of American Blacks are 1/4 to 7/8 White — during most of American history it was customary to set the boundary for being Black far over on the White side of the spectrum; more recently it has sometimes been expedient to do so. But the distinctions are all, in fact, losing importance. It is possible to envision an American society by the end of the 21st century in which concern about 'racial' criteria for distinguishing people may have lost most of its meaning.

Let us apply Russian terminology to the American ethnic situation. *Sblizhenie* and *sliianie* are words which have played an important role in discussion of ethnic issues in the USSR. *Sblizhenie* means, literally, 'coming closer' and it has been used to describe the concept of

5

nationalities living closer together, losing some of their distinctiveness and sense of separateness. In respect to language, it has meant taking more Russian terms into non-Russian languages. *Sliianie* carries the process much farther. It means, literally, 'flowing together', i.e. merging. There have been periods when the goal was said to be for the various Soviet peoples, through geographic intermingling as well as intermarriage, to merge into a single new people — to create 'Soviet Man'.

Sliianie in language was difficult to envision — a process whereby languages merged together and lost their individual character. Not even the most diligent Soviet ideologues were able to demonstrate how this process could really add up to anything more than the replacement of non-Russian languages by Russian.

We hear little about *sliianie* these days. Discussion of the subject generated antagonism. In fact, and for a considerable period of time, as latest census returns confirm, trends in the USSR, as I will discuss below, have been in the opposite direction from merging of nationalities or languages. They have even in some degree been away from *sblizhenie*. Soviet nationalities are living farther apart, not closer together.

If we apply these terms to the United States we get a very different picture. *Sblizhenie*, as far as ethnic considerations go, has always been the predominant characteristic of American society. French and Dutch colonists, after the colonial wars were over, lived side by side with Anglo-Saxon colonists. Germans and Swedes and Spaniards fit smoothly into American life. *Sliianie*, in fact, set in early among north and west European ethnic groups in America. No one saw anything unusual in the early 19th century in marriage between people of German and English, or French and Scottish background. Religion was more often a factor than nationality. In the 20th century the process broadened. Marriage between Poles and Italians, Irish, Spanish and French became common. In the generations since World War II all these trends have accelerated.[3] *Sliianie* has become characteristic of American society. In the realm of language *sliianie*, in the sense that the proponents of Russification would like to see it develop in the USSR, has always been the predominant trend in the United States — everything merges into English, but English is enriched by adoption of a steady stream of foreign words and concepts, deriving from continually more diverse sources. *Honcho, macho, gyro* have all entered English in the United States.

The Spectre and Implications of Internal Nationalist Dissent

The Russian Empire

It is ironic that approaches to ethnicity that have evolved pragmatically in the United States correspond in several respects to attitudes the Soviet leadership has recently tried to foster in the USSR — but with disappointing results. In fact, the trends, insofar as we can discern them, seem to be in the opposite direction in the Soviet Empire. The nature of the Soviet system has a good deal to do with this lack of success. The system is based on the doctrine that society must be shaped, channeled, directed and controlled by the state. Pragmatism — letting matters run their own course — is not unknown in the USSR, but it is considered irresponsible, illicit. Without pragmatic adjustments, the Soviet economy would not be able to function at all and the society would generate far greater tensions than it does. People adapt and adjust and life goes on, but always under the illusion that it conforms to a body of theory that actually represents a growing obstacle to the functioning of the system.

In respect to ethnic issues, the situation is doubly complex. Soviet nationality theory evolved as a device for justifying continuation of the Russian Empire while reducing the strains and contradictions inherent in a difficult history of nationality relations. The need to apply absolute egalitarian principles was also strongly felt. There have been many unintended consequences. Soviet leadership is now locked into a system that is likely over coming decades to generate more and more ethnic tensions while at the same time it will become increasingly difficult to change.

History predetermined very little in ethnic relations in the United States. North America was essentially an empty landscape into which Europeans expanded. They were in nearly all respects so far in advance of the sparse native peoples they encountered that there could be no serious prospect of survival of some form of native political/territorial structure. The Russians found similar circumstances in Siberia. As a result, the Yamalo-Nenets National District and the Yakut Autonomous Republic have a good deal in common with U.S. Indian reservations.

Most of the areas into which the Russian Empire expanded were different. Many were more thickly populated than Russia itself by peoples on the same or higher levels of development. This was especially true of the Baltic region, of the Ukraine and, it can be argued, of the Crimean and Volga Tatars and some of the Caucasian peoples. By the time the Russians advanced into Central Asia, the once high Muslim civilization of the region had fallen into decline as it had in most of the

Paul B. Henze

rest of the Middle East. As a political movement, the Russian conquest of Central Asia was very much like the British conquest of India or the Sudan.

The Russian Empire did not develop a unitary approach to subject peoples. Well into the 19th century it seemed apparent that a few subject peoples who retained their own governmental and religious hierarchies and ruling classes were better off than sizable portions of the Russian population itself. But on the whole the system of governorates worked against consolidation of ethnic groups as cohesive political entities. In several relatively heavily populated areas, populations were ethnically intermixed. Mixing increased as economic development progressed and cities grew. Lithuanians, Poles, Jews, Germans, Ukrainians and Russians co-existed in cities such as Vilno, Minsk, Lvov, Kiev and Odessa. The same phenomenon occurred in the cities along the Volga and in the Urals and especially in the Transcaucasus, where Armenians and Russians congregated in regional capitals such as Tbilisi and Baku in greater numbers than the Georgians and Azerbaijanis who lived in the surrounding countryside.

In Muslim areas sense of nationality, as such, was much weaker than feeling for co-religionists. Divisions between settled rural populations, nomads and urban artisans, traders and merchants were as important as criteria for identifying 'peoples' as language or sense of nationality, which was lacking.[4] Older tribal memories and allegiances were still alive in Central Asia too when the Russians arrived. So were Muslim religious orders. Finally, small groups of Arabs, Gypsies, Jews, Chinese, Persians and others occupied specialized functional niches in society and the economy, as they often did in the Caucasus. Even with substantial Slavic settlement in the North Caucasus and parts of the Central Asian steppe region, Russians remained a distinct minority in the Caucasian and Central Asian 'colonial' areas of the Russian Empire to its end. In Siberia, under circumstances comparable to those in North America, they became the majority of the population. Both the memory, and in many respects, the reality of these circumstances survived into the Soviet period and have bearing on ethnic relations in the Soviet Empire today.

Imperial rivalry with the Ottoman and Persian empires was an important factor in Russian territorial expansion from the 16th century onward. In addition to the need for military security, trade, a sense of civilizing mission, adventurism and the desire to open up new territory for settlement all played a role. So, occasionally, did missionary spirit — the desire to extend the influence of Orthodox Christianity. Cossacks —

The Spectre and Implications of Internal Nationalist Dissent

semi-outlaws and settlers who were escaping government authority — were the first Russians to penetrate many regions claimed or occupied by non-Russian peoples. In the 19th century, competition with the British for domination of Central Asia — Russian-British rivalry for influence in the entire region from the Black Sea to the Hindu Kush — became the prime motivation of Russian leaders. Strategic thinkers, including some religious personalities, developed theories of a Russian imperial mission in Palestine, the Red Sea and Horn of Africa, the Persian Gulf and Afghanistan. Russians played the Great Game with as keen a sense of high stakes as the British.

But the Russian Empire was less successful than the Ottoman Empire had been in developing a theory of imperialism. Areas conquered as the result of costly and colourful military expeditions to the Caucasus and Central Asia in the 19th century confronted the Russian Empire with problems which at the time seemed no different from those which the British and French faced as a result of conquests, annexations and protectorate arrangements in India, Sudan, North and East Africa. The fact that these conquests were territorially contiguous to Russia has made a great difference in the 20th century both to Russians and the conquered peoples.

Ottomans and Turks

Ottoman experience is relevant for comparison with Russian not only because the two empires were neighbours and rivals but also because Ottoman history, though little studied in the last 60 years, and Turkic relationships, though currently of little interest to modern Turks themselves, could become significant in the future because of the growing importance of the Muslim and predominantly Turkic peoples of the USSR to the ethnic situation there.

The Ottomans were the true heirs to the Byzantine Empire. Territorially they revived and expanded the Anatolia-centered multi-national state beyond the furthest boundaries it had enjoyed at the height of Byzantine power. This was because they adopted the religion of the Arabs — Islam — as their dynamic principle. It proved to be much more efficacious than Christianity had been during the long period of the Crusades and Byzantine decline. Under the Ottomans Islam was a more tolerant religion than it had been under the Arabs during the early centuries of Islamic expansion.

The Ottomans absorbed several streams of Turkic immigrants who came into Asia Minor but they avoided adopting a principle of ethnic exclusiveness. To an extent without parallel in history, the armed forces and the ruling class of the Ottoman Empire were consciously and systematically recruited from subjects who were neither Turks nor Muslims but converted to be Ottoman soldiers and officers. As the centuries passed, the majority of the native population of Asia Minor became Muslims, though forced conversions were rare and large non-Turkish and non-Muslim minorities remained and flourished. In the 19th century hundreds of thousands of refugees from the Russian Empire settled in Anatolia. With time the very word 'Turk' became a synonym for a backward rural type and the language of government and intellectual life lost much of its Turkic content.

Two seemingly conflicting approaches to ethnicity and religion existed side by side in the Ottoman Empire during most of its existence. They did not generate conflict or even seem contradictory until modern concepts of nationalism and religious exclusiveness began to spread in Ottoman society in the 19th century. Large ethno-religious communities which had been established in Ottoman territory long before the Turks came continued to exist — Greeks, Armenians, Albanians, Arabs, Christian Balkan peoples. Greeks and Armenians became favoured partners in administration of the Ottoman state and for long periods of time enjoyed greater economic opportunities than Turks. The *millet* system, which continued to evolve into the 19th century, gave corporate, but not separate territorial, status to these communities, and eventually to many others, based on a combination of ethnic and religious factors.

The Ottoman ruling class never became obsessed with theory but the dynamism of the state was closely linked to military effectiveness. There was an innate drive to expand. The Ottomans conquered Serbia nearly a century before they took Constantinople and came close to capturing Vienna at the end of the 17th century. Though a Polish king stopped them there, during most of their history they were allies of the Poles against the Russians.

Modern nationalist ideas infected most of the non-Turkish peoples of the Ottoman Empire before they took root among the Turks themselves. Christians were affected earlier than Muslims, but Arab nationalism, which first manifested itself as regionalism in Arab-inhabited areas such as the Maghreb and Egypt, began to develop as soon as the Ottoman Empire lost its outward momentum.

The Ottoman state found it difficult to adjust to the consequences of military stalemate and retreat. If the Ottomans had not allied

The Spectre and Implications of Internal Nationalist Dissent

themselves with European rivals of Russia, their empire might have fallen victim to Russian military pressure during the 19th century. The Russians were only narrowly prevented from attaining their age-old goal of possession of Constantinople and the Straits.

In a broad historic sense the Ottoman Empire became the victim of military decline and economic stagnation but it was also weakened by the pragmatism, tolerance, and eventually indolence, of its governing classes. Western missionaries, not always deliberately, encouraged growth of nationalism among Christian peoples, especially Armenians and Christian Arabs. The success of the Greeks in setting up a national state early in the 19th century whetted the appetites of Balkan Christians. The notion that the Ottoman Empire was destined for inevitable collapse became widely accepted but European powers could never decide what, exactly, to do about it except to avert the collapse as long as possible. This, in its essence, was what the 'Eastern Question' was all about. Imperial Russia contributed to destabilization of the Ottoman Empire by encouraging political agitation among subject peoples, especially Serbs, Bulgarians, Romanians and Armenians.

The decay was so far advanced by the time collapse came that it was a wonder that the Turkish heartland was able to reconstitute itself so effectively into a viable nation state. Turks owe their national rebirth to the genius of Mustafa Kemal Ataturk. In spirit Mustafa Kemal was a universalist, a convinced modernizer and admirer of Western civilization — like Lenin. But he was more pragmatic, lacked the dedication to conspiracy and rigid preoccupation with theory that characterized Lenin. The notion of reconstituting the Ottoman Empire had no appeal to him. He regarded it as the antithesis of the national state. Any constituency which might have favoured it became discredited and weakened to the point of ineffectualness.

The notion of a Pan-Turkic empire, on the other hand, appealed to many intellectuals and men of action in Turkey and Turkic areas of the Russian Empire. Enver Pasha went off to Central Asia to try to implement this dream. Ataturk would have nothing to do with it. He regarded Pan-Turkism as a trap which could snare and defeat the very cause it professed to champion. For him the task of building a strong Turkish national state in Anatolia was enough. By doing so he made a more lasting contribution to the Turkic cause than Enver Pasha could ever have done.

Anatolian Turks have emerged in the mid 20th century as an unusually vital people, with a capacity to modernize selectively but solidly and without damaging stresses. Their nationalism is tempered

Paul B. Henze

by an awareness of history largely devoid of emotional indulgence. They remain committed to Islam but not debilitated by it. In all these characteristics they stand above other nationalities in their part of the world. Uzbeks, Azeris, Kazakhs and the other Turks of the Soviet Empire seem to be displaying these qualities in much the same way as the Turks of Anatolia. They are thus likely to constitute one of the great ethnic challenges the Soviet system must face in the decades ahead.

The Empire Restored

The Crimean and Volga Tatars were the first Turkish/Islamic peoples of the Russian Empire to be affected by modern nationalism. From them nationalist ideas spread to others: Azeris and Central Asians. The Muslims of the North Caucasus and Dagestan, among whom the epic struggle led by the heroic Imam Shamil remains a live memory to this day, never completely reconciled themselves to Russian imperial domination, but their mountain fastnesses were both an advantage and a hindrance. Other peoples in the Russian Empire were affected by nationalism before the Muslims: Balts, Poles and Ukrainians. Georgia had not actually been conquered but sought Russian protection as the lesser of several other evils. Its aristocracy became thoroughly Russianized — Europeanized might be a better term, for essentially they became assimilated to the Europeanized Russian aristocracy — while its peasantry remained firmly wedded to the land and to ancient ways. Armenian nationalism developed among more cross-currents: fear of Muslim neighbours and eagerness to accept Russian sponsorship and protection, especially with respect to Armenians living in Ottoman and Persian territory; resentment of Russian political and social backwardness as Western ideas began to take firmer root among Russian Armenians who were affected by advancing modernization among Armenians in Constantinople; influences from Armenian religious communities long established in Jerusalem and Italy.

What is most significant about all this fascinating ferment that developed in Imperial Russia is the fact that the Tsarist government was no more creative than the Ottoman in devising a comprehensive solution for the political problems its multi-national character generated and it was less tolerant. But economic development in some parts of the Russian Empire was more rapid than in the Ottoman. Baku was the oil capital of the world by the beginning of the 20th century. Armenians and Russians benefitted more from this development than Azerbaijanis. Economic development in the Baltic region of the Empire laid the basis for the successful bid for independence which these countries were able to make when the revolution came in 1917. But it was mainly proximity to Europe which enabled them to sustain independence for 20 years. The equally energetic efforts of the three Transcaucasian republics to extricate themselves from the Russian Empire during the period 1918-21 failed. Europe was too far away and there were no states in the region which could serve as a counterweight to resurgent Soviet Russian power.

In the wake of the events of 1917 the Russian Empire came closer to falling apart than it is now fashionable to concede. It was not only a question of ethnic nationalism but of regional fragmentation as well. Soviet historians and ideologues continue to dramatize the military and political actions that had to be fought to establish Soviet power in each of these areas. They give undue weight to foreign intervention and foreign influences on native nationalist leaders. Such influences were present, but they were almost never predominant. Lack of coordination among competing nationalist leaders weakened many movements.

In Central Asia distances were vast, the situation was complicated by the presence of Russian colonists. Local nationalism was affected by many diverse currents. The situation was further compounded by the survival of the Khanate of Bukhara. The challenge for local leadership was far greater than that which Kemal faced in Anatolia where the population rallied to the idea of defending the Turkish homeland against intervention and Greek appetites for territorial expansion catalyzed nationalist resistance. A single enemy was more difficult to identify in Central Asia. No charismatic leader appeared. Other areas were more fortunate in leaders, but most of the men who led struggles for ethnic self-determination in the revolutionary period were ill-equipped to cope with the determined conspiratorial tactics the Bolsheviks employed against them.

Nevertheless, the task the Bolsheviks set for themselves — pulling the Russian Empire back together and rebuilding it as the Soviet Union — was not easy, nor was it quickly accomplished. Substantial concessions and inducements had to be offered to re-establish control and even then resistance to Soviet power continued in parts of Central Asia and the North Caucasus into the 1930's. The restructuring of the empire as a multi-national state with territorial ethnicity as the basic organizational principle, extending down to the regional and local level, was in part a concession to the strength of national feeling that had developed in the

Paul B. Henze

Russian Empire during its final decades. It was a concession that was a partial deception, and recognized as deceptive both by the architects and the beneficiaries of these arrangements. On the other hand, like so much about the Soviet system was claimed to be, it was a 'new and higher form' of deception. A great deal of bureaucratic energy and substantial funds were invested in implementing this territorial structure.

True to the spirit of the Soviet system in most other respects — systematic application of theory to form — republics, 'autonomous' republics, regions and districts were set up, staffed and vested with authority. It was a form of 'affirmative action' expected to remain limited in its consequences. What was originally often highly artificial gradually acquired substance. Eventually almost all aspects of the organization of administrative and social services conformed to the ethnic-based structure: the economy, public security, the judicial and medical systems, education and research. There were exceptions in military and national security matters, however. The Gulag system did not correspond to ethnic divisions, nor did many features of military structure.[5]

No country has ever gone as far as the Soviet Union did during the first decade of its existence in reorganizing itself territorially along ethnic lines, though the Chinese copied most features of the Soviet system in the 1950's — and may regret it today. India took more than 20 years to restructure its state system along partial ethnic lines. The Soviet structure has proven remarkably durable, but, like so many other features of Soviet society, what was originally innovation rapidly became conservative tradition, and change of any substantial sort, because of its potentially destabilizing potential, came to be seen as less desirable than prolongation of the status quo. Already in the 1920's and 1930's the Soviet government allocated impressive resources to development of national languages, to education in them, to creation of ethnic institutions and encouragement of non-political aspects of ethnic culture. Religion was permitted to play almost no role in these efforts and was, in fact, suppressed with varying degrees of severity in all non-Russian areas from the late 1920's. It began to be suppressed with even greater vigour in Russian and other Slavic areas somewhat earlier. The only religious-based territorial entity which has survived to the present in the USSR is one which began as an entirely artificial creation — the Jewish 'autonomous' region of Birobidzhan — a curious and unsuccessful effort to 'solve' the Jewish question in Russia.

Political deviations and revisionism began to plague ethnic-based political entities in the USSR almost as soon as they were formed. The

The Spectre and Implications of Internal Nationalist Dissent

effort to cast all aspects of life in an ethnic mold brought ethnic considerations into areas that would otherwise have remained unaffected by them and gave sinister political implications to relatively harmless manifestations of ethnic assertiveness. Some nationality leaders naively propelled themselves into difficulty by taking Soviet ethnic/political principles at their face value. Others more deliberately sought to exploit openings and weaknesses in the system. Sultan Galiev's effort to develop a genuine Muslim national communism[6] met with early rebuff and suppression. Language and alphabet reform were carried out so as to magnify differences between Turkic peoples and discourage intellectual exchange among them.[7] Central Asia was gerrymandered into ethnic republics designed to minimize the natural unity of the area. In the Transcaucasus the federation of the three republics was dissolved so that each would have to deal separately with Moscow. Whatever the rationalization, it was *divide et impera*. The principle still holds, though there have been adjustments and concessions.

Replacement of local nationality leaders began in some areas in the 1920's and had already gone through several phases by the time the Great Purges of the late 1930's removed practically the entire native political and intellectual elite that had been given positions of authority and influence in nationality republics and regions.

The experience of World War II demonstrated that it was not only among the leaders of these nationalities that the Soviet system had failed to develop loyalty, but among entire populations in areas that came under German occupation or prospect of it. Less than 25 years after the Russian Empire came close to disintegration along ethnic and regional lines at the end of World War I, the same spectre loomed as the USSR was forced into World War II — attacked by Hitler whom Stalin had gone to great lengths to placate. In addition to the affinity totalitarian absolutists sometimes feel for each other, Stalin may have been motivated in his conciliatoriness toward Hitler by realization of the fragility of the ethnic-based structure of the empire over which he ruled. Though shorn of their leadership by the purges of only a few years before, ethnic groups abandoned the Soviet system *en masse*. As retribution, several republics were erased from the map and millions of people were deported into Central Asia and Siberia under brutal conditions.[8] But the principle of territorial organization based on ethnicity survived the war intact. When the punished peoples were permitted to return to their territories in the 1950's, all but two — the Crimean Tatar and Volga German Autonomous Soviet Socialist Republics (ASSRs) — were restored essentially as they had existed before the 1940's.

Paul B. Henze

Growing Numbers, Greater Strength

Now, nearly forty years after the deportations of World War II and almost twenty-five years since the restoration of the majority of these peoples to their original homes, it is difficult to envision circumstances under which similar actions could take place again. Brutality and arbitrariness have been reduced in the Soviet system but this is not the only reason. Populations, especially among Muslim peoples, have increased greatly in size. It is now extremely unlikely that mass deportations could be carried out in secrecy. News now travels much faster inside the Soviet Empire and reaches the outer world quickly. Soviet involvement with the Third World, rivalry with China, status in the UN, all mitigate against mass actions of genocidal character. The problem of ethnic resistance and ethnic dissent in the USSR has acquired different dimensions. The non-Russian nationalities are stronger.

In the Western world much of the debate about the problem revolves around irrelevant considerations. It puts undue stress on developments during World War II or parallels that are inappropriate. Are the nationalities going to rise up against the Russians? Is religious dissent going to manifest itself as it did in Iran? Is religion dead? Are the non-Russians being Russified, absorbed? Poor questions produce poor answers and do not lead to better comprehension of the issues. When journalists who are looking for obvious signs of outward dissidence go to Baku and find none or are confronted by total normality in Tashkent or Alma Ata, they conclude that the non-Russian peoples are happy under the Soviet system, must be strong supporters of it and that all expectations of future problems must be unfounded. Shallow premises for enquiry produce shallow understanding.

By standards of everyday life, the non-Russian peoples of the USSR show few signs of unhappiness that are not also present among the Russians themselves. They suffer from the same problems most Soviet citizens do. In fact, a good case can be made that many non-Russians are better off than many Russians. This is in part true of Balts and Georgians, probably of Armenians as well. It may be true of many Tatars and Uzbeks. There is no reason to expect any of these peoples to revolt soon, or perhaps at all. They may never have to to gain greater control of their own destinies. Revolt is certainly not the issue now. Neither is nationality dissatisfaction in the crude sense.

Minority problems in the USSR cannot be understood without reference to the Russians themselves and to the growing nationalism that is evident among them. We have to look at Soviet society as a

The Spectre and Implications of Internal Nationalist Dissent

complex system that is affected by cross-currents and interactions, operating in different time-frames and at different speeds, conforming less and less to the political and social theories on which the governmental structure has been built and less and less amenable, in different ways, to manipulation by the leadership.

Let us consider several of the trends that have become incontrovertibly evident in the past 25 years. Most of the evidence for them derives from study of Soviet data which, though incomplete, has proven when tested to be reasonably accurate in the aggregate. The most significant single fact about non-Russians in the USSR is that they have increased enormously in numbers. This is especially true of those who least resemble the Russians and other Slavs: the Muslim peoples. While Russian, other Slavic and Baltic birthrates (except among the Lithuanians) have declined markedly over the past two decades and are now at or close to a zero population growth level, Soviet Muslims have continued to reproduce at rates which are among the highest in the world. Deathrates are still falling among these peoples while an enormous percentage of their population is young. This means that even though birthrates have already begun to decline slowly, the total increase in numbers during the next 20 years is going to be high. One out of every six Soviet citizens today is of Muslim origin and culture; by the end of the century, it will be one out of four.

Each year young men available for military service include fewer Russians and more Muslims and other non-Russians. We can be absolutely certain about this trend through the end of the 20th century, for all the young men who will be drafted in the year 2000 are already born — a third of them of Muslim origin; only half the rest are Russian. Were other trends in Soviet society in the direction of ethnic amalgamation, this would be a much less unsettling problem than it is likely to become, especially when one of the likeliest areas for use of Soviet military power is that directly south of its borders.

Religion is far from dead in the Soviet Union. No nationality has turned atheist *en masse*. Catholicism is showing great strength among Lithuanians, who are deeply affected by events in Poland. Their own Orthodox churches remain for Georgians and Armenians an essential part of their national identity. Islam is a way of life as well as a religion. While there is little evidence among Soviet Muslims of the kind of fanaticism that has accompanied the resurgence of Islam in Iran and some Arab countries, there is growing evidence of the dedication of Soviet Muslims to religious values and practices. There is also growing evidence of the resurgence of Islamic brotherhoods and of Islamic folk practices which reflect the strength of religious orders which operate outside the framework of officially tolerated Islam.[9] Islam is an important component of the sense of national identity of all Soviet Muslim peoples.

With the possible exception of some of the non-Muslim Turkic and Finno-Ugric nationalities of the Volga-Ural region and Siberia (where Russification is advancing), national self-awareness is increasing among all non-Slavs in the USSR. There is also good evidence that the sense of ethnic separateness remains strong among Ukrainians, though it has perhaps weakened among Belorussians. Though Estonian and Latvian net reproduction rates have fallen, and their republics are experiencing high Russian immigration, their national self-assertiveness is, if anything, increasing. In spite of mass deportations and acute oppression during the first years after their reincorporation into the Soviet/Russian Empire at the end of World War II, national pride and consciousness of independent historical traditions in the Baltic republics was not reduced. Georgian, Armenian and Azerbaijani sensitivity about their distinctive cultures was demonstrated a few years ago by successful agitation against efforts to downgrade their national languages in the new constitutions of these republics — the offensive clauses were withdrawn.

Russians are not as mobile a people as Americans, though the movement of explorers and settlers eastward across Siberia, into the Far North and eventually into the Asian steppes and on to the borders of China is in many ways comparable to the American westward movement in the 19th century. Not as many people were involved in these movements as in the United States. Great population movements have taken place in the Soviet period, primarily from rural areas to nearby urban centres. Forced movements — deportations — have resulted in large transfers of people not only from the abolished republics at the end of World War II but from among people who were judged to be collaborators and politically unreliable in the Baltic, Ukraine and in central and southern Russia as well as among returnees who came or were sent back from wartime labour service under the Germans. The survival rate among deportees seems to have been higher than originally estimated and many of these people, like the deported minorities, returned to their home areas in the 1950's and 1960's when conditions were eased.

Most non-Russian peoples have tended to remain in their home territories. Armenians, Jews and Germans have been classic exceptions. Among Muslim peoples, Volga Tatars have been the most mobile; their neighbours the Bashkirs much less so. Since their deportation, the Crimean Tatars have also been mobile and continually troublesome.

The Spectre and Implications of Internal Nationalist Dissent

North Caucasian Muslims, Azeris and Central Asians have generally stayed close to home. Georgians have always found their own territory and style of life so satisfactory that they have seldom gone elsewhere.

Until recently the generally sedentary habits of non-Russian peoples made little difference. Russians and Ukrainians moved to most parts of the USSR as settlers, workers in newly developed mines and industries and on large construction projects, and as officials. As Slavic birthrates have continued to decline, however, labour shortages have been developing in most Soviet industrial regions. Labour shortages have always been a chronic problem in Siberia because a large proportion of workers and settlers remain only a few years and then return to their region of origin. Higher wages and other incentives have never been sufficient to fulfill plans for increases in the Siberian population.

Projections of needs for the next two decades highlight serious shortages of labour in developed industrial regions of European Russia. There has been a great deal of debate about how they are to be alleviated. Muslim areas are producing surplus manpower — but Muslims have displayed a continual reluctance to leave their native surroundings for less favourable climatic and living conditions. Their reactions are markedly different from those of Turks, Yugoslavs, Algerians and Moroccans who compete for the opportunity to go to Germany, France and elsewhere in Europe to work — and where millions of them are temporarily settled and may eventually become permanent immigrants. The dynamic industrial societies of Europe offer such people the opportunity to earn much higher wages and experience more modern conditions of life — and eventually to return home with savings that can be invested in homes, farms and businesses. The same factors draw Mexicans and people from the Caribbean to the United States. Even the most industrially developed parts of the Soviet Union do not have this appeal for most non-Russians.

Soviet authorities have not yet made strenuous efforts to recruit Caucasians and Central Asians for labour service in other regions. There is evidence that they fear the social problems that large non-Russian populations could cause in the cities of European Russia. The dilemma of lack of labour in one part of the country and surplus in another will continue to worsen. Efforts to bring jobs to labour-surplus regions by building new industries are under discussion. Jobs for women in these areas are also becoming a problem and efforts to create opportunities for them are discussed with increasing frequency in the press. Implementation of such schemes on a scale sufficient to have serious impact would require heavy investment — difficult to provide in an

Paul B. Henze

economy where productivity and rate of economic growth are declining.

A temporary and only partial method of securing more labour for the industries of European Russia is to encourage Russians from outlying areas to migrate back. The 1979 census provides evidence that this trend has been gaining force. The proportion of Russians in the population of all Muslim republics has been declining and in some the Russian population is declining in absolute numbers. Simultaneously the proportion of the native nationality in the population of most republics is increasing. Tashkent gained an Uzbek majority in the late 1970's. In other republican capitals local nationalities have also been gaining and there has been a marked flow of some of the more scattered nationalities back to their home territory. The most striking example is Armenia. The Baltic republics present a somewhat different picture — they are the only non-Russian republics where the number of Russians has been increasing in proportion to the local population.

The overall trend in the USSR is unmistakably in the direction of concentration of nationalities into their own areas. There are many reasons to expect this trend to continue and perhaps even to gain momentum in the next few years. It is not surprising to find another resulting trend: concentration of local governmental, economic, educational and cultural activity in the hands of the native nationality. Several factors have combined to create this momentum: great availability of trained and educated natives, fewer Russians, increased assertiveness on the part of non-Russians. Non-Russians do not need to revolt or agitate to gain more control over their own affairs. They have now begun to reap decisive benefits from the 'affirmative action' programmes that have been operating for decades. Complaints are becoming increasingly frequent among Russians in non-Russian areas that they are discriminated against in jobs and university entrance and frequently in small ways in daily life. Developments of this kind become self-reinforcing. They are likely to continue indefinitely.

USA/USSR — Convergence?

Convergence theories about Western and Soviet economic and social development were popular in the 1960's. The United States, and the Soviet Union, both great continental powers with vast resources, great open spaces and expanding, mobile populations conditioned by history to think in large terms, were said by some observers to be destined to develop — by different paths perhaps — essentially in the same direction. It is difficult to make this kind of case in the 1980's.

While the American population continues to grow at a moderate rate, it is also steadily augmented by immigration, which has always been an important factor in American economic growth. The Soviet population is ethnically differentiated and becoming more so. Ethnic diversity takes much more fluid forms in the United States. If severe future labour shortages were anticipated in the United States (they are not), they could be rapidly met by increasing immigration on a temporary or permanent basis from a wide variety of sources. In contrast, no significant source of foreign labour is available to the USSR or likely to become available. Nor could the country easily utilize foreign labour without drastic alteration of current legal, social and economic practices.

With the exception of some movements of Kazakhs and other Turkic nationalities from Sinkiang into Soviet Central Asia during the 1960's, there has never been any significant migration into the USSR and there is no prospect of it in the foreseeable future. Experience in recent years with nationalities who have been permitted to emigrate — Jews, Armenians, ethnic Germans — reveals a strong desire to leave the USSR and the Soviet Union may have lost perhaps 400,000 people in this fashion over the past two decades. There is good reason to believe that potential interest in emigration extends wide beyond the particular groups whom Soviet authorities for various and periodically changing reasons have permitted to emigrate.

Could it be said that the trend toward devolution of responsibility to the states in the US — the 'New Federalism' — corresponds to the tendency in the USSR toward greater ethnic control of republics and other nationality areas? The impetus seems to be different. In both countries there is in fact momentum in both directions simultaneously. While federalism as the basis for organization of the republic operates without reference to ethnic factors in the US, federalism in the Soviet Union takes only ethnic form. Though the massive Russian Republic is officially called 'Federative', the federal principle is hard to detect in its administration.

The Soviet governmental system as a whole has much less administrative flexibility than the US system and is, therefore, much less responsive to stress and the need for adaptation and change. The fact that the ethnic principle is primary in organization and government, including the economy, causes many problems to assume an ethnic dimension from the earliest stages. The need to take ethnic factors into account introduces a degree of irrationality into many government decisions that is inconceivable in the US (where other pressures and forms of irrationality, of course, occur). Growth among non-Russian peoples both in numbers and in assertiveness means that ethnic factors in governmental and economic decision-making are likely to increase in importance.

Not only are ethnic factors significant in the official, formal side of Soviet life, they are also operative in the informal sphere. This includes the unofficial economy — which plays an increasingly important role in the USSR. Some ethnic groups — e.g. Georgians and Armenians — have long been notorious for the extent of their unofficial economic enterprise. Others play more subtle roles. We now often hear of avoidance of factory employment by Central Asian Muslims, e.g., because it deprives them of opportunities to earn from various forms of private endeavour. On the other hand, people often take regular employment or hold official positions primarily for the opportunity they provide as a base or cover for more lucrative unofficial activity.

All these phenomena are as well known among Russians as among non-Russians. The ethnic dimension affects them in various ways and leads to subtle forms of favouritism and protectionism. At all levels of Soviet society economic 'mafia' groups operate to an extent unknown and unnecessary in the developed West.

The ethnic factor in the Soviet armed forces is especially interesting. Superficially it can be argued that American and Soviet military evolution is toward convergence, for the disproportion of minorities in the US armed forces — primarily Blacks and Hispanics — is already very high. Is this not the same kind of situation toward which the Soviet Union is moving — as a larger and larger proportion of available military manpower becomes Muslim?

There are very important differences. The disproportion in the Soviet Union results from universal military service; in the US it is the result of a voluntary system. Military service is more attractive in the US, on a voluntary basis, to minorities than to the population at large. There is no evidence that this would be the case in the USSR if it depended on voluntarism as the principle for recruiting its military manpower. On the other hand, were the United States to return to conscription, the make-up of the military services would reflect the ethnic make-up of the population. The United States has a wide range of options for securing either larger military forces or a mix more representative of the ethnic composition of the population. The Soviets have very few.

The Spectre and Implications of Internal Nationalist Dissent

The US armed forces are a prime instrument for assimilation of minorities and new Americans. Women participate increasingly in this process. The role of women in the Soviet armed forces is severely limited. And while there is very little ethnic differentiation in function in the US military services, there is extreme differentiation in the Soviet Union. Most Muslims serve in construction battalions and perform related kinds of menial service, as Blacks did in the US Army until the end of World War II.

Ethnic differentiation extends all the way up through the officer corps in the USSR. The higher the rank, the more Russians; the more sensitive the category of service, the less likely it will contain minorities in any significant number at any level. Ukrainians tend to dominate the non-com level in the Soviet military. An Uzbek or a Balt as a fighter pilot is virtually unknown. Even Georgians and Armenians are rare in strategic rocket or submarine services.

The US and Soviet armed forces are not converging, but developing along very different paths. This seems to be true in respect to ethnic relations within the services. Desegregation and the principle of racial equality which have now been rigidly enforced in the US military forces for 35 years and have produced a fair degree of homogeneity at all levels are foreign to the spirit of the Soviet armed forces. There is less ethnic strain in the US armed forces than in US society as a whole. The information we have on this subject does not permit the same conclusion in respect to the Soviet Union. Ethnic tension is higher in the Soviet armed forces than in those of the US and appears to be increasing.[10] The experience of the Soviet military in Afghanistan may intensify these trends.

It is difficult to find any field where important trends in the USSR and the US are converging. While American agriculture becomes continually more productive, Soviet agriculture is stagnant. The dynamism and adaptability of the industrial and service sectors of the American economy also stand in sharp contrast to the situation in the Soviet Empire. Poor and declining Soviet economic performance places continually more severe limitations on Soviet leaders as they attempt to deal with regional and ethnic problems. Already there are signs of growing competition between republics and regions for resources for major development projects. Better educated ethnic leaders are less inclined to accept Moscow Gosplan decisions without question and protest if they find they go against their interests.

It was long claimed that the Soviet system had developed the means of delivering acceptable medical care and related social services to a

Paul B. Henze

broader segment of its population than the United States was able to do. If the Soviet Union was actually ever ahead of American performance in the field of social services, the United States outstripped Soviet performance decisively during the 1960's and 1970's. A large body of recent research has demonstrated that Soviet medical care is deficient and not improving. Rising infant mortality and declining male longevity are evidence of severe health problems in the USSR which appear to be worsening. Trends in the US and in all other developed countries are in the opposite direction. There is no question of convergence in this field and for the Soviets the problems are not easily remediable.[11]

Will the Russians Revolt?

Too often ethnic problems in the USSR are discussed only from the viewpoint of the non-Russian nationalities. The scene has to be examined from both sides — what about the Russians themselves? They are an essential part of the picture. What is happening among them? How are they interacting with their non-Russian fellow citizens? What about Russian nationalism?

Russian nationalism appears to be gaining strength too. This has been going on for a long time. It goes back to World War II, when Stalin encouraged traditional Russian patriotism as a basis for resistance to the German onslaught on his empire. It was effective. Russians are proud of the sacrifices they made in World War II. They suffered more heavily than any other Soviet nationality. They suffered after World War II as well, when the political relaxation that had been permitted during the war came to an end and Zhdanov, Beria, Molotov and the rest of Stalin's top team tightened all the screws again. The Great Russian People continued to be glorified, however, and there was no return to pre-revolutionary prohibitions on expression of Russian nationalism.

During recent years a deeper revival of Russian national pride has been apparent. It has a great deal in common with trends in many developed countries but with some additional dimensions. Heightened interest in history, 'roots', ethnic traditions and art has been evident. Religion as well. Icons are collected and studied; churches and examples of old secular architecture (wooden houses, fortifications) restored. Sumptuous coffee-table volumes featuring excellent colour reproductions of medieval frescoes, coats of arms of Russian principalities, old Russian costumes, folk art, etc. continue to pour off the presses — now often utterly devoid of even ritual mention of Marxism-Leninism.

The Spectre and Implications of Internal Nationalist Dissent

Some of the conservative currents in traditional Russian nationalism now find frequent expression — Slavophil ideas, e.g. Russia is seen as a nation with a special mission in the world, a responsibility for civilizing less developed peoples, with a role as leader of other Slavic nationalities. The necessity to justify continued Soviet domination of Eastern Europe encourages this kind of thinking. So does the sense of competitiveness with the United States.

Living under conditions that are still harsh in comparison with the standards now prevailing in most of the developed world, Russians sometimes display a defensive arrogance which is compounded of desire to be treated as equals with other major world peoples, envy and resentment that others enjoy an easier life and more respected status, and embarrassment that Russian historical development has led to a system that is not willingly recognized by any other nation in the world as a freely acceptable form of government. Thus Russians continue to live, even more so than they have through much of their national existence, with tormented souls. To reassure themselves they boast about the unique advantages of their government and society — but the reality they experience daily stands in stark contrast to these pretensions.

The dissident movement which, in spite of all efforts to suppress it, continues to produce new examples and spokesmen, feeds this collective neurosis. Though the dissidents and their *samizdat*, and now the increasingly large group of recent emigres producing *tamizdat*, appear to have little active following in the USSR, there can be little doubt that the criticisms and frustrations they express are shared by a much broader body of citizens who feel the same resentments and aspirations.

Dissidence and *samizdat* are not, of course, confined to Russians. There are manifestations of these phenomena among practically all Soviet nationalities — though they are notably weak among Muslims. Muslim dissidence has so far taken other forms. The strength and persistence of literary and political dissidence among Russians and the high quality of dissident self-expression provide more basis than any other single kind of evidence for hopefulness about the eventual evolution of the Soviet Russian Empire toward more humane and democratic forms. Russian dissidents tend to be highly nationalistic in their interests and preoccupations. The concept of the *sovetskii chelovek* — the new Soviet Man — is of little interest to them.

A fair case can be made that over a long period of time the underdeveloped regions of the USSR, and most of the areas inhabited by Muslims in particular, have in the aggregate received a disproportionate share of the national budget while the more developed areas, primarily inhabited by Slavs, have received a smaller return from their larger contribution to the revenue and income of the central government. The Ukraine, according to some calculations, seems to have been more consistently disadvantaged in allocation of investment funds than the RSFSR. Doubtlessly part of the reason for this imbalance has been a desire to raise backward regions to a level of economic and social development approximating the rest of the country. But other factors have also played a role: security requirements in border areas, development of high-priority defence industries, the space programme, mining of scarce minerals. Such requirements have necessitated heavy infrastructure development in outlying regions: roads, railways, communications facilities, power stations.

Minority advocates argue that much of the specialized security and high-technology investment that has been made in their republics has been of little benefit to them and has little relationship to their own national interests. Republics which have large deposits of oil benefit very little from it. The contrast between their situation and that of developing countries who enjoy enormous rises in national income from petroleum is striking. Non-Russian nationality leaders and peoples are increasingly aware of it.

On the other hand, there is increasing evidence that Russians, while rationalizing the benefits of exploitation of oil, minerals and other forms of natural wealth in non-Russian areas as their natural right as the leading people of the Soviet Union, resent the cost of social services and economic investments that are made for the benefit of non-Russian peoples. This is especially true of Russians still living among minority nationalities in the Caucasus and Central Asia and to a lesser extent among Russians in the Baltic and the Ukraine. Separate school systems, universities, libraries, theatres, newspapers and broadcasting services arouse Russian antagonism when non-Russians take management of them into their own hands, press for greater allocations of resources and give them real national content. Resentments of this kind contribute to the flow of Russian settlers out of non-Russian areas.

While non-Russians find themselves under increased pressure to learn Russian, and many do, few Russians learn the languages of non-Russian nationalities, even if they live among them. One of the most revealing measures of Russian attitudes toward non-Slavic and non-European nationalities is the terminology used for them. They are commonly called *chornye* (blacks), *zholtye* (yellows) and *churki* (people who speak an incomprehensible language). There are elaborations and variations of these and related terms that extend far into the obscene.

Russians are well aware that they are losing ground demographically to their Turkic and Muslim fellow citizens who commonly have families of seven or eight children, in contrast to the usual one or two in a Russian family.

Clashes between the increasingly modernized and proud native peoples and Russians are still relatively rare — but they appear to be occurring more frequently than a decade or two ago, and there have been major episodes in every republic in recent years, sometimes in connection with sports events but more often on religious anniversaries or during ceremonies honouring local historical figures. Georgians have demonstrated repeatedly to protest failure of the authorities to give precedence to their language in university teaching.

Subtle forms of expression of anti-Russian feeling are much more widespread and these are far harder for security authorities to deal with. Uzbeks may refuse to speak Russian in shops; Azeris may reserve scarce goods for fellow Muslims; Ukrainians or Balts may give Russians low priority in public services. In many non-Russian republics, Russians now complain that they are discriminated against in university admission and that local nationality teachers grade Russians more severely than native students. Official propaganda notwithstanding, trends are toward an increase of such problems rather than a reduction of them.

Thus Russians at most levels in Soviet society are increasingly aware of the pain and cost of operating a multi-national empire. Like all imperial peoples, they find that benevolent treatment of subject nations does not produce gratitude. Raising these peoples to a higher level of economic development, opening up new social and intellectual horizons for them, does not necessarily make mutual relationships easier. Some Russians react with scorn and resentment; some with open hostility; some with patience and dedication to principle; many with indifference. Russians have not developed a successful formula for turning non-Russians into Russians. Officially they have to keep denying that they are trying to do so at all. New Soviet Man has proved elusive. National feeling is intensifying, among Russians as well as non-Russians. They interact with each other and psychological barriers are mutually reinforced.

The Empire and the World

Though their ideology has compelled Soviet leaders, with greater or lesser commitment of effort, to work to influence the farthest reaches of the outer world, they have always been concerned to limit the influence of the outer world on their own empire. There is no field about which they have been more sensitive than their non-Russian peoples. The principle of self-determination to the point of separation from the USSR confronts the leadership with a dilemma which has been consistently dealt with by ensuring that the principle remains entirely theoretical. In the wake of the revolution there was active intervention from the outside in the Caucasus, Central Asia and Siberia,[12] but the desire of the great powers and the capacity of lesser ones to intervene quickly faded. For almost two decades afterward, no nation or émigré group made a major effort to have impact on Soviet minorities. The greatest political danger among Muslims was effectively dealt with by a policy of guarded friendship with Republican Turkey, which has never supported separatism in the Soviet Union.

Hitler's Germany was intensely interested in undermining the Soviet system through encouragement of separatism. Meticulous and rational planning was done before the attack in June 1941. Had the policies which intelligent Germans advocated and tried to implement prevailed, the outcome of the German onslaught on the Soviet Union might well have been different. Nazi ideology overcame better judgment and was probably the crucial factor propelling Ukrainians and Belorussians, as well as many Russians themselves, into fighting for Stalin as the lesser evil.[13]

Stalin's fears about lack of commitment to his system among practically all of the non-Slavic nationalities were justified by the uprisings that took place among peoples whose territories fell under German control and the mass defections of soldiers and civilians in 1941-42. Even severe reprisal and tight restrictions during the entire subsequent period have not prevented a trickle of defectors ever since. The only significant contrary movement was the repatriation of Armenians that took place during the late 1940's.

Intensification of the Cold War in the early 1950's resulted in Western (primarily US) financed efforts to provide emigres with the means for sustained communication with their peoples inside the USSR, including Russians. The principal result was Radio Liberty, which continues to broadcast. It has been joined by a series of broadcasting operations of several other countries, including China. These broadcasts have always drawn a more shrill and worried official Soviet response than any objective estimate of their impact could justify. The Soviet response betrays a deep insecurity among the Soviet leadership about dissidence in the broadest sense, as well as the nationality issue. This

The Spectre and Implications of Internal Nationalist Dissent

insecurity feeds the conviction that concessions to desires for genuine autonomy and communication with the outside world are bound to spiral upward and feed internal trends which would force the leadership to modify the principles on which it operates its empire.

Nevertheless, try as they will to maintain it, Soviet leaders have been steadily losing their capacity to isolate the Soviet peoples from outside influences. These come through many channels other than foreign broadcasts.[14] With so much listening to foreign broadcasts taking place, it is continually more difficult for Soviet leaders to avoid providing broader information in their own media. Soviet citizens have become skillful at interpreting information that is limited or distorted. The content of native-language broadcasts, newspapers, magazines and books is impossible to control completely. The cassette tape recorder is now widespread in the USSR, as in the rest of the world, and all kinds of forbidden information flows through the society in cassettes. The trend is clear: Soviet authorities are finding it more and more difficult to keep any of their peoples from exercising their desire to be better informed both on what is happening in their own society and in the outside world.

Educated non-Russians participate in Soviet international life in many ways. Students and visitors from other countries are brought to the USSR and given training and hospitality. Soviet official involvement with the Third World and participation in UN activities and other international undertakings brings feedback into the Soviet system. Tiny Caribbean, Indian Ocean and Pacific islands now enjoy seats in the UN; so do several dozen African and other countries whose very existence results from the accidents of 19th century colonialism. Nations of the Soviet Empire with civilizations that go back thousands of years, such as Georgia and Armenia, do not. Neither do the Baltic states, where memory of interwar independence is still alive. None of the USSR's Muslim republics — nearly all of them with populations larger than many Arab states — has a voice of its own in any international body. The UN seats of the Ukraine and Belorussia are simply a device for giving the USSR itself three votes. The 'foreign ministries' of these republics are false fronts with no reality behind them. These facts are not lost on Ukrainians and Belorussians.

It is against this background — vastly expanded knowledge which cannot be distorted beyond a limited degree, increased capacity and desire to think for themselves, heightened realization of the true meaning of human rights, political freedom, economic opportunity — that the impact of the two most serious entanglements into which the

Paul B. Henze

Soviet Empire has ever fallen, Afghanistan and Poland, must be assessed. There is already good evidence that the imbroglio in Afghanistan is having substantial impact on Soviet Muslims. The longer it continues, the greater the feedback is bound to be. The impact of Soviet oppression in Poland is greatest in the westernmost regions of the USSR — the Baltic and the Ukraine. No peoples in modern history have been more intractable in defence of their national existence than Afghans and Poles. Soviet leaders could have embarked on no venture less promising than trying to bend these vigorous and stubborn peoples to their will.

We see increasing evidence of blind conservatism — akin to that of the late Ottoman sultans even more than the tsars — which motivates Soviet leaders to avoid change and commit themselves to maintaining their grip on their empire at all costs. To a point this conservative myopia, backed by the largest array of deadly weaponry the world has ever seen, can prevail. But no weapons, no readiness to underwrite subversion and terrorism abroad, not even willingness to resort to the most brutal and inhumane methods of warfare by chemical and biological means, can create the will in a society or in its component peoples to maintain a system indefinitely that is based on oppression. The non-Russian peoples — and the Russians themselves — must be given a greater stake in their society. Here is the ultimate dilemma: give them a greater stake in Soviet society and they will press to reshape it to fit their own needs and desires. Make concessions to Afghans, and Poles and Soviet nationalities, including the Russians, will want them too.

For a society which is losing its economic momentum and showing distinct signs of psychological deterioration — growing alcoholism, serious basic demographic problems — it is difficult to envision a formula that will reconcile these mounting contradictions.

Imperial Twilight?

On the broad screen of history where the drama of the Russian/Soviet Empire may now have reached the initial scenes of its final act,[15] we might be wise to anticipate a spectacle which could turn out to parallel the long final act of the Ottoman drama, though events seem to be moving (as nearly everything has in the 20th century) at a much more rapid tempo. Like the Soviet Empire, the Ottoman Empire was unable to digest Eastern Europe. Until the end of the 17th century, the Ottoman advance into Eastern Europe seemed inevitable — to all but

The Spectre and Implications of Internal Nationalist Dissent

the East Europeans, who kept resisting it. Only a minority of the population was converted to Islam. Ties to the Christian West were never severed. The growth and persistence of nationalism was a natural by-product of this Western orientation.

Trying to maintain a hold on Eastern Europe proved costly for the Ottoman Empire in many ways. Above all it inhibited Ottoman leaders from devoting full energy to the continuing struggle on the other side of their empire in the Arab World. In the Arab lands common religion was not sufficient to overcome other differences. Even though much of Ottoman culture, including a large part of the vocabulary of the Ottoman Turkish language, was absorbed from the Arabs, the sense of common purpose between Arabs and Turks weakened with the passage of time and decline of the vitality of the Ottoman governing institutions. In the Ottoman Empire economic development in outlying regions proceeded more rapidly than it did in Anatolia, the neglected heart of the empire.

From the beginning of the 19th century onward, Turks found themselves facing disproportionate demands and making disproportionate sacrifices to maintain an imperial structure that had declining relevance to their needs as a nation. Might Russians come to look upon the Soviet Union in the same fashion?

As a people the Russians have made the greatest exertions and sacrifices to maintain the Soviet imperial structure. They have gained the largest share of psychological satisfaction — national pride — from having done so. They have seen their state become a force in world affairs well beyond the most ambitious dreams of the tsars and Slavophils. They provide the driving force and practically all the most senior and sensitive personnel for government and the armed services. They are most conscious of paying the costs of activities ranging from the Bolshoi Ballet to Venus probes that impress the world with the accomplishments of their government and social system. Lip-service to the multi-national character of their system notwithstanding, these are seen by them as essentially *Russian* accomplishments.

They also take the opprobrium for oppressing Poland and Afghanistan, for keeping Eastern Europe under heel, for nurturing subversion and terror with the aim of advancing the interests of the Soviet system beyond its borders. Soviet military and economic aid programs in the Third World, friendship treaties, and support for regimes that claim to be building 'socialism' — from Cuba to Ethiopia to Cambodia — are also regarded by the world and by the Russians themselves as essentially *Russian* efforts. Russians also see themselves as bearing the lion's share of the costs of being a world power.

Paul B. Henze

Russian support for the Soviet system appears still to be strong, far stronger than that of the other nationalities in the Soviet Empire. The satisfaction of non-Russian nationalities depends on the immediate gains and advantages they get from belonging to the Soviet state — and some of them are showing skill in gaining more. Few of the less tangible forms of satisfaction that are important to Russian national pride can be of much significance to many of the non-Russians.

Most of them are in one or more important ways denied full psychological participation in the system. There is little evidence that they desire it — but without a strong psychological bond to the system, except insofar as it delivers material returns to them, how can they be expected to uphold it as it fails to meet their rising expectations?

The Soviet Empire has been losing economic momentum for a long period of time. No end to this process is in sight. The costs of empire are rising. As the costs rise, even the marginal gains that can be shared contract. For the erstwhile underdeveloped regions of the USSR, especially the Muslim areas, the relative gains in well-being, standard of living, economic expansion and creation of the political and economic infrastructure of a modern society have been the source of real satisfaction because they have come rapidly. But these gains in satisfaction will have lasting effect only if they are felt to be secure, and if they lead to continuing advantages. Peoples who have taken their local administration and the intellectual leadership of their societies into their own hands are better able to press for further advantages for themselves. If they press but get inadequate response, relative contentment will be transformed into mounting dissatisfaction.

Abstract gratitude for political power and economic improvements is a short-lived emotion among former colonial peoples. Nothing we know about the non-Russian peoples of the Soviet Empire provides any basis for believing their reactions are different from those of the rest of mankind. Economic strains and the shifts in emotions and attitudes that they cause also put the Russian people to a severe psychological test. Nothing we know about them gives any basis for assuming that they are possessed of unusual qualities of altruism and unlimited capacity for self-sacrifice. Foreign aid has never been popular in the USSR. Facts about it are routinely suppressed. Aid for beleaguered East European economies causes resentment among Russians who have never enjoyed the level of relative well-being Poles still feel they are entitled to. The higher living standards non-Russian nationalities have secured for themselves in the USSR provoke envy and resentment too. The 1980's are likely to bring exacerbation of these conditions.

The Spectre and Implications of Internal Nationalist Dissent

Soviet leaders still take comfort in representing their system as scientific, logical and historically inevitable. They seem to have some success both in deceiving themselves and misleading the outer world. But they have been less successful in deceiving their own people. Systematic examination of the way the Soviet system actually works makes it obvious that if it goes on performing in its present manner it will fall into contradictions which could be devastating to its capacity to preserve its momentum. Ideology is no longer a binding force and is weakening. The military may be assuming a larger political role but their draft-age manpower base is contracting and becoming less Russian at a much more rapid rate than the population as a whole. Problems of labour utilization are compounded by persistent slowing of economic momentum. The longer the Afghan and Polish struggles continue, the more feedback they are bound to have into the Soviet system.

Every one of these problems is complicated by ethnic factors that are inescapable because the principle of ethnic separateness underlies the entire structure of the Soviet/Russian Empire. The Soviet system has been durable for more than sixty years but remarkably inflexible. It has developed few mechanisms for systematic change. This is its greatest weakness. Its inflexibility may be producing brittleness. Only a foolhardy historian could rate this empire as a strong prospect for survival into the 21st century without basic change. Is it too late for change from above without disruptive consequences?

By the time the Ottoman Empire entered World War I, its time had probably run out. Many people thought the same might be true of the Russian Empire as well. Lenin's tactical skill and strategic genius brought about its resuscitation. Could another political and conspiratorial genius work the same result with the Soviet Empire? If that could be done, he might have justification for claiming that it was indeed a new and higher form of political organization.

In terms of capacity for change and adaptation, the United States, both on the basis of historical experience and current performance, has to be rated far ahead of the Soviet Union. There are rigidities in its political structure too, of course, but in respect to the single factor that in the 20th century has come to predominate in the political and social life of most nations — ethnicity, nationalism — the United States, along with a few other large and similar new countries such as Canada, Australia and Brazil, has developed an approach to ethnicity which capitalizes on its positive features while minimizing its negative consequences. The melting pot principle has proved its superiority over ethnic structuralism.

Paul B. Henze

Notes

1. I am well aware that there are exceptions to every summary statement I have made. They include some of the most entertaining and fascinating episodes in American history. What I am describing here, however, is the general thrust of American historical development and evolution of American society — without allowance for the exceptions.

2. The justification for affirmative action has been that it is required to overcome the inability of particular groups to participate fully in American life because of cultural backwardness, past discrimination or other disadvantages for which society or previous governmental practice is held responsible. But it is already clear from experience with these programmes that unforeseen and unintended consequences result. Two tendencies are proving especially difficult to control. Bureaucracies created to administer affirmative action tend to maximize and extend the scope of their activity. The beneficiaries of the action often develop a vested interest in its continuation and expansion. There is a wide disparity among individuals in benefitting groups. This disparity tends to widen over time with the result that individuals who least require assistance, according to the criteria under which the action was originally justified, may capitalize most from its availability and, in effect, become a privileged minority within a still disadvantaged group. This privileged minority's continued support is difficult to justify either legally or morally — but it may become adept politically at prolonging its own advantages by championing special status for its group. Thus these undertakings can generate a dynamic for expansion and continuation and can contribute to the prolongation and exacerbation of the conditions they are designed to ameliorate and eliminate. 'Affirmative action' by other names has been undertaken extensively in the USSR. As we will see below, it has also generated unexpected consequences. These are more far-reaching in their implications for Soviet society than those of American affirmative action programmes which have much less significance for American society as a whole.

3. The practice of using both the husband's and the wife's name, hyphenated, as the name of the married couple, has acquired some popularity in the United States among couples who wish to demonstrate their commitment to equality of the sexes. It can produce combinations which illustrate how far *sliianie* is progressing in American society: I was recently told of a couple called Yamamoto-Finnegan!

4. Thus a 'nationality' prominent in the writings of 18th and 19th century travellers in Central Asia, the Sarts, has disappeared in Soviet times — not because they have fled or been liquidated — but simply because they have been redesignated as Tajiks or Uzbeks. Sarts were settled Central Asians who might speak Persian or Turkic dialects or both, but they were distinguished from rural people and nomads who spoke the same languages but had a different style of life.

5. The traditional term Turkestan, otherwise taboo, continues to be used in Soviet military organization, though the Turkestan Military District does not include all of historic Turkestan, only its central and northern sectors.

6. See Alexandre Bennigsen & S. Enders Wimbush, *Muslim National Communism in the Soviet Union*, University of Chicago Press, 1979.

7. See Paul B. Henze, 'Politics and Alphabets in Inner Asia', pp. 371-420 in Joshua A. Fishman (ed.), *Advances in the Creation and Revision of Writing Systems*, Mouton & Co., The Hague, 1977.

8. For a revealing treatment of this subject by a recent Soviet émigré see Aleksandr M. Nekrich, *The Punished Peoples*, New York, 1978.

9. For a good recent summary of the state of our knowledge of this subject

see A. Bennigsen & C. Lemercier-Quelquejay, 'L'Islam dans les Républiques Musulmanes Sovietiques' in Olivier Carré (ed.) *L'Islam et l'Etat*, Paris, 1982, pp. 157-164.

10. The most comprehensive study of the ethnic factor in the Soviet armed forces has been undertaken by the Rand Corporation during the past three years primarily on the basis of systematic interrogation in depth of recent emigres who had done military service during the preceding decade.

11. See Wm. A. Knaus, M.D., *Inside Russian Medicine*, Everest House, New York, 1981; Nick Eberstadt, 'The Health Crisis in the USSR', in *New York Review of Books*, 19 February 1981; Christopher David and Murray Feshbach, *Rising Infant Mortality in the USSR*, US Dept. of Commerce, Washington, DC (P-95/74), September 1980; and Murray Feshbach, 'A Different Crisis', in *The Wilson Quarterly*, Winter 1981.

12. There is a considerable literature on this subject. Among the most readable and informative books are: F.M. Bailey, *Mission to Tashkent*, Cape, London, 1946; C.H. Ellis, *The Transcaspian Episode*, Hutchinson, London, 1963; Firuz Kazemzadeh, *The Struggle for Transcaucasia*, Philosophical Library, New York, 1951.

13. One of the earliest accounts of the German experience remains one of the best: Jürgen Thorwald, *Wen Sie Verderben Wollen*, Steingrubenverlag, Stuttgart, 1952.

14. There is a strong case for increasing broadcasts in non-Russian languages in terms of air time, range of content and transmitter power. The desire for more broadcasts among Soviet peoples is attested by frequent reports of listening to broadcasts not specifically directed at the Soviet Union: domestic Turkish, Persian and Pakistani broadcasts, e.g., and shortwave broadcasts in English, German, French, as well as other European domestic services in many languages.

15. The most articulate and extensively argued presentation of this view in recent years had been provided by Hélène Carrère d'Encausse in *L'Empire Eclaté*, Paris, 1978; English edition: *Decline of an Empire*, Newsweek Books, New York, 1979.

MUSLIM NATIONAL MINORITIES IN REVOLUTION AND CIVIL WAR

Chantal Lemercier-Quelquejay

'For the Muslims of Russia, the February Revolution broke out ten years too early.'[1] This might be said of all other national minorities caught in the turmoil of the Russian revolution. Various nationalist movements were unprepared politically to take advantage of the collapse of the tsarist empire. In February 1917, nobody believed as yet that eight months later, in October of the same year, the Russian State would dissolve into anarchy and that the minorities would be offered a unique but brief opportunity to achieve full independence. This chapter focuses on the Muslim minorities. Their role, less known than that of Ukrainian or Latvian rifle battalions, was nevertheless significant and played an important part politically in the subsequent evolution of the USSR.

Poles, Finns, and the small Baltic nations managed to wrest themselves free of Russia, and their territories were recognized reluctantly by the Bolsheviks as sovereign states. However, their success was the result of external support from German, British, or French sources. The attempts of other nationalities, deprived of foreign help, to gain independence were easily defeated by the Bolsheviks. The defeat of the Volga Tatar, Turkestani, North Caucasians, Bashkir, Kazakh, Crimean Tatar, and Azerbaijani nationalist movements is well known, as it has been analyzed by some excellent historians, including Gerhard von Mende (who remains even today the best authority on this period) and Richard Pipes.[2] The reasons for this failure may be summarized as follows:

— lack of foreign support (with a few temporary exceptions);[3]
— absence of a well-organized, disciplined political party;
— absence of a clearly defined political programme, especially concerning their position toward Russia and the Russians: were they aiming at total independence or cultural autonomy?
— lack of political, social, and ideological unity.

The Muslim world of Russia was an immense ideological cauldron where all kinds of ideologies, from the most conservative and religious to the most radical and revolutionary, conflicted and clashed with one another. In October 1917, the moderate socialist intellectuals dominated the Muslim political scene except in the North Caucasus. They were certainly the least qualified to play the role of a third force between the Bolsheviks and the 'Whites.'

At the same time, by a strange paradox — one of those so abundant in the Russian revolution — all of the minorities, although politically immature, possessed one trump card which the Russians lacked: armed forces. Indeed, between February and October 1917, most of the national movements managed to equip themselves with national military troops. Small as they were, they represented a solid and efficient fighting instrument.

To appreciate correctly the nationalist military's role in the civil war, we must keep in mind that between February and October the immense tsarist army disintegrated in total anarchy. In October the provisional government of Alexander Kerensky collapsed in less than twenty-four hours because it had no troops — except a few cadets — to defend it. The Bolsheviks were not in a much better position. They could rely only upon the 'Red Workers Militia'; although this militia was certainly animated by real revolutionary enthusiasm, it was poorly armed and lacked the necessary training. Unable to face a serious challenge on the actual battlefield, they rapidly collapsed when met by the professional Czechoslovak legionnaires in May 1918. The sailors of the Baltic and the Black Sea (the 'beauty and the pride of the revolution' — *Krasa i gordost' Revolutsii*) were the only regular and excellent military units at the disposal of the new power. However, their number was hardly sufficient for the immensity of the empire, and, as they were led by anarchists, they were politically unreliable. In the camp of the counter-revolution the situation was even more desperate. The first White units which emerged in the winter of 1917-1918 in the Kuban consisted entirely of officers, professional warriors who were as competent and fanatically devoted to their cause as their adversaries; however, they had no troops.

The national minorities regiments, led by native officers who were generally former officers or non-commissioned officers of the tsarist army, were the only units to possess both officers and soldiers. Most of the units had been formed in haste between May and October, when the initial enthusiasm of the non-Russian nationalities for the February revolution was replaced by a more realistic understanding that democracy in Russia would not last long and that the central Russian administration was doomed. In other words, it was time to fight for a national existence.

National units appeared almost simultaneously across the entire territory of the former tsarist empire. The first Ukrainian military unit, a volunteer regiment named 'Bohdan Khmelnitski,' was formed in April 1917, in Kiev. A month later the First Ukrainian Military Congress, held in Kiev, decided to establish a permanent Ukrainian General Military Committee responsible for the formation of a Ukrainian army. Also in May 1917, Tatar nationalist leaders (right-wing socialists and moderates) formed a military committee in Kazan (the *Harbi Shura*) and began recruiting military units. On 2 August, this committee convened in Kazan the first 'All-Russian Muslim Military Congress' (*Umumi Russiyä Müsülman Harbi Kungresi*), attended by 200 delegates (soldiers and officers) who decided to replace the regular Russian army with a popular militia. And should the provisional government maintain a regular Russian army, the congress would 'proceed immediately with the formation of Muslim regiments.'[4]

The Bashkirs held their first All-Bashkir Congress in Orenburg in July 1917, under the chairmanship of Ahmed Zeki Validov (Zeki Velidi Togan), a famous orientalist and historian, later professor at the University of Istanbul. Among other decisions, the delegates called for the formation of purely Bashkir units. The Latvians were more advanced. Their national Latvian Rifle Regiments had been recruited during the war in 1915-16. On 17 May 1917, the delegates of the Latvian regiments held a Congress which, although dominated by the Bolsheviks, demanded the creation of an independent and sovereign Latvian state.[5] To these still embryonic national formations we may add the Polish, Finn, Georgian, and Armenian units, as well as the Cossack armies: those of Amur, Don, Orenburg, Terek, Ural, Kuban, Semirechie, Siberia, and Transbaikal, and the military units recruited from prisoners of war. One of the latter, the Czechoslovak Legion, equipped by the French, was to play a decisive role in the civil war.

When the Bolshevik revolution broke out, almost all minorities possessed their own well-trained military forces. Unfortunately, the efficiency of these units was greatly impaired by two factors, often overlooked by historians of the civil war. The first factor was that, although organized and dominated by moderate nationalist leaders, the units were heavily infiltrated by the Bolsheviks or by their allies, the Left SRs. This was particularly the case in the Tatar and Bashkir battalions formed by the *Harbi Shura*. The second factor was that by October 1917, the units were uncertain about which enemy they were to fight. There were so many possible adversaries. Was it the Russians in general, be they Reds or Whites? Or was it a certain category of Russians? Or was there some other foe: Armenian, Muslim, Azeri, Terek Cossack, or Chechen?

The Tatars and the Bashkirs in particular were not concerned by the October revolution, perceiving it as a purely Russian affair. Their units remained neutral in the battle for Kazan on 24 October as they refused to choose between two equally unpleasant adversaries, the Bolsheviks and the partisans of the provisional government. The only organized Muslim group which sided with the Reds was paradoxically a militant fanatical Sufi brotherhood, 'Vaisov, God's Own Regiment' (*Vaisov Bozhii Polk*).[6]

The Bolshevik assumption of power in Muslim territories was a purely Russian affair, and, consequently, Bolshevik local governments systematically excluded the natives from the exercise of power.[7] Kolesov, the chairman of the first Tashkent Soviet, justified with complete cynicism this 'colonialist' attitude when he declared at the Third Congress of the Soviet of Turkestan in Tashkent on 5 November 1917:

> It is impossible to admit Muslims to the supreme organs of the revolutionary power because the attitude of the local population toward the Soviets is uncertain and because they do not possess any proletarian organization.

In Muslim territories, the October revolution was not perceived as an historic upheaval which shook and changed the face of the world; in fact, it went practically unnoticed. The local administration of the provisional government was abolished, but its authority had already crumbled before October, and various Muslim national political organizations survived its downfall.

In the first stage, the new regime in the Muslim territories of the former empire presented a curious picture of a political dyarchy. Having seized power without serious opposition, the Bolsheviks were not ready for the second stage, as the native 'bourgeois' administration continued to co-exist with the local Soviets in a climate of uneasy truce. In February 1918, the units controlled by the *Harbi Shura* numbered some 50,000 men and officers: 20,000 in Kazan; 10,000 in Orenburg; and 12,000 to 15,000 distributed between Astrakhan, Samara, Omsk, Ekaterinburg, and Irkutsk.[8] The Red militia was still too weak to face such an adversary in a pitched battle, but it took the Bolsheviks less than five months to neutralize it completely from within. During the second stage, when the local Bolsheviks opposed the nationalists, Muslim armed units, torn between their moderate and left factions (the latter dominated by Bolsheviks and the Left SR), remained neutral once again.

On the eve of the showdown between Bolsheviks and Muslim nationalist organizations in February and March 1918, the following Muslim political organizations were functioning in the territory of Russia. In Crimea, the 'Muslim Executive committee' in Simferopol formed a National Tatar Directory in November 1917. It was the embryo of a national government, dominated by the moderate socialist *Milli Firka* (National Party).[9] In the Kazakh steppes, the Second Pan-Kirghiz Congress in Orenburg formed two Kazakh governments in December 1917. One was in Semipalatinsk for Kazakhstan East and was headed by Ali Bukeykhanov; the second was in the village of Zhambaytu near Ural'sk for Kazakhstan West and was headed by Dos Mohammedov. Both governments were dominated by *Alash Orda*, a moderate socialist national party.[10]

In Central Asia, a 'People's Council' (*Khalq Shurasy*), headed by Mustafa Chokay, was established in the city of Kokand in November 1917. In the Bashkir territory, a 'Bashkir Council' (*Shura*) was formed in December 1917 in Orenburg, headed by Ahmed Zeki Validov. It remained neutral in the conflict between the Bolsheviks and the Orenburg Cossacks, but in January 1918, it possessed a fighting force of some 2,000 soldiers. As for the Volga Tatars, they possessed the beginnings of an extra-territorial government, divided between several cities: in Petrograd, a 'Central National Council' (*Milli Shura*), chaired by Ahmed Tsalikov, founded in May 1917, and represented by an executive council (Ikomus); in Kazan, a 'Military Council' (*Harbi Shura*), founded in July 1917; and in Ufa, a 'National Directory' (*Milli Idare*), chaired by Sadri Maksudi, founded in July 1917, and a 'National Assembly' (*Millet Mejlisi*), convened in November 1917. The facade of this widespread Muslim administration appeared impressive, but there was nothing behind it, and when the local Bolsheviks marched against them, Muslim organizations collapsed without offering any resistance.

The second round began in Crimea. In January, a detachment of 3,000 Red sailors of Sebastopol marched against Simferopol, the Tatar capital. The sailors broke through the weak Tatar army on 13 January, storming the city on the next day. The Muslim Executive Committee was disbanded, its leaders arrested, and the survivors escaped to the mountains. The chairman of the committee, Chelebiev, was later murdered in Sebastopol and his body thrown into the sea. At the same time, Russian Red units from Siberia and the Urals advanced into the

Kazakh steppes without meeting any serious resistance. Akmolinsk fell on 7 January, Orenburg on 18 January, Semipalatinsk on 21 January, and Vernyi (Alma Ata) on 3 March. Members of the *Alash Orda* administration fled to the steppes.

In February, the Bolsheviks of Orenburg disbanded the *Bashkir Shura* and arrested its president, Zeki Validov. The small Bashkir army (probably the best fighting force in all of eastern Russia), torn by the conflict between its Left and Right factions, remained passive and did not intervene. Zeki Validov and his companions fled in April 1918, taking refuge in the Ural mountains where they began raising a new Bashkir army. Also in February the Russian soviet of Tashkent, challenged by the Muslim government of Kokand, launched its offensive. On 6 February its troops, consisting of Russian workers' militia and units formed of Austro-Hungarian prisoners of war, stormed the Muslim capital. After three days of massacre and plunder, the city was set on fire. According to some estimates, about 50,000 people had been slaughtered;[11] some members of the Turkestan government managed to escape the massacre and joined the Basmachis.

The Tatar National Front, appearing to be the most formidable adversary of the Bolsheviks, disintegrated as easily as the other Muslim organizations. On 27 February 1918, the soviet of Kazan arrested the leaders of the *Harbi Shura*. Those members who escaped took refuge in the Tatar suburb of Trans-Bulak and tried to reconstitute a national government, called derisively in Soviet literature the 'Zabulachka Republic'. A month later, having received a reinforcement of 300 sailors from Kronstadt, the Russian garrison of Kazan stormed the suburb and dispersed the nationalists. The units of *Harbi Shura*, influenced by the Bolsheviks, refused to march. Once again, the only Muslim unit in the struggle that took an active part on the side of the Reds was the mystical Vaisi Sufi order; their sheikh, Iman Vaisov, was killed while fighting his co-religionaries.

The battle between the Soviets and Tatar nationalists in Kazan was followed by a fast and effortless liquidation of all Tatar national agencies. On 26 March, the *Narkomnatz* closed the Petrograd headquarters and all regional branches of *Harbi Shura*. On 12 April, *Milli Shura*, *Milli Idare*, and *Millet Mejlisi* were shut down.

The last chapter of the drama took place in Baku on 20 March 1918, when the local Bolsheviks, reinforced by the Armenian militia of the Dashnaktsutun Nationalist and Socialist Party and some Muslims of the pro-Bolshevik Hümmet Party, attacked the native quarters of the city. After three days of savage fighting and massacre, during which more than 3,000 Muslims perished, the Bolsheviks seized control and formed a Bolshevik government called the 'Commune of Baku,' dominated by non-Muslims (Russians, Armenians, and Georgians).

By the end of March 1918, less than two months before the outbreak of civil war, all Muslim nationalist organizations (right-wing socialist, close to the Mensheviks or to the Right SRs, and centrist Democrats of the K.D. type) lay in ruins. Their failure was not only a result of their own inefficiency and unpreparedness but also because their native militias refused to obey orders and remained passive spectators during decisive moments. The attraction of Communism had been stronger than that of nationalism, and the victory of the Bolsheviks appeared crushing. Except for a small White Army led by General Kornilov in the Kuban, Basmachi guerrillas in the Ferghana valley, Naqshbandi mürids who held the higher valleys of Daghestan, and the regimes of the Emir of Bukhara and the Khan of Khiva, the entire territory of Russia was under Bolshevik control.

However, behind this victorious facade, Bolshevik power was still vulnerable. It still relied entirely upon the sailors of Kronstadt, the Latvian rifle regiments, and the Workers Red militia. Various national units had not been and could not be disarmed; they were still capable of fighting and were to play an active role in the third round of battle which began on 25 May 1918.

Civil War

In 1918, the Czechoslovak Legion, composed of prisoners who had belonged to the Austrian army, reorganized and rearmed by the Allies, was evacuating through the port of Vladivostok. On 25 May, the Czechs marched against the Bolsheviks and easily occupied the main towns along the Trans-Siberian railway. This occupation was a signal for action to all the counter-revolutionary elements waiting for an opportunity to take revenge on the victors of October: Don, Kuban, Orenburg, Ural, and Semirechie Cossacks, moderate socialists, partisans of the defunct Constitutional Assembly, monarchists loyal to the Romanov dynasty, and all those who refused to accept the dictatorship of the proletariat. Within less than three months, Soviet power was swept away in Siberia, the Urals, the Middle Volga, South Russia, and the Caucasus.[12]

Thus started the civil war which was to rage across the former Russian Empire for more than two years. This time there was no place for a minority 'third force' between the Reds and the Whites, who raised huge armies, commanded on both sides by professional officers. Gone was the time when native units could arbitrate between adversaries; the civil war was a Russian affair, although fought mainly on non-Russian territory. The minorities were therefore placed before a dramatic dilemma: to ally themselves with one or the other of the adversaries. As Sultan Galiev, who chose the side of the Bolsheviks, wrote:

> The decisive moment has come, not only for the individuals, but also for entire peoples and governments, each of whom must face his fate and irrevocably decide on which side of the barricade to place himself. Whether you want to or not, you must take part in this war and consciously or unconsciously become either 'White' or 'Red.'[13]

Like Sultan Galiev, very few Muslim leaders had made their choice before October 1917. The immense majority tried to dodge the dramatic decision, preferring to remain neutral spectators, since both adversaries appeared equally unpleasant. Ahmed Baytursun, leader of *Alash Orda*, explained their position with perfect candour:

> The Kirghiz (Kazakhs) received the first revolution with joy and the second with consternation and terror. It is easy to understand why. The first revolution had liberated them from the oppression of the tsarist regime and reinforced their perennial eternal dream of autonomy ... The second revolution was accompanied in the borderlands by violence, plundering, exactions and by the establishment of a dictatorial regime ... in short, it was a period of sheer anarchy. In the past, a small group of tsarist bureaucrats oppressed the Kirghiz (Kazakhs); today the same group of people, or others, who disguise themselves as Bolsheviks perpetrate in the borderlands the same regime ... Only the politics of Kolchak which promised the return of a tsarist regime forced *Alash Orda* to turn itself toward the Soviet regime, even though, judging by the local Bolsheviks, this did not appear to be a very attractive alternative.[14]

Muslim political leaders reluctantly had to join one or the other of the adversaries. A minority preferred the Whites; more by necessity than by conviction, the majority sided with the Reds. Both factions were tragically deceived and all paid dearly for their engagement.

Only the religious conservatives, the Naqshbandis in the North Caucasus and the Basmachis in Turkestan, refused to engage themselves on either side, fighting desperately against all 'Infidels' — Whites or Reds — for a complete independence under the banner of Islam. Their struggle was an anachronism, the resurgence of the medieval *Jihad* in the twentieth century; however, it lasted long after the civil war, and it represented the most terrible obstacle the Soviets were to face.

In the beginning, the White counter-revolutionary movement was not unified, either militarily or politically. It covered a wide range of opinions, trends, and reforms, from the moderate socialists (SRs and Mensheviks) to the liberal democrats and the extreme right-wing nationalists. Among its most important elements were the Cossacks, some of them traditionally opposed to their Muslim neighbours (for example, the Terek and Kuban Cossacks). Others, such as the Orenburg, Ural and Semirechie Cossacks, were eager to cooperate.

The civilian left-wing dominated the first stage of the White movement: the Komuch of Samara, the West Siberian government of Grishin-Almazov in Omsk, the Siberian government of Avksentiev, and the Crimean K.D. government led by Salomon Krym. These liberal socialist governments possessed no troops, relying entirely on the Czechoslovak legions in Eastern Russia and on the German Reichswehr in Crimea. They were eager to include Muslim nationalist units, not only because they needed their help against the growing strength of the Red army but also because they counter-balanced the importance of the Russian monarchist officers.

The second stage of the White movement was dominated entirely by professional soldiers whose political goals were vague. Some, such as Kolchak and Wrangel, were committed monarchists; others were not really committed to the restoration of the Romanov dynasty; still others even had republican sympathies. The leaders were excellent soldiers, dedicated, patriotic, and brave. However, they were technicians of war, rather than politicians, and, even worse, they were utterly unaware of the nationalities problem. The only political slogan accepted by everyone, monarchists and non-monarchists, was 'Russia, One and Indivisible' (*Edinaia i Nedelimaia*), a slogan directed more against the minorities than against the Bolsheviks. Kolchak and Denikin believed that Muslim, Ukrainian, Georgian, or Armenian separatist movements were as dangerous to the destiny of the empire as social upheaval. When they finally understood that it was the Bolsheviks who were their main foe, it was too late; the Whites' tactical errors originated in their abysmal ignorance of political conditions in Russia.[15]

In contrast, the Bolsheviks in Moscow understood the necessity of converting the minorities to the Bolshevik cause. In spite of such initial blunders as the anti-religious cavalry raids of the local Bolsheviks and the massacres of Kokand, Baku, and Simferopol, the new regime finally appeared more attractive to the Muslim masses and intelligentsia than the counter-revolutionaries.

Communism represented something new and, in particular, the possibility of modifying the relationship between the dominant Russians and the down-trodden Muslims.[16] It was perceived in the following ways by Muslim leaders:

— The vague and ambiguous promises of self-determination in Lenin's April theses were interpreted by the minorities as a chance of gaining complete independence.

— A considerable number of Muslim intellectuals believed that the revolution in Russia — in spite of its atrocities — was the first step toward the liberation of the World of Islam (and later of the entire colonial world) from European and Russian imperialism. Therefore, it was an historically positive step forward. Some Muslim leaders went so far as to discover similarities between Marxism and Islam.[17]

Stalin coopted to his *Narkomnats* a number of brilliant Muslim intellectuals who, although communists, remained loyal to their pan-Islamic national backgrounds: Turar Ryskulov, Fayzullah Khojaev, Mulla-Nur Vahitov, Mir Said Sultan Galiev, Nariman Narimanov, and Galimjan Ibragimov. These nationalist communists were responsible for bridging the immense gap between the half-medieval pre-revolutionary Islam and socialism. For, despite their local excesses, the Bolsheviks were still unknown to Muslim nationalists and therefore endowed with a capital of good will. At worst they appeared as the lesser evil, while, at the best, they were the bearers of a new doctrine of freedom and national equality.

The recruitment of Red Muslim battalions began in the Volga Tatar country soon after the revolution, in November and December 1917. The initiative belonged to Sultan Galiev, chairman of the Central Muslim Military Collegium, placed under the double control of Stalin's People's Commissariat of Nationalities (*Narkomnats*) and Trotsky's People's Defence Commissariat (*Narkomvoen*). Sultan Galiev wanted to reunite different battalions raised in 1917 in Kazan, Moscow, Petrograd, Astrakhan, Perm, and Ufa in a Muslim Workers and Peasants Red Army, led by Muslim commanders whose objective would be 'to bear socialist revolution to all the Muslim Orient.'[18] However, in August 1918, all Muslim regiments were incorporated into regular brigades and divisions of the Red army. They remained under the command of Tatar and Bashkir officers, most of whom were former tsarist officers and non-commissioned officers from the old nationalist Tatar army of the *Harbi Shura*.

These units were highly politicized. In June 1918, the Central Muslim Military Collegium founded the corpus of Muslim political commissars and organized a special seminar in Kazan where Tatar and Bashkir officers received accelerated political training. Today Soviet historians tend to minimize the role played by the Red Tatar and Bashkir units in the battles of the civil war; in reality, as emphasized by all original sources from the civil war period, their importance was enormous. It is probable that without the participation of these units the profile of the civil war would have been different. In 1921, Sultan Galiev could write without contradiction:

> The number of Red Tatar combatants increased by leaps and bounds: at the time when the Civil War was at its peak on the Eastern and Turkestan fronts, the proportion of combatants in the Red Army exceeded fifty percent of combatants and in certain units (for example in the Fifth Army) even reached seventy to seventy-five percent.[19]

It has been estimated that the total strength of Tatar units exceeded 50,000 soldiers during the winter of 1919-1920. They fought mainly on the eastern front against Kolchak and the Orenburg Cossacks; later, the Tatar units of the Fifth Red Army were engaged against the Basmachis of the Ferghana valley, from 1920-1922. They had a high proportion of Muslim soldiers and officers, fighting as well as the Russian units and deemed perfectly reliable by the Red high command even when pitted against their co-religionists. In the 1920's, revolutionary enthusiasm was still stronger than any feelings of Islamic solidarity.[20]

Tatar units were also engaged, although in smaller numbers, on the southern front against Denikin and in the Ukraine, but it is significant that there were no Muslim red units in the XIth Red army sent to Daghestan to crush the *ghazawat* ('Holy War') of the Naqshbandi *mürids* in 1920-1921. Other Muslim movements sided with the Whites, but, because of the anti-minority strategy of the White leaders, the Muslims later dramatically changed sides. This happened in three regions: Crimea, Bashkiria, and the Kazakh steppes.

In Crimea, the local Muslim national movement, dominated by the *Milli Firka* party, became strongly anti-Bolshevik after the Simferopol massacre. When the German Reichswehr occupied Crimea in April 1918, and destroyed the first Bolshevik regime, the *Milli Firka* cooperated with the Crimean government led by General Sulkevich, a Lithuanian Muslim Tatar, and in November 1918, with the liberal Russian government chaired by a Karait, Salomon Krym.

In April 1919, the Bolsheviks reoccupied Crimea. This time they tried to avoid the mistakes committed by their predecessors, and they succeeded in attracting the left wing of the *Milli Firka*. Veli Ibrahimov, its leader, accepted the portfolio of the important People's Commissariat for Foreign Affairs. However, the right and majority wing of the National Tatar movement refused to cooperate with the Reds.

The second Bolshevik regime in Crimea was destroyed by Denikin in June 1919, and all Tatar public life was forbidden, their press outlawed, and the National Tatar Directory disbanded. The right wing of *Milli Firka* joined with the left in clandestine activities and cooperated with the Bolshevik underground. In 1920 General Wrangel, the last Supreme Commander of the White movement, tried to rectify the errors of the past, promising the Tatars full cultural and religious autonomy. However, it was too late. The national movement in Crimea, dominated in 1918 by anti-Communist elements, finished the civil war solidly entrenched in the Bolshevik camp.

In Bashkiria the switch was even more dramatic. The unquestioned leader of the national movement, Ahmed Zeki Validov, was a young liberal intellectual of aristocratic origin. In July 1918, when Ataman Dutov expelled the Reds from Orenburg, Zeki Validov and his followers descended from the mountains and reconstructed a Bashkir government. Bashkir units fought the Reds on the side of the Orenburg Cossacks and the Czech legionnaires. However, in November 1918, Admiral Kolchak took command of the counter-revolutionary forces in eastern Russia. Kolchak was as strongly anti-minority as Denikin, and he made no secret of his total opposition to any Muslim minority claims to autonomy. Frictions and conflicts occurred between the Bashkirs and the White commanders at the very moment Lenin was promoting a more favourable and realistic nationalities policy.

On 6 December 1919, after a secret meeting with the Kazakhs of *Alash Orda*, Zeki Validov decided that cooperation with Kolchak was impossible; the only course of action, therefore, was to abandon the Whites and join the Reds. On 25 January 1919, Kolchak, preparing his offensive in the Urals, ordered Bashkir regiments to be disbanded. A few days later, Bashkir and Soviet delegates met behind Red lines and negotiated the method of the crossover from White to Red. On 6 February, the *Sovnarkom* granted full amnesty to any Bashkirs who deserted Kolchak, and on 18 February, some 2,000 Bashkir fighters with their officers crossed the Red lines. The next day, Zeki Validov signed an agreement with Lenin and Stalin establishing a provisional government of Bashkiria, headed by a 'Revolutionary Committee' (*Bashrevkom*) composed of Soviet and Bashkir representatives.

Bashkir soldiers fought the rest of the war on the side of the Reds. Only a few Bashkirs remained with the Whites, including the Bashkir Third rifle regiment which was isolated from other units and unable to cross over the Red lines. Thus Kolchak, whose recruitment possibilities were limited and who needed every available soldier, lost a small but highly efficient fighting force.

The unholy alliance between Bashkir nationalists and the Bolsheviks did not survive the civil war. Zeki Validov was the first of the Muslim leaders to perceive Russian imperialism behind the mask of 'proletarian socialism,' drawing the logical conclusion that a lasting understanding with the Bolsheviks was impossible. In June 1920, Zeki Validov and several of his associates escaped to Turkestan, joined the Bashmachis, and spent two years fighting the Red army once again.

The Kazakhs of *Alash Orda* were inspired by the Bashkirs. Kazakh units, less important than the Bashkir regiments, cooperated with various White forces, the Komuch, Avksent'ev's government, Orenburg, Ural, and Semirechie Cossacks, until March 1919. At that time, Kolchak's anti-Muslim strategy pushed them reluctantly into the arms of the Bolsheviks. Ahmed Baytursun, one of the leaders of *Alash Orda*, met secretly in Omsk with Jahgildih the head of the Qypchaq tribe who had been fighting on the Bolsheviks' side since the beginning. After the meeting, Kazakh units ceased to fight and retired to the central desert areas of Kazakhstan. In June 1919, Baytursun signed an agreement in Moscow establishing a joint Soviet-*Alash Orda* provisional government, the 'Kirghiz (Kazakh) Revolutionary Committee' (*Kirrevkom*).

Either because the Kazakh leaders lacked the political sophistication and acute intelligence of a Zeki Validov, or because Russian Soviet pressure was lighter in the Kazakh steppes than in industrialized Bashkiria, cooperation between the Kazakh nationalists and the Soviet regime lasted until the 1920's. The physical liquidation of Kazakh nationalists took place in the early 1930's. As a consequence:

> Until 1925, the People's Commissariat for Education, the press, and all (Kazakh) educational establishments were bastions of counter-revolutionary nationalism. Baytursun, the leader of the anti-Soviet movement, was then *narkom* for education ... and with his com-

panion Dulatov he dominated the Kazakh press ... which was completely controlled by the nationalists of *Alash Orda*.[21]

If we consider only the moderate liberal nationalist movements, the final balance of the civil war would lean heavily in favour of the Bolsheviks. In 1920, Muslim regiments led by native officers were fighting on the Bolshevik side, and the re-conquest of the Muslim borderlands appeared to be relatively easy. A long-lasting agreement between the Marxist regime and Islam was a reasonable possibility.

But reality was quite different. In the territories of the North Caucasus and Central Asia, the decisive struggle began in 1920, after the civil war, and it lasted for several years. This time, what may be called the 'second civil war' (an expression used by N. Samurskii-Efendiev in *Daghestan*, Moscow, 1925) pitted the Bolsheviks against conservative, even reactionary, religious elements, fighting for total independence under the banner of Islam against the hated Infidels.[22] This new enemy was the most dangerous the Soviets had faced on any battlefield, and, as a rule, no compromise was possible; the fight ensued with a ferocity exceptional even for the conditions of the Russian revolution. One of the two conservative religious movements, the Basmachi guerrilla in Central Asia, is relatively well known; the story of the other one, the North Caucasian uprising led by the Naqshbandi brotherhood, remains practically untold.

The Daghestan-Chechen revolt (1920-1921)[23]

The history of the 'second civil war' in the North Caucasus is outside of the scope of this paper. Suffice it to say that nowhere in Russia was the civil war[24] so confused and so ferocious. It was fought simultaneously on several fronts between four main adversaries: Bolsheviks, Whites (Terek Cossacks and Denikin), local liberal nationalists, and religious conservatives. There were also various external interventions, including the British (who equipped General Bicherakhov's army), the Turks (twice), the Azeri Mussawatists from Baku, the Armenian Dashnaks, and the Georgian Mensheviks.

However, in the spring of 1920 there remained only two adversaries to fight the final round: the Soviets and the conservatives. The Bolsheviks were either Russian, mainly workers from Petrovsk-Port (present-day Makhach-Qala), or indigenous. Until the re-conquest of Daghestan by the XIth Army in the spring of 1920, the leadership of the local Communist party belonged to the Muslim revolutionaries. These revolutionaries came from the middle and upper classes of native society, the *Uzden* class, whose grandparents had fought under Shamil. (For example, Makhach Dakhadaev, the first leader of the Daghestani Bolsheviks, was married to the granddaughter of Shamil Fatimat, daughter of Shamil's son Mohammed Shafi, a major-general in the tsarist army.)

Although the Muslim leaders were dedicated Marxists and atheists, they were also nationalists and did not under-estimate the importance of the religious factor. Most of them spoke Arabic. Nowhere in Russia were the local Bolsheviks so well qualified to lead the revolution. Unfortunately, most of them, such as Makhach Dakhadaev and Ulubii Buynakskii, perished during the civil war, and the last battles were fought by the Russians. These 'comrades from abroad' (*priezhii tovarishchi*) were, according to Samurskii (with an obvious under-statement), 'totally ignorant of the specific social conditions and of the character of the mountaineers.'[25]

The conservative religious wing consisted of deeply religious and fiercely independent members of clans and 'free societies' of upper Daghestan and upper Chechnia, organized and led by the Naqshbandi Sufi brotherhood.[26] This *tariqat* had a centuries-old tradition of *ghazawat* against the Russian invaders, from the sheikh Mansur in 1783 who died in the fortress of Schliesselburg, to Ghazi Mohammed killed in battle, to Shamil, and to the sheikh Abdurrahman of Sogratl, one of the leaders of the 1876-1878 uprising who died in a Siberian camp.

The ideal of holy war erupted in February 1917, the downfall of the monarchy being viewed as a unique occasion to restore the theocratical *Imamat* of Shamil. The Naqshbandi *tariqat* was led by two prestigious personalities: the *imam* Najmuddin of Hotso (in Russian, Gotsinski), an Avar elected supreme mufti of Daghestan in May 1917; and the sheikh Uzun Haji, a ninety-year-old Chechen and native of the village of Salty. He 'more than any other leader gave expression to the spirit and aims of the Daghestani clericals' and was 'inspired by an irreconcilable hatred for everything Russian and a passionate striving for complete independence from the Infidels.'[27]

For three years, from 1917 to 1920, the conservatives fought simultaneously and with success against the Bolsheviks and the Whites of Denikin, as well as against Bicherakov and the Terek Cossacks. In 1919, Uzun Haji created a theocratic state, an Emirate, in Upper Chechnia, placed officially under the sovereignty of the Turkish caliph. It was defended with the help of local Bolshevik units, led by the comrade Gikalo, against Denikin.

Muslim National Minorities in Revolution and Civil War

In the spring of 1920, the XIth Red army, coming from the north, occupied the lowlands of Daghestan. It was a purely Russian formation, led by Russian or European commanders, and it brought in its wake Russian political cadres whose ignorance of the local conditions was abysmal and who believed that the destruction of religion — any religion — was the first step toward sovietization. 'Several mistakes have been made,' acknowledged (with obvious under-statement) Najmuddin Samurskii, the only Daghestani Bolshevik to survive,[28] 'plundering expeditions accompanied by brutalities and atrocities generally committed by a victorious army in a civil war.' A few months later, in August 1920, upper Daghestan and Chechnia were on fire.

Soviet sources try to minimize the role of the clerics in the uprising and tend to exaggerate that of the Daghestani officers of the former tsarist army[29] and of the Georgian Mensheviks who helped them. However, the leading and decisive role belonged to the sheikhs of the Naqshbandi *tariqat*.[30] Only a Sufi brotherhood could give the rebels the iron discipline and sense of noble sacrifice which enabled them to resist the offensive of two Red armies for more than a year.

The sheikh Uzun Haji died in March 1920, several months before the revolt which began in August 1920. The Naqshbandi sheikhs who directed that revolt were the *imam* Najmuddin Gotsinski, the sheikh Sirajeddin Haji, Seyid Amin of Ansalta, Derwish Mohammed Haji of Andi, Mohammed of Balakhany, and Ibrahim of Kuchri.

Soviet commanders viewed the uprising very seriously. Two Red armies, the Ninth or 'Kuban Army' and the Eleventh or 'Terek-Daghestan Army,' helped to crush the revolt, using 27 rifle regiments, 6 cavalry regiments, 6 artillery groups, 2 special 'inner security' battalions, and one armoured car division.[31] Some 35,000 to 40,000 soldiers, officers, and political cadres participated in operations against an adversary whose maximum strength, in February 1921, did not exceed 9,690 warriors poorly armed with outdated rifles, a little amunition, and 40 machine guns taken in battle.[32]

The war was fought with extreme ferocity by both sides; no prisoners were taken[33] and the Red army suffered several severe defeats before the rebels were killed to the last man. On 30 October 1920, the 283rd rifle regiment of the 32nd division (XIth Army) and an artillery division were surrounded in the Arakan canyon and completely massacred; Safar Dudarov, head of the Daghestan Che-Ka, was one of the victims. On 30 November, the first 'Model Revolutionary Discipline' rifle regiment of Moscow, surprised by rebels on the mountain road between Vedeno (Chechnia) and Botlikh (Daghestan), was massacred. The few

51

survivors were left to freeze to death. On 8 January, it was the cavalry regiment of the Moscow cadets and one battalion of the 291th regiment that were surrounded and destroyed near the aul of Alleroy (Chechnia).

In May 1921, the revolt was crushed. Most of its leaders, religious and military, had been killed in battle, and a pitiless repression began in Daghestan. Najmuddin Gotsinski, Seyid Amin of Ansalt, and some followers managed to fight in the mountains of upper Chechnia until 1925 when they were captured and executed. The 1920-1921 uprising left an indelible memory in Daghestan-Chechnia, and they remain the two republics where anti-Russian xenophobia is strongest.

The Basmachis of Central Asia[34]

The Basmachi movement began immediately after the destruction of Kokand in February 1918. Unlike the well-organized and disciplined Daghestani *jihad*, the *Basmachestvo* had never been unified. Its leaders came from every horizon: tribal chieftains like the Turkmen Junayd Khan and Ibrahim beg, the head of the Uzbek Lokay tribe, authentic former highway robbers, the traditional *rah-zen* like Irgash, the village *aqsaqal* ('Elders'), religious leaders, and sheikhs of Sufi brotherhoods.[35] It was a typical peasant and tribal guerrilla force, effective, elusive but anarchic, and every Basmachi detachment operated independently of all others. All attempts to unify resistance (by Enver Pasha, for instance) failed. Every nationality was represented in the movement: Uzbeks, Kirghiz, Tajiks, Turkmens, and Karakalpaks. To protect the traditional way of life which was threatened by western civilization, to expel Russian rural and urban settlers, and to defend Islam against the godless new regime — these were the goals of the resistance, but the Basmachis had no ideology and no real political programme. Only a few of its leaders aimed to overthrow Russian rule in Central Asia.

In spite of its religious colouring, the Basmachi guerrilla movement never took the character of a holy war comparable to the Daghestani uprising or to the resistance of the Afghan *mojahidin*. Although deadly and dangerous, the Basmachis had neither the iron discipline nor the spirit of sacrifice characteristic of a *Jihad*. When forced, Basmachi units did not hesitate to join the Soviets, temporarily or definitely (like Madamin beg), which was unthinkable in Daghestan in 1920 or in Afghanistan today.

In 1918 and 1919 the Bashmachis controlled almost the entire Ferghana valley, the high Alay range, a refuge which was inaccessible to

Soviet troops. The number of Basmachis in Ferghana has never been important: 6,000 to 8,000 in 1919,[36] and 3,400 in early 1920.[37] One recent Soviet source cites the figure of 30,000 Basmachis in the summer of 1920, but it is obviously an exaggeration.[38] The figure of 10,000 fighters must be considered as a maximum for all of Central Asia in 1921-1922 when the *Basmachestvo* reached its peak.

In November 1919, the Red army defeated the Whites, consisting of Orenburg, Ural and Semirechie Cossacks, and Kolchak's army, and Turkestan was reunited with Soviet Russia. The Tashkent Soviet, whose atrocities were largely responsible for the Basmachi uprising, was replaced by a special 'Turkestan Commission' appointed by Lenin, and a new, more liberal, political strategy was applied to Central Asia. The doors of the Communist party were opened wide to native revolutionaries: Young Bukharans, Young Khivans, and Jadids. In May 1920, the recruitment of the native population into Red units began.[39] Finally, Marshal Frunze, probably the best Red commander of the civil war and the man responsible for the anti-Basmachi operations, abandoned the destructive tactics employed in 1918-1919 and implemented a strategy of territorial occupation and organization.

Slowly but steadily, the Red army, including a large number of Tatar officers and fighters, regained the upper hand in the Ferghana valley. In March 1920, Madamin beg capitulated and joined the Reds; he was later killed by his former companions. Some months later, Khal Hoja, one of the fiercest and most able *kurbashis*, was killed in a landslide while crossing a mountain pass. In 1921, the Soviet offensive, a superior force, cleared the Ferghana valley.

On 29 August 1920, Soviet forces occupied Bukhara and ended the regime of the Emir. In November 1921, Enver Pasha arrived in Bukhara, joined the Basmachis, and proclaimed himself the Commander-in-Chief of the insurgent army. His endeavour failed completely, for his authority was not recognized by Ibrahim beg and other tribal leaders. In August 1922, he was killed in an obscure skirmish with the Red cavalry. This was the end of the only attempt to coordinate various rebel groups, and it was detrimental to the Basmachis.

At the same time, Soviet authorities introduced a series of important reforms in Central Asia: the most unpopular laws of the Tashkent Soviet were abrogated; *waqfs* were reestablished and returned to the Muslims; religious schools reopened; and the *Shariyat* courts returned. All of these concessions placated most of Central Asia,[40] but the rebellion continued to gain new territories. In western Bukhara, the Samarkand region, the Red army in 1924 was obliged to conduct a regular campaign with airplanes, tanks, and armoured cars; this also occurred in Turkmenistan and the Khorezm under Junayd Khan. In 1928-1929, the revolt flared up again in eastern Bukhara and continued until 1931 when Ibrahim beg was finally executed. In Turkmenistan, the area of Krasnovodsk and the desert of the Karakum, the Basmachis resisted until 1932-1933; the last battle was fought in 1936.

The Balance of the Civil War

We have seen that the national minorities played an important role during the civil war, but what was the minorities' impact upon the domestic development and foreign relations of the Soviet Union? All in all, did the minorities represent an asset or a liability for the Bolsheviks?

To answer this question, we must remember that during the first five difficult and tragic years of 1918-1922, the Bolsheviks outsmarted their minority allies. Stalin was personally responsible for this remarkable success. With only a few unimportant exceptions, all Muslim nationalists — from the extreme pro-Bolshevik left to the moderate right wing, individuals and organized groups alike — terminated the civil war fighting side by side with the Reds. Their contribution to the final victory of the Bolsheviks cannot be underestimated.

The Bolsheviks also tried to convert conservative religious elements, including the well-organized Sufi brotherhoods. In Kazan the Bolsheviks obtained the total support of the Vaisi brotherhood. In the Chechen country, local Bolsheviks were able to partially neutralize the important Qadiriyq *tariqat*; the sheikh Ali Mitaev, head *mürshid* of the Bammat Giray Haji branch, cooperated with the new regime and for a short time was a member of the Chechen *revkom* — until his arrest in 1924 and execution in 1925. Even in Daghestan the Bolsheviks managed, for a short while, to oppose one religious authority against another: their ally, the Naqshbandi sheikh Ali of Akusha, against their enemy, Najmudden Gotsinski. (Ali of Akusha was also executed in 1929.) But this co-optation of religious leaders was extremely rare. It appears that the conservative Sufi 'fanatics,' whose ideology went back to the Middle Ages and who were well versed in Arabic but totally ignorant of twentieth century politics, understood the real essence of Bolshevism better than the sophisticated nationalist leaders educated in Russian and European universities.

The two popular uprisings led by religious conservatives (Daghestan and Basmachis) had a tremendous negative impact on Soviet strategy in the Muslim world abroad. While Zinoviev, Radek, and Bella Kun were urging foreign Muslim delegates at the Congress of the Toilers of the East in Baku in September 1920,[41] to unleash the holy war or *jihad* against 'British imperialism,' a real holy war was being waged against the Soviets by the Daghestani mountaineers and the Basmachi guerrillas. With these popular religious anti-Soviet uprisings just behind its borders, it was difficult for the Soviets to promote revolutionary anti-imperialist movements abroad (in Turkey and Iran) which were more or less based on Islam.

Already in 1920 Stalin had discovered the difficulty of reconciling anti-Islamic strategy at home with a pro-Islamic policy abroad. (His successors today are rediscovering this same truth in Afghanistan.) It is significant that there were no Soviet Muslim soldiers, officers, or political instructors in the Red division which was sent to Ghilan to help the *Jengeli* guerrilla fighters against the British and the Qadjar government. In the same way, relations with foreign Communist parties of Turkey, Iran, Egypt, or Indonesia were maintained exclusively by Russian or other European comrades.

It is not a paradox to claim that, in spite of the real help provided during the civil war by various fellow travellers and national Communists, Stalin and other Bolshevik leaders drew the conclusion that their Muslim allies were unreliable and could not be trusted. It is significant that when Stalin launched his first attack in 1923 against his fellow Muslim comrades, such as Sultan Galiev, Turar Ryskulov, Ikramov, and Khojanov, accusing them of 'pan-Turkist devation,' he insisted upon their connections with the Basmachis.[42] One wonders whether Stalin's accusation was simply a malignant lie or whether Muslim Communists did harbour sympathies for their 'reactionary' brethren, waging the *Jihad* against Russian comrades.

There is, of course, no evidence to support Stalin's accusation. However, we know the deep inbred respect of all Muslim intellectuals for the *ghazis*, fighters of the holy war, and it is not impossible that around 1923 some national Communists, convinced that cooperation with their Russian comrades was ending, were already considering the Basmachis as the *ultima ratio*, the final recourse against the Russians. If so, the Basmachi movement had a far deeper and long lasting impact on the general evolution of the USSR than it appeared at first sight.

Chantal Lemercier-Quelquejay

Conclusion

In 1980, the question of the Basmachis, which for years had been taboo, reappeared in the forefront of the Central Asian mass media; the historical works, memoirs, and novels on the fate of the Basmachis are being published in all languages. The meaning of this sudden reappearance is crystal clear to all Turkestanis; Soviet authorities are warning them, 'We have beaten you before, and, if necessary, we can beat you again.' They are also proclaiming to the world: 'In the 1920's, when Soviet Russia was weak and vulnerable, we defeated a well-organized and powerful rebellion in Central Asia. In the 1980's, when our army is the strongest in the world, we will easily beat the Afghan rebels.' We know that the same clever propaganda is being served to the Afghans in Afghanistan; its meaning is equally clear: 'We may have some difficulties today. It may take some time, but as we finally destroyed the Basmachis, so we will destroy you.'

There are, however, some major differences between the Basmachi revolt and the *mujahidin* guerrilla. In the 1920's, Communism was still a conquering ideology. People were ready to die for it, and the Red units, Russian and Muslim alike, fought the Basmachis with enthusiasm and ferocity. Today, the ferocity remains but the enthusiasm is gone, and Soviet soldiers in Afghanistan are not eager to die for the edification of socialism in another country. If Marxism-Leninism has lost its mobilizing power, Islam — especially its conservative fundamentalist trend — is more aggressively alive today than it was sixty years ago.

Another major difference is that, in spite of its popular character, the Basmachi movement never resembled a real Muslim holy war. A compromise was always possible between the Soviets and the *kurbashis*. Such is not the case of resistance in Afghanistan; all Soviet efforts to infiltrate the movement and influence its leaders have failed.

By 1936, Stalin had eliminated not only his declared enemies, the Basmachis and the Daghestani *ghazis*, but also fellow travellers and Muslim Party comrades. The entire pre-revolutionary native intelligentsia was physically liquidated in the bloody purges which began in all Muslim republics in 1928. Henceforward, former *ghazis* and members of the Communist party were thrown together in the dustbin of history as 'traitors,' 'the people's enemies,' 'obscurantists,' 'agents of foreign capitalism,' and 'stranglers of liberty' (*dushiteli svobody*). At least, such is the official approach.

The native population, intellectuals and masses alike, have a different attitude. While the Muslim nationalist leaders are viewed as 'victims' of Stalin, the Basmachis and *ghazis* are martyrs of the faith (*shahid*), who testified to the glory of God. It is very doubtful whether anyone in the USSR, except some historians, still remembers the names of Ahmed Baytursun, Najmuddin Samurskii, Nariman Narimanov, or even Sultan Galiev, but the Daghestani *mürids* and the Basmachis have grown to heroic proportions and belong to the glorious patrimony of resistance against the Russian conquerors. It is significant that the tomb of Uzun Haji, the intractable enemy of the Russians and Soviets, who promised to 'weave a rope to hang the engineers, the intellectuals, and all those who write from left to right,' is today the most popular place of pilgrimage in all of the North Caucasus.[43]

Notes

1. Gerhard v. Mende, *Der Nationale Kampf der Russlands Türken* (Berlin, 1936), p. 125.

2. Richard Pipes, *The Formation of the Soviet Union. Communism and Nationalism, 1917-1923* (Harvard University Press, Cambridge, Mass., 1957).

3. The only exception: Turkish troops in Baku from August to November, 1918, followed by the British who helped the short-lived Azerbaijani republic (August, 1919-April, 1920). The help provided by Afghanistan to the Basmachis was negligible.

4. Resolution of the Military Congress in Dimanstein (Edr) *Revolutsiia i Natsional'nyi Vopros*, t. III, February-October 1917, Moscow, 1930, pp. 312-314.

5. Text of the resolution of the Congress in Dimanstein, op. cit. pp. 231-233, quoting Drandin, *Oktiabrskii Rizhskii Front* (Moscow, 1922), pp. 56-60.

6. A dissident branch of the Naqshbandiya founded in 1862 in Kazan. The Vaisi *tariqa* joined the Bolsheviks because they considered the provisional government to represent 'Evil.' On this paradoxical, unholy alliance, cf. my article 'Le Vaisisme à Kazan. Contribution à l'histoire des Confréries musulmanes chez les Tatars de la Volga,' *Die Welt des Islams*, VI, no. 1-2, 1959, pp. 91-112.

7. The 20 members of the first Kazan *Revkom*, formed on 26 October 1917, were all Russian, and the 14 members of the second *Revkom*, formed on 3 November 1917, were also Russian. Out of the 11 commissars of the *Sovnarkom* of the Kazan republic formed on 17 November 1917, ten were Russian and one a Tatar. (Cf. A Bennigsen and Ch. Quelquejay, *Les Mouvements Nationaux chez les Musulmans de Russie – Le 'Sultangalievisme' au Tatarstan* (Paris-La Haye, 1960), pp. 84-85). The first *soviet* of Tashkent and of Sebastopol was also all-Russian.

8. *Zhizn Natsional'nostei*, no. 41 (97), 24. XII. 1920; also M.S. Sultan Galiev, 'Tatarskaia Avtonomnaia Respublika,' *Zhizn Natsional'nostei*, no. 1, January, 1923.

9. Crimean Tatar national party founded in July 1917, by a group of radical intellectuals. The relatively moderate right faction was close to the Russian Right SRs and the Mensheviks. The left (minority) faction was closer to the Bolsheviks.

10. 'The Horde of Alash,' (the mythical ancestor of the Kazakhs), the Kazakh national party founded in March 1917, by a group of intellectuals, including Ali Bukeykhanov, Ahmed Baytursun, Mir-Yaqub Dulatov, Dos-Mohammedov. Alash Orda was a moderate liberal group, halfway between the K.D. and the right

Socialist Revolutionaries.

11. R. Pipes, *The Formation of the Soviet Union*, op. cit., p. 176.

12. In April 1918, the Soviet regime of the Crimea, represented by the *Revkom* of Sebastopol, was destroyed by the German army occupying the peninsula; on 26 May and 28 May Georgia and Armenia proclaimed their independence. In June and July the Ural Cossacks shook off the authority of the Soviet, and on 4 July the Orenburg Cossacks re-entered Orenburg. On 20 July the Baku Commune was destroyed by an alliance of Russian Mensheviks and the Armenian Dashnaks (on 15 September the city was occupied by the Turks). In July, British units occupied Ashhabad, and, in August, the Czech legionnaires stormed Kazan.

13. M.S. Sultan Galiev, 'The Social Revolution and the East,' *Zhizn Natsional'nostei*, 38(46), 1919; English translation in Alexandre Bennigsen and S. Enders Wimbush, *Muslim National Communism in the Soviet Union. A Revolutionary Strategy for the Colonial World* (The University of Chicago Press, Chicago, 1979), p. 131.

14. Ahmed Baytursun, 'The Kirghiz and the Revolution,' *Zhizn Natsional'nostei*, no. 29(37), August 3, 1919. English translation in A. Bennigsen and S.E. Wimbush, *op. cit.*, p. 24.

15. The only White commanders who understood, to a point, the importance of the national (especially Muslim) problem were Kornilov, born in Kirghizia, and the baron Wrangel, of Swedish origin; however, when Wrangel took command in Crimea it was too late.

16. The Bolshevik government's first official 'prises de position,' in favour of Islam, tended to reinforce this feeling. Such was the famous 'appeal to all the Muslim workers of Russia and the East' of 24 November 1917, under the signatures of Lenin and Stalin, and the decree of the *Sovnarkom* of 12 December 1917, transferring the Quran of Osman from the Petrograd National Library to the Muslim Congress.

17. The great Tatar theologian Musa Jarulla Bigi, for instance, who proclaimed in 1925: 'A great revolution has triumphed in Russia, giving birth to a regime of justice and equality. Muslims enjoy equality, unity, and peace ...' Cf. A. Bennigsen and S.E. Wimbush, *Muslim National Communism, op. cit.*, p. 30.

18. R. Nafigov, 'Deiatel'nost' Tsentral'nogo Musul'manskogo Kommissariata pri Narodonom Kommissariate po delam Natsional'nostei v 1918 godu,' *Sovetskoe Vostokovedenie*, Moscow, 1958, no. 5, p. 116.

19. M.S. Sultan Galiev, 'Tatary v Revolutsii 1918 goda,' *Zhizn' Natsional'nostei*, no. 24(122), 1921; English text in A. Bennigsen and S.E. Wimbush, *Muslim National Communism, op. cit.*, p. 143.

20. This is certainly not the case today. Soviet Central Asian soldiers, engaged against the Afghan *mojahidins*, 'performed' very badly and were pulled out of Afghanistan in February, 1980.

21. A. Anushkin, 'Iz opyta korenizatsii v Kazakhskoi SSR,' *Revolutsiia i Natsional'nostei*, November 7, 1930.

22. N. Samurskii (Efendiev), *Daghestan*, Moscow, 1925, p. 131, wrote: 'For the mountaineers (of North Caucasus) Soviet power was not perceived as a Communist power, but as a Godless, Alien, Infidel power, bearer of the sinful, hated, accursed Western civilization.'

23. The history of the 1920-1921 revolt in the north Caucasus, so very similar to the war in Afghanistan, is currently a taboo topic in Soviet historiography. The best Soviet sources appeared in the 1920's: Najmuddin Samurskii (Efendiev), *Daghestan* (Moscow, 1925), and *Grazhdanskaiia Voina v Daghestane* (Makhach-Qala), 1925; A.A. Takho-Godi, *Revolutsiia i Kontrrevolutsiia v. Daghestane* (Moscow, 1927); A. Todorski, *Krasnaia Armia v Gorakh, Deistviia v Daghestane* (Moscow, 1924).

24. It began in Daghestan and Chechnia in February 1917, with the first clashes between the Muslim mountaineers and the Terek Cossacks.
25. N. Samurskii (Efendiev), *op. cit.*, p. 78.
26. In 1917, there were some 40,000 clerics in Daghestan, also called 'Arabists' — some 4% of the total population. Most of them were adepts of the Naqshbandiya. There were some 1500 religious schools (*medressehs* and *mek-tep*), Samurskii, *op. cit.*, p. 129.
27. Samurskii, *op. cit.*, p. 130.
28. Accused by Stalin of 'nationalism' and 'pan-Turkism,' Samurskii will disappear in the 1930's.
29. Several former tsarist officers played an active part in the uprising: Colonel Kaitmas Alikhanov of Khunzakh, Colonel Jafarov of Kudatl, Colonel Shamilev of Gimry, Captain Iman-Ali Ismailov of Andi, Colonel Omar Piralov of Gunib, and Lt. Hasan Abakarov.
30. Samurskii, *op. cit.*, pp. 127-129, cannot hide his admiration for his clerical adversaries: 'The *Molla* belongs to the people, he is armed with the same sword and the same rifle and in battle he is generally the leader, fighting on the forefront . . . the Daghestani clergy does not defend any class interest . . . it is the bearer of a certain democracy based on the support of the poorest and the weakest which was the quintessence of Shamil's rule . . . it is also the defender of national independence . . .'
31. A. Todorski, *op. cit.*, pp. 132-135 and 161-162.
32. *Id.* p. 135.
33. The parallel with the war in Afghanistan is, of course, striking, but, if the Afghan *ghazis* are fighting with the same absolute dedication as their Daghestani predecessors 60 years ago, the Soviet soldiers are very different from their grandfathers of 1920.
34. Soviet literature on the Basmachi is abundant. The best works were published in the 1920's and 1930's: G. Safarov, *Kolonial'naia Revolutsiia (Opyt Turkestana)* (Moscow, 1921); S.B. Ginsburg, 'Basmachestvo v Ferghane,' *Novyi Vostok*, 10-11, 1925, pp. 175-202; L. Soloveichik, *Ocherk Vozniknoveniia i Razvitiia sovremennogo Basmachestva v Bukhare* (Moscow, 1923). The post-war literature is poor and less reliable: Yv. A. Poliakov and A.I. Chugunov, *Konetz Basmachestva* (Moscow, 1976); A. Kokanbaev, *Bor'ba s Basmachestvom i uprochnenie sovetskoi Vlasti v Bukhare* (Tashkent, 1958).
Among the non-Soviet sources, the best are as follows: J. Castagné, *Les Basmatchis* (Paris, 1925); G. von Mende, *Der Nationale Kampf der Russland-Tuerken* (Berlin, 1936); and B. Hayit, *Die Nationalen Regierunge von Kokand (Choqand) und der Alash Orda* (Muenster, 1950).
35. S. Mambetaliev, *Sufizm zhana anyng Qyrgyzstandagy agymlary (Sufism and its Survivals in Kirghizia)*, Frunze, 1972 (in Kirghiz), notes that several Basmachi leaders belonged to a Sufi brotherhood; among them were Madamin beg, Janibeg Korshirmat, Islam Korbashi, Abdul Aziz Maksum, and Molla Dehkan. The last four belonged to the *tariqa* of the 'Hairy Ishans' (*Chachtuu Eshander*), a branch of the mystical Yasawiyah.
36. A Kokanbaev, *op. cit.*, p. 67.
37. *Id.*, p. 66.
38. Yu. A. Poliakov and A.I. Chugunov, *op. cit.*, p. 44.
39. According to A.I. Zevelev, 'Razgrom Kontr-revolutsionnogo Basmachestva v Turkestane,' *Uchenie Zapiski Tashkentskogo Pedinstituta im. Nizami*, quoting an order of Frunze, the commander of the Turkestan front, the mobilization involved 30,000 soldiers. About 350 Muslim officers, mainly Tatars and Bashkirs, were sent to Turkestan from Moscow; 500 native Communists served in the Red army as political instructors. (A. Kakanbaev, *op. cit.*, p. 75.).

40. *Cf.* R. Pipes, *The Formation of the Soviet Union*, Cambridge, Mass., 1957, p. 259.

41. The revolt in Daghestan broke out at the very moment the Congress of the Toilers of the East was meeting in Baku. Ordjonikidze, one of the chairmen of the Congress with Zinoviev, was obliged to leave in haste for the front.

42. Fourth Congress of the Central Committee of the RSP(b) with the Responsible Workers of the National Republics and Regions, 10 June 1923. An account of this conference has never been published. Stalin's speech appears in Volume 5 of his *Works*, 1921-23, Moscow, 1953, pp. 308-319. English text in A. Bennigsen and S.E. Wimbush, *op. cit.*, pp. 158-165.

43. It is significant that the most popular holy places of pilgrimage in Daghestan and in the Checheno-Ingush republic are the tombs of the Sufi sheikhs who fought the Russians. *Cf.* I.A. Makatov, '— Kul't Sviatykh ve Islame — Na materialakh Daghestanskoi ARRS i Checheno-Ingushskoi ARRS,' *Voprosy Nauchnogo Ateizma*, III, 1967, enumerates the most important ones: the aul of Akhulgo (Daghestan), where many murids of Shamil were killed; the aul of Uri (Daghestan), with the tomb of sheikh Abdurrahman of Sogratl', one of the leaders of the 1877 uprising who died in a Russian prison; the aul of Gergebil (Daghestan), with the tomb of the sheikh Mohammed of Balakhany, who commanded the insurgents at the battle of Arakany in 1920; the village of Qypchakh (Azerbaijan), with the tomb of Haji Murat, the hero of Tolstoy's novel who was killed by the Russians; and the village of Pervomaisk, district of Vedeno (Checheno-Ingush ASSR), with the tomb of Uzun Haji.

SOVIET NATIONALITIES UNDER ATTACK:
The World War II Experience

Alexander R. Alexiev

The Empire under Siege

Within the first few months of World War II, the German armies attacking on the Soviet front had achieved a number of quite remarkable victories. By the end of the first year of the war, German troops occupied nearly 500,000 square miles of Soviet territory and had taken more than 3 million prisoners. These same armies were to advance nearly to Moscow before their progress was arrested. Their rapid advance was based at least in part on the superior training of the German soldier, the technical superiority of German armaments (at least in the beginning), and the effective command and control structures the Germans had evolved. While these explanations are all valid — and one would have difficulty assigning priorities to them — not all German successes in the early days of the war were the result of their own technical superiority. Importantly the German attackers were rewarded in their efforts by an unusually receptive social milieu, which is another way of saying that many of the people under attack, after several decades of plunder and oppression at the hands of the Soviet Russians, welcomed them in. A great many of those extending the welcome were non-Russian subjects of the Soviet Empire, and thus it may be said that in a moment of acute crisis for Soviet power, multinationalism became a questionable strategic asset.

German advances were confined mostly to the western USSR, to the Ukraine, the Baltic states, Belorussia, and the Caucasus. In most of the territory of these regions, the Germans were regarded as liberators, and their arrival was celebrated by numerous anti-Soviet uprisings by the local populations. Soviet historians today are fond of telling how when the German onslaught began, except for a few 'anti-Soviet elements' the ethnically diverse peoples of the USSR came together as one unit to oppose the German aggressor. Of course, this is exactly what did not happen, or at best it happened only in a few regions. Rather, the German attack unleashed powerful centrifugal forces in the Soviet western borderlands, in the Caucasus, and even among Soviet Asians who were serving in the Soviet forces and elsewhere. This state of affairs was to continue in many areas until the Germans foolishly discredited themselves in the eyes of the local non-Russian peoples who had welcomed them as saviours. In other areas, where German policy on the ground was more enlightened, informed and strategically calculating, support for the German armies never flagged and the natives' anti-Soviet activities never abated, some people would argue right up to the present day.

Soviet multinational society at the time of the German invasion lacked any effective political consensus. The Baltic states (Lithuania, Latvia, and Estonia) had only recently been brought back into the Russian sphere of influence through force of arms and Soviet-German connivance after nearly two decades of independence and freedom. The Western Ukraine, like most other non-Russian territories of the former Russian Empire, had been pacified by the Red Army in the 1920s under the pretext of uniting to the new proletarian Soviet state those peoples who had 'invited' Bolshevik forces to protect them from 'foreign powers'. It made little difference in this regard that Lenin used this excuse as a way of reconstituting the historical Russian Empire; in fact, in nearly every minority region of the old Empire popular national independence movements had sprung up during the Bolshevik revolution to challenge continued Russian dominance, movements which sought, among other things, to limit or eliminate Russian interference in their national life once and for all.

Lenin's reconstruction of the Russian Empire was a brutal affair brought about by the power of the Red Army and the secret police (Cheka, GPU, or NKVD), which quickly and systematically set about to liquidate important non-Russian national leaders and cultural elites; to collectivize agriculture in the 1930s, which caused murderous famines; and to purge the national political organizations of anyone not loyal to Lenin and Stalin and, by extension, Russia. Bringing recalcitrant minorities to heel was not an instantaneous process; indeed, it required many years. By 1941, the process was yet incomplete, and it was into the chaos caused by Bolshevik policy in the minority regions that the Germans attacked. It was here that the invaders encountered in the vast non-Russian territories surrounding the Russian heartland millions of people who shared the German dream of eliminating the Soviet menace.

Curiously, only a few highly placed Germans seem to have had a proper appreciation of the advantages to be won as a result of Soviet ethnic vulnerabilities. Offered a unique opportunity to exploit this evident Soviet weakness, German planners, for the most part, proved inept. The reasons would appear to lie in the difficulty involved in convincing German political authorities, and indeed Hitler himself, to formulate a strategic policy toward Soviet non-Russians based on a body of strong evidence from the field and the sophisticated analysis of a few good specialists at home. Both sources pointed to the potential for reaping rich rewards from effective political-military action among Soviet non-Russians. In this short article, it is impossible to undertake a comprehensive examination of German trials and errors with the Soviet ethnic issue; such an examination may be found elsewhere.[1] Instead, I intend to examine German perceptions of the opportunities for waging 'ethnic warfare', and to survey their successes and failures where German forces encountered a potentially receptive audience. In this way it should be possible to develop the background for those who wish to undertake a comparison between the strategic problem as it was demonstrated in the 1940s and the residual or potential strategic problem of the same kind that may exist today.

German Ideology and Soviet Minorities

What would appear to have been the natural German advantages for projecting their military force, and hence their political objectives, through the minorities of the recently reconstituted Russian Empire were offset from the beginning by the refusal of large sections of the Nazi leadership to see this as a desirable policy. For the most part, this refusal stemmed from important facets of Nazi ideology: the imperative of territorial aggrandizement (*Lebensraum*) and the racial theories that were at the heart of Nazi belief. Hitler's desire to expand the size of the new German empire at the expense of the Soviet Union, a goal about which he spoke often,[2] in conception necessarily meant that the new German lands would be taken largely from the non-Russian subjects of the Soviet State. Territories ripe for incorporation into the Reich included the Baltic States, Belorussia, the Western Ukraine (Galicia), and the Crimea; later, plans were advanced to incorporate all of the Ukraine, parts of the Caucasus, and large expanses of Russia itself. These lands were to be exploited for the benefit of the Reich. Those populations who would be allowed to remain on the land were to be left to fend for themselves in the face of this exploitation, which the Nazi leadership recognized would lead to wholesale starvation.[3] Nearly 50 million Soviet subjects were slated for deportation and their territories were to be resettled in a way to ensure their 'Germanization'.

Nazi leaders considered most Soviet nationalities — the Baltic peoples are an important exception; they were considered to be 'Germanizeable' — as racially inferior to Aryans, much in the same way Jews were considered. Slavs came in for particular opprobium and were considered as sub-human (*Untermenschen*). All Soviet Asians were referred to collectively as 'Mongols', although they were considered to be a somewhat more vague threat to Aryan superiority than were the Slavs. Armenians, because of their penchant for trade and commerce, were thought by the Nazis to have mixed biologically with Jews. Curiously, Georgians were considered to be Aryans, and they were promised a dominant position in the Caucasus in the new German order.

These views, which were held strongly by most of the top Nazi leadership, precluded their recognizing important Soviet internal political vulnerabilities and understanding the strategic advantage the exploitation of such weaknesses could offer to German armies. Almost alone among the Nazi leadership, Alfred Rosenberg, the noted Nazi ideologue and wartime minister of the Reich Ministry for Occupied Eastern Territories (Ostministerium), saw in the Soviet minority situation an environment ripe for exploitation and began to make plans for the post-war period. Rosenberg envisaged a massive dismantling of the Soviet State, which would dramatically weaken its Russian component. To this end, he planned several separate units — which would remain under German control — that were characterized by their ethnic distinctiveness and compatability: Great Russia, Belorussia, Ukraine and the Crimea, the Baltic States, the Don region, the Caucasus, and Turkestan. It is clear that Rosenberg's more differentiated approach and his understanding of the strategic possibilities presented by the Soviet nationality issue could have paid some substantial dividends to German conduct of the war in the USSR. However, he was unable to implement his ideas, largely because of his sycophancy to Hitler.

Rosenberg's Ministry, on the other hand, perhaps because of their chief's interest in ethnic warfare as a political weapon, became a forum for debate on this issue. On one hand, a large pro-Russian group argued that the aims of German political warfare should be to drive a wedge between the Soviet leadership and the Soviet people. They rejected the notion that the Soviet state should be broken up, for this, it was argued, would antagonize 'the potentially friendly Russian population by the prospect of partitioning the Russian state'.[4] Separatist tendencies among non-Russians were not particularly strong, this group argued; moreover they should not be encouraged. This group's ultimate goal can be described as the abolition of Bolshevik rule and its replacement by a Free Russia.

A second group fought for precisely the opposite strategy: the formulation and implementation of a plan of political warfare whose main instrument would be the Soviet nationalities themselves. The German approach should be to give not only attention to the Soviet minorities but preferential treatment. They argued that Soviet minorities were the most anti-Soviet of all Soviet peoples and that this force should be mobilized to assist the German advance. Moreover, the minorities, if properly organized and controlled, represented the best bulwark against future Russian expansion. As we shall see, this group's views were to be put into practice in the Caucasus to some extent in the later stages of the war with considerable success.

Ideas in Practice

By the end of July 1941 German armies occupied the Baltic States, and by late fall the Ukraine and Belorussia also were within Germany's grasp. These were prizes of real significance, the heart of the USSR's agricultural complex. Sensible policy would have recognized the need for the enlightened administration of the populations of these captive territories, especially inasmuch as most of the Balts, Ukrainians, and many Belorussians made no secret of their pleasure at the Germans' arrival.[5] In the Western Ukrainian center of Lvov for example, Ukrainian nationalist and anti-Soviet factions staged a massive revolt even before the arrival of the Germans.

Administrative authority for occupation policy ultimately fell to Rosenberg, but he was severely constrained from the outset by the number of competing entities. For one, the SS under Himmler made and enforced its own policies in the occupied lands; for another, the economic agencies responsible for the exploitation of these territories were not under Rosenberg's control. Finally, the Army had a natural interest in the administration of the occupied territories if only to ensure logistic support to its further efforts and to promote internal security. These rivalries led to inconsistent and contradictory policies, which were usually employed at the expense of the local populations.

Lacking a consistent, well-articulated policy from Berlin, German occupation practices soon turned counter-productive, as is well known. In the Ukraine, for example, which was the real prize among the captured territories, nationalist activities were banned by the Germans, even though these were for the most part pro-German. The Germans compounded this folly by awarding a large piece of Ukrainian territory to Romania. Military jurisdiction over Ukrainian territory was soon ended and replaced by the most odious kind of Nazi civilian rule, whose methods included the systematic terrorization of the Ukrainian populace and the stripping of its economic resources — including the sending of forced labour to Germany — for the Reich's benefit. German bureaucrats took over all important government functions, despite the willingness of most Ukrainians to cooperate fully. Education in the Ukraine was emasculated; any schooling beyond the most rudimentary reading and writing skills was considered superfluous by the local Nazi leadership. 'To teach the Russians, Ukrainians and Kirghiz to read and write,' Hitler had warned, 'will eventually be to our disadvantage; education will give the more intelligent among them an opportunity to study history, to acquire a historical sense, and hence to develop political ideas which cannot but be harmful to our interests'.[6] Nazi policy also foundered on the religious issue, which could have been exploited to considerable effect. The Nazis opposed the renaissance of a unified national Ukrainian church — which had suffered terribly under Soviet rule — on the grounds that this might lead to Ukrainian nationalism, which would be hard to control. In a similar failure to enact comprehensive policy, the Reichcommissariat opposed the decollectivization of the disastrous Soviet collective farming system, despite the successes of some local German officials or military commanders, who saw this as a means of bringing the Ukrainian population to their side.

In sum, Nazi policy in the Ukraine was for the most part counterproductive. A former Soviet official captured by the Nazis explained it this way: 'We have badly mistreated our people; in fact so bad that it was almost impossible to treat them worse. You Germans have managed to do that. In the long term the people will choose between two tyrants the one who speaks their language. Therefore, we will win the war'.[7]

In the Baltic States, where the population was considered 'Germanizable' and where opposition to continued Soviet rule was vehement, German plans called for more lenient treatment than was accorded the Ukrainians, although still not equal to the superior Germans. Yet here again, Nazi racial ideology stood in the way of effective policy. Estonians were considered to be the most Aryan of the three peoples, while Latvians were thought to be polluted with Russian elements and Lithuanians with Russian and Jewish ones. Extensive Germanization was prescribed for all three nations, their nationalist activities, which were considered anti-German in spite of their strong anti-Russian character, were suppressed, and substantial parts of the native intelligentsia of all three nations were liquidated or deported. The Germans kept substantial economic assets of the Baltic peoples, which the Soviets had seized and nationalised, rather than return them to their owners, a move which would certainly have solidified Baltic support for German objectives against Russia. Eventually, even Balts were conscripted for forced labour in Germany. Thus, despite their more relaxed occupation policies in the Baltic states compared to those employed in the Ukraine, German authorities steadily lost the support of the Baltic peoples which had appeared so strong when German armies first liberated them from Soviet rule, and by late 1943 Baltic anti-German resistance groups were already beginning to appear.

Successes in the Caucasus

It is ironic, perhaps, that where the Nazis failed to take advantage of inherently advantageous ethnic situations in the Ukraine and the Baltic States and, indeed, instituted policies that were blatantly counter-productive to German short- and long-term objectives, in the Caucasus, which is one of the most complex ethnic mosaics in the world, they realized some significant successes. Like the Ukrainians and the Balts, most of the peoples of the Caucasus were devoutly anti-Russian, sentiments that went back for centuries. But unlike their policies for these regions of the USSR, the Nazi leadership recognized that, apart from Baku's important oil production, there was little to be exploited economically in the Caucasus. Moreover, most of the peoples of the Caucasus — the Armenians are a major exception — were considered by Nazi ideologues to be genetically superior to Slavs, and the Georgians were considered a superior race altogether.

German policy in the Caucasus was influenced by two factors. First was the need to cultivate Turkey, which was seen as the protector of the Turkic peoples of the Caucasian region. Second, administrative jurisdiction for the Caucasus was never passed to civilian control — the precursor to the disastrous policies in the Ukraine and the Baltic States — but remained under the Wehrmacht. Furthermore, the important German operatives in the Caucasus were of the 'realist' school, who believed that the best approach to the Soviet nationalities issue was to encourage them to support German war aims. Materials used to acquaint the troops with the ethnic situation in the Caucasus eschewed heavy racial propaganda about inferior races and Aryan superiority, concentrating instead on descriptions designed to increase the admiration of the troops for the peoples of the area.

Wehrmacht directives spelled out the Army's determination to sway the Caucasians to their side. For example, in July 1942, Commander in Chief of Army Group A, Field Marshall von List, issued the following order:

1. The population of the Caucasus should be treated as friendly nations, except when they show themselves to be anti-German.
2. The aspirations of the mountaineers to do away with the collective system should not be hindered in any way.
3. The reopening of houses of worship of all confessions and the cultivation of religious customs and traditions is to be allowed.
4. Property is to be respected and requisitioned goods should be paid for.
5. The trust of the population is to be won by exemplary conduct. Its collaboration is of great importance in the mountainous area which is difficult to control militarily, and can also considerably facilitate the further advance of the German troops.
6. All necessary war measures causing hardship to the population should be explained and justified.
7. The honour of the Caucasus women should be especially respected.[8]

The indigenous population was to be given full autonomy in cultural and educational affairs, wide-ranging self government, and considerable position in the administration of the region.[9] Religious freedom was re-introduced by the Germans, and this was received with special pleasure by the Muslim populations of the region, who had been under unrelenting Soviet anti-religious pressure for several decades.[10] School systems were allowed to operate with a minimum of German interference and were administered by local authorities.

German administrators were more serious about carrying out agricultural reforms in the Caucasus than they had been in the Ukraine and the Baltic states. Nearly 40 percent of *kolkhozes* were transformed within one year to agricultural cooperatives; in fact, in many regions of the Caucasus, peasants had already divided up the land, stock, and equipment and dissolved the hated Soviet collective farms even before the Germans arrived. Moreover, the Germans were far more restrained in applying forced labour recruitment in the Caucasus than they were in other occupied areas, depending almost entirely on volunteers.[11]

For the most part, at least until they were forced on the defensive

Soviet Nationalities Under Attack

by the advancing Soviet forces after Stalingrad, German authorities honoured these pledges, although occasional backsliding did creep in. The results were significant. The Soviets were unable to organize any anti-German partisan efforts of any consequence in the region; in fact, anti-partisan activity was left almost entirely in the hands of the indigenous peoples, who were more than ready to support the German war effort in this way. Many Caucasian national units entered the German service and fought against the Soviets. Logistic support for the German forces was secured even in this economically poor region by the willingness of the local population to assist in agriculture and industry. Anti-Soviet partisan units from the indigenous nationalities even continued to battle the advancing Soviets long after the Germans had retreated.

Soviet Nationalities in German Uniforms

It must be stressed that for the most part German policies among Soviet minority groups — with some rare exceptions — can be characterized as inept and counter-productive. While some members of Hitler's planning apparatus did understand that political warfare was as important as military might, they had little success in making themselves heard and felt in actual policy decisions. Where there were successes, as in the Caucasus, they were the result more often than not of the sensible attitude of the local German commander rather than of the implementation of central policy. And in many areas, particularly in the Ukraine and the Baltic states, few commanders would seem to have been able to assert common sense policies at the time in the face of strong resistance from those in Hitler's entourage possessed of racial theories, which seemingly made cooperation and collaboration with Soviet minorities unlikely if not impossible, and from the SS, which in the field was a law unto itself.

This being said, it must be noted that — German racial theories and brutality aside — collaboration between non-Russian nationalities and the German invaders took place on an unprecedented scale, many even taking up arms on the German side to fight the Soviets. The only plausible explanation for this development is that the minorities in question had become so convincingly anti-Soviet over the last 20 years that they were willing to cast their lot with an invader whose policies they found to be demonstrably brutal and oppressive.

At first, Nazi policy rejected the notion that Soviet minorities that fell under their control could be used to fight against the Russians. This was so for two reasons. First, of course, was the ever-present racial disdain for non-Germans. Second, Hitler feared that allowing Soviet minorities to fight on the side of his troops would lead to their advancing political demands when the war was over. To prevent this, in the first months of the war Nazis moved to disband and disarm indigenous units, such as those in the Baltic states and the Ukrainian nationalist military organization (UPA), which sprung up spontaneously when the conflict erupted.

Yet, while Nazi ideologues resisted the incorporation of non-German troops into the German fighting machine, field commanders quickly recognized the advantages of doing so, and by late fall of 1941 the practice was already well advanced. One year after the beginning of the war, one million former Soviet citizens, both Russian and non-Russian, had begun to participate actively in the German war effort. Some served as direct volunteers to the Wehrmacht or SS units; others joined indigenous ethnic units under German control and supervision.

In an attempt to redress serious shortages of reserves, local German commanders began recruiting native inhabitants directly into the Wehrmacht, where some served in front line capacities. Collectively they were referred to as Hilfswillige, or Hiwis (meaning 'little helpers'). They wore German uniforms and received the same basic rates of pay and rations as German soldiers. In August 1942 an order of the Army High Command gave divisions the right to recruit as many auxiliaries as necessary to assume full battle strength, but this number was frequently exceeded in practice.[12] Some divisions consisted of up to 50 percent auxiliaries by late 1942.[13]

It is difficult to determine how many of the Auxiliaries were non-Russians, but there is sufficient evidence to suggest that at least half were.[14] Most were recruited from released POWs, Red Army stragglers, and from the indigenous populations. Most released POWs were Ukrainian or Belorussian, for it was German practice to release only those POWs whose native lands already had been occupied. Of course, those auxiliaries recruited from the occupied territories must have been mostly from the non-Russian peoples.

Indigenous military units composed of natives from the occupied territories were intended for both front line service against Soviet troops and for service in the rear against partisans. By mid-1943 there were many of these units in operation in the Baltic states, the Ukraine, and in the Slavic areas, where they were heavily involved in anti-partisan activities. Operating along side these units were local security units — known as Guards units — or indigenous police formations, depending on the region in which they were employed. Their duties included guarding military installations and railroads and preventing partisan infiltration. While no figures are available on the numbers involved in these different units, German sources are unanimous in reporting that indigenous units represented a majority of all rear security troops. One source estimates this number to be as high as two million.[15]

National combat units also played an important part in German front line combat activities. By late 1941 the first national units had already been organized, and by 1943 hundreds of thousands of Soviet non-Russians had joined these units. Baltic units were among the first organized. Balts were quick to organize under German supervision, obviously thinking ahead to the after-war period when their participation in the fight against the Russians might win them concessions from Hitler on their long-standing objective of national independence. Estonian units performed particularly well during the Soviet winter counteroffensive of 1941-42, and on the basis of their performance, German authorities considered the possibility of a massive mobilization of Balts, an idea that was later dropped. Baltic units, however, demanded to be used only in defense of their national territories, which went against the German grain.[16] Large Baltic units were established nonetheless under the supervision of the SS beginning in early 1943, but they soon ran into difficulty attracting a sufficient number of recruits due to the brutal German policies generally in the Baltic states. Despite these limitations, by 1944 there were three Baltic divisions of the Waffen SS fighting alongside smaller units. These fought until the end of the war, compiling a distinguished combat record.

It is important to note that despite the fact that the war was fought mostly in the western regions of the USSR, the largest number of national units came from the Turkic/Muslim Central Asian and Caucasian volunteers, but there were also sizeable contingents of Georgians and Armenians as well. Again, Nazi racial theories would seem to have made these Soviet Muslims unlikely candidates for recruitment. For example, at the beginning of the war tens of thousands of Soviet Muslims who had deserted to the Germans or had been taken prisoner were summarily shot, many on the assumption that because they had been circumcised they were Jewish.

Yet by late 1941 the Nazi leadership had already embarked on a remarkable about turn. Hitler himself came to the conclusion that Soviet Muslims were among the most anti-Bolshevik of Soviet citizens and were 'by and large of good soldierly qualities'.[17] Turkey also may have exerted influence on the Germans to revise their harsh policies toward Soviet Muslims.[18]

By 1942 two special purpose national formations had been organized under the supervision of army intelligence. The first was made up primarily of Turkestanis and its mission was to incite uprisings behind Soviet lines. To this end, its members were trained in sabotage and subversive warfare. The second unit was for use in the Caucasus and had a special propaganda role.[19] Recruitment of regular 'East Legions' took place mainly in the POW camps in Poland. The call for volunteers went out, and the response was overwhelming. By mid-1943, an independent Turkic division was authorized; apart from the legions, many other units of Turkic/Muslim collaborators were formed, including under the supervision of the Waffen SS.

The exact number of participants in the East Legions is difficult to ascertain. The lowest estimates start at 250,000.[20] It is probable, in fact, that at least some Soviet nationalities may have been better represented in the German army than in the Red army.[21] These figures become more striking when one considers the appalling handicaps the East Legion troops had to overcome, including discrimination at the hands of regular German troops, poor equipment, and poor training. Beyond this, it would appear that German authorities offered the East Legion soldiers no political reward for their service, such as the promise of national independence or substantial autonomy free from Russian control. We can only speculate how powerful an instrument the East Legions might have been had such political motivation been present.

Conclusions

Several important conclusions are unavoidable. First, when faced with an onrushing army intent on destroying the Soviet state, large numbers of Soviet non-Russians (as well as Russians) turned on the Soviets by actively or passively assisting the German war effort. At this time and under these conditions, it would be impossible for Soviet scholars to deny now what Soviet political leaders knew then: Soviet multi-nationalism was a distinct liability when the very existence of the Soviet state was in question.

Second, although many Germans in positions of authority either did not realize or were prepared to discount the importance of Soviet multinationalism in the war in the East, Soviet minorities offered German political and military planners a distinct and potent strategic weapon against the Soviets. Where this weapon was employed with tact and its objectives clearly defined, it proved to be a remarkably effective instrument of German policy. Even where German policy was wrongheaded and measures toward non-Russians were brutal and oppressive, a measure of success was realized. There can be little doubt that a more sensible political leadership in Berlin could have reaped impressive rewards from the military struggle in the USSR through a thorough and positive exploitation of the nationality issue, perhaps even assuring a different outcome to the conflict.

Third, Soviet authorities recognized the inherent and real threat posed by the nationalities of the Soviet state in time of war and acted to reduce it. Stalin in his famous victory toast to 'the Great-Russian people' may have been voicing a sentiment that must have been felt by nearly all Soviet citizens in 1945: the war had been won primarily by the Russians themselves. And while it was the case that many members of other national groups fought with Stalin against the Germans, great numbers of others chose to oppose continued rule by the Russians even if it meant fighting with the detested Germans.

How much this situation has changed today is hard to judge. At the very least, in the absence of conclusive evidence that the pressures and strains that caused large parts of the Soviet empire to fragment off in time of war no longer exist it should remain a pressing strategic issue demanding our close attention.

Notes

1. The issues discussed here are examined in considerable detail and fully documented in my *Soviet Nationalities in German Wartime Strategy, 1941-1945*, The Rand Corporation, R-2772-NA, August 1982.

2. Adolf Hitler, *Mein Kampf* (Cambridge, Mass.: The Riverside Press, 1943), p. 643.

3. See Christian Streit, *Keine Kamaraden: Die Wehrmacht und de Sowjetischen Kriegsgefangenen, 1941-1945* (Stuttgart: Deutsche Verlags-Anstalt), p. 63.

4. See OKW (Armed Forces High Command)/WPr, 'Weisungen fur die Handhabung der Propaganda im Falle Barbarosa,' June 9, 1941, cited in Alexander Dallin, *German Rule in Russia, 1941-1945* (London, 1957), p. 57.

5. See for example, the intelligence report of the Army Group South, 'Stimmung und Lage beim Einmarsch der deutschen Truppen,' October 28, 1941, R6/67, Bundesarchiv, Koblenz.

6. *Hitler's Table Talk*, p. 224, cited in Dallin, p. 459.

7. Theodor Oberlander, 'Bundnis oder Ausbeutung', June 22, 1943, p. 130 R6/70, Bundesarchiv, Koblenz.

8. 'Befehl an alle im Kaukasus eingesetzten Truppen,' July 1942, R6/65,

Bundesarchiv, Koblenz.

9. See for example, 'Kaukasusrichtlinien', August 1942, R6/143, Bundesarchiv, Koblenz.

10. See for example, 'Lagebericht des Chefs der Sicherheitspolizei und des SD,' October 16, 1942, R6/143, Bundesarchiv, Koblenz; also Brautigam report to Rosenberg, December 22, 1942, R6/65, Bundesarchiv, Koblenz.

11. Alexander Dallin, 'The North Caucasus,' in John Armstrong, ed., *Soviet Partisans in World War II* (Madison: Univ. of Wisconsin Press, 1969), p. 579.

12. See Order #8000: 'Landseigene Helfskrafte im Osten,' Oberkommando des Heeres, August 1942.

13. Cited in Dallin, German Rule, p. 537.

14. See Jürgen Thorwald, *Die Illusion: Rotarmisten in Hitlers Heeren* (Zurich: Dromer Knauer Verlag, 1974), p. 12; also Peter Kleist, *Zwischen Hitler und Stalin* (Bonn: 1950), p. 202.

15. George Fischer, *Soviet Opposition to Stalin* (Cambridge, Mass.: Harvard Univ. Press, 1952), p. 45.

16. See for example, the proposal by the Latvian administration to the German authorities to set up a Latvian army of 125,000 in December 1942, R6/65, Bundesarchiv, Koblenz. On Lithuanian and Estonian positions, see 'Denkschrigt uber die Moglichkeit die Bereitschaft des litauischen Volkes fur den Kriegseinsatz zu steigern' (no date given), R6/68, Bundesarchiv, Koblenz, and 'Moglichkeiten einer Autonomie Estlands im Kriege' (no date given), R6/67, Bundesarchiv, Koblenz.

17. Joachim Hoffmann, *Die Ostlegionen 1941-1943* (Freiburg: Verlag Rombach, 1976), p. 25.

18. See Dallin, *German Rule*, pp. 234, 539.

19. For details, see Hoffman, pp. 26-27.

20 Estimates are provided by Joachim Hoffman, *Deutsche und Kalmyken, 1942 bis 1945 (Einzelschriften zur militarischen Geschichte des Zweiten Weltkrieges*, published by Militargeschichtlichen Forschungsamt, Vol. 14) (Freiburg: Verlag Rombach, 1974, p. 172; Gerhardt von Mende, 'Erfahrungen mit Ostfreiwilligen in der deutschen Wehrmacht wahrend des Zweiten Weltkrieges,' in *Auslandsforschung, No. 1, Vielvolkerheere und Koalitionskriege*, Damstadt, 1952, p. 25; Burkhart Muller-Hillebrand, *Das Heer 1933-1945*, Vol. III: *Der Zweifrontenkrieg, Das Heer vom Beginn des Geldzuges Gegen die Sowjetunion bis zum Kriegsend*, Frankfurt, 1969, p. 70.

21. After 1943 the representation of the non-Slavic nationalities in the Soviet army decreased dramatically. See S.L. Curran and D. Ponomareff, *Managing the Ethnic Factor in the Russian and Soviet Armed Forces: An Historical Overview*, The Rand Corporation, R-2640/1, July 1982, p. 28.

EMPIRE, NATIONALITIES, BORDERS:
Soviet Assets and Liabilities

Daniel C. Matuszewski

The Soviet Union is the last of the great European empires, and the multinational origins and character of the USSR provide that state with a complicated mixture of assets and liabilities. That mixture of assets and liabilities helps to explain why, on the one hand, Moscow finds it indispensable to retain an extraordinarily tight set of domestic political controls to quash potential dissidence. On the other hand, it also helps to explain critical aspects of Soviet foreign policy behaviour along the USSR's vast and sensitive peripheries where Moscow continues to enjoy certain geopolitical advantages and opportunities precisely because of its relatively successful management of the nationality question.

While the recent demographic boom among Central Asian nationalities and the 1979 invasion of Afghanistan have brought new attention to the Soviet ethnic dilemma among specialists and non-experts alike, the specific political and social consequences of that multi-ethnic feature need careful and nuanced analysis. There is an exquisite balance between Moscow's concern about potential domestic instability stemming from this nationality structure and Moscow's manipulation, to its benefit, of nationality relations across crucial segments of its borders, especially to the south and east. Understanding the dynamics of that balance is an important part of understanding Soviet foreign policy behaviour.

After centuries of expansion into the Baltic areas, the Ukraine, the Caucasus, Central Asia, and the Siberian East, the Soviet state was faced with an acute set of geopolitical options after the 1917 Revolution: should it divest itself of the vast territorial acquisitions of the tsarist past and retreat to a much-reduced Russian core, or should it move quickly to re-establish Moscow's traditional dominance of the non-Russian border areas? Once the practical steps were taken in the 1920s to retain and consolidate that territorial legacy, and decisions were made to undertake in those lands a 'modernizing' programme of systematic social engineering and transformation, the Soviet state became involved in an extremely delicate experiment which continues to condition its behaviour in a fundamental way.

Daniel C. Matuszewski

Having staked out its claim to being a unique revolutionary state with a messianic international mission, the USSR may now be compelled by the sensitivities of its own multinational structure to maintain strict ritualistic adherence to that ideology. It is commitment to that 'mission' which lends legitimacy to the regime. If the Soviet Union were suddenly to divest itself of the messianic mantle of revolution, it would overnight become simply a traditional great power — with little claim either to the maintenance of Russian dominance of the numerous minority peoples of the USSR or to the maintenance of its strict domestic political controls. Thus, a rigid ideology may well be seen by the Soviet élite as an unavoidable response to geopolitical imperatives and a *sine qua non* for Russian survival. In some very tangible ways, the Russians are now prisoners of their past and move in the realm of liberalizing reform with great caution and circumspection. Neither a Chernenko, a Sakharov, nor a Solzhenitsyn will be able to find an easy way out of this trap.[1]

The vast Russian empire had been constructed at great cost over more than half a millenium prior to the revolution of October 1917. The principality of the House of Moscow had risen from humble origins to expand its control over the neighbouring Russian principalities in the 15th and 16th centuries. When Ivan IV (the Terrible) broke the power of the Tatar khanates with the capture of Kazan and Astrakhan in 1552 and 1556, he quickly extended Russian power along the whole length of the Volga River and established the basis for subsequent Russian expansion to the shores of the Baltic to the west, to the Ukrainian plains to the south, and to the great Siberian forest expanses to the east.

The Turkic, Finnic, and Mongol tribes of the Volga region and Siberia were semi-nomadic and technologically backward; their small numbers and elemental political systems did not permit them to offer long resistance to the Muscovite freebooters in pursuit of furs and territory to the east. Moscow subdued most of Siberia in the 17th century. The end of the 17th century also witnessed Moscow's union with the ethnically and religiously kindred Ukrainian peoples to the east of the Dnieper River as the Ukrainian Cossacks sought a Russian protectorate against their Polish antagonists to the west. The eighteenth-century wars with Sweden brought Russian power to the Baltic Sea, and the small but culturally advanced Estonian and Latvian populations of that littoral were caught in what became a centuries-long tension between Germanic influences on the one side and Slavic pressures on the other. The wars of Catherine the Great at the end of that century added the important territories of the western Ukraine, great parts of the Polish-Lithuanian Commonwealth which was then being divided between Austria, Prussia, and Russia; and the north shores of the Black Sea and the Crimea.

In the first half of the 19th century Russia incorporated the remaining central regions of Poland, the Kingdom of Finland, and the Georgian, Armenian and Azerbaijani areas of the Caucasus. The great Central Asian regions were absorbed later in the century, and, with the exception of Moldavia (which would be added at Romania's expense only at the end of the Second World War), the mosaic of the sprawling multinational Russian empire was all but complete.

In varying but always fragile degrees of subordination to the Russian centre by the start of the 20th century were more than 70 million non-Russian peoples from the heart of central Europe to the seas off Japan, hundreds of ethnic groups and scores of religious sects. One German specialist at the time calculated that between the end of the 15th century and the end of the 19th century, the Russian empire grew at the rate of 50 square miles per day. Poles, Finns, Jews, Germans, Armenians, Mongols all owed allegiance to the tsar, and the Eastern Orthodox Church professed the dominant faith in a state which encompassed Catholics, Protestants, Muslims, Jews, Buddhists, fire-worshippers and others. Had the unusual sale of Alaska not taken place in 1867, some American Indians and other North American groups might have found their place within this empire as well.

Today, the Russians number some 137 million in a total Soviet population of 265 million, and the challenge of managing that vast polyethnic mosaic has become even more complicated. The Soviet state has survived barely two generations in its new imperial form and the report card must remain out on the issue of its long-term viability. Lenin's genius at the beginning of the twentieth century was to recognize the breadth of ethnic aspirations for emancipation and to utilize them by calling on the 'oppressed peoples to rise up.' This call was far more powerful and far more instrumental in the Bolshevik victory than the standard 'Workers of the world, unite.' Those ethnic aspirations have taken on newer and more complicated forms, and the Russians remain faced with the task of controlling these divergent interests.

Daniel C. Matuszewski

Ethnic Strengths and Weaknesses

The nationality question in the USSR is of central importance to the stability of the world political system. The potential fragilities of Soviet nationality structure are real, but it is essential to assess accurately their relative weight within the political life of the state and not misjudge their scope, direction, outer parameters, and limitations. We especially need a new and realistic assessment of the political, social, economic, and cultural control mechanisms available to the Soviets that have thus far successfully contained and stabilized the multinational body politic.

One feature of their policy that cannot be ignored has been the repeated, successful recruitment of native élites. One of the factors which played a substantial role in early Bolshevik successes was their ability to draw to their side and recruit substantial and influential elements from each of the non-Russian groups they sought to retain within the new Soviet state. While Red Army intervention in many of the peripheral nationality areas from 1917 on obviously played a role in determining the outcomes there, genuine civil wars splitting the indigenous populations were raging in most if not all of those areas, wars which in part at least turned on the issue of continuing close relations with the Russian centre. That issue divided, and continues to divide, substantial segments of the local élites as well as the populations at large.

Not only therefore does one find the phenomenon of new co-opted bureaucratic élites created by the Soviets with a strong immediate stake in the continuance of the current regime, but there also exists an influential crosscut of the local élites and populace which remains committed through personal conviction to the idea of a close political, economic, and military link to the Russian state. What Merle Fainsod called 'the creation of a new class of beneficiaries' had great significance for the stabilization of the regime and the system, and the replication of similar sets of beneficiaries among later generations is crucial to the stability of the state.

The appearance of such Turkic representatives as the Uzbek Sharaf Rashidov, the Kazakh Dinmukhamed Kunayev, and the Azeri Geidar Aliyev in the very highest political councils of the Politburo in Moscow is an example of the system's providing such opportunities in order to impart a sense of nationality participation. The fact that an Azeri such as Aliyev continues to be mentioned as a viable candidate for the highest post of Party General Secretary demonstrates that at times the policy is more than mere window-dressing. Seweryn Bialer has called attention to the importance of this pattern of social mobility and élite creation in the socialization and stability of the non-Russian republics:

> It is the process of formation of such native élites, of the political and social mobility that it represents, of the opportunity and satisfaction of indigenous cadres that it reflects, which forms the basis of the probably still strong commitment of these cadres to the existing system and is a key element of the explanation for the stability of nationality relations in the past decade.[2]

While this process constitutes a source of substantial strength for the regime, its termination or exhaustion would conversely have serious negative, destabilizing consequences. Faced with any such termination of opportunities in the future, indigenous élites would be motivated to press more sharply for increased autonomy from the centre. In Central Asia especially, an increasingly large number of native professionals is emerging from the grassroots and coming into sharp competition with Slavic immigrants. If the rapid development of such local talent outstrips the system's capacity to absorb it, the resulting frustration could have dangerous political effects.[3]

In addition to its efforts at élite creation and co-optation, a pattern which employs a wide range of economic, social, and political incentives to build personal stakes in regime continuity and stability, the Soviet government does not hesitate to utilize a variety of negative reinforcements. There is the obvious yet sometimes overlooked set of police and security controls at the state's disposal: extensive networks of informers; mail, telephone, and personal surveillance, legal controls on residence and internal movement within the country; plus a variety of legal and extralegal modes of incarceration and political hospitalization.[4] These techniques should not be underestimated in the shaping of habits of internalized self-censorship and ritualized adherence to official norms of behaviour which play a central role in stabilization of the system. As far as the subject nationalities are concerned, the overwhelming force of the police apparatus, and the willingness of the Muscovite élite to use that force, are also critical factors in ensuring their subservience. These coercive features are too often only enumerated briefly by Western analysts in any list of presumably equal and undifferentiated techniques for dominance.

Mention of the army itself is often taken for granted in discussions of control mechanisms over the nationalities. The structure of the

Daniel C. Matuszewski

Soviet armed forces is such as to allow Moscow — and the Russian centre — to retain virtually complete dominance. Early ideas of allowing the individual national republics to maintain their own local armies, only loosely integrated with the all-union command, were quickly shelved in practice. In 1944 a special clause which asserted the right of the individual republics to keep national military formations was added to the Soviet 1936 constitution. This clause was essentially part of an exercise intended to shape postwar diplomacy and was valid only on paper. It disappeared from the Soviet Constitution of 1977.[5]

In fact, the pattern of organization and training in the armed forces breaks down any sense of republican prerogatives, and the structure of the military clearly reflects its all-union purposes. The language employed is the *lingua franca* of Russian, the military high command is composed overwhelmingly of ethnic Russians, and troop dispositions correspond to the intent of erasing national enclaves.[6] The military instrument serves two important and distinct domestic functions. On the one hand, it is designed to break up national military units and to perform as a tool of all-union compulsion vis-à-vis the minority republics. On the other hand, it is a means of transformation and russification of non-Russian recruits.

Estimates vary on the effectiveness of the latter function. While one of the goals of this exercise is to take the non-Russian recruit out of his linguistic and cultural milieu and immerse him in a Russian-language-dominated atmosphere of command and indoctrination, some initial studies of this process suggest that its success has been far from complete. Russian language acquisition is imperfect, cultural and ethnic frictions may actually increase rather than decrease, and the results have been far from reassuring to the military and party authorities.[7] Here again, there may well be substantial differentiation in the russifying effects of military service on the various nationalities, with the comparatively monolingual and culturally vigorous Turkic peoples being at the high resistance end of the scale, and the more culturally and linguistically compatible Belorussians and Ukrainians at the low resistance end. There is testimony from such observers as the Ukrainian dissident writer Ivan Dziuba regarding the disorientation and transfer of loyalties on the part of Ukrainian recruits returning from service.[8] As in any such mass phenomenon, the results are probably ambiguous and contradictory.

Aside from the coercive features of Soviet management of the ethnic question, the regime has employed a variety of sophisticated and highly effective techniques, involving incentives, benefits, social and economic bonuses revolving around the sublimation of energies and ambitions into productive within-system channels. Moscow's establishment of a set of artificial federal republics in Central Asia in the 1920s was itself a brilliant stroke. It successfully fostered the emergence of new ethnic identities and the creation of true nationalities where there had formerly existed only tribal and clan groupings. While this introduced a special set of tensions and policy contradictions of long term significance, it initially generated and continues to generate innovative patterns of loyalty, commitment, and career development which have substantially absorbed élite, and to a lesser extent, popular energies. These energies have been diverted to intensive cultivation of social, cultural, and scientific careers at local republican levels. Stress has been laid on competition between the republics for access to federal resources, investments, and attention, with the carefully controlled, but attractive promise of entry into political life at the federal and central levels. Emphasis is placed on the advantages of within-system competition and performance in the pursuit of positions, advancement and economic well-being.[9]

This pattern of division and competition builds upon historical points of conflict between the non-Russian ethnic groups and nationalities themselves. The policy of 'divide and conquer' was not always difficult to implement since these groups had often been at each other's throats long before the Russians came on the scene. Many may view the cessation of open and violent hostilities brought about by the introduction of Russian and Soviet rule as a positive factor, a virtual *Pax Sovietica*.

In assessing this issue of minority dynamics and their implications for the stability of the system, it would be useful to keep several caveats in mind, and to recognize certain comparative and developmental signposts, in order to avoid a number of conceptual and judgmental pitfalls:

First, a careful distinction should be made between the nationalities' anti-*Russian* attitudes, which are often real and deep, and any anti-*Soviet* attitudes they may have, which are less intense as many of these peoples attempt to use the relative power and opportunities of the Soviet system for their own benefit.

Second, it is misleading to attempt to equate the intensity of the incipient nationalism of many of the Soviet nationalities with the older, more highly developed and more historically elaborate nationalism of the countries of Eastern Europe. That equation is made all too frequently and simplistically, positing a powerful political opposition which may not be present in much of the Soviet nationality spectrum.

Daniel C. Matuszewski

Third, the unstable characteristics of national republic politics should not be exaggerated. In order to balance the picture, the significance of certain Soviet achievements in the co-optation of local élites, and the relative stability created by such co-optation should be acknowledged.

Fourth, some closer attention must be paid to the developmental context out of which such co-optation arises (industrialization, urbanization, modernization, social engineering) and to the value of constructing a comparative context (Turkey, Iran, Afghanistan, China) in assessing the relative success or failure of Soviet policies. Such developmental comparisons can help to clarify the varying perceptions of the Soviet nationalities on their role within the system and the stability or instability of different points along the geographic spectrum.

Fifth, in examining the significance of ethnic and nationality linkages across given political borders around the periphery of the USSR, the differing political, socioeconomic, and cultural profile of the various ethnic groups involved should be examined closely. Suggestions regarding the presumed ease of possible political accommodation between such kindred minorities do not often pass scrutiny either on the grounds of actual minority compatibility or geopolitical feasibility.

Sixth, the consequences of all possible centrifugal scenarios must be weighed carefully. One cannot assume that any systemic breakdown in the Soviet Union involving the secession of one or more republics along its periphery would be beneficial for the international political system. The disruption entailed in any such breakdown is likely to be of such a magnitude as to make almost any prediction of likely reconfigurations unreliable.

Crossborder Dynamics — Eastern Europe

Since every Soviet Union republic is located on an external border, the balance between internal vulnerabilities and external opportunities shifts as one surveys that huge periphery from west to east. The calculus of systemic assets and liabilities is a complex one, depending as it does on the relative stability or fragility of a given republic as matched against the political cohesiveness or weakness of those states which face it across the international boundary. An assessment of that periphery reveals surprisingly few feasible geopolitical options for Soviet minority nationalities plus a dismaying number of disruptive opportunities which the Soviets might be tempted to seize across fragile state frontiers.

Empire, Nationalities, Borders

The western republics of the USSR represent an area of special sensitivities for Moscow. Here, on the rim of Russia's Eastern European empire where communist systems are clearly external phenomena imposed from the outside, certain fragilities are apparent. The Baltic republics of Lithuania, Latvia, and Estonia, and especially the large and critical Ukrainian republic have had deep historical, cultural, and political ties with Western Europe for centuries. The role which the Baltic peoples had played for a millenium in the commercial and economic world of the northern sea coasts of Europe was an important one, and served to weave them closely into the cultural and political farbic of the European community. The art, architecture, literature and music of these peoples interacted intimately with the Germanic and Scandinavian north. There can be hardly any doubt regarding the deep linkages between the Baltic and the social and cultural mainstream of northern Europe.

The Second World War and its aftermath placed these relationships in a substantially changed political framework and subjected them to new and trying strains. The incorporation of Lithuania, Latvia, and Estonia into the Soviet Union in 1940 was seen by Moscow as an essential geopolitical measure to secure the Baltic coast against potential German and western penetration and close off traditional invasion routes from that quarter. The Soviet invasion of Finland in that same year was conceived in identical terms, with the difference that the Finns were successful in resisting that move. The subsequent complicated manoeuvres of the war and postwar periods resulted in Finnish retention of independence, but the Lithuanians, Latvians, and Estonians were subsumed into the Soviet state, their political and cultural leadership broken and subordinated to the Russian | centre, and their historic ties with Europe cut off. It remains the formal policy of the United States not to recognize the legality of that military intervention and subjugation, and the Baltic states retain diplomatic embassies and missions in many Western countries.

While sensitivities have lessened over time, and the West has come by and large to recognize the fact of Soviet dominance of the Baltic, the dilemma and tragedy of small state vulnerability and conquest remain. The cultural and social, if not political, élites of these Baltic nations maintain strong feelings of national identity and a distinct European heritage, and a legacy of national independence and sovereignty lies only 40 years or so in the past. Threatened by large-scale Russian settlement patterns and an even more heavy-handed Muscovite policy of promoting 'Soviet' or 'multinational' culture in the area, these native élites are well aware of the prospects of amalgamation, absorption, and gradual disappearance.

In the face of these absorptive threats, language, literature, culture, and religion have served as national rallying points. The small size of these nations (2.8 million Lithuanians, 1.5 million Latvians, 1 million Estonians) has been a distinct handicap when set against a large and planned Russian immigration. Under the circumstances, an intensive cultivation of traditional cultural, linguistic, and spiritual traits has been indispensable for survival. Within the limits set by Soviet political authorities, the Lithuanians, Latvians, and Estonians have attempted to develop an intense, and specifically ethnic, republican cultural life. Within such limits, literature, the theatre, the film, and the world of the plastic arts have flourished. The Catholic Church in Lithuania has retained powerful links with the Church in Poland and beyond, and a broad base for dissidence obviously exists. The search for socialist renewal in Poland and corresponding new social mechanisms for worker, peasant, and intellectual expression had real resonance in the Baltic, with sympathy strikes being reported in Estonia and elsewhere.

Moscow's existing, overwhelming system of military and political controls in the region underlines its concerns about the fragility of the area and the political allegiances of the Lithuanian, Latvian, and Estonian populations. These are after all countries which were independent in the interwar period, having regained their sovereignty after World War I and having enjoyed a flourishing period of national development in the 1920s and 1930s. The initial sympathy of these peoples for the German invaders in 1941 and the bitter anti-Soviet guerrilla warfare in the forests until at least 1947 are not tempered in Soviet minds by Moscow's own convenient alliance with Hitler from 1939 to 1941. It was Suslov who was charged with breaking the back of the Lithuanian resistance after the war and with the large-scale deportation of suspected undesirables to the Siberian East. The memory of these events is still fresh on both sides, and the Russians are not likely to trust much in the allegiance of the Baltic peoples.[10]

The Belorussian lands to the south present a somewhat different picture. They have never generated a full-fledged state formation with a distinct historical experience, with a special political consciousness. Torn for centuries between Poland, Lithuania, and Russia, the essentially rural populace in Belorussia has never evolved a strong or effective nationalist movement. Language retention by comparison to other large Soviet nationalities is not high, and many professional and urban Belorussians use Russian more easily and frequently than the rural dialect. What their political loyalties might be in any crossborder conflicts is not clear, but the Belorussians did not fare well at all under the German occupation, and they have never had close affection for their Polish neighbours who had long made up the dominant urban and manorial élite in the region. Furthermore, they have since the Second World War II, when most of these territories were taken away from Poland and annexed by the Soviets, enjoyed substantial economic reconstruction and reasonable advances in their material standard of living. There is little reason to expect that they would play any overtly anti-Soviet role in a regional conflict.

The Moldavians, of course, occupy a unique place in the spectrum of Soviet republics in that they have an immediate crossborder state option, having for centuries been an integral part of the Romanian province of Bessarabia. Taken from Romania in 1945, Moldavia remains ethnically, culturally, and linguistically Romanian. Any crossborder crisis would immediately engage Moldavian sympathies for its former parent state, but here as in the Baltic case only a major global dislocation could provide the necessary context which would permit the activation of such a secessionist option. Short of a major war, it is difficult to conceive a feasible centrifugal scenario which would allow Moldavian reunification with Romania.

The Romanians meanwhile have not allowed the issue to fade, and it remains a sensitive and central one in the relations between the two fraternal socialist states. For its part, the Soviet Union will almost certainly adhere to its firm principle of never giving back any territory once acquired. If this is true in the east in the case of the militarily insignificant Kurile Islands whose retention by the Soviets continues to poison Soviet-Japanese relations beyond measure, there is no reason to expect Moscow to part easily with a whole western republic which has served as a gateway to the Ukraine.

The second largest Slavic republic, indeed the second most populous and powerful republic in the USSR, is the Ukraine. The unique and symbiotic relationship between Muscovy and the Ukraine over the last 1000 years creates a special set of challenges and sensitivities for the Russians. While arguments may persist over the degree of cultural hostility between the two peoples and the depth of both Russian and anti-Communist feelings in the Ukraine, there can be no doubt that the Russians have been reasonably successful in bringing the Ukrainians in as something of an active co-partner in the Soviet enterprise, and, in so doing, coopting a substantial portion of the Ukrainian social and political élite.

Daniel C. Matuszewski

Ukrainian openness to the West and a long history of active contact with European culture and politics have formed a distinct cultural and national tradition.[11] Nevertheless, the peculiar and tragic history of the Ukraine's interaction with Muscovy and Poland has deprived it of any but the most fleeting experience of national independence for centuries. Indeed, it has not enjoyed national independence since the very notion of national independence came into being. The consequences of this history for both popular perceptions of sociopolitical norms and for political behaviour itself have left their stamp on the structure of political life in the Ukraine today. This of course is not to say that the Ukraine is incapable of forming an autonomous state; it is simply an indication that the establishment of such a state would be likely only under the most extreme of circumstances involving a general conventional war. Given the enormous economic, industrial, and agricultural resources of the Ukraine, Moscow could hardly conceive of permitting anything resembling secession or separation of that area from the Soviet state. In a way, the Ukraine resembles Georgia and Armenia, states with deep historical and political traditions, and with the full capacity for sovereignty, but little room for manoeuvre geopolitically. With ancient antagonisms between themselves and the Poles and the Germans, the Ukraine in many ways has fallen into a reluctant partnership with the Russians. While such a relationship is far from the 'lesser of two evils' rationale which motivates the Georgians and Armenians placed between the Russians and the Turks, it is reasonably effective in making the Ukraine a quasi-partner in the functioning and direction of the Soviet state.

It would be inappropriate to cite the experience of 1941 in attempting to predict Ukrainian behaviour in future crossborder and regional conflicts in the West. The 1941 image of Ukrainian villages welcoming the German liberator and Ukrainian troops surrendering and defecting to serve against the Russians and Soviets was quite specific to its time and place. Such behaviour came on the heels of 20 years of bitter and bloody history, after the civil war, after the murderous collectivization and terrible famine of the 1930s, after the arrests and executions of the Great Purge. Such behaviour came before the policies and intent of the Nazis in the Slavic East became clear, before their atrocities, before disillusion and disgust with the Germans set in.

In many ways the experience of World War II served to close down the Western option for the Ukraine. German blunders and defeat coupled with the impressive and overwhelming Soviet victory gave the Soviet regime a legitimacy in the Ukraine which it could not have

Empire, Nationalities, Borders

enjoyed before. It was one thing for some elements of the Ukrainian population to flirt with the Germans on the heels of the disastrous collectivization and purge. It would be quite another thing for the Ukrainians to entertain that option after the disenchanting experience with German behaviour during the war, and 35 years after that war had conferred a new, and increasing, legitimacy on the Soviet regime. It is difficult to estimate the effects of continuing Soviet attacks on the Ukrainian cultural heritage and the potential backlash from the Ukrainian cultural élite, but a substantial part of that population has become a functional partner in the larger state enterprise, and it would probably be a mistake to expect a repetition of the scale of disaffection and collaboration that characterized Ukrainian behaviour in 1941. One would have to postulate a set of global circumstances which would permit the Ukrainians to function as an independent actor (not in consort with most conceivable outside intruders), and in response to some breakdown of the Soviet system which would allow them to establish an autonomous political entity without significant external pressures. Short of such an unusual concatenation of circumstances, the existing combination of systemic controls and incentives is likely to generate a substantial level of regime adherence. There are not many feasible centrifugal scenarios.

Crossborder Dynamics — The Southern Flank

Further to the east, across the Black Sea, beyond the Caucasus, along the long Soviet southern flank with Iran and Afghanistan, to the sensitive strategic borders with China, there are not only fewer feasible centrifugal scenarios, but, on the contrary, a range of opportunities for Soviet intrusion into the often more distressing minority dilemmas of its neighbours in ways that constitute substantial geopolitical assets for Moscow.

Along the southern flank of the USSR, this picture is complex, Soviet opportunities are real, and the immediate stakes for the West are far higher than those engaged for Moscow by any matching Soviet weaknesses. In the 'great game' which the Russians 'played' with the British from the early 1800s on for control of southwest Asia and the Islamic states which bordered the Persian littoral and the northwestern approaches to British India, most of the issues of the current controversy between the Soviet Union and the United States in the area were clearly laid out. What was at stake was geopolitical dominance of the remnants of the Ottoman and Persian Empires plus the buffer areas of Afghanistan, Tibet, and Sinkiang, which separated the major actors in the competition. The stakes then, as now, were very real. What has been added since is the discovery of oil and the consequent heightened significance of control of the sea lanes out of the Persian Gulf and along the adjacent coasts. If the major question in the 19th century was the security of Britain's sea lanes and access to India, secure maritime links remain the central issue, but it now revolves around Western access to oil. The essential structure of the confrontation persists: Russia, a classic land-based empire commanding extensive interior lines of communication and dominating the massive core of the Eurasian heartland, facing the West (now essentially the United States) and its fragile farflung control of the strategic sea lanes from Suez to India. Even the nature of the buffer constellation remains remarkably similar: the relatively weak successor states of the Ottoman and Persian Empires, subject to substantial internal strife and external manipulation. What has changed, however, should give policymakers in the West some pause. With the withdrawal of the British from India, Iran, and east of Suez in a staged series of moves after 1945, the West no longer has any land-based troops anywhere across that geopolitical spectrum (fleeting American attempts to substitute for the British in Iran failed with the fall of the Shah), Afghanistan is no longer neutral but occupied by a large Soviet invading force, Pakistan and Iran are vulnerable and torn by substantial internal social and political dissent, and Turkey is tentatively emerging from the imposition of martial law brought on by more than a decade of subversion and terrorism subsidized by her neighbours to the north. In this situation, all of the classic components of the 'Great Game' remain operative, and Moscow enjoys all of the advantages of almost 200 years of experience and infrastructure in the area, plus the use of ethnic cadres and operatives co-opted over that period and especially over the last 65 years of Soviet rule in the Caucasus and Turkestan. Neither the ability to use Turkic- and Persian-speaking operatives throughout that 'arc of crisis,' nor Moscow's intention to do so, should be underestimated.[12]

Within this spectrum, Turkey presents a special challenge for the Soviets. Possessed of a long imperial heritage itself during the 500-year-old Ottoman Empire, the Turks have also had a long tradition of enmity and conflict with Russia. Distrust runs deep and, on the surface at least, there would seem to be little opportunity for Soviet manoeuvre. Nevertheless, the Soviet border republics of Armenia and Georgia harbour bitter resentments over what they perceive to be Turkish abuses in the past, and Armenia retains fond hopes for the recovery of what it considers to be lost Armenian territories in eastern Turkey. When Moscow waived long-standing Soviet claims for the return of those lands in 1962, there were riots and widespread unrest throughout Armenia. The national symbol of Armenia, Mt. Ararat, remains on Turkish territory, but towers over the urban landscape of the Armenian capital Yerevan. The remaining Armenian population in Turkey's east is small, but could yet form the pretext for an irredentist movement under special crisis circumstances in the future.

Aside from the possible issue of the Armenian territories, the Kurdish question is one which would also be tempting to the Soviets. The long history of Kurdish rebellions in the East is muted at present, but future revival of Kurdish ambitions, similar to Kurdish activity in Iran and Iraq, cannot be discounted. Together with the manipulation of its Armenian and Kurdish minorities, Turkey's vulnerability is heightened by the phenomenon of international terrorism and destabilization to which it has been subject, the series of misunderstandings which have plagued its relations with its Western allies over the last two decades, and the potential disruptive effects of any revival of Islamic fundamentalism.

Turkey differs in many respects from those countries where fundamentalism has re-emerged in recent years. Ataturk and his successors were remarkably successful in converting the Ottoman realm into a secular modernizing nation-state. While Islam remains strong among the populace as a whole, the religious establishment has no significant pretensions to share social and political power with the state apparatus, and few real grievances against the secular bureaucracy. Conservative fundamentalist groups exist, and these could come to the fore in any larger social crisis. But the progress made since the 1920s in building a national consensus regarding the operation of a modern secular parliamentary democracy based upon Western models has been substantial, and it is not likely to be eroded by any but the most extreme of economic and sociopolitical crises.

While thus vulnerable in a number of respects to cross border manipulation by the Soviets, the Turks are unlikely to exercise any similar function in the Soviet republics in the near future. Ataturk and his colleagues had resolutely rejected the path of Pan-Turkism or casting Turkey's political and cultural lot with the broader family of Turkic peoples, moving instead to convert Turkey into a modern Western-oriented state with strong ties to Europe. In spite of a troubled series of controversies with Western Europe and the United States over

Cyprus, martial law, and the state of its economy, Turkey has retained that Western orientation and has, until recently, maintained a private and careful interest in its ethnic cousins to the east.

In the last few years, however, there has been a new alertness to such questions, and some intriguing work is being done in Turkey on cultural and social patterns in the Caucasus and Central Asia.[13] In similar measure, the Uzbeks, Azeris, and other Soviet Turkic peoples have reciprocated that interest with a growing attention to the Turkish film and literary worlds. There is a certain curiosity and fascination with Turkey as the only independent and sovereign Turkic state in existence.[14] On the basis of present evidence, however, it would be too much to claim that Turkey is viewed as the cultural or creative hub of the Turkic world, or as a currently feasible sociopolitical model. Such ties might well evolve over time. Over the last decade, Turkey has attempted to expand its ties with its Islamic neighbours and to enhance its role in the Middle East and West Asia.[15] To the extent that it may assume the position of a northwest bastion of a fragile set of Islamic states in that region, rather than being cast as the southeast anchor of NATO, Turkey could take on a totally different profile in the Muslim world. Under certain circumstances, e.g. economic and social stagnation leading to new centre-periphery tensions in the Soviet Turkic republics, Turkey could begin to command a great fascination among their Turkic ethnic kin to the north. In any case, Turkey's evolution over the next decade will be a crucial variable in the stability of the entire region.[16]

The Iranian situation presents a similar set of opportunities matched by some impressive pitfalls. The chaotic domestic scene, compounded by large disaffected ethnic minorities such as the Azeri, Turkmen, Kurds, and Baluchis, affords tremendous potential for meddling, intrigue and subversion. Geopolitical sensitivities and propinquity to Western oil lines and strategic interests would seem to make it unlikely that the Soviets would make any overt move into Iran even faintly resembling their suffocation of Afghanistan. Yet, Western inattention and bungling cannot be discounted. Moreover, less obvious forms of subversion and insinuation are available, and the establishment of a Soviet client regime by clandestine and covert means, so that the affair would be seen as 'an internal Iranian matter,' can hardly be ruled out. Here again, the ability of the Soviets to utilize Azeri, Turkmen, Kurd and Tajik cadres is a distinct advantage.

Nevertheless, there are aspects of the Iranian experience which must remain deeply disturbing to Moscow: the stunning success of a relatively small group of Islamic fundamentalists in holding one of the world's most powerful nations hostage for over a year, the extraordinarily rapid and unexpected reversal of social patterns within a developing and modernizing society with many similarities to the Soviet Central Asian scene; the implications of such Islamic vitality for the comparatively quiescent Muslim populations within the USSR; the possible attractions of that 'step-backward-in-time' for a Muslim population already seeking its roots and the sources of true cultural identity in the pre-Soviet period; the contagion of success against European outsiders.

One should not exaggerate Soviet vulnerabilities here, but Moscow's policymakers have always leaned towards worst-case scenarios, and their perceptions of *potential* threat from this quarter must be appreciated, however slender the actual present danger might be or the unlikelihood of feasible destabilizing patterns. Moscow has always sought *total* security along its borders and, in defining and pursuing its security needs, it has employed what is for the Soviet analyst a virtually indistinguishable blend of offensive and defensive techniques, techniques which are palpably offensive to the outside observer, but which Soviet policymakers will vigorously proclaim defensive.

Afghanistan provides a special illustration of these behavioural principles. In many social and economic categories, the Soviets have achieved remarkable progress among their Turkic and Iranian ethnic minorities over the last 65 years. The combination of material progress and substantial co-optation of local élites has produced an impressive stability in the area upon which Moscow has been able to trade in dealing with the chaotic and less developed Muslim countries and regions from Iran to the western parts of China. Whatever other great power motivations may have been involved, the overt Soviet move into Afghanistan in December 1979 was conditioned by a subtle combination of the following elements: by the very nature of their prior achievements in Central Asia, by their unwillingness to allow the uncontrolled disintegration of Iran and Afghanistan to jeopardize those achievements, by their perception of geopolitical opportunities as well as threats in that chaos, and by their determination to consolidate and extend Soviet security along that brittle and volatile southern flank.

In spite of the overwhelming disparity in forces and equipment between the Soviets and Afghans, that country will present some special problems for Moscow. In Afghanistan the Soviets face powerful hostilities in the form of Afghan notions of superiority and independence which will prove all but impossible to subjugate and eradicate.

Daniel C. Matuszewski

The features of the Afghan situation are reasonably well known. The Afghans have for centuries engaged in guerrilla warfare and resistance to external invaders, choosing the time and place of any large-scale military confrontation carefully. Techniques of terror, mutilation, and brutality, well calculated to horrify and intimidate any intruder, have raised psychological costs and barriers which have served the Afghans well. Afghan traditional disdain for outsiders works against the Russians in their military adventure in Afghanistan. There is little doubt of Soviet ability to maintain a hammerlock on that remote and landlocked country. They control all of the urban centres, have strengthened or established major air bases all around the country, and are clearly in for the long haul. But there are few points of cultural entrée which they will be able to turn to any practical use as they might attempt to extend that control and introduce programmes of ethnic and cultural manipulation similar to those used in the Soviet Turkic republics and Mongolia. Afghanistan is likely to prove an extremely tough nut to crack. Furthermore, in spite of Soviet employment of techniques of mass terror and intimidation against urban and rural areas alike, there is substantial evidence of the ability of the rebel *mojahidin* to persist and to control most of the country beyond the major cities. That continuing bloody spectacle may in turn have important repercussions for Moscow's domestic relations with its own Muslim peoples who, whatever Moscow's controls over information and the official news media, will learn of these policies and may become increasingly uneasy over their brutality and intent.[17]

The question of reverse Muslim influence on the Soviet Turkic peoples and Tajiks is an important one. The cultural identities and ultimate political allegiances of Soviet Mulsims are still somewhat malleable. Sixty-seven years after the Great October Revolution, those identities include clan/tribal, Turco-Iranian, Islamic cultural, Islamic religious, Russian, local republic, and Soviet elements in a complex amalgam. What can be said at present is that those identities definitely include a strong component of Muslim cultural, if not Muslim spiritual, colouration.

The powerful cultural renaissance among the Turkic peoples can cut both ways. If manipulated properly by Soviet authorities and imbued with a substantial Soviet element, it can play a strong role in Soviet expansionary patterns in the East. If mishandled and alienated, it would become a tremendous subversive force tending to undermine the legitimacy of the Soviet regime. At present, the Soviet content of this phenomenon remains high. This is not to say that the Soviet Turkic peoples are immune to Islamic spiritual contagion. The example of Iranian fundamentalism turning its back on modernization and westernization, together with the increasingly bloody example of Afghan resistance to Russian intrusion, are likely to accelerate the process of Turkic and Muslim ethnic and cultural solidarity and assertiveness. The habits of passive resistance, intended to build the essential base for eventual resurgence and reassertion of at least equality, if not dominance, are strong. What forms such assertiveness might take remain to be seen.

The Afghan invasion has introduced an element of doubt and concern about possible reversal of earlier trends. To the extent that the Russians become locked in an extended and brutal effort to subjugate and transform that society, questions will be raised in the Turco/Islamic communities about the scope and propriety of that effort. While Soviet Uzbeks, Kazakhs, Kirghiz, Turkmen and Tajiks enjoy a substantially higher material standard of living than their co-religionists and ethnic kin across the border, and while they might currently entertain clear notions of systemic superiority and enjoy a stake in the Soviet state, they also habour certain anti-Russian sentiments and an ultimate antipathy to European domination and abuse. Those sentiments would be exacerbated by an overly obvious display of Russian arrogance and callousness in Afghanistan. Pro-system sentiments and disdain for backward Afghan mountainmen can be eroded by such a protracted episode of ethnic and cultural destruction.

It will be difficult for Moscow to balance these assets and liabilities in the months and years immediately ahead. The obvious and proven approach will be for Soviet spokesmen to highlight the backward and brutal nature of the earlier Afghan and Iranian regimes, the oppressive and antiquated social and economic system which heightened the poverty, misery, illiteracy, and sickness of their populations. Pointing to superior social services and systems of health, education, and welfare, the Soviets will emphasize their responsibility in bringing the advantages of such social order and construction to their backward eastern brethren.[18] The Muslim and Turkic peoples of the Soviet Caucasus and Central Asia can be mobilized in a dynamic cause to bring enlightenment and improvement to their ethnic and cultural kin. It is an attractive and effective ploy, and there is more than enough objective material evidence to make it at least plausible.

The question is, will the Soviet record of material accomplishment and development in their own Muslim areas over the last 65 years sustain such an 'altruistic' expansionary thrust, or have recent patterns of cultural malaise, reinforced by shrinking socioeconomic opportunities and growing competitiveness with the Russians, not only undercut the feasibility of such an ambitious enterprise but rendered fragile the very commitment of Soviet Muslims to the stability of the system?

For the time being, the Russians enjoy substantial assets in this region and continue to use their ethnic cadres with some profit in cross border settings. However, Moscow will have to decide whether the strategic gains represented by its new air bases in Afghanistan are worth the costs incurred by its constant and debilitating punitive expeditions against the Afghan population. Its very positioning in the country offers the further temptation of another 'defensive' move through the Baluchi areas of Pakistan to an opening on the Indian Ocean. There are signs that the Soviet leadership under Chernenko believes that Soviet Army casualties there are minor and tolerable and that its new geopolitical advantages are more than worth its comparatively limited investment, especially at a time when Moscow perceives few if any incentives in an expanded political dialogue with the United States. Under the circumstances, possession of important air force facilities at Herat, Shindand, Farah, Kandahar, Bagram, Kabul and Jalalabad affords new strike capabilities into the Indian Ocean and the Persian Gulf which will make the Kremlin think twice about giving them up. The recent massive Soviet drive into the critical Panjshir Valley shows that they are serious about this investment. Their withdrawal will not be easy under any circumstances.

Yet, the Afghan gamble has not only raised the costs of such expansionary exercises, but could begin to jeopardize the assets of Soviet ethnic structure as well. The Soviets are seriously overextended, their stagnating economy is not good for the Central Asian republics with their growing labour surpluses, and there have been signs that Soviet Muslims are uncomfortable with the spectacle of Moscow's calculated policy of decimation in Afghanistan. The fact that logic and the global context dictate withdrawal does not mean that Moscow will follow that logic.

Nevertheless, whatever new sensitivities may be engaged by this complex of issues, it is likely that Moscow still retains substantial assets in this area in its cross border relations with China. The legacy of age-old patterns of Chinese assimilation of minority peoples is such that, in any conflagration involving Sino-Soviet hostilities, the Mongols, Uighurs, Kazakhs, and Uzbeks of China's western border areas might be expected to welcome Russian intervention. Historically, Chinese patterns of nationality assimilation have been far more powerful and effective than those practised by the Russians. By comparison, the Russians have tended to preserve individual ethnic and religious identities, indeed enhance them to the extent it serves their broader state purposes, while absorbing and transforming their native élites. In the event of armed hostilities in the area, in the near future, the Soviets might yet enjoy certain advantages among the nationalities on their Inner Mongolian and Turkic Sinkiang flanks. This has been true repeatedly.

In recent years a new enlightened tolerance has appeared on the part of Peking, and the Chinese have begun to devote far more attention to the care and handling of these minorities as they have come to appreciate the fragilities involved. There is some indication that Peking intends to design more sophisticated policies for treatment of China's border nationalities, recognizing the potential Achilles heel that this issue may represent for Moscow. The new Chinese constitution under review in the late spring of 1984 includes provisions for substantial cultural, social, and administrative liberties and privileges for the non-Han and Muslim peoples: schooling and administration in their own languages, artistic and religious freedoms including the construction of new mosques, and the right to establish ethnic and nationality organizations which might foster a stronger sense of minority identity. The long-term effect of such policy shifts is unpredictable but intriguing.[19]

Under the present circumstances, a further serious disintegration of Soviet-American relations would open the door to two equally unattractive developments for United States policy in the region. On the one hand, if such a disintegration coincided with a sharp Soviet-Chinese confrontation, the Soviets might be unable to resist some territorial meddling on China's Turkic and Mongol eastern flanks. Once before, at the time of the Ussuri border clashes in 1968-1969, East European diplomats floated several trial balloons with their Western colleagues regarding possible Soviet surgical strikes into Sinkiang and Manchuria. Strong private representations by Western governments helped prevent such an eventuality, and the very intensity of the crisis contributed to a search for more conciliatory arrangements and a later striking realignment of relations between the Soviet, Chinese, and American principals. However, a recurrence of such negative coincidences, and new Soviet opportunities in the area, cannot be discounted.

On the other hand, given Chinese sensitivities to such a geopolitical eventuality, and their recent heightened criticism of American softness as a potential global ally, it might be expected that they would manoeuvre successfully to avoid such an outcome, shifting to new forms of careful accommodation with the Soviets. Neither eventuality is terribly attractive for the Western alliance.

Conclusions

How does one assess the range of assets and liabilities which this multinational framework presents for Moscow? Is there an internal instability so serious as to undercut Soviet ability to take advantage of chaotic minority conditions in critical adjacent states, especially along the southern and eastern flank? Does such instability override Western concerns about Soviet manipulative opportunities in those areas? With some cautious reservations, the simple answer to the last two questions is no, and the western analyst ought not to exaggerate the fragility of the system. A brief summation of current internal trends should put this response in some perspective.

In spite of the impressive Soviet performance in stabilizing and controlling its minorities issue over the past 65 years, the problem which remains is a fundamental one which will continue to challenge Soviet social management prowess in the decade to come. There has been a striking emergence of new and intense forms of ethnicity and nationalism within the last 20 years. The emergence of these phenomena can be traced to the general breakdown of the attempt to create a New Soviet Man, a *homo sovieticus*, and to the search by Russians and non-Russians alike for more genuine and satisfying social and cultural roots. The *homo sovieticus* experiment itself was simply an unusually oppressive variant of the developmental pattern of industrialization, urbanization, and modernization. From the 1930s on, in the interests of economic rationality and state efficiency, the Soviets put a very high premium on the need to sever the individual from his or her place in a largely agricultural or rural society and to redefine that individual as a producer for the state, a patriotic cog in an industrial machine. In the Soviet Union, as in other similar developing societies, such a narrow definition of human roles has not proven to be a very satisfactory one and, over the last two decades, a search has begun for more comforting and personal forms of human community.

This search has quite naturally focused on ethnic and religious communities with linguistic, cultural, and spiritual roots deep in the pre-Soviet past. The phenomenon has taken on impressive forms in virtually every public from the Baltic through Central Asia. The renaissance of Islamic and pre-Islamic cultural patterns in the Turkic republics is especially striking, but it would be a mistake to ignore these trends in the Caucasus, the Ukraine, and the western peripheries as well.[20] For the time being this phenomenon is fairly well circumscribed in the cultural sphere, but it has obvious long-term social and political potential as well. Cultural and social identities are being elaborated of a new depth, richness, and complexity. As these new, more vigorous and assertive identities are established and come to interact with the urgent economic and political pressures troubling the Soviet scene, new and more obvious vulnerabilities will arise.

It is one thing to deal with flagging industrial production, labour shortages, energy shortfalls, regional investment dilemmas, and military recruitment when the state disposes of a reasonably disciplined populace homogeneous from the point of view of political culture. When that culture begins to fragment and each of the problems of political economy becomes complicated by the underlying ethnic and national issue now on the Soviet horizon, the question of potential destabilization is raised, and the need for intelligent and careful management of that multinational mosaic becomes more urgent.

While the current sum of in-system advantages may persuade most nationality groups to continue to identify themselves as Soviet citizens (and to continue to function in that capacity loyally), any drastic decline in that sum of advantages would bring new incentives for many to identify themselves more actively and immediately as Ukrainians, Lithuanians, Turkic Muslims, or with other ethnic designations carrying far less Soviet political content.[21] Such calculation or dissimulation shapes the daily habits of most nationalities in the USSR, as these groups balance to varying degrees the advantages which the current system provides against the costs of attempting to confront and change that system, the costs of constructing a viable, alternative political structure, or the costs of seeking a feasible set of external alliances (almost certainly under high cost, crisis conditions) which would promise or produce greater benefits and more group autonomy.

It would be an error to ignore Soviet successes to date in managing the multinational state it has constructed since 1917, and to underestimate the control mechanisms of both incentive and coercion it continues to have at its disposal. Nevertheless, the multinational factor remains the single most urgent issue threatening the legitimacy of the Soviet regime. On the one hand, faced with the need to maintain tight controls over a multi-ethnic state, Soviet decision makers will find it all but impossible to jettison the legitimating rationale of their revolutionary ideology, both on the domestic scene and in the international

Daniel C. Matuszewski

arena, and extraordinarily costly and difficult to sustain. On the domestic scene, this entails continuing strict subordination of the non-Russian peripheries to the dominant Moscow centre, a subordination more grudgingly acknowledged as economic growth slows and regional investment patterns become more complicated and hotly contested. In the international arena, this has meant virtually obligatory, and very expensive, support for a variety of revolutionary groups in the Third World which have sought Moscow's assistance. It has also meant the maintenance of a sophisticated and extensive pattern of involvement in the ethnic politics of such sensitive border areas as Iran, Afghanistan, Pakistan, Sinkiang and Mongolia.

Given the magnitude of the task, Moscow's record in retaining the allegiances of its nationalities has been surprisingly successful. Yet that performance now stands in some jeopardy. To date, Moscow has assured the stability of this system, and the use of those nationalities in a variety of cross border opportunities, through a mixture of economic incentives, cultural and social flexibility, and relatively moderate police controls. Nevertheless, recent economic stagnation, the potential exhaustion of economic and political opportunities for the minorities, and potential closure of their pattern of social mobility, together with serious overextension in military ventures abroad, have brought the Russian-dominated leadership to an important crossroads. How the centre handles these issues will have fateful consequences. Too primitive and repressive an approach by Moscow to the legitimate and increasing cultural, social, and economic aspirations of its minorities could reverse previous successes, releasing those very centrifugal tendencies which it fears most and transforming the several current assets of its nationality structure into ominous liabilities.

Notes

1. The importance of ideology is only loosely related to the degree of personal conviction of the party, military and security élite. However cynical the latter might be, ideology is indispensable to them and the current regime as a legitimating rationale for Moscow's dominance of the non-Russian minorities and for Soviet global activism. The linkage between that ideology, the peculiar multinational structure of the Soviet state, and Soviet international behaviour will be all but impossible to dissolve. Cf. William E. Odom, 'Whither the Soviet Union?' *The Washington Quarterly*, Spring 1981, pp. 30-49.

2. Seweryn Bialer, *Stalin's Successors*. (Cambridge University Press, Cambridge, 1980), pp. 216-17.

3. Gregory Massell, 'Modernization and National Policy in Soviet Central

Asia,' in *The Dynamics of Soviet Politics*, ed. Paul Cocks, et al. (Cambridge, Massachusetts, 1976), p. 282.

4. Zbigniew Brzezinski, 'Soviet Politics: From the Future to the Past?' in Cocks, *Dynamics*, pp. 337-351. In this intriguing article, he attempts to identify a series of critical structural characteristics which link the Soviet state to its tsarist imperial past, marking the Bolshevik Revolution as an 'act of revitalized Restoration.' Concentration of power in the political rather than social sector, limitation of that power to an extremely small group around the ruler, subordination of all other groups to the central power, the absence of any notion of a loyal opposition and the equation of opposition with treason, and a number of other features of extreme centralization.

5. Hélène Carrère d'Encausse, *Decline of an Empire*. New York, 1980, p. 130.

6. Bialer, *Stalin's Successors*, p. 220.

7. S. Enders Wimbush and Alex Alexiev, *The Ethnic Factor in the Soviet Armed Forces*. The Rand Corporation, R-2787/1, Santa Monica, California, March 1982.

8. Ivan Dziuba, *Internationalization or Russification?* (London, 1968), p. 137.

9. Gail W. Lapidus, 'Social Trends,' in *After Brezhnev*, ed. Robert F. Byrnes (Indiana University Press, Bloomington, Indiana, 1983), pp. 221-233.

10. Romuald J. Misunas and Rein Taagepera, *The Baltic States: Years of Dependence, 1940-1980* (Berkeley and Los Angeles, University of California Press, 1983).

11. Roman Solchanyk, 'Poland and the Soviet West,' in this volume.

12. David Fromkin, 'The Great Game in Asia,' *Foreign Affairs*, Spring 1980, pp. 936-951.

13. See, for example, the new journal of translations and commentary on Soviet Turkic literature and culture, *Kardas Edebiyatlar*, inaugurated in Erzurum in 1982 under the editorship of Ibrahim Bozyel.

14. Kemal H. Karpat, 'The Turkic Nationalities,' *Soviet Asian Ethnic Frontiers*, ed. William O. McCagg, Jr. and Brian D. Silver (New York, 1979), pp. 117-146. In September 1967 the Turkish Prime Minister Suleiman Demirel visited the Soviet Union, including in his itinerary some of the Turkic parts of Central Asia. The story is told of the delegation's visit to Tashkent where the group examined a number of educational institutions and spoke with representatives of the Ministry of Higher Education. After being reassured that the basic language of instruction in the schools was the local Turkic language Uzbek, one of the visiting Turkish dignitaries asked what the second language of the schools was. When he was told that it was Russian, he blurted out naively but quite urgently, 'But why not English?' His host answered slyly and with a shrug, 'Fate, my friend! Fate!'

15. Nuri Eren, 'Comments on Turkey,' *Middle East Perspectives*, ed. George S. Wise and Charles Issawi (Princeton, 1981), pp. 181-204.

16. Geoffrey Kemp, 'Strategic Problems in the Persian Gulf Region,' *ibid.*, pp. 71-80.

17. Claude Malhuret, 'Report from Afghanistan,' *Foreign Affairs*, Winter 1983-1984; Edward Girardet, 'Russia's War in Afghanistan,' and Hans Bräker, 'The Implications of the Islamic Question for Soviet Domestic and Foreign Policy,' *Central Asian Survey*, vol. 2, no. 1, July 1983; Alexandre Bennigsen, 'Soviet Islam Since the Invasion of Afghanistan,' *Central Asian Survey*, vol. 1, no. 1, July 1982.

18. The Soviet representative at the Geneva arms talks, Kvitsinskii, once complained of Western exaggeration of the Soviet role in Afghanistan, and was quoted as saying, in effect, in private: This is virtually a Soviet internal matter.

Give us a little time, and we will civilize the backward Afghans and bring them into the twentieth century as we have our own Turkmen and others. *New York Times*, December 1, 1981, p. A6.

19. In August-September of 1981, a special society was established in China to study the philosophical and ideological history of the western and northern minorities. A symposium on these questions was organized in Urumchi and further work will be coordinated through the Institute of Nationalities of the Chinese Academy of Social Sciences. *China Exchange News*, vol. 9, no. 4 (December 1981), p. 25. Cf. also June Teufel Dreyer, 'The Islamic Community in China,' *Central Asian Survey*, vol. 1, nos. 2/3 (October 1982-January 1983) and Geng Shimin, 'Recent Chinese Research in Turkic Studics,' *Central Asian Survey*, vol. 1, no. 1, July 1982.

20. Daniel C. Matuszewski, 'The Turkic Past and the Soviet Future,' *Problems of Communism*, July-August 1982 (vol. XXXI).

21. Alexandre Bennigsen has used the concept of 'tactical identities,' i.e., the simultaneous existence for one and the same individual of a variety of forms of self-identification. Thus, at different times in any given day a citizen in Tashkent might identify him- or herself variously as a member of a clan, as an Uzbek, as one of the family of Turkic peoples, as a Muslim, or as a Soviet. The suggestion is that the identification of oneself as Soviet is far more superficial than it often appears to be to the outside observer, masking a form of political dissimulation endemic to Soviet society. See for example his recent 'Comments,' *Conference on the Study of Central Asia* (Kennan Institute for Advanced Russian Studies, Washington, D.C. 1983), edited by David Nalle, pp. 39-42. Cf. also in that same collection the articles by Azade-Ayse Rorlich, 'Notes on the Dynamics of Religion and National Identity in Central Asia,' pp. 29-38, and Timur Kocaoglu, 'What are the Most Important Traditional, Reformist, and Revolutionary Attitudes of Central Asians towards their Own Societies Today?' pp. 17-28.

NATIONALITY DYNAMICS IN SINO-SOVIET RELATIONS

Hans Bräker

Sino-Soviet relations, since the takeover of power by Mao Tse-tung, have been appraised in the Western world primarily from the standpoint of the controversial interpretation of the teachings of Marx and its consequences as regards the mutual relations between the two largest Communist-ruled countries, and as regards their respective policies within the world communist movement. For the countries of the West, these differences have always been an important calculation in the formulation of their policies against a background of conflict between East and West.

With the recent events in the Middle East and in Central Asia, and in particular with the growing political dynamism of the Islamic renewal movement, the awareness has grown that the evolution of the conflict between the two countries has been influenced by other factors, too, that have little or nothing to do with their ideological differences. These include, above all

— the activities pursued by the Peking leadership since 1950 with a view to settling the PRC's relations with its immediate neighbours, and, as a direct result of this,
— the spread of Soviet-Chinese rivalry to include what have come to be known as the developing countries, and in particular the Middle East and Central Asia.[1]

The following chapter examines the difficulties with which relations between Soviet Russia and China are faced as a result of these developments.

The Core Differences between Soviet Russia and China: The 'Unequal Treaties'

The PRC's relations with its neighbours in Asia have, from Peking's point of view, always been encumbered by differences of interpretation

101

as regards the course of the national borders 'imposed upon' China in centuries past, what China calls the 'unequal treaties'. It is thus only logical that Peking's foreign policy since the early 1950s should have been geared, above all, to the rectification of these 'unequal treaties'; and, in fact, China managed, in protracted and, in some cases, difficult negotiations to conclude by the mid-1960s treaties with Burma (January 1980), Nepal (March 1960/October 1961), Pakistan (March 1963) and Afghanistan (November 1963) in which its boundaries with these countries were corrected or re-established. In the process, China was able to set up a kind of 'pacified zone' in its South-East Asian approaches.[2]

The result of this for Soviet policy towards Asia was that for a long time, it was able to initiate in Asia activities directed against China only in those areas were China had not succeeded in arriving at formal settlements of the kind described with its neighbours. Foremost among these was India, upon which, precisely for this reason, Soviet policy towards Asia has been largely focused since 1962. Soviet policy on India has, without doubt, been able to chalk up significant successes, culminating in the Soviet-Indian 'Friendship Treaty' signed in August 1971; this had the effect of tying India closer to the Soviet Union.[3]

Russia's Colonial Expansion — The Destruction of Turkestan as a Geopolitical Entity

Peking's endeavours to clarify the — in its eyes — still unresolved problems with the Soviet Union at the state-to-state level likewise remained fruitless. As in the case of China's relations with all its other neighbours, the problems involved with the Soviet Union are border disagreements — even if the terms of reference are wider than just those of international law. They touch upon that field of political relations between the two countries that is in many ways the most sensitive spot even today.[4]

The Soviet Union's border with China, stretching over a length of some 2,500 kilometres between Mongolia and Afghanistan, derives from the course of Tsarist Russia's colonial expansion towards Central Asia in the second half of the 19th century. This line was based on the Sino-Russian Treaty of Peking (14 November 1860), the Chuguchak Protocol (Tarbagatai, 7 October 1864) which supplemented it, the Treaty of St. Petersburg (24 February 1891) and the treaty between Russia and Britain (known as the Pamir

Agreement, 11 March 1895). These in effect brought Russia territorial gains amounting to 580,000 square kilometers — regions to which China raises nominal claim even today.

Russia's colonial advances into Central Asia also pushed the power boundary of the Tsarist Empire far out to the south. The occupation of Tashkent (1864) first brought the thinly populated Kazakh steppes under Russian control. The threat posed to these newly-gained positions by the Islamic khanates of Khorezm (Khiva), Bukhara, and Kokand (Ferghana) eventually yielded the excuse for further thrusts: by the end of the 1870s, Russia had managed to secure Khiva and Bukhara under treaty as protectorates, while Kokand was integrated into the new Russian province of Kazakhstan. By the early eighties, all of Central Asia was under Russian rule. And by the end of the 19th century, Russia and Britain, the other European colonial power that was pressing forward into this region from the Indian subcontinent, were facing each other along the line that is now the border of the Soviet Union with Afghanistan, Iran and Turkey and were mutually blocking each other's further advances in the region.[5]

The European powers delimited their mutual interests in a number of agreements and accords: in 1885 they first established the northern border of Afghanistan, which remains in force to this day. In 1888 they concluded an agreement on the course of the Afghani-Persian border. And with the St. Petersburg Convention of 31 August 1907 they eventually reached a settlement on Persia to the effect that that country nominally retained its independence but was divided up into three zones of interest. The whole of the North — the provinces of Gilan, Mazandaran and Khorasan — were allocated to the sphere of interest of Tsarist Russia. Great Britain, for its part, was awarded the southeast of Persia as its interest zone.[6]

The consequences of this course of development during the 19th century are plain to see: Russia's colonial advances practically destroyed the unity of Turkestan, a region that stretched from the Caspian Sea well into Central Asia towards China and from the borders of Kazakhstan well into Persia and Afghanistan. The peoples living in this region — almost without exception Turkic peoples of Islamic religion — are very different in their ethnic, linguistic and religious characteristics from the populations of either Russia or of China.

In other words, the shift in the power boundaries of the Russian Empire up to the end of the 19th century divided closely related peoples or even tribes and clans. Since then, Islamic Turkic peoples have been living on both sides of the Soviet Union's present-day borders:

north and south of its borders with Iran and Afghanistan, and west and east of its border with China; in the south Azerbaijanis, Tajiks, Uzbeks, Turkmens, and Kirghiz, and in the east Uighurs, Kazakhs, Khirgiz and Uzbeks. These peoples have always regarded themselves as one entity and as an integral part of the *Umma*, the world-wide community of Muslims, or more precisely, the best community according to the Qoran, the one provided for in the divine plan of creation and salvation.[7] For that reason, they, like all the other peoples of the *Umma*, had never known or recognised national or state boundaries and, also for the same reason, they have to this day never given up their Islamic identity. On the contrary, their religious persuasion was even strengthened, as a result of the 'new order' in Central Asia brought about by the Tzarist occupation, by the addition of a national component unknown in the Islamic world until that time.

Since then, the Turkic peoples of Central Asia have made their profession of Islam identical with their awareness of their not belonging to the Russian European or to the Han Chinese, or, in terms of religious history, not to the Russian Orthodox or to the Chinese Confucian 'new nation'. The implication of this for both Moscow and Peking has been that the twin problems of minorities and religion, i.e. Islam, in their Central Asian regions can no longer be solved independently of each other. It is against this multi-level and extremely complex background that the true yardsticks emerge by which relations between the Soviet Union and China and their political rivalry in Asia should be judged.

For this reason, it is necessary to turn our attention briefly to the most important forces that have been acting in this region and that have formed it for centuries into one of the political and cultural centres in the development of the Asian continent as a whole.

The Turkic Peoples and Islam

The foundations for the original almost complete self-reliance and independence of this region were established as early as in the 6th century A.D. when the Turkic Karashanids set up their first empire in the Altai Mountains. From this starting point, the Turkic peoples spread by migration and conquest in the course of the following centuries to the geographical region between Siberia and the Balkans, between the middle reaches of the Volga and Anatolia, and throughout

Turkestan and the northern parts of Iran and Afghanistan. For a long period of time — practically up until the dissolution of the Ottoman Empire — they also ruled vast parts of the Arabian region and of southeast Europe.[8]

An important link between the Turkic peoples has always been their common language; the languages of the various individual peoples are so closely related that they can be regarded almost as dialects of one and the same language.

The other feature linking all the Turkic peoples even in the present day is their religion. Shortly after the establishment of their first empire, the Turks came into contact with the missionaries of the world religions. First, Manichaeism established itself in the Great Empire of the Uighurs (742-840). At the same time, Nestorian Christianity gained influence among various Turkic tribes. The missionary influence of Indian Buddhism on the Turks, and especially on the Uighurs, lasted longer and had a more enduring effect than its two forerunners.

But it was Islam that was to be of decisive importance. It turned into a catalyst for all the Turkic peoples and tribes; its spread was so rapid that none of the other religions could withstand it. Immediately after the death of the Prophet Muhammad, the Arabs brought Islam to Iran and from Afghanistan, which they had reached in the year 651, across the Oxus (now River Amu Darya) into Inner Asia. Even as early as in the first half of the 8th century, there were already mosques in Bukhara and Samarkand.[9] After the Arabs' victory over the Chinese in the Talas mountains in 751 — that is to say, only 80 years after the death of the Prophet — the Turks came more and more under the influence of Islam. Once the ruler of the Turkic Karashanids with his residence in Kashgar had gone over to Islam with his people, the foundations were laid for the spread of this people's dominion over all of Transoxania. This process was concluded with the conquest of Bukhara and Samarkand in the year 999. Since then, Transoxania has remained under the 'dominion' of Islamic Turkic peoples.[10]

The Arabs' advance towards Central Asia was likewise an essential precondition for the spread of Islam in China. China had made its first contacts with Islam at the time of the Tang dynasty (618-906) by virtue of its trading relations with the Near East along the Silk Road and above all by sea. However, it was not until the age of Mongol rule (1219-1367) that Islam was able to gain a firm footing in China, Central Asia, and over vast expanses of the Muscovite Empire. The cosmopolitanism that was characteristic of the Mongols — one of the prominent features of which was a religious tolerance previously unknown in China — established favourable conditions for the large-scale influx of Turkic Muslims from the Central Asian region. This migrant flood discharged into the Western provinces of China, into Sinkiang (Xinjiang), but also further beyond to Ningxia, Gansu, and even as far as Yunnan.[11]

An important conclusion can be drawn from this history for an appraisal of the national minorities issue in the Soviet Union and China: Central Asia does not belong to the homeland of Islam but to those areas that were converted by missionary activity. It has been made into a part of the *Umma* by *jihad*, or holy war. *Jihad* — it should be remembered in this context — is an instrument serving both the expansion and the defence of the sphere of influence and jurisdiction of Islam to become the universally dominant religion. It is directed against all non-Muslims, who are regarded as infidels. As long as the infidels are 'book-owners', that is to say, Jews or Christians, the *jihad* ends with their subjugation but does not require their conversion to Islam. 'Non-book-owners', however, must be fought until they adopt Islam.[12]

It is these two features of the *jihad* — expansion and defence — that have formed Islam in the regions that today belong to the Soviet Union and to the People's Republic of China. Islam pressed forward into the areas that are now the five Republics of the Soviet Union of Kazahkstan, Kirghizia, Turkmenistan, Uzbekistan and Tajikistan and into the Caucasian region as of the first half of the 8th century. For the purposes of the *jihad*, this invasion was an immediate advance by the Arabs into 'heathen regions'. In the 10th century, Islam was finally established here in its Sunnite form by the Iranian Samanid dynasty. The *jihad* had fulfilled its objective: the faith preached by the Prophet had become the determinant element in the culture of the region. Since then, these regions have been an important constituent part of the *Umma*. Central Asia developed into a centre of Islamic culture, in particular of Persian scientific, scholarly and theological literature. It was not until the Tsarist colonial drive in the 19th century that Islam in Turkestan was forced onto the defensive.

In China, too, when the Muslims were being constantly harassed under the Ming (1368-1644) and Qing (1644-1911) dynasties that followed the Mongols, it was above all among the Turkic peoples of East Turkestan — the Uighurs, Kazakhs, Kirghiz and Uzbeks — that Islam was able to hold its own. By contrast with the other religions originating in Anterior Asia, Nestorian Christianity and Manichaeism, Islam gave them its support and deepened their feeling of belonging to a community. Unlike in Russia, therefore, the defensive character of the *jihad* became an essential feature of Islam in China at a very early stage.

Respect for Autarky and Relative Independence

The Grand Dukes of Moscow and the rulers of Tsarist Russia respected the autarky of the Central Asian region, based as it was on its ethnic and religious structure, practically up to the middle of the 19th century. The most obvious indication of this is the fact that when Moscow's colonial expansion set in in the 16th century it was directed not south but east. Within the space of one century, Moscow was able, starting with the subjugation of Kazakhstan (1552), to conquer wide regions of Siberia and finally to reach the Pacific Ocean.

Treaties with the Chinese Empire — the Treaties of Nerchinski (September 1689) and Kiakhta (November 1727) — established the border between the two great powers in Asia, thus consolidating the *status quo* as regards Moscow's newly gained Siberian possessions. The Russian Empire had reached the goal of its colonial expansion, but had at the same time come up against the limits of its potential for expansion. Today, Peking counts these treaties among the 'Unequal Treaties'. Nevertheless, they brought not inconsiderable advantages for China too: their conclusion practically put an end to the incursions by the 'barbarian' peoples from the north for the first time since Emperor Ch'in Shita Huang-ti (221-205 B.C.) had united the Empire and built the 2,400 kilometer long Great Wall to defend it against the constant threat from the north and northwest, without being able to avert that threat in the long term.

A further consequence of the treaties with Tsarist Russia was that China was able to disengage forces to be put to use with profitable results on the other borders of the Empire — in particular against the Mongol Oyrats, who were attempting to set up a major empire in Central Asia with China as one of its tributaries. This empire also covered Tashkent, large parts of Kazakhstan, the Ili region as far as the Lakes Balkhash and Zaysan, the valleys of the Syrdarya and Amudarya rivers. Once the Oyrats had been subjugated, the Manchu were able to impose their own rule in this region: thus, over two million square kilometers of what is now the territory of the Soviet Union was either in Chinese possession or at least in an — albeit very loose — tributary relationship with China.[13] China's strength, dominion and right to possession in this region were not disputed by Moscow. The peaceful coexistence between the two neighbours was reflected above all in the fact that Russia respected a border that ran east-west from Lake Zaysan via Ust-Kamenogorsk, Semipalatinsk, Omsk, Petropavlovsk, Presnovodsk, Zverinogolovsk, Orsk, Ilinsk, Orenburg, Talisheva, Ilezki Gorodok, Uralsk and Sakharnya to the Caspian Sea (to the West of Guryev).

The 'Dream' of a Great Islamic Empire in Central Asia

It was Russia's colonial advance beyond this border as of the middle of the 19th century that marked the turning point in the neighbourly relations between the two countries. This advance was triggered by the rapidly deteriorating power of the Chinese Empire as of the fifth decade of the 19th century. This, in turn, was the result of the penetration of China from the east by Great Britain, France and the USA (the Opium War, the 'Unequal Treaties', the cession of Hong Kong) and of the spread of the spheres of influence of the two European colonial powers to encompass China's southern 'tributary' states (Burma, Indochina); also of the permanent threat posed to Chinese mastery over Turkestan by the constant incursions by western Mongols. In this period of weakness, Peking was forced to grant the Turkic peoples of East Turkestan a major degree of autonomy. The entire internal administration of Sinkiang was left to the Islamic leadership elite. Peking's presence in this region was for a long time of symbolic nature only. The Tsarist government had no qualms about exploiting China's weakness for its own colonial penetration into West Turkestan.

Of no less significance in our present context, however, was the fact that at about the same time the Uzbek Khan Ya'qub Beg, born in the region of Kokand (West Turkestan) in 1820 and resident in Kashgar (East Turkestan) since 1867, was pursuing a plan of setting up an Islamic state in Central Asia which was to unite all the Islamic Turkic peoples of West and East Turkestan and was to take its political bearings from the Ottoman Empire, the centre of the *Umma* at that time. The establishment of diplomatic relations with the Sublime Porte and the conclusion of trading agreements with Tsarist Russia (Baron Kaulbar) in 1872 and with British India (Douglas Forsyth) in 1874 nurtured Ya'qub Beg's hopes of realizing his objectives.[14] In reality, however, this was to spark off the controversies between China and Russia over this area, especially since Russia had already occupied

Chinese territory by taking over the Ili basin in 1871.[15] For the dream of an Islamic state in Central Asia to come true, China would have had to give up its sovereignty in East Turkestan and Russia would have had to refrain from exercising its newly gained mastery over West Turkestan. But for neither country was this at any time a subject of political consideration. A more important factor in the assessment of the historical and contemporary rivalry between Russia (and the Soviet Union as its successor) and China is that the goals of Tsarist colonial expansion were never limited to the occupation of West Turkestan. The Russian penetration into the Ili basin was one of the first obvious signs of Russia's intention to extend its influence to East Turkestan, that is, to Sinkiang.

This period of historical development has been discussed because it is in this period that all the problems become evident that were to dominate relations between Russia and China in Central Asia in the years to follow: The figure of Ya'qub Beg personifies the sense of identity of the Islamic Turkic population of East and West Turkestan, who had always thought of themselves as a part of the Islamic world. As long as the ethnic, cultural and religious peculiarity of the Islamic population was respected by the Chinese central government and was allowed an — albeit limited — degree of administrative autonomy, Peking's sovereignty in this region was always felt to be a nominal one, and for that reason only seldom needed to be challenged. And the ill-defined borders at that time had little adverse effect on the links between the Islamic Turkic peoples of West and East Turkestan.

Since the Tsarist takeover of West Turkestan, Russian policy has always looked at these complex problems as a point of departure: any deterioration in relations between the Islamic population of East Turkestan and the Chinese central government could only be of advantage to Russian policy. For this reason, the latter exploited every opportunity for promoting such tensions, or even for creating them in the first place. The most effective means to this end was to support separatist movements. This support came up against its limits, however, as soon as these movements proved to have their roots in pan-Islamic ideals and the creation of a greater Islamic state as their objective. For this would of necessity draw into question Russian mastery over West Turkestan. Russian policy towards Central Asia was governed by down-to-earth power-political and economic interests, and not by any sympathies towards the Islamic population or by ideals of religious tolerance.

Hans Bräker

East Turkestan under Pressure of Russian/Soviet Expansion from 1911

It has always demanded a great measure of flexibility and diplomatic skill on the part of the Chinese central government to assure for Sinkiang a status and a course of development that could not be jeopardized by Russian encroachment. This became evident immediately after the 1911 Chinese revolution, when the conversion of China into a republic brought a threat to the unity of Sinkiang: Ili threatened to set up its own government, in Hami the Islamic population rose against the Manchus, in many parts of the province the Muslim Chinese troops were on the point of breaking away from control from Urumchi; and assaults on Russian subjects living in Sinkiang were the order of the day.

These events were bound to provoke Russian intervention. Under the pretext that the Russian consulates in Kashgar and Kuldja were obliged to guarantee the security of the Russian citizens there, the consulate troops were reinforced massively until they totalled 1,000 Cossacks by mid-1912. For a time there was danger of Sinkiang either being completely annexed by Russia or at least being forced into accepting a protectorate status such as that exercised by Russia over Outer Mongolia at that time.

It was thanks to Yang Tseng-hsin, the former head of the regional administration of Urumchi recently promoted to Governor General of Sinkiang, that this danger was averted. The reason why Yang was eminently predestined for this office was that the Muslim troops were unquestioningly loyal to him, and his not very friendly attitude towards the republic met with widespread acclaim in Sinkiang.[16] Yang Tseng-hsin succeeded in stabilizing the situation by peaceful means: he was able to arrive at an agreement with the Ili rebels, to bring about, with diplomatic support from Russia, the withdrawal of the Mongolian troops and thus to secure the border between Sinkiang and Outer Mongolia, to restore the Governor General's authority among the Chinese troops, and finally to put an end to the Muslim uprising in Hami.

The success of Yang Tseng-hsin's politics was due to no mean extent to the fact that he treated Sinkiang as an autonomous region. In this way, he was able not only to screen the province against influences from abroad but also to isolate it from the domestic turmoil that was shaking China in the wake of the revolutionary events of 1911. Yang Tseng-hsin saw his main task in the foreign-policy field as being not to provoke Russia but rather to avoid anything that could give that country an excuse to intervene. The following are some of the steps he took that provide evidence of the great diplomatic skill with which he mastered this task:

— In 1916, some 300,000 Kazakhs fled to Sinkiang in order to avoid being conscripted to military service. Even before his Eastern neighbour could intervene, Yang Tseng-hsin joined Russia in negotiations and succeeded in obtaining amnesty for and the repatriation of the majority of the Kazakh fugitives.
— A similar situation arose in 1918 when about 7,000 defeated White Russian troops under the command of General Anenkov fled into Sinkiang. In this case, too, having disarmed and interned the fugitives, Yang was able to obtain in difficult negotiations with the Bolsheviks an amnesty for the Russians and the conclusion of an agreement which made it possible for them to return to the Soviet Union.[17]
— When, however, other sections of the fugitive White Guard (about 3,000) under the command of the Generals Bashchich and Novikov, fled into the Altai region where they began to cause difficulties, Yang reached a formal agreement with the Soviet Union whereby the Army was allowed to enter Sinkiang for a limited period for the purpose of helping Yang to expel the fugitives across the border to Outer Mongolia.[18]
— Many of Yang's diplomatic tactics can be explained by the fact that Sinkiang was economically dependent upon the continued exchange of commodities with Russia. For this reason a trade agreement was concluded with the Soviet Union in 1920,[19] and in 1924 the two governments agreed on the opening of five Soviet consulates (in Urumchi, Tarbagatai, Ili, Altai and Kashgar) and of five Chinese consulates in the Soviet Union (in Tashkent, Andizhan, Alma Ata, Zaysan and Semipalatinsk).[20] The Soviet consulates in Sinkiang were able to continue their activities without restriction even after Chiang Kai-shek's *de facto* break with the Soviet Union in 1927; relations were not officially severed until 1929.[21]

The effect of screening Sinkiang against influences from abroad which resulted from this 'foreign policy' enabled Yang to make the province economically almost completely independent and to implement social and economic reforms with a view to the long-term stabilization of the country on the basis of administrative autonomy. Thus, for example, he abolished the trade monopolies, prohibited the requisitioning of means of transport for civil service officials from the population at large, and put an end to the usurious practices of moneylenders by placing a ceiling on interest levels.

All these measures reflect Yang Tseng-hsin's wise and circumspect policies. On the one hand they gave the Islamic populace no reason to criticise the Chinese provincial administration, much less to rebel against it; experience had shown that such criticism could readily be coupled with pan-Islamic objectives and thus could be directed both against Chinese rule in Sinkiang and against Russian rule in West Turkestan. On the other hand, these policies made sure that Russia was given no pretext for encroachment of any kind. Such encroachments had in the past been the rule whenever Chinese policy in Sinkiang had run contrary to the interests of the Islamic population.

Nevertheless, it would be a mistake to attribute the reserve exhibited by Russian and later Soviet policy towards Central Asia up to 1928 solely to the wise policies pursued by Yang Tseng-hsin. The reasons for this reserve are also to be found in the fact that, because of the war in Europe, the problems of Central Asia were of minor importance to the Tsarist regime up to 1917. And for the Bolshevik leaders the consolidation of the Soviet system was of utmost priority; for this reason, they had to mark time on all foreign-policy fronts.

The Double-Track Approach of Soviet Policy towards Central Asia from 1928

After 1928, the situation for Soviet foreign policy was a fundamentally new one. Yang Tseng-hsin's successor as Governor General of Sinkiang, Tsin Shu-yen, (he proclaimed himself Governor General after his predecessor's assassination) was likewise a civil servant of the old school. However, he proved unsuitable for such a difficult government office. Corruption and nepotism, such as had been the order of the day in Sinkiang prior to 1912, once more became dominant. Only a short time after Tsin's takeover all that Yang Tseng-hsin had painstakingly built up was mostly destroyed.

Tsin Shu-yen's mismanagement was bound to be at the expense of the Muslim population; it provoked their opposition and eventually drove them to rebellion. Revolt broke out among the Muslim Uighurs in Hami, spread like lightning to Kashgar, and caused the Kazakhs and Kirghiz in Sinkiang for their part to take up arms against Chinese rule. The decisive event in the course of this uprising and for the further development of Sinkiang was that the Islamic Dungans of Kansu under the leadership of their 23-year-old General, Ma Ch'ung-ying, hastened to the aid of their co-religionists in Sinkiang. Thanks to this intervention, which brought Ma Ch'ung-ying's army right to the gates of Urumchi, the uprising of the Uighurs of Hami developed within a very short time into a wide-based popular movement. It made the whole question of continued Chinese rule in Sinkiang uncertain.[22]

Ma Ch'ung-ying was a highly talented young officer. For religious and national reasons, he was an irreconcilable opponent of the Soviet Union. He had surrounded himself mainly with Turkmen advisors and was revered by his warriors with great devotion, by many even as the long-awaited Mahdi. This was connected with the fact that the objective of his intervention in Sinkiang went far beyond merely the rendering of aid to his brothers in faith but was rather — as in the case of Ya'qub Beg's goals in the 19th century — to create an Islamic state that was to encompass all of Central Asia, that is, both West and East Turkestan. This meant that the Muslim rebel movement constituted a threat to Chinese predominance in Central Asia and also confronted the Soviet Union's foreign policy with an extremely sensitive situation.

The possibilities open to the government in Moscow under these circumstances were several. It could intervene on behalf of the Muslim rebel movement in Sinkiang, which would have opened up the possibility of neutralizing that movement, of controlling it and of using it at the same time to serve Soviet interests. Because of the 'susceptibility' of the Muslims in Soviet West Turkestan to the Ma Ch'ung-ying idea of a united Islamic state in Central Asia, such a policy would have been accompanied by serious risks. Alternatively, the Soviets could exploit the debility of the Chinese central government — without taking any notice of Ma Ch'ung-ying's rebel movement — to achieve those political and, above all, economic concessions that up to that time had been denied to the Soviets directly by Yang Tseng-hsin and indirectly by the Chinese central government.

The policy actually pursued by the Soviets was, though somewhat confusing, nevertheless revealing in its singleness of purpose: they supplied weapons and other material to Tsin Shu-yen, thus supporting him directly in his fight against the Muslim rebellions. This is the reason why it proved possible to halt Ma Ch'ung-ying's advance before the gates of Urumchi. At the same time, however, Tsin Shu-yen was compelled, by way of return, to sign a secret agreement accompanied by four supplementary agreements (1 October 1931)[23], affording the Soviet Union extensive economic concessions and privileges, namely[24]

Hans Bräker

- the right to open trading offices in Urumchi, Chuguchak, Ili and Kashgar and to conclude via authorized agents trading contracts with private merchants in Turfan, Karashar, Aksu, Yarkand and Khotan;
- the right to unrestricted freedom of movement for the employees of the trading offices and for other Soviet citizens throughout the territory of Sinkiang for the purpose of facilitating commercial intercourse;
- preferential tariffs for all commodities of Soviet origin;
- the establishment of a cable link-up between Chuguchak and Bakhti and permission for radio communications between Sinkiang and the Soviet Union;
- Tsin Shu-yen was also obliged to accept large-scale technological aid from the Soviet Union — deliveries of machinery and the secondment of Soviet experts for the economic development of the province.

The conclusion of these agreements was an outrageous step because it was a flagrant violation of China's sovereignty to sign such agreements with a provincial government, and that at a time when there were no diplomatic relations between the two countries.[25] But more than that, the Soviet Union did not even stop at open intervention in Sinkiang: under the absurd pretext of strengthening the position of the central government in Peking, but in reality to protect the concessions it had newly gained from the agreement of 1 October 1931, the Soviet Union 'repatriated' 10,000 soldiers of the North Manchurian army to Sinkiang who had been forced over the Soviet border by the Japanese in 1932 and had been kept in internment in the Soviet Union since then.

Parallel to its support for the government in Urumchi, however, the Soviet consul in Kashgar at the same time supplied the Civil Governor of Kashgar, Ma Shao-wu, with weapons and ammunition from the Soviet Union, thereby backing the Muslim rebels in their uprising against the Chinese central government — and thus, of course, against its representative Tsin in Sinkiang.[26] The ambivalence of Soviet policy could hardly have shown itself more strikingly.

As it was, the consequences of Tsin Shu-yen's mismanagement in Sinkiang were in all respects as Soviet policy had expected them to be: this policy had extorted wide-ranging economic concessions and thus had for all practical purposes also got its grip on the entire 'New Province'. And his agreement with the Soviet Union by no means saved the day for Tsin Shu-yen. On the contrary, on 12 April 1933, he was toppled by his own Chief of Staff, Sheng Shih-ts'ai. The civil war in the country not only was not abated but, just the opposite, it was heated up further by the Soviet Union's two-sided interference.

Whether the Soviet Union intended to exploit the confusion it had created to put permanent ties on Sinkiang need not be discussed on this occasion. At all events, it is the person of Shen Shi-ts'ai who is the centre of interest in this context. Sheng had been educated in Japan, where he developed sympathies for communism. In 1938 (presumably in September), he joined the Communist Party of the Soviet Union.[27] At the time he took over the government, Sheng declared his objective to be to keep the province free from 'Japanese agents'[28] and to improve the conditions of the non-Chinese population.[29] In the implementation of this latter goal he proclaimed an eight-point programme with which he promised the population of Sinkiang equality among nationalities, freedom of religion, agrarian reforms, a radical fiscal reform, the systematic establishment of an educational system, reform of the administration and the judiciary, and, last but not least, the right to administrative autonomy.

The declaration of these ambitious targets was intended to show the people that an attempt was to be made to return to the policies pursued prior to 1928. It evidently was not very convincing, however, as it failed to put an end to the troubles that were plaguing the country. The Muslim uprisings flared up again, even more vehemently than before, and Ma Ch'ung-ying was able to gain control over large parts of Sinkiang. The Dungans offered to join Ma in marching on Urumchi; other Muslim leaders in Sinkiang either openly supported Ma or maintained secret links with him. The situation was aggravated still further for Sheng when Shang Pei-yuan, the Commander of the Ili garrison, also revolted and marched against Urumchi, significantly, after having been kitted out by the Soviet Union. This placed Sheng in a position in which he had no other recourse but to appeal to the Soviet Union for help. Thus the situation evolved that the Soviets had systematically worked towards in quest for their ultimate goal — the *de facto* political and economic annexation of Sinkiang.

The further course of events went according to plan. First, wide-ranging secret talks were held in December 1933 at which the Soviet Union was represented by General Pogodin.[30] To this day it has never been revealed whether any written agreement came of the talks at all. The events that followed, however, indicate that a comprehensive agreement must have been reached whereby the Soviet side declared itself willing as a first step to 'pacify' the province by military force, in return for which Sheng committed himself to affording the Soviet Union economic rights in Sinkiang that went far beyond the earlier concessions. At any rate, the secret talks had hardly been concluded when the Red Army started with the liquidation of the uprising. In early 1934 some 7,000 men — equipped with tanks and artillery[31] — were poured into Sinkiang to tackle Ma Ch'ung-ying. Soviet combat aircraft also took part in the campaign. Ma's troops were largely demoralized by the use of gas bombs.[32] Ma withdrew to Kashgar, from where, for some time, he continued to put up resistance. Then he disappeared from Kashgar, too. He is thought to have 'emigrated' to the Soviet Union with the 'aid' of the Soviet trade agency in Kashgar.[33] In his book *The Flight of the Great Horse*, Sven Hedin reported from his immediate experience on the birth of the legend that elevated the personage of that Muslim leader to a figure reminiscent of the 'occult Mahdi':[34]

> A thousand rumours passed from mouth to mouth, after General Ma Chung-yin with his Dungans had travelled like a whirlwind through the steppes and deserts of Dzungaria and East Turkestan, overtaking and rectifying one rumour and refuting another. Only Ma himself could have written down what really happened, but he did not keep a diary . . .
>
> The last we heard as we set off on our journey to the Lop-nor was Colonel Salomakhin's news that Ma was encircled with 800 men in Bai, between Kucha and Aksu and that there was no escape possible.
>
> But when, months later, we returned from the wandering lake and came to Urumchi there were completely different rumours and versions of the fate of Ma Chung-yin. There the Soviet Consul General Apresoff reported that, according to a reliable letter from Kashgar, General Ma had fled with 120 men via Irkeshtam onto Soviet territory. He and his followers had been disarmed and brought to Tashkent. . . .
>
> Rumours, rumours! Another had it that Ma had first fought his way through to Kashgar with the remnants of his army, had later gone on to Khotan, taking the oasis after bloody street fighting. He would soon return to Korla to attack the Northern Army from the rear.
>
> When almost a year later, in February 1935, I was again in

Nationality Dynamics in Sino-Soviet Relations

Nanking, all the papers bore the surprising news that Ma Chung-yin had arrived in Peking. A month later I travelled to Peking, where the press reported that Ma had gone to Nanking to talk to Chiang Kai-shek. And another month after that the German Consul in Novosibirsk, Grosskopf, informed me that the Soviets had brought Ma to Alma-ata, where he was presumably being held prisoner. There were also some who considered it likely that the Great Horse had gone on to India in order, with English aid, to gather arms for a new campaign against East Turkestan. And others again feared that Ma had stolen out of Bai, had drifted down the Tarim to the Lop-nor on ferryboats, and was now marching with an army from Tung-hwang to Kansu. Nothing was beyond the Great Horse. When I remarked on hearing this latter rumour that such a march through the desert under the sweltering heat and with a shortage of water was impossible, the answer was: 'Yes, for anybody else it would be impossible. But Ma can do it. He has already performed such feats in the past. No sandy deserts or snowy mountains can deter him. He is a daredevil and he always pulls through. If he is beaten at one point, he will appear again at another!'...

This flight to the Soviet Union was for me a completely unfathomable step in the Great Horse's restless and unresting career. Must he not hate Russia? Had the Russian regiments in Urumchi and the Russian pilots at the Davankh defile not been the feather that tipped the scales in favour of Sheng Shih-Tsai's Provincial Army? Had his military situation deteriorated so far beyond hope that it left no other way open to him? And what about his notions of the great Mohammedan empire that he had cast out to an enthusiastic audience of 1,000 in the Yamen courtyard at Kucha, had these dreams come to an end, or had they been merely fleeting soap-bubbles blown by an adventurous lad?

The Binding of East Turkestan to the Soviet Union

After the liquidation of Ma Ch'ung-ying's insurgent movement, General Pogodin set about the pacification of the province. The White Russian corps in Urumchi was also among the victims of his large-scale purge. With the occupation of Hami, 560 kilometers east of Urumchi, by the so-called 'Altai Volunteers' (in reality a 3,000-strong armoured division of the Red Army disguised in Chinese uniforms), Pogodin gained control of the access to Sinkiang from Kansu. The reason given for the occupation of Hami was that Sinkiang had to be protected against possible Japanese incursions. In reality, however, the intention was to ensure that the sovietization of Sinkiang could progress without major impediment.

This infiltration and *de facto* incorporation of Sinkiang into the Soviet sphere of hegemony was brought about primarily by economic means. The foundation stone for this had already been laid under Tsin Shu-yen: as early as in 1930, the Turkestan-Siberia railway line had already been largely completed and, thus, the most important link with the Chinese border established. The treaty of 1 October 1931 had afforded the Soviet Union exploitation concessions for petroleum, gold and other mineral resources. In 1935, Soviet experts began, without the authorisation of the provincial government, to prospect for oil in the vicinity of Tu-Shantse (about 380 km west of Urumchi). On the basis of this prospecting, the total oil deposits in Sinkiang were estimated in 1937 to amount to at least 120 million tons. In 1939 a refinery was built in this region; by 1942, 35 oil wells with a daily output of 67·3 metric tons were in operation.[35]

The economic penetration of Sinkiang was accompanied by a large-scale 'anti-imperialist' campaign which at first kept the Indian and British traders under constant pressure and in 1939 forced them to leave the province, leaving all their stocks behind them. This action was followed by a boycott campaign against the British Consulate General in Kashgar.[36] Typical of Soviet policy towards East Turkestan in the first phase of Sheng Shi-ts'ai's period of government were the negotiations held in 1933-34, which ended in the awarding of a Soviet credit of 5 million gold roubles to be repaid in the form of cattle.[37] In this way, the financial burden of financing the Soviet development schemes was placed on the provincial government, for the credit was to be used to improve the communications system, to build factories, and to construct a refinery in the vicinity of Urumchi for the exploitation of the oil deposits in the region of Karamay — all projects of which the Soviet Union was the sole beneficiary. The credit was also intended to help stabilize the currency of the region, which had been in ruins since Yang Tsen-hsin's attempt to make the province economically autonomous by means which had included experimenting with paper money.

By the end of 1937, the Soviets had achieved the almost complete economic link-up of Sinkiang to the Soviet Union. This is indicated by all the economic measures adopted by the provincial government: Sheng announced the first Three Year Plan to run from 1938 to 1940 for the economic development of the province along the lines of the

Soviet planning model. Even in 1936 he had already re-interpreted the eight points of his 1933 government programme with this in mind. According to this interpretation, the basis was to be the fight against the Japanese and the British and 'friendship with our Soviet brother nation', that is to say political and economic orientation towards the Soviet Union, but not towards the Chinese central government.

In the years between 1940 and 1943, the Soviets were able to pursue their more far-reaching plans openly and without consideration for the central government in Peking. The conditions were favourable for this, since the Japanese invasion in 1937 had put China in an extremely precarious position: by 21 August 1937, the Chinese government was in such straits that it was forced to conclude a non-aggression pact with the Soviet Union.[38] This pact was followed by three credit agreements, which secured for China Soviet credits totalling 250 million dollars by mid-1939 to be used to finance the intensification of its war effort against Japan.[39] On 16 June 1939, China finally concluded a trade agreement with the Soviet Union.[40] In short, the critical situation in which China found herself forced Peking to re-organize completely its relations with the Soviet Union; and in fact it is said that the Soviet Union gave China more material aid in these years than did the USA and Great Britain together.

At any rate, the Japanese invasion of China appears not to have come as an inconvenience to the Soviet Union as regards the implementation of its plans for East Turkestan. And it was able to plan its decisive thrust towards Sinkiang under even more favourable conditions after it had concluded the pact of August 1939 with the German Reich, which safeguarded its rear politically, economically, and also militarily in Europe.

The Culmination of Soviet Influence: the Treaty of 26 November 1940

It is worth recalling in this connection that Sheng Shi-ts'ai had joined the Communist Party of the Soviet Union after a personal talk with Stalin on the occasion of a visit to the Soviet Union in 1938.[41] This act was of consummate importance to the further course of developments in Sinkiang, for without this precedent the conclusion of the agreement signed on 26 November 1940 between Sheng Shi-Ts'ai as the 'Representative of the Government of Sinkiang' and Karpov and Bakulin as the 'Representatives of the Government of the USSR' would hardly have been conceivable. The most important provisions of that agreement, reproduced below,[42] leave no room for doubt that its purpose was to legitimate one-sided rights on the part of the Soviet Union and one-sided duties on the part of Sinkiang:[43]

> Article 1: The Government of Sinkiang agrees to grant the Government of the USSR exclusive rights to the prospecting, investigation and exploitation of tin deposits and related secondary deposits of other minerals within the territory of Sinkiang.
> Article 2: The Government of the USSR is entitled, on the territory of Sinkiang,
> — to exploit and investigate tin deposits and related secondary deposits of other minerals and to carry out expedient geological and geographical investigations. . .;
> — to utilize all natural water sources, with the right to construct hydroelectric power plants and other facilities;
> — to construct electric power plants including hydroelectric power plants, to instal high-voltage transmission systems, transformer stations, etc.;
> — to import all the goods necessary for the usufruct of the concessions, with the right to use all the means of transport available on the territory of Sinkiang, to construct transportation routes, to deliver all the construction equipment required for the construction of transportation routes including railway lines, and to organize and to use means of transport of all kinds;
> — to import into the territory of Sinkiang, without let or hindrance to all technical equipment and material required for the repair and for the construction of all machines, utensils and associated parts, and to transfer them at liberty from one works to another;
> — to hire labour in Sinkiang and to employ engineers, technicians and workers from the USSR;
> Article 4: For the purpose of the implementation of these provisions the USSR will set up a trust with the function of prospecting for and exploiting tin deposits and related secondary deposits of other minerals; this trust shall be given the name 'Sin-Tin' and shall be invested with all the rights and privileges of an independent legal person. Its operations will be governed by a Statute which will be formulated in accordance with the pertinent statutory provisions of the law of the USSR. 'Sin-Tin' shall be entitled to open without let or hindrance branch offices, subsidiaries and agencies throughout the territory of Sinkiang.

Article 5: For as long as the present agreement remains in force, the Government of Sinkiang will undertake to guarantee the provision of land, including the felling of timber, the mining of coal, and the extraction of natural materials for building on specially designated plots of land to the extent that this is necessary for the due implementation of the various works mentioned in this agreement. The Government of Sinkiang will evacuate the entire resident population from the regions allocated to 'Sin-Tin'. Such plots of land shall be allocated to 'Sin-Tin' at its request...

Article 7: For the first five years from the date of the signing of this agreement, 'Sin-Tin' will make over to the Government of Sinkiang five percent of the tin and other marketable mineral secondary products recovered in Sinkiang... Products made over to the Government of Sinkiang under the provisions of paragraph 1 of this Article shall be offered for sale to the Government of the USSR, and the price shall be equal to the annual average price (during the year preceding the sale) at the main locations of the world market for time and marketable mineral secondary products...

Article 8: In return for the privilege of exemption from all customs duties, 'Sin-Tin' shall pay to the Government of Sinkiang annually the sum of two percent of the price of all products exported by 'Sin-Tin', the basis for the determination of the prices being as laid down in Article 7 of this agreement...

Article 10: 'Sin-Tin' shall be entitled to conduct business with its entire capital, to take out loans, to maintain current bank accounts in local and foreign currency, to engage in remittance and bill exchange transactions inside or outside the territory of Sinkiang, to convert foreign currency into Sinkiang currency and vice versa.

Article 12: 'Sin-Tin' shall be entitled to mount armed guards to protect its houses, buildings, factories, plants, stockyards, etc. and to safeguard its transport services.

Article 15: The period of validity of this agreement shall be 50 years, dating from the day on which it is signed.

Sheng Shi-ts'ai later reported on the negotiations that preceded the conclusion of the agreement in a detailed letter to Chiang Kai-shek. The following excerpts from the original wording of the letter are quoted here because they illustrate the methods used to coerce Sheng into unconditionally acceding to the Soviet demands:[44]

> Completely unexpectedly, the Soviet Union sent an emissary to Sinkiang in the November of 1940 with a letter addressed to me and marked strictly confidential. This document was all about the leasing of the Sinkiang tin deposits under downright ridiculous and inequitable conditions and, moreover, it was couched in extremely aggressive terms. At that time I insisted that the conditions be revised and the duration of the lease be shortened. The emissary explained, however, that not a single word of the text was open to change, and, besides, as a member of the CPSU I should comply with the instructions of the Party and should stand up more energetically and aggressively for the interests of the Soviet Union.
>
> At that time the Altai uprising was just brewing and, besides, I was ill. Under these circumstances I found myself forced to put my seal to the document. On top of that, he also demanded that I should affix the seals of the Provincial Government and of the Defense Commissariat, as well, but I refused to do that. This agreement was originated by the Soviet Union and was placed before me (in its final condition) by the Soviet Union. The wording, however, said that it had been drawn up in consultation with the Provincial Government of Sinkiang, which, of course, is contrary to the actual facts of the matter. I demanded that this be rectified, but I was told I should not let that bother me; I would understand the whole thing better after I had had a talk with Stalin about it. I also demanded that the exploitation of the tin deposits should be vested in a mixed Sinkiang-Soviet company. The emissary replied that I should first remember that I was a member of the CPSU and secondly that a lot of Russian blood had been shed in Sinkiang during the Muslim uprising under Ma Ch'ung-ying, for which Soviet Russia had not yet received any compensation.

As Article 1 of the text quoted shows, the treaty afforded the Soviet Union practically every possible facility for the exploitation of all the mineral resources in Sinkiang. Whether full use was actually made of these rights, or to what degree, has not emerged very clearly to date. According to the Chinese government, the Soviet experts' investigations concentrated on the large-scale tungsten deposits in the southern foothills of the Altai. With the aid of sixty engineers and technicians and 3,000 conscripted labourers, more than 150 metric tons of tungsten are thought to have been removed from the area without the knowledge or consent of the authorities in the period from April 1941 to 1943.[45]

But the height of Soviet pressure on Urumchi was not reached even with the treaty of 26 November 1940: in July 1942, the Deputy Foreign Commissar of the Soviet Union, Dekanosov, confronted Governor Sheng on the occasion of a visit to Urumchi with further demands which amounted to the granting of comprehensive petroleum exploitation concessions. The Soviet draft consisted of a total of 18 Articles, including the following provisions: [46]

- The oil fields were to be made the property of a joint company — the 'Sinkiang-Soviet Oil Company' — under the management of a Director General and under the control of a Chief Engineer, both of whom were to be appointed by the People's Commissariat for the Petroleum Industry in Moscow.
- The Soviet Union agreed to give the Provincial Government a three-year credit (from 1 April 1942 to 1 April 1945) at 4.5 percent interest for an amount that would be sufficient for it to be able to pay off at certain scheduled dates half of the cost of the equipment to be installed in the vicinity of Tu-Shantse by 1 January 1942.
- The repayment instalments and interest paid by the Provincial Government to the Soviet Government were to be used for the purchase and duty-free export of cattle, wool and gold of Sinkiang production.
- The Provincial Government was to undertake to guarantee the free availability of land for exploratory drilling and for the exploitation of petroleum deposits and the free availability of construction materials and manpower. All machinery and materials imported from the Soviet Union for the purposes of the company were to be exempt from customs duties and all other levies.
- The People's Commissariat for the Petroleum Industry in Moscow was to be given the right to perform the planning work and give technological assistance in the building up of the petroleum industry and related industrial branches, to second Soviet advisers and technicians, and to train the Chinese labour and technical cadres required at the expense of the company.
- Half the production was to be bought from the company by the Provincial Government and the other half by the Soviet Government at a price to be agreed between the two governments and subject to duty-free export conditions.
- The agreement was to run for 25 years, after which it was to be extended for further periods of 5 years until such time as the Provincial Government had acquired the entire company by purchase. The Provincial Government was not to be allowed to use

foreign capital to finance its take-over of the Soviet share in the company; nor was it allowed to transfer its rights in full or in part, by assignment or by sale, to the government, private persons or companies of any third country.

The Forced Withdrawal of the Soviets from East Turkestan

These demands brought forward by Dekanosov, however, caused Sheng to become extremely cautious, if not sceptical, especially since his brother, Brigadier Sheng Shi-chi, had been murdered shortly before and the investigations into the assassination had revealed a plot against himself and his Provincial Government. His disenchantment became strikingly evident in his aforementioned letter to Chiang Kai-shek:[47]

> The sincerity of my intentions not only went unrewarded, but, on the contrary, my close association with the Soviets was used at every opportunity to the detriment of Sinkiang. In this context, for example, the numerous sporadic but without exception unsuccessful attempted *putsches* should be mentioned. On closer investigation, every single one of them turned out to be the result of Soviet machinations. But more perfidious and injurious than any of the others was the plot that was geared towards a *coup d'état* during the conference on 12 April 1942. It was not only well-planned in terms of timing and organisation, but this time there were more influential politicians and military personnel involved than in any of the earlier revolts, and in addition all the Soviets in Sinkiang, including the consuls, advisers and instructors, and the communists in the Chinese workforce. Their objectives were very ambitious, and besides myself all the important political and military leaders were on their black list. We were all going to be murdered. Their plan was to overthrow the acting administration and to set up a Soviet regime, controlled by the Soviets in conjunction with the Chinese communists, and independent of the Chinese Government...

The Soviet Union's worsening situation in Europe as a result of the adverse course of the war against Germany encouraged Sheng Shi-ts'ai to extricate himself more and more from the control of the Soviets. With his letter of 7 July 1942 to Chiang Kai-shek, from which the above quotes were taken, he appealed to the Chinese central government in Chungking for backing. Only ten days later he informed the

Soviet Foreign Commissar in a letter that Sinkiang was a province of China and the Soviet Union would have to negotiate the question of oil concessions in Sinkiang directly with the Chinese government in Chungking. In his reply of 20 August 1942, Molotov expressed his agreement with that proposal. In the period from October 1942 to March 1943, protracted negotiations were held between the Soviet Ambassador to China, Panyushkin, and the competent Chinese authorities in Chungking; these negotiations ended without any agreement being reached.[48]

Sheng then went one step further: he revoked the agreement of 26 November 1940 and demanded the immediate withdrawal of the Soviet technical personnel from Sinkiang.

He also had a large number of communist and leftist officials of his own administrative apparatus arrested. These events left the Soviet Union no other option than to start withdrawing from Sinkiang. On 10 April 1943 the Soviet Consul General in Urumchi informed Sheng that work in the tin mines was going to be discontinued, the technical staff withdrawn and the installed machinery disassembled. At the same time, Panyushkin broke off the talks on oil concessions in Chungking and announced the dismantling of all installations in Tu-Shantse. He also announced that the trading company 'Sovsintorg' would discontinue its activities, that the Soviet advisers would leave the province, and that the Soviet regiment stationed in Hami would be redeployed to Outer Mongolia.

During the last phase of their withdrawal from Sinkiang, the Soviets offered on 2 November 1943 to sell to the central government the drilling equipment they had left behind[49] for a total of two million dollars and the buildings for 490,000 dollars. The price for the installations and buildings was eventually reduced to a total of 1.7 million dollars, which the Chinese central government paid into the Soviet State Bank's account at the Chase National Bank in New York. This marked the end of this chapter in the history of Soviet policy towards Sinkiang: for the first time since 1912 — when Yan Tsen-hsin took office — Sinkiang was once again under the full control of the Chinese central government.

Moscow's Last Intervention before Mao

How little this withdrawal had detracted from the Soviet government's interest in East Turkestan became apparent only a short time later, when the Soviet Union, shortly before its victory over Germany in the Second World War, was at the zenith of its power within the coalition of the opponents of Germany. In February 1944 the last great Muslim uprising before Mao Tse-tung's takeover of power was launched in the form of the rebellion of the Kazakh tribes under their leader Usman Batur. This revolt revealed all the features that had always been characteristic of the Muslim uprisings in Central Asia — the quest for the greatest possible degree of autonomy from the Chinese and Russian giants. Uprisings in Sinkiang had always tended to ignite spontaneously precisely whenever either the Chinese central government had attempted to assert its sovereignty with all the means at its disposal or when political and economic interest on the part of Russia and later the Soviet Union raised fears of too close a link-up of East Turkestan to Moscow.

The uprising in early 1944 originated from the disaffection of the Muslim population with the policies of the Chinese central government. It thus once more indirectly offered the Soviet Union a foothold from which to influence the course of development in Sinkiang: the rebel Kazakh tribes under Usman Batur were armed with weapons and ammunition from the Soviet Union. They were backed up by Mongolian troops under the leadership of Soviet officers and by the Soviet Air Force, which flew hefty bombing attacks against Chinese government forces from bases in Outer Mongolia. Without this assistance, the complete annihilation of three Chinese regiments by Usman Batur and his Kazakh troops would have been inconceivable.

The reason given by the Soviet Union to justify its intervention on behalf of Usman Batur was that Chinese troops in Sinkiang had allegedly violated the territory of Outer Mongolia.[50] A TASS statement on these events even threatened further 'countermeasures'.[51] The timing of the Soviet Union's renewed intervention in Sinkiang was extremely well chosen: at this time, 'Russophilia' had reached a peak in the USA. Roosevelt and his Administration were giving top priority to the war in Europe and to the co-operation with the Soviet Union that was essential to its termination. They thus did everything in their power to prevent the outbreak of conflicts between America's allies — in this case between China and the Soviet Union. For this purpose, the American Vice-President, Henry A. Wallace, travelled to the region affected between 20 May and 10 July 1944, visiting first Outer Mongolia, then Soviet Central Asia, from there to Urumchi, where he conferred with Sheng Shi-ts'ai,[52] and finally to Nanking for detailed talks with Chiang Kai-shek. Wallace explained the objective of this trip to the Sino-Soviet border area and to China in precise detail: Roosevelt 'wanted in this way', he writes, 'to form an opinion as to how far any future border conflicts between China and Russia can be reduced to a minimum'.[53]

Sheng Shi-Ts'ai's recall to Chungking in July 1944 to take over a ministry was largely attributable to Wallace's influence.[54] This conclusion is suggested by records (drawn up by John Carter Vincent) of the talks between Wallace and Chiang Kai-shek. These show that Wallace was at pains to convince the Chinese President that it was necessary for the sake of preserving the peace in the Central Asian border regions to make concessions to the Soviet Union. The records also reveal that Chiang Kai-shek's emphatic warning not to place too much trust in the Soviet Union and the Chinese communists met with deaf ears if not indignation on the part of the American Vice-President.[55]

The recall of Sheng did not bring the stabilization the Americans had expected but rather — just the opposite — paved the way for the even more unimpeded development of Soviet activities in Central Asia: as early as 7 November 1944, a new rebellion broke out among the Muslim population in Ili. This rebellion in turn grew into a popular uprising that the Muslim Uighurs also joined and which was backed by the Soviet Union. The troops of the Chinese garrison were forced in bloody battles to retreat. The Muslim rebel forces were brought to a halt about 100 kilometers from Urumchi. This once more assured the Soviet Union of control over the mineral resources in the Ili, Tacheng, and Altai regions. In Urumchi, the Republic of East Turkestan was proclaimed on the grounds of the right of the non-Chinese population to self-determination. Its government was headed by Akhmed Djan, a Soviet citizen; his Russian name was Kasimov.[56]

The assurance given by the Soviet government in the Treaty of Friendship and Alliance concluded with China on 14 August 1945[57] that 'in the light of recent events in Sinkiang' it did not harbour 'the intention of interfering in China's internal affairs' had thus been made completely meaningless by this consolidation of Soviet influence. It was born of the realization that even at that time the Kuomintang was no longer in a position to assert its legitimate claim to sovereignty in Sinkiang. One local view of Soviet policy towards East Turkestan at this time was given by the Kazakh leader Usman Batur: he had first operated together with the Ili rebels but had broken with them in the April of 1946, returning to the side of the Chinese central government:[58]

On 6 September 1945, 6,000 men of the Ili troops entered Chenghua, the capital of the Altai region. They were wearing Russian uniforms and they were speaking Russian, too ... They were under the orders of a Lieutenant-General Birkdorff; the latter had under his command two regimental commanders by the name of Leskin and Dostgonov. I co-operated with them until 1 April 1946. Then I went on to Peitashon. Along with the Ili troops there came a Russian Police Chief by the name of Sambayev. They fetched me to a conference in Ili and demanded that I should transfer my entire Kazakh formations to Ili while they themselves wanted to take over the garrison of the Altai region. I refuse to do so. For this reason, and because they brought Kazakh women to Ili, I turned away from them. I also dismissed their demand that we should hand over our weapons to them. The Ili people also confiscated 28,600 ounces of gold from the office of the Ashan gold mines that by rights actually belongs to the Government. Now the Russians have taken over the exploitation of the gold and tungsten mines and are increasing the output day by day.[59]

The result of the break by Usman Batur and his Kazakhs with Soviet-controlled policy was what was known as the 'Peitachan Affair', which also deserves mention here. When Usman Batur found himself forced to retire to Peitachan (Baitik Bogda), he was chased by Outer Mongolian troops. These were backed up by formations of the Mongolian Air Force, which on 5 June 1947 bombarded the Chinese positions in Peitachan. A protest by the Chinese Foreign Ministry against this 'Peitachan Affair' was rejected by the Soviet Union as not conforming with the facts and as 'a provocative misrepresentation'. The battles were continued despite this *dementi*. The explanation for this is probably to be found in the fact that this region, some 200 kilometers from the border of Outer Mongolia, is rich in uranium deposits.

Also in this connection, the air attacks on Chinese security posts and villages in the Pamir region and along the south-west border of Sinkiang should be mentioned; these aircraft took off from the Soviet military airfield in Qizil Rabat in Tajikistan.[60] In this case, too, the Soviets had taken advantage of uprisings by Muslim Tajiks in Sinkiang who threatened Kashgar, occupied Kaghilik (Yehcheng), and attempted to capture Yarkand (Shache). According to a report by the British Consul in Kashgar[61], the rebels were equipped with weapons and ammunition from the Soviet Union and had been reinforced with formations of

Nationality Dynamics in Sino-Soviet Relations

Muslim Tajiks from the Soviet Union. All these uprisings inspired by the Soviet Union did much to further Moscow's economic interests in Sinkiang. In those regions that had shaken off control by the provincial government in Urumchi and by the Chinese central government, the exploitation of the oil fields and the tungsten mines was resumed immediately.[62]

The Chinese central government after the war was no longer in a position to influence the course of events in Sinkiang. For this reason, it was left to the provincial government to take up negotiations with the government of the Republic of East Turkestan which had constituted itself in Kuldja. These negotiations led in the summer of 1946 to the admission of the leader of the Kuldja Group to the provincial government in Urumchi, of which the Chinese General Chang Chi-chung became President. The latter was later replaced by the Uighur Masud Sabri, the first non-Chinese President since Ya'qub Beg, and eventually, in December 1948, by Burkhan, a second non-Chinese.

How helpless the Chinese central government was in the face of this course of events is illustrated by the fact that the proposals it had put to the Soviet government on 4 November 1946 regarding the establishment of settled economic relations between Sinkiang and the Soviet Union had still found no reply by the end of January 1949. The draft of a three-year trade agreement submitted by the Soviet Consul General in Kashgar on 24 January 1949 to the Provincial Government in Urumchi in complete disregard of the competence of the central government provides evidence of the more and more advanced decline of the power of the Kuomintang. In that draft, the Soviet Union demanded the right to unrestricted export and import to and from Sinkiang while offering nothing in return and called for the conclusion of a treaty with a term of 50 years on the formation of joint Sino-Soviet companies for the prospecting and exploitation of Sinkiang's mineral and petroleum deposits. It further demanded to be given a share in the exploitation of all raw material deposits still undiscovered at that time. Finally, the draft treaty contained provisions to the effect that the managing directors of all joint companies to be founded should be nominated by the Soviet government.[63]

The Chinese central government, too, was by all means interested, as its proposal of 4 November 1946 to the Soviet Union showed, in extending economic relations between Sinkiang and China's neighbour to the west. However, it did not want to sign away half of all Sinkiang's oil and mineral deposits as the price for such improved relations. For this reason, the negotiations on the Soviet draft made very slow progress. They were broken off after Chang Chi-chung and representatives of the Kuldja Group had attended the meeting of the political People's Council held by the Communist Party of China in Peking in the September of 1949 and after both the military and the political leadership of Sinkiang had broken off relations with the Chinese central government and had formally gone over to the communist camp. On 17 December 1949, finally, a provisional People's Government was installed in Urumchi.

The Turkic Peoples of Central Asia in the Sino-Soviet Tug o'War

The takeover by Mao Tse-tung was to have far-reaching consequences for the Russian-Chinese confrontation in Central Asia, but the full importance of those consequences was not to make itself evident until much later.

At first, the impression was bound to arise that the Soviet Union would be granted without major disagreement by the Communist Party of China what it had not been able to wrest from the Nationalist government in the protracted negotiations undertaken since the end of January 1949.

During Mao Tse-tung's two-month stay in Moscow, a friendship, alliance and mutual assistance pact was worked out between the two countries;[64] a delegation from Sinkiang under the leadership of Saif ad-Din (Saifuddin), the Deputy Chairman of the new Provincial Government in Urumchi, had also been summoned to attend these consultations on 30 January 1950.

On 27 March 1950, an agreement on the foundation of two joint Soviet-Chinese companies for the extraction of mineral oil and the exploitation of noble and light metals was concluded in Moscow to cover a period of thirty years.[65] This agreement granted the Soviet Union half of Sinkiang's mineral and oil output. For all practical purposes, this amounted to China having renounced its sovereignty in Sinkiang — a goal that the Soviet Union had been striving to achieve with its draft treaty of 24 January 1949. The full extent of the obligations and commitments which China was forced to undertake in respect of Sinkiang has never been revealed. It must, however, be assumed that it goes far beyond just the formal agreement concluded on 27 March 1950.

According to one Indian source,[66] Moscow is said to have forced the People's Republic of China to accept a secret agreement that secured for the Soviet Union control over all uranium deposits in Sinkiang. The mining areas were accordingly said to have been declared 'no-go areas' to which only Soviet scientists, technicians and specially skilled workers had access. The uranium ores mined are supposed to have been transported to a processing facility in the Soviet part of Central Asia. Such a degree of 'obligingness' on the part of China can only be explained by the possibility that, after 30 September 1949, the Communist Party must have had to give the stabilization of its newly-gained power absolute priority. Against this background, the new communist government may well have regarded the 'sovietization' of Sinkiang as the lesser evil for the time being.[67] That Peking did not consider this to represent any irreversible renunciation of its sovereignty in the Chinese part of Central Asia was evident long before the first harsh-worded altercations between the two countries after the start of the Cultural Revolution. On the contrary, even China's very first measures, adopted with the aim of calming down the situation in Sinkiang, made Peking's stance apparent: immediately after 1 October 1949 it recognised Sinkiang's special national status within China.[68] Regions in which national minorities predominated were to be given an 'autonomous law'. By the end of 1954, this precept had led to the foundation of a Dunga, a Kirghiz, an Uighur, and a Kazakh Autonomous District (Chou).[69] These reflected the ethnic composition of the region and — whether intentionally or unintentionally — the various currents striving for autonomy within the Muslim population of Sinkiang, which had always been directed against either Russia or China. But this measure was to prove to be merely an *ad hoc* transitional arrangement by means of which it was possible to create expedient conditions for the restoration or consolidation of the Chinese central government's authority in Sinkiang: even as early as on 1 October 1955, all of Chinese Central Asia was re-united under the designation of 'Uighur Autonomous Region of Sinkiang'. The man appointed as the first Governor of the Autonomous Region was the Deputy Governor of the old provincial government, Saif ad-Din (Saifuddin).

A further instrument used to tie Sinkiang more closely to China and thus to ward off the sovietization of East Turkestan was the relatively lenient policy towards Islam pursued by Peking until the mid-fifties.[70] China's Muslims were largely able to preserve the identity of religious life and everyday life even after 1949. And the communist leaders of Party and State in China accordingly allowed themselves to be guided for a time by the realisation that any attempt to change the customs of the everyday life of the Muslim population would have been interpreted by that population as an attempt to assail or even to eliminate its religion. Under such circumstances, even the very existence of Islam would without doubt have faced the leaders of Party and State in China with problems of immense consequence to the country's domestic and foreign policy, for Islam as a religious community not only regards itself as an organic part of the *Umma*, it is also, as Nasser expressly pointed out in his work 'Philosophy of the Revolution', considered by the leaders of the Islamic states, too, as the integrating component of that community.[71] To have suppressed the Islamic minority within its own borders would therefore inevitably have had adverse repercussions on China's relations with the Islamic countries of the Near and Middle East and of Southeast Asia.

This explains the relatively moderate policy towards Islam pursued by the leaders of the Chinese Party and State in the early years after 1949. Following the example of the Soviet Union in the twenties, China sent functionaries of the Communist Party into the regions peopled by the national minorities in order to win over the Muslims for active co-operation in Party work. They were to be schooled and, so to speak, 'transformed' by persuasion and by psychological ruses.[72]

Again, following the Soviet pattern, non-Muslim Han Chinese were also re-settled in the regions of Sinkiang that were only thinly populated by Muslim Turkic peoples under the pretext that Sinkiang's rich raw material resources could only be developed by Chinese experts. The Islamic communities were also directly affected by the land reforms that were carried out throughout China, since they held vast expanses of land. However, the Muslims were given preferential treatment by comparison with the other religious communities in that for a while they were allowed to keep and cultivate the land belonging to the mosques.

This relatively moderate policy had very little to do with religious tolerance, however, as is demonstrated by numerous examples. For instance, a new Chinese translation of the Qoran was published in Shanghai in early 1952 under the title *Outline and Special Characteristics of the Qoran*. This contained only such *surahs* and verses as were suitable for demonstrating the validity of Communist doctrine. This translation constituted an attempt to adapt the doctrine of Islam to Marxist-Leninist dogma. There can be no doubt that the leadership in Peking expected the use of the new translation as the basis for the Qoran readings in the mosques, the training of religious teachers in the *madrassahs*, and the education of children to bear great fruit.

Another measure adopted against the Muslim population of China was the undermining of the Muslim dietary laws. In compliance with the requirement that believers may eat only the meat of animals slaughtered in accordance with a certain rite, the Muslims have always bought their beef and mutton from slaughterhouses run by the mosques. When the Chinese authorities closed down these slaughterhouses the Muslim population was forced either to buy its meat from the State shops, thereby violating its religious precepts, or to do without this form of nutrition altogether.

Finally, the foundation of two central organisations should be mentioned in this context, the 'Chinese Islamic Society' and the 'Hai Cultural Association', which made it possible for the Chinese Party and State leadership to influence, or at least keep under control, the religious, social and political life of China's Muslim minorities. These organisations were also used to establish and cultivate contacts with the Islamic countries — a highly effective move to which the respectable successes achieved by Chinese foreign policy in the Near East, in Africa and in Southeast Asia up to about 1963-64 can be attributed. At any rate, all measures directed against Islam up to that time were undertaken with great caution and discretion.

Peking's relatively soft policy towards Islam was by no means incompatible with the doctrine of Marxism-Leninism on the question of religion. Nevertheless, it enabled the new Chinese leadership to keep the sovietization of Sinkiang in check or even to counteract it in the period up to 1955, during a time when Moscow's predominance in the region was apparently inevitable. Nor was it an indication of any willingness on the part of Peking to grant the Muslim population any real degree of autonomy within the People's Republic.

This became plainly evident after China had succeeded in forcing the Soviets to agree in a treaty to withdraw from Sinkiang.[73] The consolidation of the new regime brought with it a perceptible tightening-up in policy towards the national minorities: the limited 'freedoms' granted to the nationalities were curtailed or even retracted altogether. The repulsion of Soviet influence created clear-cut 'fronts' also as regards the confrontation between the Islamic Turkic peoples and the communist State in that all measures directed against them could now be clearly seen to proceed exclusively from the Communist Party of China.

Hans Bräker

Moscow's Hand in the Escalation of Tensions

An assessment of the subsequent course of events is made difficult by the fact that, because of the policy of tight restrictions on information concerning the goings-on within Sinkiang pursued by the government and Party of the People's Republic of China in the period as of 1955, only a scanty picture can be gained of the actual situation within the province.

From the few items of news that reached the outside world, however, the conclusion can be drawn that Chinese policy towards the Islamic minorities came up against growing opposition as of 1955, and that that opposition became increasingly well organised. On 26 July 1955, for example, Saif ad-Din pointed out in a speech made before the National People's Congress[74] that it was necessary to combat the growing counter-revolutionary activities in Sinkiang. He pointed to an attempted revolt that had been launched in December 1954 in Khotan (Hotien). This revolt seems to have been on quite a large scale. Even as late as in September 1959 there were reports from Urumchi that, referring back to the events in 1954, the reasons for unrest continued unabated in Khotan:[75] counter-revolutionary elements had again launched an agitation campaign based primarily on religious and nationalist slogans. And a year later the same source announced[76] that all-out operations were planned for the 'next winter and spring' to liquidate the remaining elements of this uprising.

The course of events apparently became particularly turbulent in 1958. Wang En-mao, a local Party leader and high-ranking officer, described the tense atmosphere in Sinkiang by stating that everything indicated 'that the local nationalists are hoping for something along the lines of the events in Hungary in order to be able to eliminate the democratic dictatorship of the people'.[77] The events of that year appear to have been the result of an instruction issued by the government in Peking to the institutions of higher education in Sinkiang to the effect that the languages of the nationalities should no longer be used in instruction but that all teaching was to be done in Chinese. In connection with this change-over, the local teachers were also to be gradually replaced by Chinese teachers. The reaction by the Chinese authorities to the unrest among the pupils and students that this move triggered off and that became apparent in the form of attempted strikes and protest gatherings was first to withdraw the offenders' food ration cards and later — when this measure had proved ineffectual — to expel many teachers and students from the colleges and universities. There is only little information available as to the extent of the unrest in Sinkiang. According to a report by a Uighur refugee in Hong Kong, about 60,000 Muslims were involved in the insurrection of 1958.[78] A report by the Chinese news agency Taipeh claimed that in mid-1958 members of the underground liberation movement had proclaimed a government of the 'Uighur Republic'.[79]

Naturally, the fragmentary information yielded by such reports and news items can only yield general leads for the purposes of any analysis of the actual events. What appears certain, however, was that the main centre of insurrection was Khotan. According to the report by the Uighur refugee in Hong Kong, the Soviets, after years of keeping a low profile, once more openly exploited the disturbances of 1958: of the 60,000 involved in the uprising, about half had been trained by Soviet instructors and armed with Soviet weapons. The 'rebels' had succeeded in digging themselves in for more than two months in the mountains along the border to Kazakhstan; the Chinese had had to launch a major military effort in order to break the resistance at all. An eye-witness report by a Uighur who had fled to Pakistan, published in a French daily, claimed that in the course of the uprising about 10,000 'rebels' had occupied a prison in the vicinity of Khotan, had released about 600 convicts and killed about 50 Chinese.[80]

Nor was the Chinese government able to put down the rebellion in the years that followed. On the contrary, it appears to have gained considerably in intensity because the insurgent Muslims were given direct aid more and more openly by the Soviet Union. When, for example, in July 1962 the diversion of large quantities of foodstuffs to other regions of China caused a severe supply crisis in Sinkiang, the local population in the border towns of Kuldja and Chuguchak (Tacheng) clashed with the Chinese administrative and military authorities, leaving many dead and wounded.[81] The Kazakh demonstrators had gathered in front of the Soviet consulate in Kuldja and had requested armed assistance in their quest to force the Chinese to leave Sinkiang and to make the country independent. But the Soviet Consul had refused to intervene in any way and had persuaded the demonstrators to disperse. Thereupon many families fled to the Soviet Union, where they were received as 'living examples of Chinese brutality'. Although the Soviet consulate formally denied having had anything to do with these events and disclaimed all responsibility for them, the Chinese closed not only the Sino-Soviet border but also the Soviet Consulate General in Urumchi.

Although public order in Kuldja was superficially restored in

September 1962 thanks to a slight increase in food rations, the unrest continued to spread: thus, the Indian press again and again brought reports of outbreaks of bloody rebellion, behind which the Chinese identified the 'wire-pullers' in most cases as Kazakhs, but also Uighurs, Kirghiz, Uzbeks and Tatars.[82] It would appear that in 1962 the workers in the Tu-shan-tsu oilfields went on strike and that many of them left their jobs. The workforce is said to have numbered only 10,000 in October 1962, as opposed to 15,000 in 1959, and oil production is reported to have dropped to only 75 percent of the 1960 level. Persistent uprisings were reported from the Altai region, the border region to Outer Mongolia: the Chinese communication lines had been interrupted, bridges blown up, and numerous armed attacks launched. The Soviet Union is thought to have backed up the activities of the rebel bands by secretly supplying them with weapons.

Peking's Reaction — Pressure on the Turkic Population

These reports have never been confirmed nor refuted by official Soviet or Chinese statements. For despite the deterioration in Sino-Soviet relations, both sides still exercised a relatively high degree of restraint in their public media.[83] But even at this time it would already have been an overstatement to speak of normal relations between the two.[84]

Nevertheless, the documents published in 1963 marking the open outbreak of the conflict between Moscow and Peking underline the credibility of the reports quoted above. Thus, for example, an editorial published on 6 September 1963 in the Chinese newspapers *Hung ch'i* and *Yen Min Yih Pao* corroborated the reports on the events in 1962 in Sinkiang by reproaching and launching attacks on the CPSU:[85]

> From April to May 1962 the leaders of the C.P.S.U. provoked ... some thousands of Chinese citizens who, with the support of the Soviet Government and its accredited official representatives in Sinkiang, had launched into subversive activity on a large scale in the Ili District to flee to the Soviet Union. Heedless of numerous protests and appeals by the Chinese Government, the Soviet Government has ... refused to repatriate these citizens. This affair has still not been settled. This is an atrocious incident for which there is no precedent in the relations between socialist countries.[86]

Despite drastic measures, the Chinese government was not able to bring the situation in Sinkiang under control in the following years. Thus, the Turkish newspaper *Yeni Istanbul* reported in early 1966:[87]

> A further 60,000 Chinese soldiers were recently transferred to the Soviet-Chinese border in East Turkestan. This measure shows that the Chinese administration in East Turkestan has still not been successful in containing the exodus of the Kazakhs and the Uighurs into the Soviet Union ... But it is not only the refugee problem that has got the leadership in Peking worried. The fact is that armed clashes have persisted unabated for years in this region between the Kazakhs, Uighurs, and other Turkic peoples on the one hand and Chinese occupation troops on the other. The partisan movement of East Turkestani patriots continues to disturb not only just the mountainous Tarbagatai region but also the valley of the Ili and the regions around Kashgar and Aq Su (Wen Su). According to what are in most cases very cautious estimates, about 40,000 well-armed Uighur and Kazakh partisans were recently still operating on the territory of East Turkestan. They were raiding and destroying Chinese garrisons, blowing up bridges and railway lines, derailing troop transport trains, etc. The Chinese military leadership is forced to keep about 100,000 soldiers stationed here just to protect the communications routes.

Under increasing pressure from China, the Turkic populace of Sinkiang evidently had no other choice but to flee or to stay and put up armed resistance. In support of this fight, a National Centre for the Liberation of East Turkestan was founded in Istanbul and on several occasions appealed to world public opinion to voice its support for the rights of the peoples of East Turkestan and to protect them against complete annihilation by the Chinese. In this connection the Turkish paper *Yeni Gazeta* reported in February 1966 on an interview given by the President of the National Centre for the Liberation of East Turkestan, Isa Yusuf Alptekin, to a number of American journalists[88] that his organisation intended to bring the 'case of the illegal occupation of East Turkestan' by the Chinese before the United Nations for review. He accused Peking of offences against humanity, of genocide, and of the expulsion of the peoples of East Turkestan on religious, racist and nationalist grounds.

Reports by Turkic refugees from Sinkiang living in the Soviet Union[89] speak of the Turkic partisans operating in Sinkiang from Soviet bases. According to these accounts, a former Major General of the

Chinese People's Liberation Army, the Uighur Zunun Taipov, was in command of an army operating in Sinkiang from a base in Alma Ata. Taipov is said to have been involved as regimental commander in the 1944 revolt against the Chinese and to have fled to the Soviet Union in 1963 after an uprising he had organised failed. *Izvestiia* published an exhaustive letter penned by him in September 1964, in which he wrote:[90]

> It is a depressing thought that on the other side of the border thousands of my brothers — Uighurs and Kazakhs, Kirghiz and Mongols — are subject to inconceivable persecution and oppression ... I myself have experienced how the Chinese are acting more and more despotically towards the national minorities. Peking is hardly attempting any more to conceal its intention of sinifying Sinkiang and isolating it from its neighbour, the Soviet Union, by a solid wall.

In his letter, Taipov went on to accuse the Chinese leaders of attempting to smuggle anti-Soviet literature into the Soviet Union and to provoke clashes on the Soviet-Chinese border.

The account quoted here corroborates the existence of secret training camps in which refugees from Sinkiang were given instruction in partisan warfare and administrative questions. It also states that the high-ranking partisan officials trained in these camps were being infiltrated into Sinkiang on a regular basis. The number of Turks that had fled to the Soviet Union since 1962 was given — with a reference to the fact that the stream of refugees had previously flowed in the other direction — as about 300,000.

The Soviet Union as the Advocate of the National Minorities in East Turkestan

The reports on the Soviet Union's moral and material support for the resistance of the Turkic population of China against Peking has been confirmed by the Soviet press, too, since 1963. The material for these reports came from refugees from Sinkiang. For example a Kazakh writer by the name of Bukhar Tyshkanbayev reported in September 1963 in *Literaturnaia Gazeta* on his experience of a so-called 're-education camp'[91] to which the East Turkestani intellectuals were sent after they had been forced by the Chinese to indulge in self-criticism.

After his release from the camp, Tyshkanbayev was forced to denounce the playing of ethnic folk songs and folk music. He was compelled against his will to write a literature textbook for Kazakh schools in which it is claimed that Kazakhs of Chinese origins are of the same culture as the Chinese; thus there was no difference between Chinese and Kazakhs. Most of the interned intellectuals, he claimed, had already been held in Kuomintang prisons. Finally, Tyshkanbayev reported that the campaign for the 'de-nationalisation' of Central Asia had been backed up by mass resettlement of Uighurs, Kazakhs and Kirghiz in the interior of China and of Chinese from central and eastern China in Sinkiang.

There can be no doubt that the Chinese campaign against the Muslim Turkic populace reached its climax during the Cultural Revolution. The author of an article published in *Literaturnaia Gazeta* in early 1967, Anur Alimzhanov, even went so far as to maintain, on the basis of reports given by refugees, that even with their 1955 '100 Flowers' campaign the Chinese had already been pursuing no other objective in Sinkiang but to identify the nationalist forces opposing the Communist Party of China in order to be able to eliminate them.[92]

The aim of such articles and reports was plainly evident. The issue of the national minorities in East Turkestan was just the excuse Moscow needed to underpin its own positions in the controversy with China within the Soviet Union itself, within the socialist camp, and in the non-communist world, and thus to make those positions more credible.

The Kazakhs of Sinkiang embodied, according to Alimzhanov, by no means primarily the Muslim nationalists that Peking made them out to be but rather 'sincere communists of Sinkiang'. And if the Communist Party of China was levelling the charge that these 'Muslim nationalists' had 'attempted to set up a Khanate uniting not only the Kazakhs of China but also those of Mongolia and the Soviet Union', then it was only because their own intentions of assimilating the Kazakhs, Uighurs, and Kirghiz of East Turkestan had run aground. Peking's claim that these peoples were Chinese and shared with the Chinese 'a common homeland . . . stretching from China to the Aral Sea' was untenable. Instead, the 'imperialist chauvinism of the leaders of the People's Republic of China' was in direct contrast with the historical bonds shared by East Turkestan and Russia. Eye-witness reports were also produced in support of the Turkic populace's continued awareness of these bonds, in this case, for example, that of a 'former Lieutenant-Colonel of the People's Liberation Army of China' by the name of Balkash Bafin, 'decorated with three Chinese orders and five medals, ... today a Kazakh journalist'. He gave as the motive for his flight from Sinkiang: 'The only reason why I was relieved of my command was because I was a Kazakh. Without waiting for the further course of events, I decided to put into practice an age-old dream and the legacy of my father who had died in the prison of the Chiang Kai-shek people. I went over the border and returned to the land of my forefathers'.

Other eye-witness reports whose narrators Alimzhanov names as the 'former Chinese citizens S.M. and Y. Daurabkayeva and O. Magomedov, who lived in Sinkiang until last autumn' are called upon to underline the solidarity of the persecuted populace of Sinkiang with the Soviet Union: 'First of all, they [the so-called 'Hungweipingists'[93]] demolished the building in which the Soviet consulate had previously been located. They pulled up all the flowers out of the flower-beds and cut down all the trees near the building, shouting that they had been planted by "Revisionists".'

In all the refugee reports quoted, unanimous criticism is levelled at the 'forced assimilation' of the populace of East Turkestan: one of the reports quoted from here states, for example, 'They take the Kazakh, Uighur and Kirghiz girls away from their parents and force them under pain of death to marry Chinese. The leaders of the Hungweipingists claim that Chinese blood must prevail in the veins of every human being ... They destroy everything: books, records, furniture, household utensils. They cut the women's and girls' pigtails off and forbid them to wear national costume ...'

And finally, the economic importance of the traditional ties between East Turkestan and the Soviet Union are repeatedly brought into play. These are reflected in the fact that even as late as 'only ten years ago the convoys of trucks were driving in an endless stream from the [Soviet] Republic of Kazakhstan to Sinkiang and an exchange of goods was in progress that gave rise to trading activities of benefit both to us and to China.' It was 'historical, centuries-old traditional links' — this is the conclusion drawn by Alimzhanov from the refugees' reports, most of them published in *Literaturnaia Gazeta* — that had been severed through no fault of the Soviet Union. The blame was to be placed firmly with those 'who by the hour proclaim via Radio Peking, Urumchi [Urlumuqi], and Kudja [Yining] in the Russian, Kazakh and Uighur languages "victories" of the "Cultural Revolution" and a "Marxist" solution of the national issue in China'.

All these reports in the Soviet press confirm — intentionally or unintentionally — that it is the pronounced self-awareness of the Turkic populace that has really been the basis for the confrontation between the Soviet Union and China in Central Asia. The disputes about this region reflect again and again Moscow's struggle to gain positions of economic, political and territorial power. Both sides resort to ideological arguments in their altercations. But in the final analysis, this rivalry has little to do with ideological differences. And if the Soviet side devotes major efforts to criticising Peking's attempts to combat Islam, this only serves to confirm that Moscow is very well aware of the insoluble links between Islam and the national minorities that exist throughout the Central Asia region — that is to say, not only in the Chinese territories. In Kuldja (Yining) alone, according to a detailed TASS report by Shakir Gubarbakiev, the editor-in-chief of a Turkic periodical *The Sinkiang Liberation Army*, widely circulated (underground) in Sinkiang,[94] 'there were once more than 150 mosques. Now there are only three, a Uighur one, a Dungan one, and an Uzbek one. The possessions of the places of worship that have been closed down have been confiscated. Recently a mosque in the district of Nilkhe was attacked by Hungweipingists just as the Friday service was in progress. There were bloody clashes between these rowdies and those who had gathered for the service.' And a Uighur poet whose name is given as Abdulkhai Ruzi in the same TASS report tells in detail of how the Arabic alphabet is being replaced by the Latin throughout Sinkiang, against the wishes of the Islamic population — despite the phonetic peculiarities of the native language. The schoolchildren were being prevented from learning their own history because Chinese had been made the only language in which classes were held.

The flood of reports in the major organs of the Soviet press dealing with the events in East Turkestan in mid-1966 was unmistakeably directed towards influencing the attitudes of the countries of Southern Asia and of the Near and Middle East. The resonance was remarkable. As of 1966, the publication of reports about outrages perpetrated against the Muslims in China escalated abruptly in those countries. These publications could without exception be traced back to reports and news items that had appeared earlier in the Soviet press. Here, too, just a few examples will suffice: in October 1966, the Indian newspaper *Patrika* reported, with reference to the 'Soviet press', that Islam had been made a prime target for attacks by the Red Guard in China:[95]

... it is being accused of spreading superstition, of opposition to Mao's thoughts, and of spreading revisionist ideas. Oppression of the adherents of Islam, however, was already a shameful characteristic of the communist regime in China even long before the appearance of the Red Guards. The dreadful oppression of the Muslims in Sinkiang, which has led to thousands of them seeking refuge abroad, must not be forgotten so soon.

At about the same time, the *Hindustan Times* reported that a 'revolutionary combat group for the elimination of Islam' had been set up. This had proclaimed a ten-point programme for the 'elimination of the Islamic superstition' which included the closure of all mosques, the 're-education' of all religious leaders in labour camps, the abolition of fasting and of public prayer, a ban on readings from the Qoran, the abolition of circumcision and of giving children names from the Qoran.[96]

In December 1966, Moroccan newspapers published a photograph of a wall-poster containing an ultimatum to the Muslims of China. This read:[97] 'From now on it will no longer be permitted for you to hide behind your religious mask — we will exterminate you. You will no longer be allowed to waste your time with prayer, because all your mumbling in Arabic is anti-Chinese. It will also be forbidden for you to read your so-called Qoran.' The *Ceylon Daily News* reported that in Peking Red Guards had stormed mosques and mistreated their clergy. A Muslim scholar of Chinese descent who had become well-known for his translation of the Qoran into Chinese is reported to have been chased around the streets with a fool's cap on his head.[98]

Nevertheless, even if the references in the reports published in other countries to publications in the Soviet press did a great deal to foster public interest in the non-communist countries of Asia in the goings-on in Sinkiang, this did not imply that these countries came to any more positive appraisal of the policies towards the national minorities and the religions pursued by the Soviet leaders in their own part of the Central Asian region. On the contrary, an article that appeared in the *Times of India* in October 1966[99] recalled that anti-Islamic currents had not originated in China but were rather the inevitable consequence of the anti-religious doctrine of Marxism-Leninism. It was only in the interests of its own foreign policy strategy for Asia that Moscow was covering up its true attitude on this question. Since the beginning of the October Revolution in Russia, the Soviet leadership had been unconditionally geared to the elimination of Islam, just as the Chinese leadership had been since 1949. Muslims throughout the world must therefore recognize that communist radicalism was wholly and without reservation a constant threat to Islam.

The Moroccan newspaper *Eshaab* — to give one last example in this context — also referred to the events in China to call to mind the unbridgeable gap between Islam and communism in general[100]: if persecution in China was directed primarily against the Muslims, this was because Islam constituted the greatest obstacle to the expansion of the communist sphere of influence throughout the world. Only Islam was capable of solving those problems which communism had for decades been trying in vain to master. And Islam could do this without destroying the spiritual needs of mankind. Communism was able at best to offer people recipes for their material pursuits, but it destroyed the human spirit.

The Islamic Revolution and the Turkic Peoples in the Soviet Union and China

The leaders of Party and State in Moscow have, without doubt, made a good job of exploiting the turbulent events in China during the Cultural Revolution and even up to the death of Mao Zedong to promote the objectives of their own traditional power policies in Central Asia. Above all, they were able to profit in this phase of Soviet-Chinese confrontation in Central Asia particularly from Peking's ideologically induced ignorance of the problems of the national minorities in Sinkiang. The best that could be said of Chinese policy towards Central Asia was that it was based on a dreadfully inaccurate appraisal of the survival capabilities, deeply rooted in their cultural heritage, of the Islamic Turkic peoples living within the Chinese borders.

On the other hand, the analysis has made clear the continuity of Russian policy towards Central Asia since the 19th century: the Bolshevik October Revolution was not a departure from this course, although this was at first expected in the light of the 'Message to the working Muslims of Russia and the Orient' signed by Lenin and Stalin on 3 December 1917, which contained the words: '. . . From now on your Faith and your customs, your national and cultural institutions are declared to be free and inviolable . . . Build up your national life freely and without hindrance. This is your Right.'[101]

Despite such declarations, Soviet policy in Central Asia has continued to adhere to the standards and methods on which Tsarist policy before it had been based. And these foundations have remained determinant for Moscow's policies even after the radical upheaval in China of September/October 1949. After all, Mao's takeover of power had turned China into a communist 'brother state' which raised claim — a claim that Moscow readily accepted — to being one of the twin centres of the world communist movement.

The leaders of the Soviet Party and State have not been able with their offensive policy towards East Turkestan to shift attention from the difficulties they are themselves experiencing with the Turkic peoples in their own Central Asian Union Republics.

One can reasonably assume that the Soviet leaders were aware of the complexity of the problems presented by the national minorities and by Islam in Central Asia. This is indicated, at least, by the strategy and style of their policy on East Turkestan/Sinkiang. Despite all its experience, however, the Soviet leadership has evidently been suffering since the end of World War II under the delusion that this many-faceted and complex problem had been solved with the aid of the instruments and methods of Marxism-Leninism typical of the Soviet system. At any rate, it was convinced, even in the most recent past, that it had succeeded, thanks to its policies towards the national minorities and religions, in permanently integrating the ethnic minorities of Islamic culture into Soviet society.

With a certain persuasive power, Moscow believed that the reason for this was to be found in the progressive consolidation of its power in the Union Republics of Central Asia, that is to say the presence beside each non-Russian top-level official of a Russian. And it is indeed true — at least to the superficial observer — that signs of anti-Soviet national stirrings having their ideological and organizational motive forces in an ethnic-religious self-perception, that is, in Islam, are just as little in evidence today as are expressions of dissatisfaction by Muslims on a scale comparable with the activities of religious dissident groups in other parts of the Soviet Union.

Still, ever since the latter half of the 1960s Soviet orientalists and Islam specialists have been warning more and more urgently against attempting to judge the external appearance of the Central Asian Union Republics by the standards of Marxist-Leninist development doctrine alone. They have expressly pointed out that their 'investigations into the extent of religious conviction among the population show that the percentage of believers in the Republics of the Soviet East is considerably higher than in the other Soviet Republics'. And they admit to having only 'scanty knowledge of the number of modern Muslims, of their spiritual world, of their psyche ...'[102] But such warnings have found mainly deaf ears among the leaders of the Soviet Party and State.

It may be coincidence that such cries of warning came at about the time that the campaign in the Soviet media against Chinese policy towards the national minorities and Islam was reaching its climax and that they then proceeded to become louder. But there can be no doubt that Moscow's openly taking sides with the Muslim Turkic peoples in Sinkiang also gave new impetus to the self-awareness of the Muslim Turkic peoples within the Soviet Union itself. This logical consequence is one which the Soviet leadership appears not to have allowed for, to have deliberately ignored, or to have consciously accepted in the interests of demonstrating the 'rightness' of its own Marxist-Leninist self-perception in the conflict with China.

It is a veritable irony of history that it has taken the political explosions set off in the Near and Middle East by Khomeini's Islamic revolution in Iran and by the militant Islamic resistance to Moscow's puppet regime in Afghanistan to make the Soviet leadership aware of the unsolved problems inherent in its own domestic situation as regards the Muslim minorities. It has now been forced to realize that its own complex Central Asian national minorities problem had never been solved and is now taking on a more dangerous aspect.[103] The Soviet Union's minority problems in Central Asia have not been isolated. These problems affect not only the Soviet Union's bilateral relations with the People's Republic of China but are also linked with the political developments in the Middle East/Central Asia region. Because of the political interests of the Western Powers in this region, these border land minorities are inevitably involved in the theatre of the conflict between East and West.[104]

In the relatively short time since Mao's death, but especially since 1979, the leaders of Party and State in Peking have been making significant modifications to Chinese policy towards the minorities, and this again complicates Moscow's problem. These changes were the outcome of the open (and public) admission of fundamental mistakes in policy towards the national minorities and the religions under Mao's leadership, which had had particularly catastrophic repercussions on the Turkic peoples of Sinkiang. This radical about-turn away from Mao's policies was and is all the more convincing and credible in that considerably greater rights and freedoms of religious activity have again been granted in the Constitution: thus, for instance, the 1978 Constitution states that the citizens of the People's Republic of China are free to believe or not to believe and free to preach religion or atheism (Article 46). And in the Draft Constitution of 1982, this 'basic right' was elucidated to the effect that the citizens of the People's Republic of China have freedom of religious belief (paragraph 1), that no organ of the State, no public organization and no individual has the right to force the citizens to believe or not to believe or to discriminate against them by reason of their belief or non-belief (paragraph 2), that the State shall protect the religious activities it has legitimated, but that no person may misuse religion for counter-revolutionary activities which destroy public order, run counter to the wellbeing of the citizens, or call into question the State educational system (paragraph 3); and, finally, that religious activity may not be influenced by foreign States (paragraph 4).

What is more important, however, is that the revision of policy towards the minorities and the religions has by no means been restricted to merely formal changes or amendments and additions to the Constitution. These have been followed by concrete steps that show that Government and Party are prepared to implement the reforms not only symbolically but also swiftly and with great material effort. These steps are manifested in numerous measures that can not only be gleaned from official and semi-official publications in the People's Republic of China but which can be quickly recognized by visitors to the Islamic regions who are familiar with this problem. Only a few can be pointed out here. For instance, even as early as in March 1980 a publication by the re-constituted Chinese Islamic Association, which now appears to be working largely independently and without outside interference, was able to present for the first time since 1949 concrete figures about the ethnic minorities professing Islam.[105] These figures were even at this time, as later official publications revealed,[106] of a value equal to official statistical data. According to these figures, it could be taken for granted that at that time there were still — in spite of the activities directed against Islam during the Cultural Revolution — at least 13 million Muslims living in the People's Republic of China[107]; these are spread over the whole of China, but of course the greatest concentration can be found in the Western provinces.[108] It can be taken as certain that these numbers are today considerably higher. This can be deduced just from the fact that the Turkic minorities are expressly exempt from all government's population control measures. Five to ten or even more children can still be regarded as quite normal, if not as the general rule, in this region today.

Particular interest naturally accrues to the data on the mosques re-opened since 1979. The numbers given for the period up to 1981 show, for example, 1900 in Sinkiang alone[109] and 1200[110] for Ningxia. These figures can be expected to rise still further in the near future if allowance is made for the mosques that have not yet been opened but are now in the course of restoration or construction; their numbers cannot even be approximately ascertained in concrete terms.[111] The

Nationality Dynamics in Sino-Soviet Relations

same applies to the restoration of old and the building of new *madrassahs* for the training of next generation of spiritual leaders (*ahongs*); the majority of the *ahongs* now in office (again) are very advanced in years. Finally, it must also be mentioned that a new edition of the Qoran has recently been published by the Chinese Islamic Association — apparently in a very large printing.[112] The author was able to see for himself during a period of several weeks spent in Sinkiang in the spring of 1984 that all of the many mosques he visited during that time were in possession of at least one copy of this new edition of the Qoran. This edition differs from all others printed since 1949 in that it is an unabridged reprint of the modern-day definitive Cairo edition in the Arabic original.

Of course, these data are not nearly enough to elucidate even in approximate terms the full scale of the new policies that the Peking leadership has been pursuing towards the Central Asian Turkic and Muslim minorities since 1979. But the material available is such that there can be no doubt that these new policies have led now to a marked improvement in the situation of the minorities, above all in Sinkiang. This is reflected also in reports by natives who were forced to emigrate from Sinkiang after 1949 and above all during the Cultural Revolution and have now been able to re-visit the Western provinces of China.[113]

Of course it would be inaccurate to draw from the appraisal of this unusually far-reaching course of development the conclusion that the reasons for Peking's change of policy are to be found in any fundamental transformation of the basic attitude of Chinese Marxism-Leninism toward Islam or to the issue of religion as a whole. It is without doubt primarily the pragmatic consequence of tremendous errors and misguided trends in domestic policy during the Cultural Revolution. But the unsparingly self-critical openness with which these shortcomings and their effects are now being treated and radically corrected by State and Party in the People's Republic of China today is without precedent in any other country of the communist-ruled world and is a dramatic contrast to policies in the Soviet Union.

As regards China's foreign policy in the Middle East, this radical about-turn in domestic policy has been of considerable benefit. One consequence has been that Peking can now take a more impartial position vis-à-vis the Islamic renewal movement in the Middle East and can thus appear more credible in lending its political and economic support to the Islamic resistance in its battle against Moscow's puppet regime in Kabul and against the Soviet occupation troops in Afghanistan. In the light of all historical experience, it cannot be ruled out that these changes in China's policy towards its own minorities could have

Hans Bräker

an effect on the relationship between the Muslim Turkic populations of East and West Turkestan. Whether and what consequences these could have on future Soviet-Chinese relations cannot be known at the present time, but the seeds of change have been planted.

Notes

1. Cf. Hans Bräker, 'Die Sowjetunion und China im Wettbewerb um die Entwicklungsländer', *Die internationale Politik 1963*, (Munich/Vienna, 1969); idem, 'Die sowjetisch-chinesische Rivalität in Asien und Afrika', *Die internationale Politik 1968/69*, (Munich/Vienna, 1974).

2. The texts of China's border treaties with these countries were published (in German translation, in some cases extracts only) in *Verträge der Volksrepublik China mit anderen Staaten, Schriften des Instituts für Asienkunde in Hamburg*, Vols. XII/1-XII/8, (Wiesbaden, 1962-1981) (Burma: XII/1, pp. 20 et seq.; Nepal: XII/1, pp. 214 et seq. and pp. 219 et seq.; Pakistan: XII/4, pp. 258 et seq.; Afghanistan: XII/4, pp. 9 et seq.).

3. On India's endeavours since 1979 to extricate itself again from these close ties, however, see Hans Bräker, 'Die indischsowjetischen Beziehungen und die 7. Gipfelkonferenz der Blockfreien', in *Aktuelle Analysen des Bundesinstituts für ostwissenschaftliche und internationale Studien*, No. 7/1983.

4. On the issue of the border between China and Russia and of the Soviet borders in Central Asia, H. Pommerening, *Der chinesisch-sowjetische Grenskonflikt. Das Ende der ungleichen Verträge*, (Olten and Freiburg, 1968); D. Frenke, 'Der Begriff der ungleichen Verträge im sowjetisch-chinesischen Grenzkonflikt', *Osteuropa-Recht*, Vol. 2/1965, pp. 869 et seq.; idem, 'Die Gebiesforderunger der Volksrepublik China gegenüber der Sowjetunion', *Europa-Archiv*, Series 21/1965, pp. 812 et seq.

5. A compilation of the literature on the Russian expansion in the Caucasus and on the spread of Russian power in Central Asia is given in Dietrich Geyer, *Die Sowjetunion und Iran. Eine Untersuchung zur Aussenpolitik der UdSSR im Nahen Osten*, (Tübingen, 1955), pp. 5 et seq. Also of importance on this subject, H. Übersberger, *Russlands Orientpolitik in den letzten beiden Jahrhunderten. I. Bis zum Frieden von Jassy*, (Stuttgart, 1913); E. Sarkysianz, *Geschichte der orientalischen Völker Russlands bis 1917*, (Munich, 1961); Richard A. Pierce, *Russian Central Asia 1867-1917. A Study in Colonial Rule*, (Berkeley, 1960); O. Hoetzsch, *Russland in Asien. Geschichte einer Expansion*, (Stuttgart, 1966); David D. Dallin, *The Rise of Russia in Asia*, (New Haven, 1949).

6. On the St. Petersburg Convention (31st August 1907) see Roger F. Churchill, *The Anglo-Russian convention in 1907*, (London, 1939) and the dissertation by D. Linnenbrink, *Die anglisch-russische Entente vom 31.8.1907 und Deutschland*, (Münster, 1930). This Convention concerned not only Persia but also Russian-British relations in Afghanistan and Tibet.

7. On the concept of the *Umma*, |C.A.O. Nieuwenhuize, 'The Umma – an Analytical Approach', *Studia Islamica*, 10.1059, pp. 5-22; W.M. Watt, *Muhammad at Medina*, (Oxford, 1956); R. Paret, entry on the Umma in *Encyclopaedia of Islam*, 1st Edition, (Leiden); W.F. Abbonshi, *Political Systems of the Middle East in the 20th Century*, (New York, 1971).

8. On the early history of the Turks in Central Asia see W.M. McGovern, *The Early Empires of Central Asia*, (Chapel Hill, 1939); R. Giraud, *L'empire des Turcs*

celestes: les règnes d'Elterich, Qapghan et Bilgä, pp. 680-734, (Paris, 1960); W. Samolin, *East Turkestan to the Twelfth Century*, (Den Haag, 1964); H.A. Gibb, *The Arab Conquest of Central Asia*, (London, 1923); J.R. Hamilson, *Les Ouighours à l'époque des cinq dynasties (907 á 960)*, (Paris, 1955); Liu Mau Tsat, *Die chinesischen Nachrichten zur Geschichte der Osttürken (T'u-küe)*, 2 vols., (Weisbaden, 1958); W. Barthold (V.V. Bartol'd), *Zwölf Vorlesungen über die Geschichte der Türken Mittelasiens*, (Darmstadt, 1962) (unamended reprint of the Berlin 1935 edition); *Histoire des Turcs d'Asie Central*, (Paris, 1945); *Turkestan down to the Mongol Invasion*, (London, 1928). The works by Bartol'd are now readily accessible again, since they are being re-edited since 1963 in Moscow by the Institute of the Peoples of Asia of the Academy of Sciences of the USSR. The following have appeared up to now, *Sochineniia*, Pt. I, 1963; Pt. II (1), 1963; Pt. II (2), 1964; Pt. III, 1965; Pt. IV, 1966; Pt. V, 1968; Pt. VI, 1968. In all, 12 volumes will probably be published.

    9. Cf. G.A. Pugachenkova, *Samarkand, Bukhara* (Moskva, 1968).

    10. On the historical evolution of the Central Asian region in general, K. Brokelmann, *Geschichte der islamischen Staaten und Völker*, (Munich, 1939); G. Hambly (Ed.), *Zentralasien*, (Grankfurt am Main, 1966), (*Fischer Weltgeschichte* series, Vol. 16). On the penetration of Islam into Central Asia see also the two volumes of *Fischer Weltgeschichte* on Islam, Claude Cahen (Ed.), *Der Islam I. Vom Ursprung bis zu den Anfängen des Osmanenreiches*, (Frankfurt a.M., 1968) (Vol. 14); G.E.V. Grunebaum, *Der Islam II. Die Islamischen Reiche nach dem Fall von Konstantinopel*, (Frankfurt a.M., 1971) (Vol. 15).

    11. On the history of Islam in China, F.S. Drake, 'Mohammedanism in the T'ang Dynasty', *Monuments Seria* 8/1948, pp. 1-40; J. Gernet, *Le Monde Chinois*, (Paris, 1972) (quoted from the German edition, *Die chinesische Welt*, (Frankfurt a.M., 1979), pp. 240 et seq.); M. Hartmann, 'Vom chinesischen Islam', *Die Welt des Islams*, I/1913, pp. 178-210; idem, *Zur Geschichte des Islams in China*, (Leipzig, 1921).

    12. On the *Jihad* issue in general, E. Tyan, entry on the *Jihad* in *Encyclopaedia of Islam*, 2nd Edition, (Leiden); M. Khadduri, *War and Peace on the Law of Islam*, (Baltimore, 1955); A. Noth, *Heiliger Drieg und Heiliger Kampf in Islam und Christentum*, (Bonn, 1966); J. Harris (Ed.), *Islam and International Relations*, (London, 1965).

    13. On the Treaties of Nerchinsk and Kiakhta see H. Pommerining, op. cit. (Note 4), pp. 106 et seq., and the titles listed in the bibliography thereto.

    14. Ya'qub Beg had fought against the Russians at the time of their advance to Kokand but eventually had to join forces with the chief of the Khodja clan, Buzurg-Khan, when the latter returned to Kashgar in 1865 from his exile in Kokand. In 1867 he took Buzurg-Khan prisoner, sent him into exile and took his place himself. On this and the following see T. Yuan, 'Jakub Bek (1820-1877) and the Moslem Rebellion in Chinese Turkestan', *Royal Central Asian Journal*, No. 6/1961, pp. 134-167; J.C.Y. Hsü, 'British Mediation of China's Wars with Yakub Bek, 1877', *Royal Central Asian Journal*, No. 2/1964; on the general course of development, V.G. Kiernan, 'Kashgar and the Politics of Central Asia 1868-1888', *Cambridge Historical Journal*, (1953-55).

    15. The 'Ili Crisis' has been analysed in detail by J.C. Hsü, *The Ili Crisis. A Study of Sino-Russian Diplomacy 1878 to 1881*, (Oxford, 1965); for general treatment of this subject see Roger Levy, 'Les confrontations territoriales Sino-Russes: particulièrement dans la règion de l'Ili au Sinkiang', *Politique Etrangère*, No. 2/1966, pp. 157 et seq.

    16. Except as specifically quoted, the following account is based on R. Yang, 'Sinkiang under the administration of General Yang Tseng-hsin 1911-1928', *Royal Central Asian Journal*, No. 1/1981.

17. The basis for the return of the troops to the Soviet Union was the Border Traffic and Repatriation Agreement concluded between the two countries in Kuldja on 27 and 28 May 1920. For the text see *Sovetsko-kitaiskie otnosheniia 1917-1957 gg., Sbornik dokumentov*, (Moskva, 1959), p. 47; for the English see also J. Degras, *Soviet documents on foreign policy*, Vols. I-III, (London, 1951-1953), Vol. I, p. 483, and L. Shapiro, *Soviet treaties series. A collection of bilateral treaties, agreements and conventions concluded between the Soviet Union and foreign powers*, Vol. I: 1917-1928; Vol. II 1929-1939, (Washington D.C., 1950-1955), Vol. I, p. 47.

18. This co-operation with the Red Army was pursued on the basis of an 'Agreement with the High Command of the Soviet Troops in Turkestan to Combat White Guardsmen on the Territory of the Chinese Province of Sinkiang' signed on 17 May 1921 (*Sovetskokitaiskie otnosheniia*, op. cit., p. 434) and of a further 'Agreement on the Crossing of the Border to Sinkiang by Soviet Troops to Combat White Guard Forces in the Altai Region' signed on 26 September 1921 (ibid., p. 59; cf. also: *Voprosy Istorii*, No. 3/1957, p. 147).

19. This trade agreement is mentioned only by R. Yang in the above article (Note 16). It is not referred to however, in any of the – in most cases incomplete – documentation consulted for present purposes.

20. This was made possible by an exchange of notes with the provincial government of Sinkiang in October 1924. Cf. Cheng Tien-fong, *A history of Soviet-Chinese relations*, (Washington, 1957), p. 168 and also W. Whiting, *Sheng Shih-ts'ai, Sinkiang: pawn or pivot*, (East Lansing, Mich., 1958), p. 9. The Russian consulates in Kashgar and Kuldja had been closed in 1918.

21. Cf. *Izvestiia*, 18 July 1929; *Sovetsko-Kitaiskii Konflikt 1929g. Sbornik dokumentov*, (Moskva, 1930), p. 31.

22. The most detailed account of the Muslim insurrection movement under Ma Ch'ung-ying against the Chinese central and provincial governments to my knowledge is to be found in Sven Hedin's *Die Flucht des grossen Pferdes*, (The Flight of the Great Horse), (Leipzig, 1935), of which a new, slightly abridged edition appeared in Wiesbaden in 1964. It is from this abridged edition that the following excerpts are quoted. Sven Hedin was engaged in an expedition to Sinkiang on behalf of the Chinese government for the purposes of investigating the feasibility of his plan 'to join up East Turkestan and Dzungaria to the Middle Kingdom by two great highways' (p. 10). This plan had originated as a memorandum which Sven Hedin had drawn up at the request of the Chinese government. The Swedish explorer explained the political considerations behind the project to the Chinese Vice Foreign Minister of the day, Lin Chung-chieh, orally in the following terms: 'Of the buffer states that Emperor Chien Lung once established in a semicircle around the Middle Kingdom, only a single state is left. Since China has been a republic it has lost Tibet, Manchuria and Jehol, and even Inner Mongolia is threatened. Sinkiang is still Chinese but is now torn apart by Mohammedan uprisings and civil wars. If nothing is done to protect the province, it, too, will be lost!'. Sven Hedin's own comments on the subject matter of his memoranda are of particular interest in the context with which we are dealing here: 'I limit myself ... to the questions of trade and of transportation routes. Russian trade had put a stop to Chinese trade and was in the process of ousting English trade from India. The Russians maintained excellent, constantly improved routes up to the border of Sinkiang and were advancing in the vicinity of Kashgar, Kuldja, Chuguchak and in the Altai region. Chinese trade had been based from time immemorial primarily on camel caravans through the Gobi to Hami and Urumchi. The caravans were on the road for three months. If automobiles were used instead, and given good roads, this time could be reduced to ten to twelve days, and it would be possible to enter into competition successfully' (pp. 9 et seq.).

23. Cf. especially *Recueil des traités (Société des Nations). Treaty series (League of Nations)*, Vols. 1-205, (Geneva, 1920-1946) especially Vol. 122, p. 439; J. Degras, op. cit. (Note 17), Vol. II, p. 507; L. Shapiro, op. cit. (Note 17), Vol. II, p. 36.

24. Quoted here after the details summary of the text in Aitchen K. Wu, *China and the Soviet Union. A Study of Sino-Soviet Relations*, (London/New York, 1950), pp. 376 et seq.

25. Diplomatic and consular relations between the two countries were not resumed until 12 December 1932 in the form of an exchange of notes in Geneva. For the wording of the notes see, *Izvestiia*, 13 September 1932; *Sovetsko-kitaiskie otnosheniia* (Note 17), p. 156; L. Shapiro, op. cit. (Note 17), Vol. II, p. 62.

26. After the report by Dr. Cherbakoff, 'In Kashgar, December 1921 – October 1931', *Royal Central Asian Journal*, October 1933, pp. 532 et seq.

27. Cf. Note 41.

28. A brief account of Japan's influence on the developments in Inner Mongolia and the related risk of encroachment on Sinkiang is to be found in B.C. Olschak, 'Die Mongolenfrage als aussenpolitisches Problem', *Ost-Probleme*, Vol. 17 (1965), pp. 17-27, especially pp. 24 et seq.

29. The most detailed account of this period is to be found in W. Whiting, *Sheng Shi-ts'ai, Sinkiang: pawn or pivot*, (East Lansing, Mich., 1958).

30. The secret negotiations are mentioned only by Li Chang, 'The Soviet Grip on Sinkiang', *Foreign Affairs*, April 1954, pp. 491 et seq. As far as I have been able to determine, there is no information to be found on these talks in Soviet sources.

31. Li Chang, op. cit., who mentions the dispatch of the Soviet troops, maintains that they were placed in Chinese uniforms for their mission.

32. A very colourful and vivid account of such an attack on Ma's troops in Korla, during which 28 bombs were dropped in a single day, is given in Sven Hedin, op. cit. (Note 22), pp. 101-119.

33. *Royal Central Asian Journal*, Jan. 1935, p. 102. Here verbatim: 'When the Chinese Northern Army reached Kashgar, the Soviet Russian Consul General there advised the Dungan General Ma Ch'ung-ying to travel to Russia. The General was escorted to the border by the Secretary and some other members of the Trade Agency of the Soviet Consulate. It is reported that he died on arrival in Moscow'.

34. Sven Hedin, op. cit. (Note 22), pp. 155 et seq.

35. These figures are given by Li Chang, op. cit. (Note 30).

36. *The Times*, 25 March 1939.

37. Cf. *Vneshniaia torgovlia SSSR s sotsialisticheskimi stranami*, (Moskva, 1957), p. 31 (Trade and Loan Agreement between the Soviet Foreign Trade Organisation 'Sovin'torg' and the Trade Organisation of Sinkiang 'Tuchangunsy'); significantly, the agreement was not signed until 16 May 1935, owing to repeated protests lodged by the central government in Nanking. On the Soviet side, the agreement was signed by the then head of the Soviet Foreign Trade Bank, Svanidse, a brother-in-law of Stalin.

38. Text of the agreement in, *Izvestiia*, 30 August 1937; *Vedomosti Verkhovnogo Soveta SSSR*, Moskva, 15 June 1938, No. 7; for the English also: L. Shapiro, op. cit. (Note 17), Vol. II, p. 185.

39. According to *Sovetsko-Kitaiskie otnosheniia 1917-1957 gg.* (Note 17), the credit agreements concerned were the following: 1 March 1938 – 50 million dollars (p. 167); 1 July 1938 – 50 million dollars (p. 172); 13 June 1939 – 150 million dollars (p. 176).

40. Text of the 'Trade Agreement with Annex on the Legal Status of the Soviet Trade Agency in China', *Vedomosti Verkhovnogo Soveta SSSR*, Moskva,

15 June 1940, No. 16; for the English also, J. Degras, op. cit. (Note 17), Vol. III, p. 341, and L. Shapiro, op. cit. (Note 17), Vol. II, p. 203.

41. According to a later letter by Sheng to Chiang Kai-shek (Source: Note 42), Sheng probably joined the CPSU in September 1938. In this letter, Sheng writes: "In September 1938, while I was travelling through the Soviet Union and paid a visit to Stalin, I again brought up the question of my joining the CPCh. However, I was instead urged to first join the CPSU and then have myself transferred to the CPCh ... But since my application for transfer remained unprocessed even long thereafter, I inevitably became suspicious ...."

42. Cf. *Soviet Economic Aggression in Sinkiang* (in Chinese), (Taipei, 1950) (edited by the Nationalist Chinese Foreign Ministry in Taipeh). This treaty is not mentioned in any of the pertinent Soviet or Western sources analysed for the present purposes, probably due to the fact that it was rescinded again by the Chinese side long before it became known. It was thanks to the Union Research Institute, Kowloon, that I was able to study the work quoted here in Hong Kong.

43. Translated and quoted from a photocopy of the Russian original, in *Soviet Economic Aggression in Sinkiang*, ibid., pp. 45 et seq.

44. Letter by Sheng Shi-Ts'ai to Chiang Kai-shek dated 7 July 1942, ibid, pp. 64 et seq.

45. Figures from Li Chang, op. cit. (Note 30).

46. Summarized from a photocopy of the original of the Russian draft in *Soviet Economic Aggression in Sinkiang* (Note 42), pp. 82 et seq.

47. Wording of Sheng's letter to Chiang Kai-shek, op. cit. (Note 44), pp. 61 et seq.

48. The exchange of correspondence between Sheng and Molotov is mentioned in Li Chang, op. cit. (Note 30).

49. The following figures are likewise taken from Li Chang, op. cit. (Note 30).

50. The Soviet Union based its intervention on the 'Protocol on Mutual Assistance' (text in J. Degras, op. cit., Vol. III, p. 168 and L. Shapiro, op. cit., Vol. II, p. 162) signed between the Soviet Union and the Mongolian People's Republic in Ulan Bator on 12 March 1936, against which, by the way, China lodged a sharp protest on 7 April 1936 (*Izvestiia*, 9 April 1936), and on the 'Joint Declaration on the Territorial Integrity of Manchukuo and the Mongolian People's Republic' (text by J. Degras, op. cit., Vol. III, p. 486), made in the context of the Soviet-Japanese 'Neutrality Pact' signed in Moscow on 13 April 1941.

51. TASS, 3 April 1944; quoted after Li Chang, op. cit. (Note 30).

52. In his book, *Soviet Asia Mission* (German translation, Zurich, 1947), however, Wallace makes not a word of mention of this. All he describes (pp. 134 et seq.) is how he had given Sheng's wife some strawberries given him by the Russians on his departure from Alma Ata and had shown her how to plant them.

53. Ibid., p. 15.

54. However, neither Wallace's report, nor Chiang Kai-shek's detailed portrait of Soviet-Chinese relations (Chiang Kai-shek, *Soviet Russia in China*, German translation, Bonn, 1959) gives any indication of whether this action was a direct result of Wallace's trip.

55. Cf. anon., *United States Relations with China. With Special Reference to the Period 1944-1949*, (Washington, D.C., 1949), for a description of the mission, pp. 55 et seq.; complete texts of the minutes of the talks, pp. 549-560. In this context, Wallace's comment in his book (p. 135) on Chiang Kai-shek's recalling of Sheng is interesting. The reason for the transfer, he writes, had been the 'stupidity' with which Sheng was kindling 'anti-Soviet sentiment' in his province. He also comments on the Russian withdrawal from Sinkiang in 1943 with the following words: '... in the light of the anti-Soviet intrigues in Sinkiang, the Russians withdraw to avoid an open break with Chung King.'

56. Cf. on these events D. Dallin, *Soviet Russia and the Far East*, (New Haven, 1948), especially pp. 366 et seq.

57. Text of the Treaty of Friendship and Alliance in, *Sovetsko-Kitaiskie otnosheniia 1917-1957 gg.* (Note 17), p. 196. Cf. also, G.F. Hudson, 'The Sino-Soviet Alliance, Treaty of 1945, *St. Antony's Papers*, No. 2, (London, 1957), pp. 13 et seq. On the same day, an 'Exchange of Notes on Soviet Assistance, on Manchuria and Sinkiang' took place in connection with this treaty (text, ibid., p. 205). It was not until 25 February 1953 that this treaty was declared null and void by the government of (Nationalist) China.

58. Cf. on this and the following, Ian Morrison, 'Some Notes on the Kasakhs of Sinkiang', *Royal Central Asian Journal*, January 1949.

59. Ibid., p. 70.

60. According to N.L.D. McLean, 'The New Dominion', *Royal Central Asian Journal*, (April, 1948), p. 133.

61. Eric Shipton, *Mountains of Tatary*, (London, 1950), pp. 52 et seq.; also Diana Shipton, *Antique Land*, (London, 1950), p. 129.

62. According to Li Chang, op. cit. (Note 30), who refers, however, to otherwise unconfirmed 'reports submitted to the Chinese Ministry of Defence in 1948', the situation in the tungsten mines in the districts of Wenchuan and Polo developed as follows: in 1945, 3,000 workers extracted 150 tonnes; in 1946, 10,000 workers extracted 450 tonnes; in 1947, 20,000 workers extracted 1,000 tonnes. In the districts of Fuyun and Chenghua along the border to Mongolia, there were 1,000 Soviet technicians, 3,000 workers, and 120 armed watchmen. Besides the tin and tungsten reserves, diamond, gold, bismuth, beryllium, talc, asbestos, gypsum and mercury deposits were also found.

63. According to Chang, op. cit. (Note 30), who refers to a detailed 'Telegram from the Foreign Commissariat of Urumchi to the Chinese Foreign Ministry', of which, however, he provides no further evidence.

64. Text of the 'Treaty on Friendship, Alliance and Mutual Assistance' signed by Vishinskii and Chou En-lai in, *Sovetsko-Kitaiskie otnosheniia 1917-1957 gg.* (Note 17), p. 219. A number of supplementary agreements and exchanges of notes were also linked with this treaty, for example the nullification of the Treaty of Friendship, and Alliance of 14 August 1945 (for text see, *Izvestiia*, 15 February 1950).

65. Cf., *Sovetsko-Kitaiskie otnosheniie 1917-1957 gg.* (Note 17), p. 227 and *Izvestiia*, 29 March 1950.

66. Amar Lahiri, 'Communist New Deal in Sinkiang', *United Asia*, No. 2/1950, pp. 141 et seq.

67. The extent of this sovietization can be measured on the basis of the following reports: (quoted after B. Hayit, *Das Vorgehen der Sowjets im Orient*, supplement B XXVII/55 to the weekly *Das Parlament* of 6 July 1955). On 24 August 1951, Radio Urumchi announced that Usman Batur and 25 of his leading comrades-in-arms had been demonstratively hanged in Urumchi before 90,000 people. On 28 April 1951, the Secretary of the Communist Party of East Turkestan, Sho Li-hin, announced that 13,569 followers of Usman Batur, 889 members of the units commanded by Muhammed Niyaz (one of the leaders of the insurrection) and 300 followers of Masus Sabri (who even as late as in 1949 had been appointed Governor by the communists but had been arrested on 8 April 1951 for supporting the Nationalists) had been liquidated. According to Sho Li-hin, more than 30 national organisations had been uncovered in Sinkiang since the communists had come to power. In a speech broadcast by radio, the former Governor of Sinkiang, Burkhan, declared: 'In the course of three years, the anti-revolutionary movement has been put down. The purging of our public institutions from insurgent bandits, nationalist foes, and henchmen of the

imperialists has been successfully completed. We have succeeded in destroying 120,000 of these enemies of the people.' According to figures given in the periodical *Milli Türkistan* (No. 75/1951, pp. 8 et seq.) there were 66 hostile engagements between the insurgents and communist troops during the period in question.

68. According to B. Hayit, op. cit., the communists assumed that there were a total of 14 'nations' living in East Turkestan.

69. *Sovetskaia Kirgiziia* reported on 18 November 1954 that a Dungan and Kirghiz Autonomous Region had been established in East Turkestan and that the foundation of an Uighur and Kazakh Autonomous Region was imminent. According to Hsinhua, 1 December 1954, the Kazakh Autonomous Region had been founded on 28 November 1954. It encompassed Kuldja, Tarbagatai and Altai.

70. There have been few useful publications available on Chinese policy towards the religions, and in particular towards Islam, since 1949. Some pointers are given in S. Chandra Sarker's essay, 'China's Policy towards Minorities', *The World Today*, No. 10/1959, pp. 408-416 and by Chan Wing-tsit, *Religious Trends in Modern China*, (New York, 1953). The following account of Chinese policy towards Islam in the 'early days' is based primarily on three minor works: Yang I-fang, *Islam in China*, (Hong Kong, 1957); idem, 'Unruhe unter den Muslimen in der Chinesischen Volksrepublik', R. Italiaander (Ed.), *Die Herausforderung des Islams*, (Göttingen – Berlin – Frankfurt, 1965); anon., *Moslem Unrest in China*, (Hong Kong, 1958). Reference should be made at this point to the following more recent works: R. Israeli, *Muslim in China: A Study of Cultural Confrontation*, (Atlantic Highlands, N.J., 1979); anon., '20 years of Chinese Communism', *Religion in China*, October 1969; R. Israeli, 'The Muslim Minority in the People's Republic of China', *Asian Survey*, No. 8/1981; J. Dreyer, 'China's Minority Nationalities in the Cultural Revolution', *China Quarterly*, No. 35/1968; ibid., *China's Forty Millions*, 1976; ibid., 'The Islamic Community of China', *Central Asian Survey*, Vol. 1/Nov. 2/3, Oct. 1982-Jan. 1983; R. Silde-Karlins, 'The Uighurs between China and the USSR', *Canadian Slavonic Papers*, Nos. 2 and 3/ 1975; L. Pye, 'China: Ethnic Minorities and National Security', *Current Scene*, No. 12/1976; R.C. Bush, *Religion in Communist China*, (Nashville, 1970).

71. G.A. Nasser, 'Die Philosophie der Revolution', F.R. Allemann (Ed.), *Die arabische Revolution. Nasser über seine Politik*, (Frankfurt am Main, 1958), p. 56.

72. For more detail see Hans Bräker, 'Die Stellung des Islams und des islamischen Rechts – Sowjetunion und Volksrepublik China', W. Ende, U. Steinbach, *Der Islam in der Gegenwart*, (Munich, 1983).

73. The formal basis for the withdrawal of the Soviet Union was: the 'Joint Communiqué on the Transfer of the Soviet Shares in the Joint Soviet-Chinese Companies 'Sovkitneft', 'Sovkitmetall', 'Skoga' [civil aviation] and 'Sovkitsudostroi' [shipbuilding and ship repairs] to the Ownership of the PRC' dated 12 October 1954 (*Sovetsko-Kitaiskie otnosheniia 1917-1957 gg.*, p. 303) and the 'Protocols on the Conclusion of the Transfer of Soviet Shares in the Joint Soviet-Chinese Companies to the Ownership of the PRC' dated 30 and 31 December 1954 (*Izvestiia*, 31st December 1954 and 1 January 1955).

74. Süleyman Tekiner, 'Sinkiang and the Sino-Soviet Conflict', *Bulletin. Institute for the Study of the USSR*, Vol. XIV, No. 8, August 1967, p. 10.

75. Hsin Chiang Yih Pao, 23 September 1956, (quoted after Süleyman Tekiner, op. cit.).

76. Hsin Chiang Yih Pao, 16 October 1956, (quoted after Süleyman Tekiner, op. cit.).

77. In *Penminpibao*, 27 June 1958.

78. He is mentioned by Süleyman Tekiner, op. cit., p. 11.

79. Central News Agency, 13 July 1958.
80. Report in, *Le Monde*, 2 July 1959.
81. After Süleyman Tekiner, op. cit., p. 11 et seq.
82. The article by Süleyman Tekiner from which these details are taken (p. 12), is based primarily on reports in the Indian daily *Indian Express*.
83. For their mutual criticism, the two sides at this time were still, as a rule, using comparable points of departure and trends in other 'brother countries', above all in Yugoslavia and Albania. Cf. on this and the lead-up to the Sino-Soviet conflict, Harry Hamm and Joseph Kun, *Das rote Schisma*, (Cologne, 1963) (with 22 documents), in particular the introductory analysis 'Ursachen und Motive des Schismas' (causes of and motives for the schism), pp. 8-45.
84. The literature on the Soviet-Chinese conflict has reached such proportions by now that it would be superfluous to give a list of individual titles in this instance.
85. Quoted here from the English-language version of this article: 'The Origin and Development of the Differences Between the Leadership of the C.P.S.U. and Ourselves, Comment on the Open Letter of the Central Committee of the C.P.S.U.', *Peking Review*, No. 37, 13 September 1963, pp. 6-20, passage quoted here, p. 18.
86. The Italian daily *Il Messaggero* reported on 16 July 1963 that a total of 60,000 Kazakhs and Uighurs had sought political asylum in the Soviet Union.
87. *Yeni Istanbul*, 9 January 1966 (quoted after Süleyman Tekiner, op. cit., p. 12 et seq.).
88. *Yeni Gazeta*, 20 February 1966 (quoted after Süleyman Tekiner, op. cit., p. 13).
89. Cf., 'Die Türkvölker zwischen China und Russland', *Neue Zürcher Zeitung*, 3 February 1967. Incidentally, this report describes Alptekin as the 'Head of the Government of East Turkestan until the Chinese communists took over power there in 1949'. It also expressly points out that 'his information (has) always proved correct up to now'.
90. Zunun Taipov, 'Po tu storunu granitsy. Pis'mo byvshego generalmayora narodno-osvoboditel'noi armii Kitaia', *Izvestiia*, 13 September 1964, p. 4.
91. 'Eto — neprikrytyi shovinizm. Rasskazyvayet pokinuvshy Kitai pisatel' Bukhara Tyshkanbayev', *Literaturnaia Gazeta*, 26 September 1963.
92. Anur Alimzhanov: 'Tragicheskayia istoriia odnogo lozunga' (The tragic history of a slogan), *Literaturnaia Gazeta*, 25 January 1967, p. 14.
93. 'Hungweiping' — Red Guard. This Chinese term designating the Red Guard is used throughout the Soviet press as well, probably to discount from the very beginning any association with the 'Red Guard' ('Krasnaia Gvardiia') of early Soviet days.
94. TASS report dated 10 February 1967.
95. *Patrika*, 17 October 1966.
96. *Hindustan Times*, 30 September 1966.
97. For instance in, 'Le Petit Marocain', 16 December 1966 and in, *L'Opinion*, 17 December 1966.
98. *Ceylon Daily News*, 19 September 1966.
99. *Times of India*, 21 October 1966.
100. *Eshaab*, 23 January 1967.
101. Full text of this plea, 'Obrashchenie k vsem trudiashchimsia musul'manam Rossii i Vostoka' (7.12. 1917), in Yu.V. Kluchnikov i A. Sabanin, *Mezhdunarodnaia politika noveishego vremeni v dogovorakh, notakh i deklaratsiiakh*, T. II, (Moskva, 1926), pp. 94-97 (English translation in, Jane Degras, *Soviet documents on foreign policy*, Vol. I, (London, 1950), pp. 15-17).

102. E.g., M.V. Vagabov, 'Bol'she vnimani sovetskomu islamovedeniia', in, *Voprosy filosofii*, No. 12/1966.

103. Cf. Hans Bräker, 'Die Islam-Frage als Problem der sowjetischen Religions- und Minderheitenpolitik', *Sowjetunion 1980/81*, (Munich, 1981) (English edition, 'Islam as a Problem of Soviet Religious and Minority Policy', *The Soviet Union 1980-81*, (New York and London 1983).

104. Cf. Hans Bräker, 'The Implications of the Islamic Queston for Soviet Domestic and Foreign Policy', *Central Asian Survey* (Oxford), Vol. 2, No. 1, July 1983, and ibid., 'Die islamische Erneueungsbewegung und die Kräfteverschiebung in Nah-Mittel-Ost und Zentralasien', *Moderne Welt, Jahrbuch für Ost-West Fragen 1983*, (Cologne, 1983).

105. Haj Ilyas Shen Wiawi (Chinese Islamic Association), *General Conditions of Muslims in China*, (Beijing, March 1980).

106. According to the Sinkiang regional service of Radio Urumqi (28.10.1982), the following nationalities were living in Sinkiang in 1982: 5,949,661 Uighurs; 5,286,533 Han; 903,370 Kazakhs; 570,788 Hui; 117,460 Mongols; 112,979 Kirghiz; 27,364 Sibos; 26,484 Tajiks; 12,433 Uzbeks; 9,137 Manchus; 4,360 Tahurs; 4,106 Tatars; 2,662 Russians; 54,335 members of other nationalities.

107. According to the source named in Note 105, these could be broken down into (in table form):

Ethnic group	Estimated numbers	Main settlement areas
Hui	more than 6.4 million	Widely scattered throughout all of China but concentrated in cities and some regions; large centres in the Ningxia Hui Autonomous Region (North-West China)
Uighurs	more than 5.4 million	Uygur Autonomous Region Sinkiang (Chinese Central Asia)
Kazakhs	approx. 800,000	Kazakh Autonomous District Ili, Sinkiang
Kirghiz	approx. 97,000	Parts of Sinkiang
Tajiks	approx. 22,000	Parts of Sinkiang
Tatars	approx. 2,900	Parts of Sinkiang
Uzbeks	approx. 7,500	Scattered over Sinkiang
Dongxiang	approx. 190,000	Autonomous County Dongxiang in the Province Gansu
Salas	approx. 56,000	Autonomous County Sala of Xinhua and County Hualong in the Province Qinghai
Paoans	approx. 6,800	Province Gansu
Total	approx. 13 million	Total population of China over 1,000 million

108. The figures given in Note 106 are also interesting in that they reflect the sharp increase in the proportion of Han Chinese in the population of Xinjiang to about 40% as a result of the resettlements during the Cultural Revolution. As late as in the 1950s, the percentage of Han in the total population of Sinkiang had been at most 14%.

109. Cf. on this subject the data in my article, 'Sowjetunion und Volksrepublik China', W. Ende, U. Steinbach (eds.), *Der Islam in der Gegenwart. Entwicklung und Ausbreitung. Staat, Politik und Recht. Kultur und Religion*, (Munich, 1983).

110. According to Xinhua News Agency, 7 May 1983.

111. The Government has obviously earmarked considerable sums for the restoration and the construction of new mosques and *madrassahs*: the amount involved could not, however, be ascertained. In all the cases I had occasion to review in the Provinces of Sinkiang and Gansu in the spring of 1984, however, the Islamic congregations had declined to draw upon these funds and were using only the services provided free of charge by the transportation facilities of the central government and/or the local communities to assist in the delivery of the materials required for the restoration of existing mosques and *madrassahs* and for the construction of new ones. In all these cases, the money to meet the construction costs (including materials) was found exclusively by the adherents themselves (zakāt).

112. The precise number of copies printed could not be ascertained even at the source (Peking); according to the Xinhua News Agency on 7 May 1983, however, 10,000 copies of this edition of the Qu'ran were distributed in the Ningxia Autonomous Region alone.

113. E.g. Erkin Alptekin in his report in *Central Asian Survey* (Oxford), Vol. 1, No. 4, March 1983.

POLAND AND THE SOVIET WEST

Roman Solchanyk

Viewed from the perspective of Soviet multinational polity, the significance of developments in Poland since the summer of 1980 — the emergence of Solidarity as an independent trade union, its transformation into a national movement of opposition to the established political system, and the resulting crisis in the Polish United Workers' Party — lies primarily in the realm of ideology. 'Polonism is revolution,' argued Metternich, advising Tsar Alexander I against granting political concessions to the Poles in 1815.[1] One suspects that the Austrian chancellor equated 'Polonism' with the development of a modern political nation. Tsarist Russia proved unable to halt that process; its successor is faced with the task of precluding variants of 'Polonism' from taking shape within the USSR.

The greatest potential for the diffusion of ideas and influences from Poland is in the Soviet West,[2] particularly among those nations whose historical experience has been inter-twined with that of its western neighbour (Lithuanians, Belorussians, and Ukrainians). Yet, unlike other factors that impact on national relations and nationalities policy in the Soviet Union, the transmission and reception of outside stimuli is a process that, by its very nature, is not easily discerned, nor does it lend itself to systematic analysis.[3] Thus, any discussion of the implications of events in Poland on the Soviet nationalities scene must be approached with a note of caution. Above all, it must be recognized that in most cases it is virtually impossible to determine to what extent, if any, specific developments in the USSR are the result of a cause-and-effect process having its origins in Poland. This is particularly true of developments 'from below' such as strikes and demonstrations. Tempting as it may be, the fact that workers in Tartu and Kiev staged work stoppages after the strikes in Gdansk should not lead us to draw hasty conclusions about Poland's spillover effect on the Soviet Union.[4] Neither labour disputes nor public disorders are entirely novel phenomena in the USSR. At the same time, it is clear from the reporting of Western journalists and from *samizdat* materials that the opposition movement in Poland has evoked sympathy and understanding, often mixed with envy and a sense of resignation, within segments of the Soviet population. It is equally clear that such attitudes have been more pronounced and widespread in the Soviet West than in other regions.[5] The reaction 'from above' — i.e., measures taken by the Soviet leadership to dilute the unwelcome ramifications of the Polish crisis — has been much more apparent. Soviet officials have on various occasions voiced their concern about the situation in Poland in terms that are directly relevant to social, economic, and political problems in the USSR.

Both sets of responses, official and unofficial, will be discussed below in the context of the national question and the important role of the Catholic Church in the Soviet West. The choice of *gestarum locus* is not arbitrary. While not discounting the implications of Poland for other issues (for example, labour relations), the approach that informs this study of Polish-Soviet linkages recognizes that the combination of historical, cultural, and religious factors that define the Soviet West render it the most susceptible to 'Polonism.'

Differential Development, Political Culture, and the National Question

The central preoccupation of Soviet nationalities policy is with unity (*edinstvo*). It is the underlying theme running through all of Soviet writing on the national question, be it pseudo-scholarly or primitive agitprop. Thus, the USSR is officially defined as 'a single union multinational state,' and the Soviet economy as 'a single national-economic complex.' Both concepts are enshrined in the 1977 Constitution. Anyone familiar with the literature will also recognize: 'the single Soviet culture,' Soviet 'all-national pride' (*obshchenatsional'naia gordost'*), and the idea that all nations of the USSR are united by 'the indivisibility of their historical destinies.' Increasingly, the Russian language is viewed as an important integrating factor by virtue of its assigned role as 'the language of inter-nationality communication.' All of these elements are said to be attributes of 'the Soviet people' (*sovetskii narod*), which is described as 'a qualitatively new historical community of people' that has evolved organically in the process of building communism.[6] In short, from the standpoint of ethnicity, Soviet society is projected as a monolith.

For the most part, Soviet scholars and propagandists disseminate these notions in a fairly straightforward manner, as if they were self-evident truths requiring little or no elaboration. From time to time, however, we are reminded of certain realities that render this picture of ethnic uniformity and unanimity suspect. Thus, at the Twenty-sixth Congress of the CPSU in February 1981, the late Party leader Leonid Brezhnev assured his listeners that 'the unity of the Soviet nations is stronger today than ever before.' Nonetheless, he continued,

> this certainly does not mean that all questions in the sphere of national relations have already been solved. The dynamics of development of such a large multinational state as ours raises many problems that require the tactful attention of the Party.[7]

His successor, Iurii Andropov, also warned that

> the successes in solving the national question by no means signify that all of those problems brought about by the very fact that a multiplicity of nations and nationalities live and work within the framework of a single state have disappeared.

Indeed, Andropov suggested that the source of these problems lies in 'the inevitable growth of national consciousness' within the Soviet multinational polity.[8] More recently, CPSU general secretary Konstantin Chernenko has spoken of 'problems and contradictions' in the context of 'the distinctive features of national psychology and culture' that continue to make themselves felt.[9] Finally, moving from the abstract to the concrete, what is one to make of the much heralded unity of the Soviet people when the Latvian Party leader confesses that some people in Latvia would prefer that large enterprises not locate in *their* republic because of the resulting influx of non-Latvians?[10]

Such revelations illustrate the need for minimal contact with reality in what Leszek Kolakowski has termed 'the ideological empire.'[11] In the Soviet West, the reality of the national question surfaces when the ideological secretary of a Western Ukrainian obkom raises the question of the impact of 'prolonged alienation of the toilers of the Western Ukrainian lands from their blood-related (*edinokrovnykh*) brothers in the East,' or when the first secretary of Estonia emphasizes the need to consider 'the relative youth of Soviet power in Estonia' in the process of conducting internationalist upbringing among the population.[12] Implicit in the foregoing is the perception that differential development in the Soviet West — i.e., the diversity of historical, cultural, and religious experience — impacts on political behaviour. This may be conceptualized in terms of the existence within the official Soviet political culture of specific 'horizontal subcultures,' the most obvious and important of which are those of a national or ethnic character.[13]

The Polish crisis has focused renewed attention on the implications of such fragmentation for 'the Soviet way of life'; one of its byproducts appears to be a reevaluation of the forces at work both in the Soviet Union and in Eastern Europe. Consider the following passage from Andropov's speech at the June 1983 plenum of the CPSU Central Committee:

> The Programme of the CPSU talks about the new type of relations that emerged between socialist countries. But the last two decades have enriched our notions about the world of socialism, graphically illustrating how diverse and complex that world is. There are major differences among the individual socialist countries in the economy, in the culture, and in the ways and methods of solving the tasks of socialist development. This is natural, even if in the past it seemed to us that it would be more uniform.... The time comes when the dues have to be paid for mistakes in politics. When the leading role of the communist party weakens, the danger arises of slipping on to a bourgeois-reformist path of development. When the tie between the party and the people is lost, the resulting vacuum is filled by self-declared claimants to the role of spokesmen for the interests of the toilers. When nationalist sentiments are not rebuffed, inter-state conflicts — for which there is seemingly no basis in the socialist world — make their appearance.[14]

Several months before the plenum, a round-table discussion on socialist international relations was organized by the Moscow branch of the USSR Philosophical Society, the Academy of Sciences' Institute of Economics of the World Socialist System, and the editorial board of *Nauchnyi kommunizm*. The participants were concerned primarily with the disparities within the socialist community, and the degree to which the conventional Soviet wisdom about the unity of its member states is removed from reality. Significantly, one of the contributions was devoted to the political cultures of socialist countries, emphasizing 'the particular urgency (*aktual'nost'*) and importance of the question of the influence of the past on the political culture of the present in socialist countries.'

> Frequently, attention is fixed in the literature on elements of the socialist political culture, but there is insufficient analysis of

> fragments of past political culture, which continue to play a not insignificant role in some socialist countries and the underestimation of which may yield a distorted picture of the political culture as a whole. Thus, the question of the role of religion in the formation of political culture in this or that country remains a timely one. In this respect, it is important to bear in mind the influence of religion on the activities of social movements and organizations (trade union, youth, and the like).[15]

Clearly, the references to Poland in the course of this discussion were not entirely fortuitous.

It may take quite some time before this kind of forthright approach devolves to the area of national relations in the USSR and begins to inform Soviet nationalities policy. Some movement in this direction is already visible in spite of the fact that the convoluted jargon about simultaneous flourishing (*rastsvet*) and drawing together (*sblizhenie*) of nations followed by their eventual merger (*sliianie*) continues to predominate. The few occasions on which Andropov addressed the national question showed him to be more attuned to the issues than his predecessor. The recognition that national consciousness is on the rise, that 'negative phenomena' can not be explained wholly in terms of 'survivals of the past,' that the Party has been guilty of miscalculations in the past, and that national languages and histories are not trifles, reflects this heightened awareness.[16] Particularly relevant to our discussion are the forays of Soviet theoreticians into such areas as the relationship between history and national consciousness. Thus, two of the most prominent experts on the national question have recently written that

> the national consciousness of a people, like that of the individual, rest to a significant degree on the properties of memory. The self-realization of an individual as a stable entity is impossible if he does not remember his past and is not conscious of the continuity of his motives and activities. In exactly the same way, a people becomes conscious of its common character above all through the community of its culture, historical destinies, and traditions. National consciousness is always historical consciousness, establishing the continuity of the present and future with the past.[17]

In a similar vein, Soviet scholars are now beginning to take a closer look at something called ethnopsychology, its relationship to such concepts as national spirit, national culture, and national consciousness, and their implications for national relations and nationalities policy.[18]

In their search for unity, Soviet policymakers can be expected to apply the findings of social science research in seeking to transform the myth of the Soviet people into reality. The commitment to this goal was unequivocally reaffirmed by Andropov in his speech marking the sixtieth anniversary of the USSR in December 1982. The Party, he said, is interested not only in the drawing together of nations but in their merger.[19] The outcome will depend not only on demographic changes, linguistic assimilation, and other tangibles, but also on what may properly be called a reorientation in the structure of thinking.[20] Kolakowski has defined the problem as follows:

> The art of forgetting history is crucial: people need to know that the past can be changed overnight — from truth to truth. In this manner they are cut off from what would be a source of strength through which they could identify and assert themselves by recalling their collective past ... people know that what they are taught today is both 'objectively' true and true for today only, and that the rulers are masters of the past. If they get accustomed to this situation, they become people without historical consciousness, thus without the ability to define themselves except in relation to the state — they are non-persons, *perduta gente*.[21]

The danger that Poland poses for the ideological empire in the Soviet West, and particularly with regard to those nations who have shared a common past with the Polish people, lies in the potential for reinforcing national identities that define themselves in terms other than the Soviet people.

The Reaction 'from Above'

The immediate Soviet reaction to developments in Poland was to insulate the population from outside sources of information. On August 20, 1980, jamming was resumed of radio stations that had previously been exempted from interference. Western correspondents reported that as of mid-October all Polish newspapers and journals were removed from sale in Latvia and Lithuania, and the routine flow of tourist traffic and family visits across the Polish-Lithuanian border was drastically curtailed.[22] Other measures, also preventive in nature, followed. First, the media initiated a campaign emphasizing mass-elite linkages in Soviet society which continues to the present day. One of its initial characteristics was the readily transparent effort to brighten the image of Soviet trade unions by, among other methods, criticizing and exposing specific cases of malfeasance on the part of trade union officials. Characteristic was a report from the Lithuanian Council of Trade Unions in November 1980 stating that the director of the Vilnius gas equipment works was removed from his post at the request of the republican trade union of local industry for failing to meet the housing construction plan. Indeed, the report claims that 'this year alone the Council investigated more than twenty conflicts between trade unions and enterprise managements and they were all resolved to the benefit of the working people.'[23] This public relations exercise, which subsided after the imposition of martial law in Poland, was accompanied by efforts to strengthen Party influence in the trade unions. Already at the end of October 1980 Ukrainian Party first secretary Volodymyr Shcherbyts'kyi was calling for 'a significant increase in the level of work of the primary Party organizations and the strengthening of their influence in the workers' collectives.' At the same time, he revealed that the Ukrainian Politburo had worked out 'concrete measures' in this regard. Eventually it was learned that in October 1980 the Central Committee of the Ukrainian Party had adopted a resolution 'On Improving Ideological-Upbringing Work in Workers' Collectives' and another 'On Further Improving the Work of Primary Party Organizations and Strengthening Their Influence on the Life and Activity of Workers' Collectives.'[24] Addressing the all-Union seminar of ideological workers held in Moscow in April 1981, Ukrainian Central Committee secretary Oleksandr Kapto reported that 'one of the important elements of the restructuring of the ideological process is the transfer of the centre of ideological-upbringing activity directly into the workers' collectives.'[25] The concern shown by the authorities in Ukraine is understandable in view of the fact that the first attempt in recent times to organize an independent trade union in the USSR was made at the end of 1977 by coal miners in the Donbass led by Vladimir Klebanov.[26]

Another element of the campaign has been the sustained attention devoted to *glasnost'* or 'openness.' Party and government officials are being urged to mingle with the masses and make themselves more visible and accessible; the bureaucracy and the press are continually exhorted to improve their handling of citizens' complaints; and the practice of holding so-called open letter days — public forums at the workplace organized by newspapers during which officials are expected to respond to questions and grievances — has been instituted.[27] The object lesson in all of this, of course, is Poland, which was made clear by Brezhnev in his Central Committee report to the CPSU Congress:

> Events in Poland once again convincingly demonstrate how important it is for the Party, for the strengthening of its leading role, to listen attentively to the voice of the masses; to struggle decisively against all manifestations of bureaucratism and voluntarism; to actively develop socialist democracy and conduct a balanced and realistic policy in external economic relations.[28]

Brezhnev went on to criticize Soviet trade unions for their lack of initiative in 'exercizing their broad rights,' pointing to their cavalier attitude towards the fulfillment of collective agreements and labour safety regulations, violations of labour legislation, and other issues affecting workers.

Keeping in touch with the common folk also has the practical advantage of providing insight into the overall mood of the population. In September 1981 *Pravda* carried a lengthy theoretical article extolling the virtues of utilizing scientifically conducted public opinion surveys to discern 'what the people are thinking and what they want.' Citing Brezhnev's remarks at the Party Congress, the author argued that survey research acts as 'a barometer providing a timely and clear warning about those contradictions and conflicting situations that arise in the very process of social development and the increasing complexity of social relations.'[29] Less than two years later, at the June 1983 plenum of the Central Committee, it was resolved to establish an All-Union Centre for the Study of Public Opinion. Chernenko has emphasized that its purpose would be 'not only to study public opinion but also to purposefully develop it.'[30] It is interesting to note that in Ukraine plans to set up a single republican centre wedding sociological research to ideological work were already underway in early 1981.[31] Public opinion studies have also been used to gauge the effectiveness of foreign radio broadcasts to the USSR. In the Brest oblast of Belorussia, for example, a sociological survey was recently conducted to determine the impact of religious programmes, including those intended for listeners in Poland, on the local population.[32] The Brest region forms part of the Western Belorussian territories which were annexed from Poland in 1939 and where the overwhelming majority of Belorussia's 2.25 million Catholics (approximately a quarter of the republic's total population) are to be found.[33]

Perhaps the most revealing indication of Soviet uneasiness over developments in Poland was the 'election,' in January 1981, of blue-collar workers to the bureaux of the central committees of five republican Party organizations: those of Latvia, Lithuania, Georgia, Armenia, and Azerbaijan. This is the first time in at least twenty-five years that genuine workers have been represented at the highest level of decision making in the republics.[34]

The second area that has been affected by the Polish crisis is the ideological arena. The Soviet propaganda apparatus had no difficulty realizing that Solidarity was not simply the product of a labour-management dispute, but rather a force for political change. Accordingly, the media began to emphasize the dangers of Western influences, urging increased vigilance against attempts to subvert the Soviet system and the socialist community from within. In an article published in April 1981 the current head of the KGB, Viktor Chebrikov, singled out the harmful ideas of 'political pluralism' and 'competition' in a one-party state in the context of Western attempts to inspire nationalist and religious sentiments among Soviet youth. Chebrikov's arguments were echoed several months later by the late Semen Tsvigun, a deputy chairman of the KGB, in the authoritative Party journal *Kommunist*.[35] Similar articles by Vitalii Fedorchuk, at that time head of the Ukrainian KGB, were published in Party journals in Kiev.[36] Unlike his colleagues in Moscow, Fedorchuk openly referred to developments in Poland:

> These events plainly confirm the incontrovertible truth that any kind of belittlement of Marxist and communist ideology, any mistake, shortcoming or violation of the economic laws of socialism, any relaxation of ideological and political upbringing of the masses, boomerang with the onslaught of bourgeois ideology. They graphically illustrate that the primary objective of counterrevolutionary forces, supported morally and materially from the outside, is to disorient the masses, ideologically disarm and disorganize the Communist Party, and remove it from the leadership of society with the aim of seizing power in the country and creating conditions for the restoration of capitalism.[37]

In late November 1983 a press conference for foreign and domestic journalists was organized in Kiev to publicize the detention in Poland of a Ukrainian tourist from France alleged to have been caught in the act of transferring 'spying instructions, money, and microfilms' to a Soviet citizen. The featured speaker at the press meeting was an associate of the Ivano-Frankivs'k Medical Institute, Mykhailo Kukhtiak, who disclosed that he had been given published materials by a Ukrainian nationalist organization abroad which included 'appeals to learn from Walesa and Solidarity and apply these methods of counterrevolution to the situation of the population of Soviet Ukraine.'[38]

In the Soviet West the ideological offensive was mounted relatively early and tailored to local conditions. At the Twenty-sixth Congress of the Ukrainian Party, which was held at the beginning of February 1981, Vitalii Solohub, chairman of the Ukrainian Council of Trade Unions, raised the issue of independent trade unions in the context of the ideological struggle. Although he did not refer to either Solidarity or Poland by name, the source of Solohub's concern is clear from his remarks:

> Understandably, nothing but anger and indignation are evoked by the intrigues of enemies of the working class who, speculating on the demagogic slogans of independent trade unions, blasphemously instruct the trade unions of the socialist countries how they should work and who and how they should defend. We know that all kinds of anti-socialist elements, donning the robes of champions of human rights, speculating on the sacred feelings of proletarian solidarity and abusing the trust of the workers, and incited by the most reactionary imperialist and clerical forces, would like to set the trade unions against the Marxist-Leninist parties and socialist states, and in so doing try to shatter the socialist system from within. This will never come to pass.[39]

Several weeks later, at the CPSU Congress in Moscow, Petras Griskevicius, first secretary of the Lithuanian Party, was the only republican Party head to openly mention Poland, noting the 'anxiety' with which developments across the border were being followed in the USSR; Karl Vaino, leader of the Estonian Party, emphasized his republic's susceptibility to foreign propaganda because of its geographic location.[40] In July 1981 the Latvian Party *aktiv* met to discuss further improvement of the effectiveness of ideological work in the republic. Party first secretary Avgust Voss used the occasion to cite the situation in Poland as an example of 'the serious economic, political, and moral costs' that result from underestimating 'the slightest shortcomings and omissions, including the area of ideological work.'[41] In 1982 Riga and Tallinn hosted major all-Union conferences on the related themes of national relations, patriotic and international upbringing, and the exacerbation of the ideological struggle. Once again the issue of the Baltic states' differential development and their 'exposed' positions vis-a-vis Western influences served as the point of departure in the presentations made by Voss and Vaino.[42] At the Riga conference (June 1982) the Ukrainian ideological secretary Kapto returned to the workers theme, noting that Western radio stations had begun to focus their attention on the Soviet working class. 'It is no secret,' he said, 'that with the development of the resources of radio propaganda the ideological opponent has gained access to a wide audience in our country.'[43] The keynote speaker at the Tallinn conference (October 1982) was Konstantin Rusakov, CPSU Central Committee secretary responsible for relations with ruling communist parties. At the top of his list of lessons learned from the Polish crisis stood 'the necessity for the Party not to allow itself to be alienated from the working class.'[44]

Two additional aspects of the Soviet reaction to developments in Poland need to be considered. The first involves the potential for stimulating anti-Polish feelings in such areas as Western Ukraine and Lithuania by recalling Polish designs on territories that were formerly part of the interwar Polish republic. The rise of Solidarity gave a powerful boost to nationalist and patriotic sentiments among the Poles, which was reflected in some political groupings by the revival of the idea of a Polish confederation including Ukraine, Belorussia, and the Baltic states.[45] Also, the large volume of uncensored publications circulating in Poland have provided a forum for diverse points of view on a wide variety of problems, including such sensitive issues as Poland's eastern border and relations with its immediate neighbours in the USSR.[46] In Ukraine this was easily translated into political capital by portraying 'extremists from "Solidarity" and their Western patrons' in the role of territorial revisionists.[47]

The Response 'from Below'

As mentioned earlier, the paucity of reliable information makes it difficult to draw firm conclusions about Poland's impact on Soviet society. It seems fairly clear, however, that developments in Poland did arouse considerable general interest, and that in the Soviet West the authorities had good reason to be concerned about the possible ramifications of the Polish crisis. The fact that the Soviet public was keenly interested in Polish affairs was confirmed in the summer of 1981 by Spartak Beglov, a leading political commentator for the Novosti Press Agency. Citing his own experience, Beglov noted that 'today, regardless of what kind of Soviet audience one addresses with a lecture or discussion on a topic of international affairs, the first question asked of the speaker inevitably touches on Poland.'[48] A similar picture emerges from an analysis of the kinds of questions that Estonian audiences posed to Party lecturers and propagandists in 1981. The study shows that forty-five percent of all questions about international affairs concerned the current situation and future development of the world socialist system. This marked 'a considerable increase' over 1980. There were also more inquiries about security and cooperation in Europe, which the study attributes 'above all to the events in the Polish People's Republic.'[49] A revealing insight into the popular response as well as the official reaction to developments in Poland was provided by the ideological secretary of the Brest obkom in Western Belorussia:

> During the period of crisis in Poland, the toilers of the Brest region, like all Soviet people, followed the events in the Polish People's Republic with deep anxiety and uneasiness, evaluating them from class positions ... The fraternal interest and the readiness to come to the aid of a neighbouring socialist republic was so great among the Soviet people that, on the basis of decisions of Party and public organizations, a single political day (*edinyi politden'*) as well as several other measures were undertaken in the Brest oblast allowing the population to express its views and wishes.[50]

The impression that one forms is that 'the Party and public organizations' in the Brest region were primarily concerned about channeling local interest in Polish affairs into the proper direction. There is reason to believe that, as in other parts of the Soviet Union, shortages of meat, milk, and other foodstuffs in 1981-1982 contributed to increased public disaffection in Belorussia.[51]

The response to developments in Poland by the dissident community in the Soviet West is reflected in the *samizdat* literature. Already on September 11, 1980 twenty Baltic human rights activists, eleven Lithuanians and nine Estonians, sent a short statement to Lech Walesa greeting him and his countrymen 'on the occasion of the start of democratic reforms [in Poland], which are needed in the entire socialist camp.'[52] A similar statement is reported to have been sent to the Solidarity leader by Leonid Siryi, a worker from Odessa, during the initial strikes in Gdansk.[53] In January 1981 eight political prisoners of various nationalities, including two Ukrainians and a Lithuanian, sent a message of support to Solidarity from the Perm strict-regime Camp No. 36 in the Urals.[54] The first anniversary of Solidarity was another occasion for thirty-six activists from Lithuania and Latvia to greet Walesa, noting that 'the historic campaign of Poland's working people on behalf of human and national rights is significant for the Baltic nations as well.'[55]

A worker's perspective on developments in Poland is presented in a letter from the Ukrainian political prisoner Mykola Pohyba, who was sentenced in 1979 to a five-year term for campaigning for workers' rights. Addressed to the Ukrainian Helsinki Group and the United Nations Human Rights Commission, the letter, dated November 4, 1980, argues that conditions in the Soviet Union are such that independent trade unions could be formed there on the Polish model:

> The recent events in Poland have clearly shown that the working class is capable of waging a struggle for its rights and freedoms, for a real improvement of its well-being, and that the efficacy of this struggle depends on the degree of solidarity of the working class and on its level of self-organization.[56]

In 1981 the full text of the Gdansk agreement concluded between the Interfactory Strike Committee and the Polish government in August 1980 was reproduced in an Estonian *samizdat* journal.[57]

At the end of October 1980 the Western press widely publicized a reported strike on October 1 and 2 at a tractor factory in the Estonian city of Tartu in which anywhere from 115 and 1,000 workers are said to have participated. The initial reports came from Estonian circles in Stockholm, who were quick to suggest that the strikers were influenced by the example of Solidarity. That the strike did in fact occur was confirmed by residents of Tartu (although denied by local authorities),[58] but it remains problematical whether or not the strike movement in Poland played a role. Obviously, the great amount of publicity generated by Solidarity in the Western media in the fall of 1980 can not be discounted, particularly in Estonia where workers could easily tune in to Finnish radio and television to learn of the latest developments in Poland. The same sources also made public a document from a previously unknown group called the Democratic National Front of the Soviet Union. Dated June 1981, it listed a series of demands, including an end to Soviet intervention into Poland's internal affairs, and urged a half-hour general strike throughout the USSR beginning on December 1 and continuing on the first working day of each following month.[59]

'The initiative,' according to these sources, 'is clearly inspired by developments toward a new political and economic scene in nearby Poland.'[60] The strike call was largely ignored, but the authorities nonetheless conducted arrests of activists believed to have been linked to the movement and subsequently put them on trial. In an article in *Kommunist*, Estonian Party leader Vaino later noted that the calls to take part in work stoppages in Estonia were 'similar to those advanced in Poland by "Solidarity".'[61] In 1981 Western correspondents were told about work stoppages and walkouts in Lithuania and Latvia,[62] and dissident sources described a total of six strikes that were said to have occurred in Kiev between March and August.[63] There are no indications that any of these were motivated by events in Poland, although in Western Ukraine, leaflets are reported to have been disseminated in February and March 1982 urging support for Solidarity and calling on workers to strike.[64]

Religion and Nationalism

An important element linking Poland and the Soviet West was the election of Cracow's Cardinal Karol Wojtyla in October 1978 to the throne of Saint Peter in Rome. The Soviet leadership has been forced to reckon with a very outspoken and popular Polish Pope in the person of John Paul II who has had a major impact not only in his native Poland, but throughout Catholic communities in Eastern Europe and the Soviet Union. From the very beginning of his pontificate, John Paul II made it clear that he had a special interest in the fate of the Catholic Church in the Eastern bloc. This was dramatically illustrated during his first visit to Poland in June 1979. His statements on that occasion — emphasizing not only religious liberty and human rights but also the rights of nations — and his references to 'the brother peoples' and 'those often forgotten nations' in terms of his own unique position as the first Slavic Pope could not but be viewed with consternation in Moscow.[65] A recently published and highly sophisticated Soviet analysis of the Vatican's Ostpolitik argues:

> It is absolutely clear that the activity of the new Pope, who has devoted a great deal of attention to East European Catholicism, introduces a new element in the politics of the national churches and in their relations with the socialist states. This, in turn, can not but have an impact, to one degree or another, on the mind-sets

(*umonastroeniiakh*) of believers in individual countries of socialism.[66]

Within a month of the Pope's return from Poland a conference of secretaries of the central committees of ruling communist parties was held in East Berlin to review international and ideological questions. Although not announced at the time, the meeting also discussed the implications of John Paul II's pontificate for the Catholic Church in the Eastern bloc. It was concluded that

> the policy of the Vatican towards the socialist countries has entered a new phase, which is marked by a sharp increase in the activity of the Roman Catholic church, by a desire to turn it into a political opposition in the socialist countries.[67]

The Pope has been subjected to personal criticism in the Soviet press, including a vilifying article in the Belorussian literary monthly *Polymia*.[68]

John Paul II's efforts on behalf of the Catholic Church in Lithuania and Latvia, and his support for the outlawed Ukrainian Greek Catholic (Uniate) Church have had a perceptible impact. On 13 November 1978, less than a month after his installation in the Vatican, five Lithuanian priests founded the Catholic Committee for the Defence of the Rights of Believers. On the same day they sent the new Pope a letter stating that their action was inspired by his determination to defend 'the Church of Silence.'[69] In the fall of 1981 the uncensored Polish journal *Spotkania* published a letter to John Paul II from a group of Ukrainian Catholics who declared their intention to struggle for the legalization of their Church in the Soviet Union. A year later, on 9 September 1982, three priests and two laymen from Western Ukraine formed the Initiative Group for the Defence of the Rights of Believers and the Church, which set itself the same task.[70] Several months earlier, at the Riga conference, the head of the Propaganda and Agitation Department in Kiev, Leonid Kravchuk, characterized the situation in Western Ukraine as follows:

> We have information that in the republic, especially in its western oblasts, the propaganda of the Vatican and other bourgeois clerical and clerical nationalist centres\is finding a response among certain circles of listeners. Among them are Catholics, former Uniate priests and monks, and nationalistically inclined individuals. There is also a

certain revival of religious activity within several of the registered communities of sects. The Catholic clergy has become more active under the influence of hostile propaganda. The former Uniate clergy has tried to promote the psychological preparedness of believers with a view towards putting forth demands for the resumption of the activity of the Uniate Church.[71]

In the Baltic states the authorities have responded by combining the carrot with the stick. In June 1982 the Vatican was successful in pushing through the appointments of two new Lithuanian bishops and a new Latvian bishop. This was followed, in January 1983, by the elevation of Riga's Bishop Julijans Vaivods to cardinal, the Soviet Union's first resident cardinal in history and, in April, by the unprecedented *ad limina* visit to Rome by four Lithuanian bishops. At the same time, criticism of the Church's activities and repressive measures against the Catholic clergy and faithful have been stepped up. For the first time in over a decade priests in Lithuania have been arrested and put on trial, including members of the Catholic Committee.[72] In Ukraine there have been no compromises vis-a-vis what are routinely described as 'the Uniate remnants.' The Soviet Ukrainian press has been filled with attacks on the underground Catholic Church, the Vatican, and the Pope. In December 1982, three months after the formation of the Initiative Group, the authorities arrested its chairman, Iosyf Terelia. Terelia was subsequently tried and sentenced, and other members of the group have been subjected to harassment.[73]

The stature of Pope John Paul II and the important role played by the Polish Church as the bastion of national interests seem also to have contributed to a reorientation of atheist propaganda in the USSR. Specifically, a campaign has been launched to discredit the idea that religion and nationality exist in a symbiotic relationship. Thus, a correspondent for *Izvestiia*, visiting a cathedral in Warsaw, finds it strange that the walls are decorated with portraits of Polish historical and cultural figures. Five years ago, he claims, these portraits were not to be seen. Conclusion: 'A perfectly obvious attempt to transform the church into a pantheon of national memory and to represent churches as its only depository.'[74] The notion that religion has never been a 'progressive' factor in the life of a nation is not, of course, a new element in Soviet atheistic propaganda. Recently, however, this theme has been given priority status both in the general press and in specialized publications. Numerous articles on the subject have been published in Lithuania and Ukraine. Thus, Lionginas Sepetys, the Lithuanian ideological secretary, argues:

> Some clergymen, in appealing to religious feeling, are inciting nationalist sentiments and superstition. They are trying to show that the Catholic Church is the only protector of Lithuania's national values, the guardian of its culture and uniqueness, incorrectly identifying national traditions with religious ones. Attempting to compromise scientific atheism, they claim it is being used as an instrument to denationalize the culture of the Lithuanian nation.[75]

The same approach was taken by representatives of the Ukrainian ideological establishment at the June 1982 conference in Riga. Kapto, the ideological secretary, maintained that

> the ideologues of clericalism are attempting to represent everything that is religious as national, and to portray the processes of atheistic upbringing as 'denationalization of the people.' Hostile propaganda is forcibly thrusting upon our people the stereotype of clerical ideologues that every 'Ukrainian is a Greek Catholic,' every 'Uzbek is a Muslim,' every 'Lithuanian is a Catholic,' and every 'Jew is a Judaist.'[76]

Kravchuk, the agitprop chief, devoted his entire presentation to the subject of atheism and the tasks of counterpropaganda. Uniates and nationalists, he noted, are proclaiming

> the thesis about some kind of mystical conformity of the spiritual make-up of Ukrainians with the fundamental postulates of Christian religion, as a result of which the Ukrainian people and the church are supposedly 'inseparably linked' inasmuch as it is precisely 'Christianity that has moulded the Ukrainian soul' and 'the Ukrainian spirit.'[77]

A branch of the Institute of Scientific Atheism of Moscow's Academy of Social Sciences has now been set up in Vilnius similar to the interrepublican branch already existing in Kiev. One of its tasks is to coordinate research projects on problems that are also being studied in Belorussia, Latvia, and Estonia.[78] The relationship between religion, culture, history, and nationalism is being closely examined by experts in scientific atheism.[79] At the end of 1981 a philosophical seminar on culture and religion was organized, and specialists from various fields were later invited to share their views on the pages of *Nauka i religiia*.[80] A recent conference in Warsaw on 'Religion and the Church in Socialist

Society' also revealed that efforts are under way to draw experts on religion from Eastern Europe into closer cooperation with their Soviet colleagues.[81]

The dilemma confronting the nations of the Soviet West has been given eloquent expression by the Ukrainian poet and political prisoner Vasyl' Stus in a document entitled 'From a Camp Dairy.' Stus writes of his admiration for Polish defiance of Soviet despotism and offers Poland as a model for Ukraine. 'We Ukrainians,' he says, 'are psychologically close, perhaps the closest of all, to the Polish character, but we lack the most important of all things — the ardent patriotism that consolidates the Poles.' According to Stus, Ukraine's position on the easternmost fringes of the West and the resulting exposure to Moscow and Orthodoxy is the source of its misfortune:

My thoughts turn to the one thousandth anniversary of Christianity in Ukraine. I think that was when the first mistake was made — the Byzantine-Muscovite rite, which linked us, the easternmost part of the West, to the East. Our western individualistic spirit, weakened by despotic Byzantine Orthodoxy, could not in the final analysis free itself from this spiritual duality, a duality which with time created a hypocrisy complex.[82]

In a conversation with George Urban a decade ago, Francois Bondy suggested the validity of projecting 'the notion of a "Western" Eastern Europe further back into the multinational Soviet state itself, for it may well be that the dividing line runs deeper than we normally think.'[83] That dividing line continues to set the Soviet West apart, and it may well have been reinforced by the Polish experience.

Notes

1. Roman Szporluk in the *Los Angeles Times*, April 2, 1981.
2. The concept of the Soviet West is applied in the case studies by V. Stanley Vardys, Yaroslav Bilinsky, and Stephen Fischer-Galati in Roman Szporluk, ed., *The Influence of Eastern Europe and the Soviet West on the USSR* (New York: Praeger Publishers, 1975). See also Roman Szporluk, "Defining Central Europe's Power, Politics, and Culture," in Ladislav Matejka and Benjamin Stolz, eds. Cross Currents: A Yearbook of Central European Culture 1982 (Ann Arbor: University of Michigan, 1982), pp. 30-38.
3. Western scholarship has devoted considerably more attention to the Soviet impact on Eastern Europe. The reverse process is treated by Zvi Gitelman, 'The

Impact on the Soviet Union of the Eastern European Experience in Modernization,' in Charles Gati, ed., *The Politics of Modernization in Eastern Europe: Testing the Soviet Model* (New York: Praeger Publishers, 1974), pp. 256-274, and *idem*, 'The Diffusion of Political Innovation: From East Europe to the Soviet Union,' in *The Influence of Eastern Europe*, pp. 11-67.

4. See, for example, 'Vliianie pol'skikh sobytii na SSSR i strany Vostochnoi Evropy: Kruglyi stol zhurnalov "Kontakt", "Kontinent", "Badashte" i "Svedetstvi", Parizh, 22 iiunia 1982 g.,' *Kontinent*, No. 33 (1982), 423-439.

5. This is largely an impressionistic judgement based on the reports of Western correspondents in the Soviet Union. For example, Dusko Doder wrote in *The Washington Post*, July 25, 1981: 'Travelers reaching here [Moscow] from the Baltic republics, Western Ukraine and Western Byelorussia also report considerable public sympathy for the Poles and a greater understanding of gut issues, largely because of the access to Polish television.' Although complete breakdowns by nationality are not available, attitudinal studies conducted by Radio Free Europe-Radio Liberty Area Audience and Opinion Research show greater support for the Polish strike movement among non-Russians, particularly non-Slavs. See *Attitudes in the USSR toward the Right to Strike*, AR 1-81, January 1981; *Attitudes of Soviet Citizens to the Strike Movement in Poland (September 1980-February 1981)*, BGR 3-81, May 1981; *Developing Soviet Citizen Attitudes toward Poland*, AR 8-81, October 1981; *Attitudes of Some Soviet Citizens to the Solidarity Trade Union Movement: Comparison of SAAOR Data with Unofficial Soviet Poll*, AR 5-82, May 1982; and *Soviet Citizen Attitudes toward Poland since Martial Law: Agitprop, Western Radio and the Evolution of Opinion*, AR 6-82, September 1982.

6. *Razvitoi sotsializm* (Moscow: Izdatel'stvo politicheskoi literatury, 1978), p. 260.

7. L.I. Brezhnev, *Otchetnyi doklad Tsentral'nogo Komiteta KPSS XXVI s"ezdu Kommunisticheskoi partii Sovetskogo Soiuza i ocherednye zadachi partii v oblasti vnutrennei i vneshnei politiki* (Moscow: Izdatel'stvo politicheskoi literatury, 1981), p. 76.

8. Iu. V. Andropov, *Shest'desiat let SSSR* (Moscow: Izdatel'stovo politicheskoi literatury, 1982), p. 13.

9. *Materialy plenuma Tsentral'nogo Komiteta KPSS 14-15 iiunia 1983 goda* (Moscow: Izdatel'stvo politicheskoi literatury, 1983), pp. 58-59.

10. A. Voss, 'V edinom narodnokhoziaistvennom komplekse,' *Kommunist*, 1978, No. 14, 66.

11. 'A Conference of Soviet and East European Dissidents: Politics and Ideology,' *Partisan Review*, Vol. 50, No. 4 (1983), 499-500. See also Kolakowski's 'Ideology in Eastern Europe,' in Milorad M. Drachkovitch, ed., *East Central Europe: Yesterday-Today-Tomorrow* (Stanford: Hoover Institution Press, 1982), pp. 43-53.

12. D.A. Iaremchuk, 'Kontrpropaganda – odna iz vazhnykh form ideologicheskoi deiatel'nosti partiinykh komitetov,' in *Neprimirimost' k burzhuaznoi ideologii, perezhitkam natsionalizma: Po materialam Vsesoiuznoi nauchnoprakticheskoi konferentsii 'Razvitie natsional'nykh otnoshenii v usloviiakh zrelogo sotsializma. Opyt i problemy patrioticheskogo i internatsional'nogo vospitaniia' (Riga, 28-30 iiunia 1982 g.)* (Moscow: Mezhdunarodnye otnosheniia, 1982), p. 59; K. Vaino, 'S tochnym znaniem obstanovki,' *Kommunist*, 1983, No. 4, 51.

13. Stephen White, *Political Culture and Soviet Politics* (London: The Macmillan Press, 1979), pp. 143 ff.

14. *Materialy plenuma Tsentral'nogo Komiteta KPSS 14-15 iiunia 1983 goda*, pp. 20-21. See also, in this context, his earlier remark about 'illusions that had to

be discarded and mistakes that had to be paid for.' Andropov, *op. cit.* p. 18.
  15. 'Sotsialisticheskie mezhdunarodnye otnosheniia,' *Nauchnyi kommunizm*, 1983, No. 5, 133-134.
  16. Andropov, *op. cit.*, pp. 13-14.
  17. Iu. V. Bromlei and M.I. Kulichenko, 'Natsional'noe i internatsional'noe v obraze zhizni sovetskogo cheloveka,' *Nauchnyi kommunizm*, 1982, No. 4, 10.
  18. See the discussion initiated by A.F. Dashdamirov's article 'K metodologii issledovaniia natsional'no-psikhologicheskikh problem,' *Sovetskaia etnografiia*, 1983, Nos. 2, 3, and 4, and Dashdamirov's 'Nekotorye metodologicheskie voprosy issledovaniia natsional'no-psikhologicheskikh problem,' in *Razvitie natsional'nykh otnoshenii v svete reshenii XXVI s"ezda KPSS* (Moscow: Izdatel'stvo 'Nauka,' 1982), pp. 302-326.
  19. See Roman Solchanyk, 'Merger of Nations: Back in Style?,' *Radio Liberty Research*, 84/83, February 18, 1983.
  20. 'Surmounting "national" unscrupulousness (*nedobrosovestnost'*) and narrow-mindedness, be it intentional or unintentional, is a problem that is far more complicated than it may appear at first glance. It is a problem of deep-seated *structure of thought*, not just facts, views or opinions.' Gustav Naan, 'Mnogoobrazie edinogo: Natsional'nye kul'tury v epokhu nauchno-tekhnicheskoi revoliutsii,' *Kommunist Estonii*, 1983, No. 1, 35 (emphasis in original).
  21. Leszek Kolakowski, 'Totalitarianism & the Lie,' *Commentary*, Vol. 75, No. 5 (May 1983), 36.
  22. 'Jam Today, Jam Tomorrow,' *The Economist*, August 30, 1980, 39; David K. Willis in *The Christian Science Monitor*, November 17, 1980; R.W. Apple, Jr., in *The New York Times*, November 24, 1980; David Satter in the *Financial Times*, July 29, 1981; and Andrew Nagorski in *Newsweek*, August 13, 1981, 19.
  23. Tass dispatch from Vilnius, November 20, 1980. See also Robert Gillette in the *Los Angeles Times*, December 22, 1980, and V. Stanley Vardys, 'Polish Echoes in the Baltic,' *Problems of Communism*, Vol. 32, No. 4 (July-August 1983), 33.
  24. *Radians'ka Ukraina*, October 30, 1980; *Trud*, April 14, 1981; *Radians'ka Ukraina*, June 9, 1981; *Radians'ka Ukraina*, July 24, 1981; A. Kapto, 'Povyshat' deistvennost' ideologicheskoi raboty,' *Kommunist*, 1981, No. 18, 58; and *Pravda*, February 10, 1982.
  25. A.S. Kapto, 'Kommunisticheskomu vospitaniiu – kompleksnost' i tseleustremlennost',' in *Za vysokoe kachestvo i deistvennost' ideologicheskoi raboty: Materialy Vsesoiuznogo seminara-soveshchaniia ideologicheskikh rabotnikov. Moskva, 20-25 aprelia 1981 g.* (Moscow: Izadatel'stvo politicheskoi literatury, 1981), p. 439.
  26. Victor Haynes and Olga Semyonova, eds., *Workers Against the Gulag: The New Opposition in the Soviet Union* (London: Pluto Press, 1979), pp. 16-22.
  27. Various aspects of the renewed attention that the Soviet media have devoted to labour themes since the emergence of Solidarity are discussed by Roman Solchanyk, 'Nervous Neighbors: The Soviets and Solidarity,' *Workers under Communism*, No. 1 (Spring 1982), 16-18; Elizabeth Teague, 'Channeling Discontent: Workers Complaints in the Soviet Media,' *ibid.*, 33-35; Betsy Gidwitz, 'Labor Unrest in the Soviet Union,' *Problems of Communism*, Vol. 31, No. 6 (November-December 1982), 25-42; and Blair A. Ruble, 'Soviet Trade Unions and Labor Relations after "Solidarity",' in Joint Economic Committee, Congress of the United States, *Soviet Economy in the 1980's: Problems and Prospects*, Pt. 2 (Washington: U.S. Government Printing Office, 1983), 349-366.
  28. Brezhnev, *op. cit.*, p. 13.
  29. *Pravda*, September 25, 1981.
  30. *Materialy plenuma Tsentral'nogo Komiteta KPSS 14-15 iiunia 1983 goda*,

p. 79, and K. Chernenko, 'Delo vsei partii, dolg kazhdogo kommunista,' *Kommunist*, 1983, No. 15, 26.

31. Kapto, *Za vysokoe kachestvo i deistvennost' ideogicheskoi raboty*, p. 439; *idem*, 'Sotsial'naia struktura obshchestva i differentsirovannyi podkhod k organizatsii vospitatel'noi deiatel'nosti,' *Sotsiologicheskie issledovaniia*, 1981, No. 4, 103; and *idem*, 'O sovershenstvovanii stilia ideologicheskoi, politiko-vospitatel'noi raboty,' *Voprosy istorii KPSS*, 1983, No. 10, 9.

32. S. Pavlov, 'Vazhnyi uchastok partiinoi ucheby, kommunisticheskogo vospitaniia trudiashchikhsia,' *Politicheskoe samoobrazovanie*, 1983, No. 7, 117.

33. Marite Sapiets, 'The Situation of the Roman Catholic Church in Belorussia,' *Religion in Communist Lands*, Vol. 10, No. 2 (Autumn 1982), 178.

34. Ann Sheehy, 'Blue-Collar Workers Elected to Central Committee Buros in Five Union Republics,' *Radio Liberty Research*, 57/81, February 5, 1981.

35. V.M. Chebrikov, 'Bditel'nost' – ispytannoe oruzhie,' *Molodoi kommunist*, 1981, No. 4, 28-34; S. Tsvigun, 'O proiskakh imperialisticheskikh razvedok,' *Kommunist*, 1981, No. 14, 88-99.

36. V.V. Fedorchuk, 'Vysoka politychnia pyl'nist' radians'kykh liudei – nadiinyi zaslin pidryvnym pidstupam imperializmu,' *Kommunist Ukrainy*, 1980, No. 10, 10-26, and *idem*, 'Ideolohichni dyversii-broia imperializmu,' *Pid praporom leninizmu*, 1981, No. 19, 10-17.

37. *Ibid.*, 13.

38. Radio Kiev, November 23, 1983. See also *Radians'ka Ukraina*, *Pravda Ukrainy*, *Robitnycha hazeta*, *Sil'ski visti*, *Komsomol'skaia pravda*, and *Trybuna Ludu* for November 23, 1983; *Literaturna Ukraina*, November 24, 1983; and *Izvestiia*, November 23 and 25, 1983.

39. *Radians'ka Ukraina*, February 12, 1981.

40. *Pravda*, February 26 and 27, 1981.

41. *Sovetskaia Latviia*, July 19, 1981.

42. *Sovetskaia Latviia*, June 29, 1982, and *Sovetskaia Estoniia*, October 13, 1982.

43. A.S. Kapto, 'Problemy aktualizatsii internatsional'nogo i patrioticheskogo vospitaniia v usloviiakh obostrivsheisia ideologicheskoi bor'by,' in *Vospityvat' ubezhdennykh patriotov-internatsionalistov: Po materialiam Vsesoiuznoi nauchno-prakticheskoi konferentsii 'Razvitie natsional'nykh otnoshenii v usloviiakh zrelogo sotsializma. Opyt i problemy patrioticheskogo i internatsional'nogo vospitaniia' (Riga, 28-30 iiunia 1982 g.)* (Moscow: Izdatel'stvo politicheskoi literatury, 1982), 65-67. See also Shcherbyts'kyi's remark that 'bourgeois propaganda is now being reoriented' and 'is increasingly addressing itself to the audience of workers' in *Radians'ka Ukraina*, November 5, 1981.

44. *Sovetskaia Estoniia*, October 13, 1982.

45. Nigel Wade in *The Daily Telegraph*, November 17, 1980.

46. For example, a Tass dispatch from Warsaw, September 23, 1981 refers to a Solidarity bulletin issued by the Katowice metallurgical plant that ostensibly 'published openly provocative articles which distort the events connected with the liberation of the peoples of Western Ukraine and Byelorussia. This dirty and slanderous material puts the Soviet Union on the same level with Nazi Germany.' Cf. 'O co walczy Konfederacja Polski Niepodleglej?,' *Niepodleglosc. Biuletyn informacynyj Konfederacji Polski Niepodleglej* (Cracow), Vol. 2, No. 2 (February 2, 1983), 1-3 (typescript).

47. See the report by Arnol'd Shlepakov, director of the Institute of Social and Economic Problems of Foreign Countries, to the general assembly of the Ukrainian Academy of Sciences in *Visnyk Akademii nauk Ukrains'koi RSR*, 1982, No. 7, 42.

48. Solchanyk, *Workers under Communism*, 17.

49. G. Sillaste, 'O chem govoriat voprosy,' *Kommunist Estonii*, 1982, No. 6, 11.
50. V.I. Boris, 'Organicheskoe edinstvo internatsionalizma i patriotizma,' in *Sotsialisticheskii internatsionalizm v deistvii: Po materialam Vsesoiuznoi nauchno-prakticheskoi konferentsii 'Razvitie natsional'nykh otuoshenii v usloviiakh zrelogo sotsializma. Opyt i problemy patrioticheskogo i internatsional'nogo vospitaniia' (Riga, 28-30 iiunia 1982 g.)* (Moscow: Izdatel'stvo 'Nauka,' 1982), p. 85.
51. See Bobo Scheutz in *Svenska Dagbladet* (Stockholm), October 8, 1982.
52. Arkhiv Samizadata No. 4452.
53. *Svoboda* (Jersey City, N.J.), October 11, 1980.
54. Arkhiv Samizadata No. 4428.
55. Vardys, *Problems of Communism*, 25.
56. Arkhiv Samizdata No. 4321. An English translation of the letter was published in *The Observer*, August 16, 1981.
57. Vardys, *Problems of Communism*, 25.
58. Staffan Teste in *Dagens Nyheter* (Stockholm), October 27, 1980.
59. Arkhiv Samizdata No. 4503. A Reuter dispatch from Stockholm on November 19, 1981 reported that the document was printed in the Russian, Ukrainian, Estonian, Latvian, and Lithuanian languages, and that it had been distributed in Moscow, Leningrad, Kiev, and the Baltic states.
60. Associated Press dispatch from Stockholm, November 13, 1981.
61. Vaino, *Kommunist*, 52. See also Dusko Doder in *The Washington Post*, April 20, 1983.
62. See Ned Temko in *The Christian Science Monitor*, June 4, 1981, and Robert Gillette in the *Los Angeles Times*, August 3, 1981.
63. Arkhiv Samizdata Nos. 4354 and 4496, and *Vesti iz SSSR/USSR News Brief*, 1981, No. 16 (August 31, 1981), 8.
64. *Vesti iz SSSR/USSR News Brief*, 1983, No. 7 (April 15, 1983), 8.
65. Alex Alexiev, *The Kremlin and the Pope*, The Rand Paper Series P-6855, April 1983, 2-3, and *The Pope in Poland* (Munich: Radio Free Europe Research, 1979), 68-72.
66. A.F. Shevtsova, *Sotsializm i katolitsizm (Vzaimootnosheniia gosudarstva i katolicheskoi tserkvi v sotsialisticheskikh stranakh)* (Moscow: Izdatel'stvo 'Nauka,' 1982), 9.
67. Quoted by Ivan Hvat, 'The Ukrainian Catholic Church, the Vatican and the Soviet Union during the Pontificate of Pope John Paul II,' *Religion in Communist Lands*, Vol. II, No. 3 (Winter, 1983), 267.
68. Ales' Bazhko, 'Pakruchastyia stsezhki bahaslova z Vadovits,' *Polymia*, 1981, No. 4, 138-167. See also V. Makhin, 'Religiia v ideinom arsenale antikommunizma,' *Politicheskoe samoobrazovanie*, 1982, No. 12, 115-122.
69. Marite Sapiets, 'Religion and Nationalism in Lithuania,' *Religion in Communist Lands*, Vol. 7, No. 2 (Summer 1979), 87-89.
70. Hvat, *op. cit.*, 271-276.
71. L.M. Kravchuk, 'Ateisticheskoe vospitanie trudiashchikhsia i zadachi kontrpropaganda,' in *Neprimirimost' k burzhuaznoi ideologii, perezhitkam natsionalizma*, 41-42.
72. Vardys, *Problems of Communism*, 31-32. See also Kestutis Girnius and Saulius Girnius, 'Relations between the Kremlin and the Vatican as Mirrored in Lithuania,' *Radio Liberty Research*, 190/83, May 11, 1983, and *idem*, 'Five Years of the Catholic Committee in Lithuania: Its Achievements and Dispersal,' *Radio Liberty Research*, 431/83, November 11, 1983.
73. Hvat, *op. cit.*, 276-277.
74. *Izvestiia*, August 10, 1983.

75. Quoted by Kestutis Girnius, 'Atheist Campaign in Lithuania Intensified,' *Radio Liberty Research*, 136/83, March 30, 1983. See also his 'Soviet Authors Deny that Lithuanian Nationalist and Catholic Interests are Identical,' *Radio Liberty Research*, 345/82, August 26, 1982.

76. Kapto, in *Vospityvat' ubezhdennykh patriotov-internatsionalistov*, p. 75.

77. Kravchuk, *op. cit.*, p. 38.

78. *Sovetskaia Litva*, September 15, 1982.

79. See for example, V.A. Zots, *Kul'tura, religiia, ateizm* (Moscow: Izdatel'stvo politicheskoi literatury, 1982). Zots is a doctor of philosophical sciences based in Kiev.

80. M. Danilova and Z. Tazhurizna, 'Kul'tura i mirovozzrenie: Problemy i diskussii,' *Nauka i religiia*, 1982, No. 10, 19-22; Ia. Minkiavichius, 'Religiia i tserkov' v natsional'noi zhizni naroda,' *Nauka i religiia*, 1982, No. 12, 31-33; and V. Zots, 'Mistifikatsiia kul'tury,' *ibid*., 34-36.

81. *Trybuna Ludu*, November 16, 1983.

82. Arkhiv Samizdata No. 5062. See also Bohdan Nahaylo, 'Ukrainian Dissident Comments on Events in Poland,' *Radio Liberty Research*, 437/83, November 11, 1983.

83. Francois Bondy and George Urban, 'Cultural Exchange and Its Prospects,' *Survey*, Vol. 20, No. 2-3 (Spring-Summer 1974), 37-38.

INSTITUTIONAL RELIGION AND NATIONALITY IN THE SOVIET UNION

Bohdan R. Bociurkiw

The image of the Soviet Union as not just an atheist state, but one inhabited by peoples of different religions, has probably encountered fewer cultural and ideological barriers in permeating the Western public mind than the perception of the USSR as a multinational empire. The impressive growth in Western scholarship on both aspects of the Soviet state has yet to be matched by a comprehensive examination of the inter-relationship between religion and nationality in the Soviet political and social context.[1] This is a problem of considerable importance for an understanding of the dynamics of Soviet nationality politics and of the ethno-cultural persistence that has outlived a succession of ideological 'solutions'; this interdependence of religion and nationality must also be considered in assessing the impact of political integration and cultural-linguistic assimilation upon the survival of different religions in the USSR.

This study can only partially and tentatively fill that void by exploring the dimensions, ramifications, and implications of the complex and varied relationship between institutional religion and nationality in a state both committed to the eventual 'melting' of its many nationalities into a 'single Soviet' (and Russian, at least linguistically) 'people' and determined ultimately to eliminate each and every religion from among its subjects.

As for the Communist party leaders, they have long been aware of the problems posed for Soviet religious and nationality policies by the interdependence of religion and nationality. Significantly, it was only during the Brezhnev era that these problems have been given high priority in Soviet political socialization and adult indoctrination programmes — predominantly among non-Russians — ranging in form from the so-called 'internationalist-atheist education,'[2] to the synthetic 'new Soviet rites.'[3] While the Kremlin leaders have been increasingly reaching to Soviet Russian nationalism for more credible integrating and legitimizing symbols, to compensate for the widespread cynicism about 'Marxism-Leninism' — Russian Orthodoxy, the legitimizing faith and the principal integrating institution of the old Tsarist Empire, has been gaining converts among the Russian intelligentsia and the youth. The markedly ambivalent reaction of the regime to the new popularity of Russian Orthodoxy[4] reflects the basic dilemma facing the Soviet leadership; on the one hand, Orthodoxy with its historical links to the *ancien régime* and traditional Russian nationalism poses a growing challenge to both the legitimacy of the Party dictatorship and its rule over the non-Russian and, in particular, non-Orthodox peoples. On the other hand — as the old supranational symbolism is losing its cementing value, and as the demographic balance in the USSR continues to shift in favour of non-Russians, particularly in Central Asia — the potentialities of Russian nationalism and Orthodoxy as vehicles for the Russification of Ukrainians, Belorussians, Moldavians and some other European nationalities and their integration into a smaller, 'white' version of the 'one Soviet People' may be becoming more attractive to some elements of the Soviet political elite.

The Patterns

The nature and mutability of the interrelationship between institutional religion and ethnicity in the contemporary USSR varies not only from one nationality to another and amongst religions, but also within individual nationalities; in virtually all cases it has been affected to a greater or lesser extent by political, social and demographic changes. Of all the factors reshaping the traditional ethno-religious patterns, a nationality's loss of political control over its own collective fate has perhaps been the most important.

Four indicators could be employed to identify the principal patterns linking institutional religion and nationality in the USSR:

(a) the (positive or negative) historical relationship between religion predominating within a given nationality and ethno-cultural persistence and nation building;
(b) the extent to which particular religions and religious institutions have been employed by the imperial (Tsarist or Soviet) regime as vehicles for supranational integration and destruction of the subject peoples' ethnic, cultural, and linguistic distinctiveness ('nation-unmaking');
(c) the impact (including the duration and intensity) of 'Sovietization' (more specifically, Soviet political re-socialization, modernization,

and inter-republican migration) on the traditional interdependence between religion and nationality; and

(d) the characteristics of a given religion, involving its attitude to the state, the nature of its organization, and the location of its ultimate spiritual authority (within or outside the Soviet sphere of control); the numbers, strategical location, and political influence of its co-believers abroad; the extent of its adaptability to political and social change; and the degree of its vulnerability to Soviet penetration and control.

The application of these indicators makes it possible to identify seven principal patterns linking institutional religion to nationality in the Soviet Union: 'the imperial church'; 'national churches'; 'traditional native sects'; 'transnational religious communities'; 'ethno-religious diasporas'; 'modern cosmopolitan sects', and 'nationalist religious cults'.

The Imperial Church

The model of an 'imperial church' derives from the Byzantine tradition of 'symphonic' relationship between the *sacerdotium* and *imperium*. Translated into practice this 'symphony' amounted to the submission of the Church to the Emperor and involved legitimation and enforcement of his authority through ecclesiastical teachings and discipline, in return for the Emperor's maintenance and protection of the Church against domestic heresies and alien faiths. The territorial jurisdictions of Church and the Empire were perceived as co-extensive in scope, as expressed in a late 14th century message of the Ecumenical Patriarch to the Grand Duke of Moscow:

> It is inconceivable for a Christian to have a church and not have a Tsar; for the state and the church are closely united and it would be impossible to separate them one from another.[5]

In the multinational Byzantine empire, the imperial church not only served as the chief agency of supranational integration and socialization, but it also employed ecclesiastical sanctions (including excommunication and anathema) against those challenging the integrity of the Empire or legitimacy of the ruler, just as the latter employed imperial authority to prevent the emergence of separate national churches

183

threatening to diminish the power of the imperial church within the borders of the state.[6]

Within the USSR, only the Russian Orthodox church fits the traditional pattern of an 'imperial church', with obvious qualifications arising from the atheist orientation of the Soviet state. At the same time, it remains the historical national church of the Russian people and an heir to two not entirely reconcilable traditions of Russian history of church-state relations. One of these was the doctrine of Moscow — the Third Rome, developed by Russian churchmen after the unilateral declaration of autocephaly (ecclesiastical independence) by the Muscovite Church in 1448, separating it from the Patriarchate of Constantinople. This doctrine invested both the Muscovite state and the church with the providential mission of uniting the whole of Christendom around Moscow — the Third Rome — 'the last universal earthly kingdom preceding the coming of the heavenly kingdom'[7] — a theocratic formula for rationalizing political and ecclesiastical expansion of Moscow. As noted by Berdyaev,

> under the symbolic messianic idea of Moscow as the Third Rome there took place an acute nationalizing of the Church. Religion and nationality in the Muscovite kingdom grew up together ... But the religious idea of the kingdom took shape in the formation of a powerful state in which the Church was to play a subservient part.[8]

The second element in the historical legacy of the Russian Church which superceded but did not entirely eliminate the messianic formula of the Third Rome, was the 'Erastian' pattern of state-dominated church,[9] transplanted to Russia from Protestant countries of North-Western Europe by Peter the Great.

The expansion of the Russian Orthodox Church paralleled the expansion of the Russian rule over the neighbouring East Slavic peoples: the gradual absorption of the Left-Bank Ukraine into the Russian Empire after the Treaty of Pereiaslav 1654 brought about the annexation of the Kievan Orthodox metropoly in 1685.[10] What follows was the eventual reduction of the Ukrainian Church to a number of provincial eparchies directly dependent on the Holy Synod in St Petersburg, and Russification of its hierarchy, rites and language; a similar fate awaited the remaining Orthodox eparchies of the Right-Bank Ukraine and Belorussia after the partitions of Poland.[11] In 1839 the Uniate Church of Belorussia and Right-Bank Ukraine was forced into so-called 'reunion' with the Russian Orthodox Church,[12] surviving

Institutional Religion and Nationality in the Soviet Union

henceforth only under Austrian and Hungarian rule in Galicia and Transcarpathia. Earlier, the annexation of Bessarabia opened the way for the assimilation of the Moldavian Church into the imperial ecclesiastical structure.

After its initial confrontation with the Soviet regime, the Russian Orthodox Church eventually resumed some of its pre-revolutionary functions of imperial integration with regard to the Ukrainians, Belorussians, Moldavians and some smaller non-Slavic nationalities which had been converted to Orthodox Christianity. Characteristically, even while it was being violently attacked by the new Communist regime, the Moscow Patriarchate fought bitterly against the Ukrainian autocephalist movement that since 1917 sought to de-Russify and democratize the Orthodox Church in the Ukraine and make it independent from Moscow;[13] this struggle continued throughout the 1920s until Stalin's regime intervened to destroy the Ukrainian Autocephalous Church under charges of 'bourgeois nationalism' and 'counter-revolution'.[14] When the Ukrainian Autocephalous Church re-emerged during the war-time German occupation of the Ukraine, the Moscow Patriarchate joined with Stalin's regime in propaganda war against this Church and its equivalent in Belorussia, and as the Soviet armies retook the two border republics the liquidated autocephalist parishes were forced back into the Russian Church.[15]

It is significant that the historic shift in Stalin's nationalities policy from the Leninist formula to the hardly disguised reliance on Russian nationalism as the cementing force of the Soviet multinational state was by 1938 accompanied by the official 'rehabilitation' of the historical role of the Russian Orthodox Church in building the Russian centralized state.[16] Though decimated by the two decades of religious persecution, the Russian Church was entrusted, following the Nazi-Soviet partition of Poland in 1939, the welcome task of bringing under the ecclesiastical and political control of Moscow the large Orthodox dioceses in the annexed Western Ukraine and Belorussia;[17] similar extension of the Moscow Patriarchate's jurisdiction followed the 1940 annexation of the Orthodox Bessarabia and Bukovyna and of the three Baltic states with their minority Orthodox Churches.[18]

But by far the most dramatic manifestation of the new 'symphony' between the Russian Church and the Kremlin (symbolized in Stalin's and Molotov's meeting with senior Russian hierarchs in September 1943)[19] was the post-war liquidation of the Ukrainian Greek Catholic (Uniate) Church in Galicia and Transcarpathia, which was forcibly 'reunited' with the Russian Orthodox Church, with the Soviet secret policy assuming the unprecedented role of 'missionaries' for the imperial church.[20]

Epitomizing its role of integrating above all the 'younger brothers' — Ukrainians and Belorussians — with the Russian 'backbone' of the empire, the Orthodox Church is the only Union-wide multinational institution in the Soviet Union that has retained its pre-revolutionary name ('Russian') as well as its 'monarchic' (Patriachal) centralised structure; only the ancient Georgian Orthodox Church, thanks to Stalin's refusal to 'reunite' it with the Moscow Patriarchate, has escaped the embrace of its ecclesiastic 'big brother', after it had reclaimed its autocephaly in 1917.[21] In its limited sphere, the Russian Orthodox Church symbolically represents what the Soviet leaders apparently conceive to be the essence of the 'new historical entity' — the 'Soviet People' — the 'merger' of the Ukrainians and Belorussians with the Russians into a 'new Rus'. On this kind of 'merger', there is, it seems, a fundamental agreement between the Patriarchate and the Kremlin and a broad concensus linking the regime and most Russians within and outside the USSR.

National Churches

National churches represent a unique symbiosis of religious and national identities which sustain and reinforce each other. A national church claims as its faithful members of the given nationality, usually excluding — unlike an imperial church — other nationalities. This religious-ethnic symbiosis expresses itself institutionally in terms of an independent or autonomous ecclesiastical structure based in the nation's territorial homeland and integrating members of that nationality at home and in dispersion. The latter function acquires additional dimensions and special significance for a subject nationality of the empire that has lost its independence or is aspiring to its own nation-state. In the absence of other autonomous ethnic structures, a national church becomes a haven for national traditions and culture; it legitimizes the struggle for their preservation and, at least implicitly, for the national liberation, and assumes the role of a spokesman for the 'geniune' national interest. Accordingly, both the imperial government and imperial church strive at breaking that religio-ethnic symbiosis by a variety of means ranging from 'conversion' or at least 'co-optation' of the ecclesiastical elite to severe restrictions or even outlawing of the national church's activities.

Within the USSR, the 'model' of a national church can presently be exemplified by the ancient Armenian-Gregorian Church which unifies Armenians within and outside the USSR, the Georgian Orthodox Church, the Lithuanian Roman Catholic Church, and the Ukrainian Greek Catholic (Uniate) Church. The latter two churches may also be included under another category of founded[22] transnational religions (Catholicism), but given the intimate interdependence of religion/rite and nationality in Lithuania and the Western Ukraine, they have to be classified as 'national' Churches. Both churches have become associated with Lithuanian and Ukrainian nationalism respectively and have been treated as such by the Soviet regime.

Implicitly recognised by the regime as a 'national' institution, the Armenian Gregorian Church has many more adherents in the Armenian diaspora abroad than within the USSR.[23] Its head, the 'Catholicos of All Armenians' has indeed been encouraged by the Soviet authorities to maintain extensive external relations and to compete with the Lebanon-based Catholicos of Cilicia for not just ecclesiastical but also political loyalties of the Armenians abroad.[24] While its loyal leadership has enjoyed material benefits and other privileges reserved for the top Soviet elite, the Armenian Church in the USSR has been under close control of the state authorities and its domestic domain (monasteries, seminaries and churches) has been reduced to a mere shadow of its pre-revolutionary strength.[25] Given the geographical location of Armenia and depth of Armenian-Turkish hostility, Armenian religious nationalism has not apparently been perceived by the Kremlin as a significant threat to its rule over Transcaucasia.

In contrast, the Georgian Orthodox Church still retains a living memory of oppression by the Russian empire and the imperial church. Dating as the established church of Georgia since the first half of the fourth century, the Georgian Orthodox Church was forcibly absorbed into the Russian Church in 1811, ten years after the annexation of Georgia.[26] In place of the Catholicos, St Petersburg appointed Exarchs, all but the first of whom were Russians, and introduced the completely alien Church Slavonic language. It was only after the 1917 Revolution that the remaining Georgian bishops declared the restoration of the Georgian autocephaly, which the Moscow Patriarchate refused to recognise until it was apparently 'persuaded' to do so by Stalin in the fall of 1943.[27] Only a small fraction of the Georgian monasteries and churches survived Stalinist rule and Khrushchev's anti-religious campaign of 1959-64. By 1972, about 60 (of the 2,455 churches before 1917) were still active in the Republic, with stories of vandalism, desecration, and looting of the national church treasures by corrupt Party and church leaders surfacing in *samizdat* during the last decade.[28] Religious and national sentiments in Georgia have taken a stronger anti-Russian direction than in Armenia. Lacking, unlike the latter, a massive and prosperous foreign constituency, the Georgian Church has been more vulnerable to Soviet pressures, but since the 1970s it has received strong support from the ranks of Georgian intellectuals and even from some officials.[29]

The Lithuanian Roman Catholic Church, having come under Soviet rule during World War II has not experienced, as had the Georgian and Armenian Churches, the antireligious terror of 1929-1938. While its symbiotic relationship to Lithuanian national consciousness does not date back more than two hundred years (beyond the partitions of Poland in the late eighteenth century)[30] the inter-war period of independence of Lithuania has completed the process of religio-ethnic consolidation. After the Soviet destruction of independent Lithuanian statehood, the Church has remained the only ethnic Lithuanian institution in the USSR, speaking for the national interest not only in relation to the Soviet regime, but to the Vatican as well. It suffered Soviet repressions for its refusal to condemn the nationalist resistance movement after the war.[31] The early Soviet attempts to bring about the Lithuanian Church's separation from Rome have failed despite massive use of force against the hierarchy and the clergy.[32] The Church's continued canonical subordination to the Pope has frustrated so far Soviet attempts to penetrate the hierarchical core of Lithuanian Catholicism, while religious-ethnic solidarity of Lithuanians made it possible to compensate for the Soviet banning of Catholic monastic, educational and publishing institutions, by an 'underground' ecclesiastical substructure operating in the shadow of the legal Church. The underground *Chronicle of the Catholic Church in Lithuania*, a 'mainstream' *samizdat* periodical in Lithuania which has been appearing since 1972, epitomizes the close inter-dependence of religion and nationalism in Lithuania and the continuing nation-integrating (and, conversely, empire-disintegrating) role performed by the Lithuanian Catholic Church.[33]

The Ukrainian Greek Catholic (Uniate) Church in Galicia (and, to a somewhat smaller degree in Transcarpathia[34]) represents a similar symbiotic relationship between religion (as well as distinct religious rite) and ethnicity, which was completed by the end of the last century in those parts of the Ukraine which until recent times have never been part of the Russian empire.[35] Dating since the end of the 16th century, the once common Ukrainian-Belorussian ('Ruthenian') Uniate Church within the Polish-Lithuanian kingdom was wiped out in Belorussia and in most of the Ukraine after the partitions of Poland, as a result of joint action by the imperial government and the Russian Orthodox Church.[36] The Union's survival in Austrian-annexed Galicia was of decisive importance for the nation-building process in this part of the Ukraine; the Church — now given equal rights with the Roman Catholic Church of the politically and economically dominant Polish minority in Eastern Galicia — initially provided the central structure, leadership, and resources for the national movement, which by the beginning of the 20th century assumed a mass character with clearly irredentist objectives and modernizing secular leadership.[37] The dramatic contrast between the attitude taken by the once national Orthodox Church towards the Ukrainian Revolution and statehood after 1917, and that shown by the Greek Catholic Church to the short-lived Western Ukrainian Republic illustrate the nation-destroying and nation-building capabilities of institutional religion. In the now solidly Orthodox Eastern Ukraine, not a single local bishop could be found in 1917-19 to supply leadership and legitimacy to the movement for the Ukrainianization and canonical emancipation (autocephaly) of the Ukrainian Church.[38] The hierarchy of the Orthodox Church openly sided with the Russian Whites in combating Ukrainian 'separatism', preaching the inseparability of Orthodoxy and integrity of Russia and depicting the Ukrainian autocephalist movement as strictly political, un-Orthodox adventurism and anticlericalist fringe elements preparing the ground for Union.[39]

In contrast, the Ukrainian Greek Catholic Church in Galicia supplied spiritual and organisational support to the Ukrainian statehood proclaimed in 1918, and ensured solidarity of the Galician Ukrainians in their defence of the West Ukrainian Republic against invasion by the reborn Roman Catholic Poland.[40] After the Polish victory, the Uniate Church provided the backbone to the Ukrainian national movement under the inter-war Polish rule. For more than forty years (1901-44), the Church's primate, Metropolitan Sheptyskyi served not only as the spiritual patron and chief moral arbiter for Galician Ukrainians, but also as the most widely recognised spokesman for their national interests.[41] It was therefore not accidental that having failed to force the Church into condemning Ukrainian nationalist resistance after the Soviet re-occupation of Galicia in 1944, the Kremlin proceeded in 1945-46 to suppress this national Church by imprisoning and exiling its entire hierarchy and several hundred clergymen who refused to join the Russian Orthodox Church.[42] The intensity

Bohdan R. Bociurkiw

of the intertwined religious and national consciousness among Ukrainians of Galicia proved to be stronger and more durable than expected by the Soviet authorities; not only has the Uniate Church survived nearly a decade of Stalinist persecution but, in the post-Stalin era, it managed to rebuild, in conditions of illegality and constant harassment, its organisation and hierarchy in Western Ukraine.[43] Even the forcibly 'converted' clergy have overwhelmingly remained loyal at heart to the Union, while the rank-and-file believers refused to accept Russian or Russified parish clergy, which helped to retain — in contrast to Eastern Ukraine — a continuing Ukrainian character of the nominally Russian Orthodox dioceses in Galicia.[44] As will be shown later, the post-Stalin *détente* between the Vatican and Moscow evoked considerable bitterness among the West Ukrainian Uniates, leading a fraction of them to break away from the Catholic Church and form an eschatological Penitent (*pokutnyky*) sect.

The Armenian, Georgian, Lithuanian and Ukrainian Greek Catholic churches exemplify variations in the roles and status of 'national churches' within the USSR. They are not the only 'national churches' in the country. One must mention in particular the Lutheran Churches of Latvia and Estonia which, for a variety of reasons (particularly their German origin and their traditional deference towards political authority) have not displayed as close an inter-relationship between religion and ethnicity as the four churches discussed above.[45] On the other hand, Lutheranism among the exiled Germans in the Asiatic part of the USSR has been very much a rallying point for ethno-cultural maintenance.[46]

Roman Catholicism in Latvia represents a 'mixed' pattern: not a national church, it is nevertheless firmly rooted in history[47] and clearly differentiates Latvians from Russians. On the other hand it is more illustrative (than Lithuanian or Uniate churches) of Catholicism as a transnational religion. Not accidentally, the Riga See and seminary serve as a focal point for Soviet Catholics *in partibus* (Poles, Germans, etc.)[48]

Traditional Native Sects

Several religious groups in the USSR may be categorised as traditional native sects[49] sharing such characteristics as direct or indirect origin in seventeenth-century protest against perceived 'innovations' in Muscovy's Orthodox ritual (Old Believers) or in rejection of the 'sacramental and hierarchical organisation'[50] of the state church ('spiritual

Christians'); close association with Russian ethnicity; non-proselytism and self-isolation combined in many instances with a communal way of life; and traditional distrust of the state authority. These features have caused great difficulties in these groups' adaptation to Soviet political, economic and social conditions and have contributed to the rapid decline of 'traditional native sects' with their 'descendants' either joining the pietistic currents within Russian Orthodoxy or moving further away from it into 'modern cosmopolitan sects' of Western origins.[51]

The doctrinally and organisationally divided Old Believers overlap the categories of 'national churches' and 'traditional native sects'. The 'Co-Believers' (*edinovertsy*) among them actually recognise the authority of the Moscow Patriarchate,[52] and the 'Priestly' (*popovtsy*) majority of the Old Believers — the Belo-Krinitsa hierarchy[53] and the 'Fugitive-Priest' (*beglopopovtsy*) branch[54] — can now well be classified as independent Russian churches. It is the 'Priestless' (*bezpopovtsy*) groups ranging from the recognised and institutionalised Pomorskoe and Fedoseev 'concords' to the officially persecuted, apocalyptic currents of ascetic 'Avoiders' (*stranniki*)[55] — that clearly fall into the 'native sects' category, with some of them (the 'Fugitives', 'Hermits', and 'Concealers') becoming indistinguishable from remnants of the catacomb 'True Orthodox Christians'.[56]

More typical of 'traditional native sects' in the USSR are the rapidly declining 'Spiritual Christians', represented by the nearly extinct 'Castrators' (*skoptsy*)[57] and 'Christ-Believers' (*Khrystovery*) or 'Flagellanti' (*khlysty*).[58] The latter's nineteenth-century offshoots — the Old and New Israel sects, and the better known Dukhobors ('Spirit-Wrestlers')[59] and Molokans ('Milk-Drinkers')[60] — who, too, emerged from *khlysty* (in the 18th century) — have been once favoured by Lenin's regime on account of their communal agricultural way of life and pacifism.[61] Stalin's collectivisation and antireligious terror of the 1930's have decimated these communal sects which now survive largely as Russian ethnic islands in the countryside of Transcaucasia.[62] Similarly, the Old Believers have best survived (and have experienced least antireligious pressure) in non-Russian borderlands of the USSR (e.g. the Baltic republics, the Ukraine, Belorussia, Moldavia and the Caucasus)[63] where their isolationism, non-proselytism, and communal ways have helped maintain their Russian ethnic identity.

Transnational Communities

Islam in the Soviet Union represents a transnational religious community that without destroying, disrupting or impeding the ethnic loyalties of the Turkic and Iranic-speaking peoples, integrates them in the *Ummah*. It sharply differentiates them from the dominant Russians and other European nationalities while linking them with the Islamic nations outside the USSR. The Soviet regime attempted to break up a pan-Islamic and pan-Turkic consciousness through the formation of several union republics and a number of autonomous republics, oblasts and districts.[64] However, the Soviet promotion of nation-building processes within their boundaries have failed to substitute new 'Soviet' national identities and loyalties for the traditional Muslim values and norms that — as in today's Afghanistan — once inspired a prolonged Basmachi resistance to Soviet Russian rule in Central Asia.[65] In fact this *divide et impera* policy, along with far-reaching destruction of institutional Islam, has contributed to a potent synthesis of those elements of Islam which were not seriously affected by modernisation with the emergent ethnic consciousness of the Turkic and Iranic-speaking peoples. Thus the religious and the secular components of the new 'socialist nations' were inseparably linked in the historically Islamic areas of the USSR in an overarching, self-designation *musulmanin* (Muslim).[66] The simultaneous processes of a demographic explosion in the Turkic and Iranic-speaking areas of the Soviet Union and of a dramatic rise in strategic, economic, and political importance of the Islamic nations of the Third World — have combined to imbue Soviet Muslims with an optimistic assessment of their future.[67]

Four Spiritual Administrations were established with the Soviet government's approval after World War II to direct official Muslim activities in Central Asia and Kazakhstan, European Russia and Siberia, Azerbaijan, and North Caucasus respectively.[68] Closely controlled by the regime, they have been relied upon to confine the religious fervour of the believers within the narrow limits prescribed by Soviet laws. At the same time, together with other officially recognised religious centres in the USSR, the Muftiates have been employed by the Kremlin for external propaganda activities among their co-believers abroad in support of Soviet foreign policy objectives. The Spiritual Administrations led by the chief Mufti for Central Asia and Kazakhstan have been particularly instrumental in rationalising away in theological terms (through *fetwa* rulings) Soviet restrictions on Muslim religious practices, as well as many contradictions between Islam and Soviet norms and policies. While helping to adapt the Muslim doctrine and practices to Soviet conditions, they thus facilitated the survival of modernised Islamic values.[69] The Muslim establishment has not been

Institutional Religion and Nationality in the Soviet Union

able, however, to cope with tradition-bound 'unofficial Islam' and has been facing a growing challenge from the secret, fundamentalist *Sufi* orders condemning both the Soviet Russian policies towards Islam and charging the Muftiates with a betrayal of the basic tenets of the faith. The Soviet invasion of Afghanistan and the continuing resistance of the Muslim guerrillas has put to the test the political loyalty of the Muftiates as well as their credibility with the believers and deepened the tension between the official Islamic leaders and their fundamentalist opponents.

Ethno-Religious Diaspora

The principal example of an ethno-religious diaspora in the USSR is supplied by Soviet Jewry.[70] Once religiously defined, Jewish ethnicity has survived in conditions of territorial dispersal and a high degree of social mobilisation partly through the adoption of a secularised notion of Jewish nationality, partly due to the reluctance of the dominant nationality to absorb assimilated Jews, and partly as a result of Soviet policy (including passportisation) which made it almost impossible to change one's nationality.[71] Only among the Oriental Jewish communities in Central Asia and the Caucasus, and among the Holocaust survivors in the Western areas annexed by the USSR since the last war, had Judaism remained a viable factor in shaping Jewish national consciousness.[72]

In aggregate terms, Soviet Jewry displays the highest level of modernisation among Soviet nationalities and — not surprisingly for Soviet conditions — the lowest indicators of religiosity.[73] The establishment of the State of Israel had a profound impact on the perception of their own nationality among the Soviet Jews, especially after the Six-Day-War in 1967, just as the same developments have significantly affected Soviet policies towards the Jews.[74] The resurgence of Jewish national consciousness during and after World War II has had little impact on the remnants of institutional Judaism in the USSR, despite the fact that since the late 1940's the synagogues have remained the only ethnic Jewish institutions in the USSR. Repeated attempts by resurdent Council of Churches of Evangelical Christians Baptists, which has a make synagogues rallying points for the manifestation of their Jewishness on major Judaic holy days, have not translated themselves into a Judaic religious revival.[75] Ironically, a number of assimilated Jewish intellectual dissidents converted to Russian Orthodoxy, and a few to

Bohdan R. Bociurkiw

Catholicism — in itself a reflection on the condition of institutional Judaism in the USSR. The rising anti-Semitic tone of Soviet anti-Zionist and anti-Judaic propaganda has very likely contributed more to the mass emigration movement among the Soviet Jews, than any religious sentiments on their part.

Modern Cosmopolitan Sects

In contrast to the rapidly declining old Russian sects, modern (Western-origin) sects — with their egalitarian and activist orientation, strict and unambiguous doctrinal and moral norms, and conversionist orientation uninhibited by Soviet legal restrictions or ethno-cultural barriers — have been the most rapidly growing religious communities in the Soviet Union. These sects — particularly the Evangelical Christian-Baptists, the Pentecostals, and the Seventh Day Adventists — have in many ways been unintended beneficiaries of Soviet nationality and religious policies aimed at the breakdown of traditional linkages between nationality and religion and the penetration and corruption of the traditional church hierarchies.

In the Ukraine, where, reportedly, about one half of all the sectarian congregations are located,[76] the latter have been spreading particularly in the more industrialised, urbanised areas, where Khrushchev's anti-religious campaign has closed down the great majority of Orthodox churches. The sectarians' reliance on Russian as a *lingua franca* and their indifference to the Ukrainian (or, in Belorussia, Belorussian) language and ethno-cultural values may have been generated as much by Evangelical 'cosmopolitanism' and practical missionary considerations, as by the effects of Soviet political socialisation. Only within the dissident Council of Churches of Evangelical Christian Baptists, which was a strong following in the Ukraine, have concessions been made in the 1970s to the Ukrainian language in the Council's *samizdat* publications.[77]

Characteristically, Soviet policies have aimed at the maximum possible centralisation and institutionalisation of sectarianism in order to maximize state control over the 'servants of cult'. The internal tensions between the 'co-opted' leaders of the official All-Union Council of the Evangelical Christian-Baptists and the fundamentalist elements of the group erupted into a schism in the early 1960s, when the Khrushchev regime proceeded to use the former to enforce restrictions on Baptist conversionist activities.[78] The secessionist Council of

Churches of the Evangelical Christian-Baptists has been denied governmental 'registration' and has been subject to repeated waves of persecution, with some 180 dissident Baptists currently imprisoned in the USSR.[79]

Among the most persecuted sectarian groups in the USSR have been the Jehovah's Witnesses. For historical reasons, the core of this group has come from the Western Ukraine and the Ukrainian language has been widely used in its clandestine operations and publications.[80] This, combined with their uncompromising hostility to the Soviet regime has led to Soviet charges that the Jehovah's Witnesses had offered a haven for Ukrainian nationalists (apart from serving 'American spymasters').[81] Ukrainian *samizdat* sources, however, have depicted *iehovisty* as a group absolutely alien to Ukrainian national aspirations and, by virtue of its linguistic appeal, more destructive of Ukrainian national loyalties than other sectarian groups.[82]

Nationalist Religious Cults

A sharp contrast to the Jehovah's Witnesses is presented by another West Ukraine-based illegal religious group — the Penitents (*pokutnyky*). In terms of their doctrinal peculiarities, religious practices, and the nature of their organisation (or, more correctly, the paucity of structural features) they have to be classified as a nationalist religious cult. Dating since 1954, the Penitents first emerged on the fringe of the outlawed Ukrainian Greek Catholic Church as a local apocalyptic Marian cult in Subcarpathia.[83] It centred around an alleged Fatima-like apparition of the Virgin Mary witnessed by a woman who has since become the 'medium' for transmission of 'Marian' prophecies, warnings and messages to cult followers. They were interpreted, expanded upon and combined with select elements of Catholic doctrine, Uniate tradition, and Ukrainian nationalism into a Penitent theology of alienation and salvation that could be summarised in the following terms: The Soviet regime which has destroyed Ukrainian 'faith ... nation, the people, the country and humanity'[84] is but the fulfillment of apocalyptic prophecy about Satan taking over the world before the end of the world and the Last Judgement. Since 1958, after the death of the last true Pope, Pius XII, Satan has captured Rome and the centre of true Catholicism has moved to the long suffering Ukraine, where the last battle is being waged between Satan and God.[85] As instructed by messages from the Virgin Mary, a true Catholic Christian must completely repudiate the Satanic Soviet system, refuse Soviet passports, services, schools, and reject participation in Soviet elections, work for Soviet institutions, and service in the Red Army.[86] Against the 'false popes' in Rome (from Roncalli to Wojtyla) a true successor to Pius XII has been selected by God in Western Ukraine in the person of the cult's founder and charismatic leader, priest Ihnat Soltys (who assumed the name of the 'last pope' Peter II and, later, Emmanuel).[87] He was subsequently declared a reincarnation of returning Christ.[88] At the imminent end of the world, only Penitents are to be saved. For the cult members special Penitent rituals, in particular its *deviatnytsia* (nine days of penitence), have been devised and different levels of devotion and subordination to the Penitent 'pope' have been prescribed.[89]

While breaking away from Rome in 1958, the Penitents have also repudiated the underground Uniate Church for allegedly 'making peace' with the Communist regime, and thus 'betraying' its people and faith.[90]

The Soviet authorities who may have initially favoured a split in the Uniate ranks, soon turned against the Penitent movement that has been attracting large numbers of pilgrims to the 'Holy Mountain' near the Subcarpathian village of Serednie (the site of the reported Marian apparition) and spreading its message through chain letters and wandering Penitent proselytisers. The leaders of the cult have been repeatedly arrested and sentenced to increasing terms of imprisonment and exile, the Penitent parents have been deprived of their parental rights, and rank-and-file *pokutnyky* have been continuously harassed by the police for their alleged 'parasitic way of life'.[91] Despite their nationalist rhetoric, the Penitents have found little sympathy among the vast majority of Ukrainian Uniates, becoming more of an embarrassment than a threat to the underground Church.

A distant analogy to the Penitent cult can be found in the 'True Orthodox Christians' in Russia, who also totally reject both the 'Satanic' Soviet regime and the official Moscow Patriarchate which, they believe, has lost divine grace, having 'sold itself out' to the regime when Metropolitan Sergii made his compromise with the Kremlin in 1927.[92] Traditionally nationalist and monarchist, this remnant of what was once the Russian Catacomb Church (led by bishops who refused to accept Sergii's 1927 Declaration) has also been severely persecuted by the authorities.[93]

Conclusion

The proposed typology of religious groups in terms of their patterns of relationship between religion and nationality and between the given religious group and the Soviet state needs yet to be refined and extended to apply to some smaller religious groups in the USSR.[94] Yet even at this preliminary stage, I believe it should help to clarify the important links between religions and churches, on the one hand, and the processes of empire-building (imperial integration) and national persistency, on the other hand.

Soviet religious policy and antireligious propaganda have long displayed acute awareness of the mutually supportive and protective roles performed by national and religious sentiments and have early identified this overlap of ethnic and religious loyalties as the main obstacle to Soviet political socialization in national republics and an opening for anti-Soviet diversions from emigré 'bourgeois nationalists' and Western propaganda agencies. This symbiotic relationship of religion and nationality has become a special target for Soviet 'internationalist, patriotic indoctrination'.[95]

The highly selective treatment of this problem by Soviet mass media can be illustrated with the data supplied in a recent study of atheist indoctrination in seven oblasts of the Western Ukraine.[96] The survey shows that only 13.3% of the anti-religious articles published in the seven oblast Ukrainian newspapers from 1971 to 1979 were directed against Orthodoxy (claiming the overwhelming majority of all religious congregations in these regions). Significantly, the majority of these articles attacked the national church which officially has been long suppressed — the Ukrainian Autocephalous Orthodox Church (nearly 30% of articles in the Volyn oblast newspaper and over 20% in the Rovno oblast organ); only a few articles were addressed to the Russian Orthodox Church, but only to its 'reactionary' activities before 1917.[97] The main target of Soviet anti-religious press campaigns has been the officially 'non-existent' Ukrainian Greek Catholic Church to which has been devoted 23.7% of all articles (including over 47% of all atheist articles in the Lviv daily, over 31% in Ivano-Frankivsk, 25.5% in Ternopil, and 23.3% in Transcarpathia); between 1957 and 1977, the Ivano-Frankivsk *Prykarpatska pravda* alone published 200 anti-Uniate and anti-Catholic articles.[98] The other targets of the seven newspapers were, in the order of newspaper space devoted to them, Jehovah's Witnesses (14%), Baptists (8.4%), Judaism (7.2%), Pentecostals (3%) and Adventists (3%). In Volyn, the local oblast daily aimed over 32% of its antireligious articles against Baptists; in Transcarpathia, the oblast daily devoted one-third of all material to attacks against Jehovah's Witnesses; while in Bukovyna the local daily directed almost 18% of its antireligious materials against Judaism.[99]

This striking partisanship of the Party's antireligious propaganda underlines once more the appreciation by the Soviet authorities of the integrating, 'patriotic' role performed by the imperial church in the non-Russian parts of the USSR and, conversely, demonstrates their special hostility to the 'disintegrative' 'bourgeois nationalist' national churches, 'disloyal' 'cosmopolitan' sects and nationalist cults. The sharpening of East-West ideological tensions over the last years, the developments in Poland, the activities of the Polish Pope, and the nature of the resistance encountered by the Soviets in Afghanistan — have all sharpened the attention of the Kremlin leaders to the deeper domestic and external political implications of religion and nationalism in the USSR.[100]

Within the 'imperial' Church, dissident voices have been penetrating the facade of harmony between the Moscow Patriarchate and the regime, accusing the loyal Church leaders of cowardice, materialism and betrayal of their spiritual and patriotic duty by silently complying with the arbitrary orders of state officials seeking to further undermine the Church's influence and credibility in society. Initially slow and relatively mild Soviet reaction against Russian Orthodox dissidents has escalated into arrests and trials, as some of them, led by Fr. Gleb Iakunin and his Christian Committee for the Defence of Believers' Rights, have assumed a more nationalist position, gravitating towards the monarchist Russian émigré Church and attacking from national and religious positions the unholy alliance of the Patriarchate and the atheist regime.[101] It is significant and perhaps indicative of the post-Brezhnev policy trends that the KGB has assumed sponsorship of a fringe group of the 're-educated' Orthodox dissidents (Shimanov, Karelin et al.) now preaching a kind of Orthodox National Bolshevism, with a tinge of antisemitism, obviously aiming its appeal at the chauvinist elements among the believers.[102]

To conclude, the confluence of religion and ethnicity is likely to remain a major obstacle to the Soviet strategies of denationalization and secularisation at the time when the regime has entered into a crisis, not only of social-economic nature, but also one of legitimacy that touches upon the fundamental assumptions underlying its religious and nationalities policies. It is doubtful whether this multiple crisis can be resolved by the further escalation of coercive measures. Whatever

Institutional Religion and Nationality in the Soviet Union

solutions will be offered by the new generation of Soviet leaders after the transitional Chernenko phase, they will have to address themselves to the inter-related problems of religion and ethnicity that have not been made irrelevant by modernization — as once expected by the founders of the Soviet system.

Notes

1. Among the few Western scholarly studies of the problem are Walter Kolarz's important *Religion in the Soviet Union* (London, 1961); David M. Lang, 'Religion and Nationalism; A Case Study: The Caucasus', in Max Hayward and William C. Fletcher (eds.), *Religion and the Soviet State: Dilemma of Power* (New York, 1969), pp. 169-186; this writer's 'Religion and Nationalism in the Contemporary Ukraine', in George W. Simmonds (ed.), *Nationalism in the USSR and Eastern Europe in the Era of Brezhnev and Kosygin* (Detroit, 1977), pp. 81-93; Vahakn N. Dadrian, 'Nationality in Soviet Armenia — A Case Study of Ethnocentrism', *ibid.*, pp. 202-258; Christopher Doersam, 'Sovietization, Culture, and Religion', in Edward Allworth (ed.), *Nationality Group Survival in Multi-Ethnic States: Shifting Support Patterns in the Soviet Baltic Region* (New York, 1977), pp. 148-193; Christel Lane, *Christian Religion in the Soviet Union* (London, 1978), Chs. 9, 10; Stanley Vardys, *The Catholic Church, Dissent and Nationality in Soviet Lithuania* (New York, 1978); Marite Sapiets, 'Religion and Nationalism in Lithuania', *Religion in Communist Lands*, VII, 2 (Summer 1979), pp. 76-85 and Hélène Carrère d'Encausse, *Decline of an Empire: The Soviet Socialist Republics in Revolt* (New York, 1981), Ch. VII: 'Religion and National Sentiment', pp. 219-248. Proportionately, the largest number of recent publications on the interrelationship between religion and nationality focused on Islam and the Turkic and Iranic-speaking nationalities of the USSR; see, in particular, Alexander Bennigsen and C. Lemercier-Quelquejay, *Islam in the Soviet Union* (London, 1967); Geoffrey Wheeler, 'National and Religious Consciousness of Soviet Islam', in Hayward and Fletcher, *op. cit.*, pp. 187-198; and Azade-Ayse Rorlich, 'Notes on the Dynamics of Religion and National Identity in Central Asia,' in Davie Nalle (ed.), *Conference on the Study of Central Asia, March 10-11, 1983* (Washington, D.C.: The Wilson Center, 1983, pp. 29-38.

2. See Volume 22 of *Voprosy nauchnogo ateizma* (cited subsequently as *VNA*) (Moscow, 1978) published semi-annually by the Party's Institute of Scientific Atheism, in particular A.T. Veshchikov, 'Ed instvo internatsionalisticheskogo i ateisticheskogo vospitaniia' (pp. 178-189), and M.I. Ivanesko and V.E. Leshan, 'Vzaemosviaz patrioticheskogo i ateisticheskogo vospitaniia' (pp. 190-198); as well as A.V. Shuba, 'Leninskie printsipy kritiki soiuza religii i natsionalizma,' *Voprosy ateizma* (Kiev), Vol. 16 (1980), pp. 122-129, M.G. Mustafaeva, 'Mezhnatsionalnoe obshchenie, internatsionalisticheskoe i ateisticheskoe vospitanie,' *VNA*, Vol. 26 (1980), pp. 51-66, and V.I. Titov, 'O vzaemosviazi patrioticheskogo i ateisticheskogo vospitaniia,' *ibid.*, Vol. 29 (1982), pp. 126-137. Recently, the Party convened an all-Union Scientific-Practical Conference on 'Development of National Relations in Conditions of Mature Socialism: The Experience and Problems of Patriotic and Internationalist Upbringing' (Riga, June 28-30, 1982). Selected materials of the Conference's Section XI (which focused on domestic 'counter-propaganda') were published in a separate volume entitled *Neprimirimost k burzhuaznoi ideologii, perezhitkam natsionalizma* (Moscow,

1982). Several papers were devoted to the struggle against religion and nationalism in non-Russian republics, in particular in the Western Ukraine, Lithuania, in Moslem republics, and among the Soviet Jewry; see, in particular, L.M. Kravchuk, 'Ateisticheskoe vospitanie trudiashchikhsia i zadachi kontrpropagandy' (pp. 35-50), and M.A. Goldenberg, 'Nasionalizm i religiia v planakh sovremennogo klerikalnogo antikommunizma' (pp. 153-162).

3. Note a 1964 Soviet Russian decree 'On the Inculcation of New Civil Rites into the Life of Soviet Citizens,' in *Sobranie postanovlenii Soveta Ministrov RSFSR*, No. 3, 1964, pp. 41-45; analogous decrees have been adopted in the Ukrainian SSR and other republics. See P. Kampars and P.P. Zakovich, *Sovetskaia grazhdanskaia obriadnost* (Moscow, 1967), and V.G. Sinitsyn, *Nashi prazdniki (sovetskie obshchegosudarstvennye, trudovye, moldezhnye i semeino-bytovye prazdniki, obriady, rituaty)* (Moscow, 1977). Cf. Christel Lane, *The Rites of Rulers* (Cambridge U.P., 1981).

4. See, in particular, *VNA*, Vol. 18 (1975), on the general theme of 'Atheism and Religion in the Contemporary Ideological Struggle,' which attacks Roman Catholics (esp. in Lithuania), Ukrainian Catholics, Judaism, and Islam, but spares the largest religious group — the Russian Orthodox Church. Of special interest is a topical volume 20 of *VNA* (1976) on 'Timely Problems of the History of Atheism and Religion,' especially articles by Ia. N. Shchapov and A.M. Sakharov seeking to minimize the role of the Orthodox Church in Kievan Rus and the rise of a centralized Russian state. Cf. A.V. Shuba, 'Modernizasiia pravoslavno-bogoslovskoi interpretatsii natsionalnykh otnoshenii,' *Voprosy ateizma*, Vol. 18 (1982), pp. 113-119. Differences within the Soviet ideological establishment on the treatment of Russian Orthodox tradition and of artistic and historical monuments of the Church surfaced at the 1982 Riga Conference. See a summary of the paper by the chief editor of *Kommunist*, R.I. Kosolapov, 'Klassovye i natsionalnye otnosheniia na etape razvitogo sotsializma,' in *Sotsialnaia politika i natsialnye otnosheniia* (Moscow, 1982), containing selected materials of Section III of the Conference.

5. Cited in Paul Miliukov, *Outlines of Russian Culture*, Part I: *Religion and the Church* (Philadelphia, 1943), p. 18.

6. Note the opposition of the Patriarchate of Constantinople to the autocephaly of the Russian (15-16th c.), Hellenic (19th c.), and Bulgarian (19-20th c.) Orthodox Churches. Similarly, the Moscow Patriarchate opposed since 1917 ecclesiastical independence of the Orthodox Churches in Georgia (recognized only in 1943), Ukraine, Belorussia, and Poland. More recently, the Serbian Orthodox Church has refused to recognize the autocephaly of the Macedonian Church proclaimed in 1967.

7. William K. Medlin, *Moscow and East Rome: A Political Study of the Relations of Church and State in Muscovite Russia* (Geneva, 1952), pp. 93-95.

8. Nicholas Berdyaev, *The Origin of Russian Communism* (London, 1955), p. 10.

9. See Luigi Sturzo, *Church and State* (Note Dame, Ind., 1962), Vol. II, pp. 283-284.

10. Mykhailo Hrushevskyi, *Z istorii religiinoi dumky na Ukraini* (Lviv, 1925), pp. 84-85.

11. *Ibid.*, p. 86.

12. See Wasyl Lencyk, *The Eastern Catholic Church and Czar Nicholas I* (Rome, 1966), especially Chapters VIII and IX. The Empire's only surviving Uniate diocese of Kholm was forcibly 'reunited' with the Russian Orthodox Church in 1875.

13. See this writer's 'Ukrainization Movements within the Russian Orthodox Church, and the Ukrainian Autocephalous Orthodox Church,' in I. Sevcenko and

F.E. Sysyn (eds.), *Eucharisterion: Essays Presented on Omeljan Pritsak on His Sixtieth Birthday* (Harvard Ukrainian Studies, Vol. III/IV, 1979-80), Part I, pp. 92-111.

14. See this writer's 'The Ukrainian Autocephalous Orthodox Church, 1920-1930: A Case Study in Religious Modernization,' in Dennis J. Dunn (ed.), *Religion and Modernization in the Soviet Union* (Boulder, Colo., 1977), pp. 310-347.

15. For the Moscow Patriarchate's attacks against Archbishop Polikarp (Sikorskyi), who headed the Ukrainian Autocephalous Orthodox Church in the German-occupied Ukraine, see Moscow Patriarchate, *Russkaia Pravoslavnaia Tserkov i Velikaia Otechestvennaia voina. Sbornik tserkovnykh dokumentov* (Moscow, 1943), pp. 13-23, 66-69. Cf. this writer's 'Modernization movements,' *loc. cit.*, pp. 109-110. For a historical analysis of the unresolved nationality problem in Orthodoxy in Ukraine, see Frank E. Sysyn, 'The Ukrainian Orthodox Question in the USSR,' *RCL*, XI, No. 3 (Winter 1983), pp. 251-263.

16. See Nicholas S. Timasheff, *Religion in Soviet Russia (1917-1942)* (London, 1943), pp. 47, 112-118.

17. See Ivan Vlasovskyi, *Narys istorii Ukrainskoi Pravoslavnoi Tserkvy*, Vol. IV, Part I (South Bound Brook, N.J., 1966), pp. 193-199.

18. Ironically, at the time the Moscow Patriarchate proceeded with the Kremlin's blessings to expand its jurisdiction over several Orthodox dioceses in the newly-occupied lands with their numerous churches, seminaries, monasteries, and convents — its own organization within the 'old' Soviet borders had been reduced by Stalin's terror to four bishops (two of whom were now dispatched as 'exarchs' to the 'liberated' territories) and fewer than one hundred operating churches (cf. Nikita Struve, *Christians in Contemporary Russia*, New York, 1967, p. 57).

19. On the September 1943 meeting and the Church-state accord see William C. Fletcher, *A Study in Survival: The Church in Russia, 1927-1943* (London, 1965), pp. 112-114. For the genesis, implications, and rationalizations of the new 'symphony' between the Patriarchate and the Kremlin, see this writer's 'Church-State Relations in the USSR,' *Survey*, no. 66 (January 1968), especially pp. 16-24.

20. See this writer's 'The Uniate Church in the Soviet Ukraine: A Case Study in Soviet Church Policy,' *Canadian Slavonic Papers*, Vol. VII (1965), pp. 89-113; and Ivan Hrynioch, 'The Destruction of the Ukrainian Catholic Church in the Soviet Union,' *Prologue*, No. 1-2 (1960), pp. 5-51.

21. See Elie Melia, 'The Georgian Orthodox Church,' in Richard H. Marshall, Jr. (ed.), *Aspects of Religion in the Soviet Union, 1917-1967* (Chicago, 1971), pp. 223-237.

22. Joachim Wach's distinction which derives major world religions from identifiable founders, incl. Christianity, Buddhism, Mohammedanism, and Confucianism (*Sociology of Religion*, Chicago 1971, pp. 130-133).

23. See Dadrian, 'Nationalism in Soviet Armenia,' *op. cit.*, pp. 224-253.

24. *Ibid.*, p. 246. Cf. Mesrob K. Krikorian, 'The Armenian Church in the Soviet Union,' in Marshall, *Aspects of Religion*, pp. 253-54.

25. In the entire Armenian republic, only ninety-six parish priests, sixteen archimandrites, and six bishops were reported in 1975 by Dadrian in his 'Nationalism in Soviet Armenia,' *loc. cit.*, p. 244.

26. Kolarz, *op. cit.*, pp. 97-99.

27. *Ibid.*, pp. 103-105.

28. See Peter Reddaway, 'The Georgian Orthodox Church: Corruption and Renewal,' *RCL*, III, No. 4-5 (July-October 1975), pp. 114-23.

29. On recent protests against increasing repression of the Georgian Orthodox Church, see *RCL*, XI, No. 1 (Spring 1983), p. 78.

30. See Vardys, *op. cit.*, pp. 2-18.

31. *Ibid.*, pp. 70-72.
32. *Ibid.*, pp. 74-79.
33. See Saulius Girnius, 'The Tenth Anniversary of the Lithuanian Chronicle,' *Radio Liberty Research*, RL 160/80 (April 14, 1982), pp. 1-12.
34. Between World War I and the 1930's, the numbers of Orthodox among the Ruthenian-Ukrainian population of Transcarpathia (officially designated then in Czechoslovakia as Subcarparthian Ruthenia) rose to some 112-130,000. While both the Uniate rite and Orthodoxy distinguished the Ruthenian-Ukrainians in Czechoslovakia from Hungarians, Czechs and Slovaks, Ukrainian national consciousness has prevailed in the popular masses only in the course of this century. Cf. Paul R. Magocsi, *The Shaping of a National Identity: Subcarpathian Rus, 1848-1948* (Cambridge, Mass., 1978).
35. Including, Bukovyna.
36. See fn. 12 above.
37. John-Paul Himka, 'Priests and Peasants: The Greek Catholic Pastor and the Ukrainian National Movement in Austria, 1967-1900,' *Canadian Slavonic Papers*, XXI, No. 1 (March 1979), pp. 1-14.
38. See this writer's 'The Church and the Ukrainian Revolution: The Central *Rada* Period,' in Taras Hunchak (ed.), *The Ukraine, 1917-1921: A Study in Revolution* (Cambridge, Mass., 1977), pp. 220-246; and his 'Ukrainization Movements,' *loc. cit.*, pp. 92-96.
39. See this writer's 'The Church and the Ukrainian Revolution,' *loc. cit.*
40. See 'Documents which Refer to the Attempts to Form an Autonomous Ukrainian Orthodox Church in 1917-1918,' collected by Peter T. Sheshko and appended to Part II of his 'Russian Orthodox Church *Sobor* of Moscow and the Orthodox Church in the Ukraine (1917-1919)', *Analecta Ordinis S. Basilii Magni* (Rome), Section II, Vol. X(XI), No. 1-4 (1979), pp. 229-355. Cf. Friedrich Heyer, *Die Orthodoxe Kirche in der Ukraine von 1917 bis 1945* (Koeln-Braunsfeld, 1953), pp. 36-77.
41. See Cyrille Korolevskij, *Metropolite Andre Szeptyckyj, 1865-1944* (Rome, 1964); Ivan Hrynioch, *Sluha Bozhyi Andrei – Brahovisnyk Iednosty* (Munich 1961); and Stefan Baran, *Mytropolyt Andrei Sheptytskyi* (Munich, 1947).
42. See this writer's 'The Uniate Church,' *loc. cit.*; and *First Victims of Communism: White Book on the Religious Persecution in Ukraine* (Rome, 1953); on the suppression of the Greek Catholic Church in Transcarpathia, see Vasyl Markus, *Nyshchennia hreko-katolytskoi tserkvy v mukachivskii ieparkhii v 1945-50 rr.* (Paris 1962).
43. See Vasyl Markus, 'Religion and Nationality: The Uniates of the Ukraine,' in B.R. Bociurkiw and J.S. Strong (eds.), *Religion and Atheism in the USSR and Eastern Europe* (London, 1975), pp. 101-122; this writer's 'The Catacomb Church: Ukrainian Greek Catholics in the USSR,' *RCL*, V, No. 1 (Spring 1977), pp. 4-12; and Ivan Hvat, 'The Ukrainian Catholic Church, the Vatican and the Soviet Union during the Pontificate of Pope John Paul II,' *ibid.*, XI, No. 3 (Winter 1983), pp. 264-280.
44. See this writer's 'Religious Situation in Soviet Ukraine,' in Walter Dushnyck (ed.), *Ukraine in a Changing World* (New York, 1977), pp. 173-194.
45. Lane, *op cit.*, pp. 192-200. See also Tönu Parming, 'Nationalism in Soviet Estonia Since 1964,' in Simmonds (ed.), *op. cit.*, p. 128; significantly, the two articles on Latvian nationalism in Simmond's symposium do not even mention the Lutheran Church or religion in general. For a historical context, see Kolarz, *op. cit.*, pp. 256-270. Cf. Wilhelm Kahle, 'Baltic Protestantism,' *RCL*, VII, No. 4 (Winter 1979), pp. 220-225; and Edgar C. Duin, 'Soviet Lutheranism after the Second World War,' *ibid.*, VIII, No. 2 (Summer 1980), pp. 113-118.

46. 'Lutheraner in der Sowjetunion. Deutsche Diasporagemeinden,' *Glaube in der 2. Welt* (hereafter *G2W*), IX, No. 7-8 (1981), pp. 255-326.
47. 'Die Katholiken in der USSR,' 2 ('Lettland'), *G2W*, IX, No. 6 (1951), pp. 213-214.
48. *Ibid.*, pp. 217-219; and Part 1, *ibid.*, IX, No. 5 (1981), pp. 166-167. On the late Ukrainian Catholic Bishop Oleksander Chira of Mukachiv-Uzhhorod diocese, who had been deported to Kazakhstan where he served until his recent death, the exiled Uniate Ukrainians, as well as German and Polish Roman Catholics, see memoirs by an exiled Polish priest from Kazakhstan, Ks. Wladyslaw Bukowinski, *Wspomienia z Kazachstanu* (London, 1979). See also Juchym Wolf, 'Begegnungen mit Pfarrer Olexander Chira,' *G2W*, XI, No. 4 (1983), pp. 22-24. Catholic diaspora in Central Asia was also served for several years by another secretly ordained Ukrainian Catholic Bishop, the late Iosyf Fedoryk, when he was exiled to Kirghizia.
49. The concept of a 'sect' as used in sociological literature, can only conditionally be applied to Russian native sects, which lack as a rule voluntary, elective membership. Cf. Joachim Wach, *Sociology of Religion* (Chicago, 1971), Ch. 5; Lane, *op. cit.*, pp. 19-20; and 'O soderzhanii poniatiia religioznoe sektantstvo, v usloviiakh sotsialisticheskogo obshchestva,' *VNA*, Vol. 24 (1979), pp. 14-41.
50. Wach, *op. cit.*, p. 192.
51. Cf. Kolarz, *op cit.*, Ch. XI, A. Katunskii, *Staroobriadchestvo* (Moscow, 1972); I. Malakhova, *Dukhovnye khristiane* (Moscow, 1970); and in particular, *VNA*, Vol. 24 (1979), devoted to the theme 'Evolution of Christian sectarianism in the USSR.'
52. Kolarz, *op cit.*, pp. 147-148; Lane, *op. cit.*, p. 116.
53. The largest of the Old Believer groups, headed by Archbishop of Moscow and All Rus. See Katunskii, *op cit.*, pp. 47-48.
54. A declining group, with its own hierarchy, apparently being absorbed by the Belo-Krinitsa branch of *staroobriadtsy* (*ibid.*, pp. 48-49; cf. Lane, *op. cit.*, pp. 115-116).
55. V.F. Milovidov, *Staroobriadchestvo v proshlom i nastoiashchem* (Moscow, 1969), pp. 102-104.
56. Lane, *op cit*, pp. 116-122.
57. See Kolarz, *op. cit.*, pp. 356-358; Lane, *op. cit.*, pp. 94-95; and Malakhova, *op. cit.*, pp. 35-46.
58. Malakhova, *op. cit.*, pp. 9-34.
59. *Ibid.*, pp. 47-77; Lane, *op. cit.*, pp. 95-100.
60. *Ibid.*, pp. 100-111; Malakhova, *op. cit.*, pp. 78-123; and, especially, 'Vliianie sotsialisticheskogo obraza zhizni na ideologiiu 'dukhovnogo khristianstva',' *VNA*, Vol. 24 (1979), pp. 181-191.
61. Encouraged by V. Bonch-Bruevich, Lenin signed a special decree in January 1919 exempting sectarians from military service, and gave his blessings to the preferential treatment of communal sectarians by the People's Commissariat of Agriculture in the early 1920's designed to turn sympathetic religious dissenters into propagandists of collectivized agriculture among the peasants. See this writer's 'Lenin and Religion,' in Leonard Schapiro and Peter Reddaway (eds.), *Lenin. The Man, the Theorist, the Leader: A Reappraisal* (London, 1967), pp. 107-134.
62. Lane, *op. cit.*, pp. 107-111; see, in particular, 'Krizis khristianskogo sektantstva i osobennosti ego proiavleniia v razlichnykh regionakh strany,' *VNA*, Vol. 24 (1979), pp. 42-64.
63. Katunskii, *op. cit.*, pp. 48-50.
64. See this writer's 'The Changing Soviet Image of Islam: The Domestic

Scene,' *Journal* of the Institute of Muslim Minority Affairs (Jeddah), Vols II, 2, and III, 1 (Winter 1980-Summer 1981), pp. 9-25; and Ie.G. Filimonov *et al.* (eds.), *Islam v SSSR. Osobennosti protsesa sekuliarizatsii v respublikakh Sovetskogo Vostoka* (Moscow, 1983).

65. See *ibid.*, pp. 39-46.
66. Rorlich, *loc. cit.*, p. 34; cf. this writer's 'Changing Soviet Image of Islam,' *loc. cit.*, p. 21.
67. Carrère d'Encausse, *op. cit.*, p. 9.
68. Alexandre Bennigsen and Chantal Lemercier-Quelquejay, "'Official' Islam in the Soviet Union," *RCL*, VII, No. 3 (Autumn 1979), pp. 148-159.
69. Rorlich, *loc. cit.*, pp. 31-33.
70. With some qualifications, one may also speak of an Armenian diaspora outside the Armenian SSR, the German and the Poles diasporas, as displaying that particular interdependence of religion and ethnicity in conditions of demographic dispersal.
71. Zvi Gitelman, 'Moscow and the Soviet Jews,' *Problems of Communism*, XXIX, No. 1 (Jan-Feb 1980), pp. 18-34; Kolarz, *op. cit.*, Ch. XX; see also this writer's 'Soviet Religious Policy and the Status of Judaism in the USSR,' *Bulletin on Soviet and East European Jewish Affairs* (December 1970), pp. 13-19.
72. Joshua Rothenberg, 'The Jewish Religion in the Soviet Union since World War II,' in Marshall, *op. cit.*, pp. 352-353; cf. I. Shapiro, 'Iudaizm v SSSR,' *Nauka i religiia*, No. 9 (1980), pp. 38-39.
73. According to Shapiro (*loc. cit.*, p. 38), there are some 60,000 practising religious Jews in the USSR, which would amount to slightly over 3% of the officially reported Soviet Jewish population in 1979. Cf. Havdallah Wein, 'A Religious Minority Among Soviet Jewry,' *RCL*, VI, No. 4 (Winter 1978), pp. 244-247. Surveying post-1971 Soviet Jewish immigrants to the United States, Zvi Gitelman found only 8% of them identifying themselves as religious ('Soviet Immigrant Re-settlement in the United States,' *Soviet Jewish Affairs*, XII, No. 2, May 1982, p. 16). On the other hand, a much higher proportion of religious believers was found by Gitelman among Soviet Jewish immigrants to Israel in 1971-72 (46% of his random sample; among Georgian Jews the proportion was 77%); see his 'Judaism and Modernization in the Soviet Union,' in Dunn, *Religion and Modernization*, p. 302.
74. Rothenberg, *loc. cit.*, pp. 343-351; Gitelman, 'Moscow and the Soviet Jews,' *loc. cit.*, pp. 25-34.
75. See Moshe Davis, 'Jewish Spiritual Life in the USSR: Some Personal Impressions,' *RCL*, IV, No. 4 (Winter 1976), pp. 20-23.
76. 'Krizis khristianskogo sektantstva,' *loc. cit.*, p. 46.
77. A *samizdat* collection of religious songs and poetry in Ukrainian, *Pisni spassennykh* published by the Baptist underground press 'Khristianin' in 1975.
78. See Michael Rowe, 'Soviet Policy towards Evangelicals,' *RCL*, VII, No. 1 (Spring 1979), pp. 4-12.
79. See a bulletin of the International Representation for the Council of Evangelical Baptist Churches in the Soviet Union (Elkhart, Ind.), February 1984, p. 3. Kolarz, *op. cit.*, pp. 338-344; Lane, *op. cit.*, pp. 185-191.
80. 'Evoliutsiia religioznogo soznaniia i deiatelnosti sviditelei Iegovy,' *VNA*, Vol 24 (1979), p. 135. During the 1960's, a Ukrainian-language version of *The Watchtower* was illegally published in Tomsk, Siberia.
81. N. Vozniak, *Ikh spravzhne oblychchia* (Uzhhorod, 1974), pp. 108, 116-117. Cf. V. Konyk, *Illiuzii s viditelei Iegovy* (Moscow, 1981), pp. 148-149.
82. Valentyn Moroz, 'Amid the Snows,' in *Boomerang. The Works of Valen-*

tyn Moroz (Baltimore, 1974), p. 82.

83. Among the invariably hostile Soviet accounts of *pokutnyky*, note Iu. M. Hryhor'ev, *Buzuviry* (Lviv, 1974); M. Kosiv, 'Pokutniki — kto oni?' *Nauka i religiia*, No. 8, 1975, pp. 56-57; A. Shysh, *Uniiaty-pokutnyky — khto vony?* (Uzhhorod, 1978); and B. Orlyk, 'Neblahovydni diistva 'pasazhyriv pershoho klasa,' *Liudyna i svit*, No. 2, 1983, pp. 52-56.

84. Cf. a handwritten Penitent *samizdat* appeal to 'all races and nationalities, on all continents' protesting against the arrest of the *pokutnyky* leader Ihnatii Soltys ('the Holy Father' and 'reincarnated Christ') on January 21, 1981, (3 p.). (This writer's archive.)

85. *Ibid.* See also a handprinted 1981 'open letter' 'To Our Family — Close and Distant' which outlines Soltys' 'succession' to Pius XII and the basic tenets of the Penitent beliefs. (8 p.) (This writer's archive). For Soviet version of the sect's origins and activities, see Shysh, *op. cit.*

86. *Ibid.*, pp. 61-79. In many instances, Soviet authorities have deprived Penitents of their parental rights.

87. Cf. *samizdat* documents cited in ftns. 84 and 85. In another handprinted *pokutnyky* appeal from 'participants, contemporaries and eyewitnesses' of the Lviv trial of 70-year-old Soltys on May 12-15, 1981, the latter is identified as having served as 'priest, bishop, cardinal, exarch, the pope, and finally — Christ himself' (4 p.; this writer's archive). Echoing Soltys' trial at which he was sentenced (for a third time) to 5 years imprisonment ('severe regime') and 5 years exile, is a February 1983 article in the Soviet Ukrainian antireligious monthly, *Liudyna i svit* (Orlyk, *loc. cit.*). During Soltys' previous imprisonment in the 1960's, the sect was lead by another former Uniate priest, A. Potochniak, who, too, was arrested and sentenced along with other sect leaders in 1968 (cf. Ie. Pryshchepa, 'Lyk uniiatskoho dushpastyria,' *Liudyna i svit*, No. 11, 1968, pp. 36-39).

88. See 'To Our Family — Close and Distant.' According to Ivan Hvat's annotations of this document, some of the *pokutnyky* claims about a 'Satanist' conspiracy in the Vatican that 'accelerated through poisoning' the death of Pope Pius XII, have been adopted from a Polish 'expose' of post-1958 'machinations' in the Roman Curia, T. Breza, *Spizowa brama* (Warsaw, 1960), that was subsequently published in a Russian translation (*Bronzovye vrata. Rimskii dnevnik*, Moscow, 1964).

89. Hryhor'iev, *op. cit.*, pp. 61-65.

90. See the 1981 handprinted appeal 'To Our Family', accusing the illegal Uniate clergy of having allegedly 'betrayed' Christ's Church and abandoned their flock by "secretly making peace"' with the Godless regime.

91. Shysh, *op. cit.*, pp. 133-135; see also *pokutnyk* documents mentioned above.

92. See William C. Fletcher, *The Russian Orthodox Church Underground, 1917-1970* (London, 1971), Chs. VII and VIII.

93. See this writer's 'Church-State Relations in the USSR,' *loc. cit.*, pp. 16-19.

94. Fletcher, *op. cit.*, Ch. X; Lane, *op. cit.*, Ch. 4; and 'Nekotorye osobennosti istinno pravoslavnogo khristianstva,' *VNA*, Vol. 24 (1979), pp. 192-204.

95. See ft. 2; as well as materials of an all-union scientific-atheist conference on 'Atheism, Religion and Their Place in the Contemporary Struggle of Ideas,' which was held in Kiev, on October 30-31, 1973, and focused in particular on the Uniate Church and nationalism in the Ukraine (five out of 16 papers in section 'Religion in the Plans of Anticommunism'), Garadzha, V.I. *et al.* (eds.), *Ateizm i religiia v sovremennoi borbe idei* (Kiev, 1975). Note also I.V. Poluk, *Zblyzhennia natsii i rozvytok masovoho ateizmu v SSSR* (Kiev, 1976); A.V.

Ipatov, 'Voprosy ateisticheskogo vospitaniia v svete etnokonfessionalnoi spetsifiki religii,' *VNA*, Vol. 23 (1978), pp. 88-106) — a sympathetic assessment of the importance of Orthodoxy in the development of the Russian national consciousness and culture; a section 'Internationalism and Atheism' (containing three articles on 'internationalist' and anti-Islamic propaganda in Northern Caucasus) in *VNA*, Vol. 26 (1980), pp. 22-66; and an article by S.A. Bublik (a lecturer of the Kievan Higher School of the MVD), 'Rol' patrioticheskogo vospitaniia v formirovanii ateisticheskikh ubezhdenii,' *Voprosy ateizma*, Vol. 18 (1982), pp. 55-61.

96. Akademiia nauk Ukrainskoi RSR, Instytut istorii, *Stanovlennia i rozvytok masovoho ateizmu v zakhidnykh oblastiakh Ukrainskoi RSR*, ed. by Iu. Iu. Slyvka (Kiev, 1981).

97. *Ibid.*, pp. 183-184; see also pp. 144-145.

98. *Ibid.*, pp. 183-184.

99. *Ibid.*, p. 184.

100. See, in particular, S.T. Mashchenko, "'Khristianskii' natsionalizm uniatstva — orudie antikommunizma,' *Voprosy ateizma*, Vol. 17 (1981), pp. 106-114; I.I. Myhovych, 'Uniatsko-natsionalisticheskii al'ians na sluzhbe imperializma,' *VNA*, Vol. 28 (1981), pp. 89-104; and a paper by the head of the propaganda department of the CC CPU, L.M. Kravchuk, 'Ateisticheskoe vospitanie trudiashchikhsia i zadachi kontrpropagandy,' in *Neprimirimost k burzhuaznoi ideologii, perezhitkam natsionalizma*, pp. 35-50. Lithuania and the Western Ukraine appear to have been singled out for 'internationalist atheist' indoctrination. According to *Nauka i religiia* (No. 6, 1982, p. 3), in the Lviv oblast alone, Society 'Knowledge' has 'elaborated 23 cycles of lectures on the problems of unity of the atheist, patriotic, and internationalist upbringing.' Of some interest is the first systematic Soviet treatment of the problems of moral, political and psychological training of the Soviet Armed Forces draftees, prepared by faculty members of the Lenin Military-Political Academy under the general editorship of Colonel-General Zheltov, *Soldat i voina* (Moscow, 1971); the authors urge officers and NCO's to uncover and 're-educate' soldiers who 'conceal' their 'national and religious superstitions,' especially if they belong to 'prohibited' religious groups, and to break up any informal friendship circles of soldiers 'infected with national and religious biases' pp. 111-112, 94-95). Elsewhere, the authors stress that 'commanders and political workers, officers should always remember that inculcation of the hatred of enemies represents an inseparable part of the moral, political and psychological preparation of soldiers for a modern war, a part which, moreover, in many ways determines other component elements of this preparation' (p. 110).

101. See Gleb Yakunin's 'Report to the Christian Committee for the Defence of Believers' Rights on the Present Situation of the Russian Orthodox Church and the Prospects for Religious Revival in Russia,' dated August 15, 1979, reproduced in *Volnoe slovo*, (Frankfurt a.M.) No. 35-36 (1980), pp. 5-78. On the Committee, see Jane Ellis, 'The Christian Committee for the Defence of Believers' Rights in the USSR,' *RCL*, VIII, No. 4 (Winter 1980), pp. 279-291. For a sample of official attacks on Yakunin and the CCDBR, see V.A. Kuroedov (Chairman of the Council on Religious Affairs, attached to the USSR Council of Ministers), *Religiia i tserkov v Sovetskom gosudarstve* (Moscow, 1981), pp. 187-195.

102. See John B. Dunlop, '*Mnogaia leta*: Advocate of a Russian Church-Soviet State Concordat,' *RCL*, XI, No. 2 (Summer 1983), pp. 146-160, Cf. an early *samizdat* article by Gennadii Shimanov, 'Kak ponimat' nashu istoriiu i k chemu v nei stremitsia (v sviazi s pismom Solzhenitsyna),' dated June 2, 1974, *Materialy samizdata* (Munich: RFE-RL), no. 43/82, December 31, 1982. For Soviet propaganda use of 'confessions' and 'appeals' by 'repentant' Russian Orthodox dissenters, see Kuroedov, *op. cit.*, pp. 185-192.

SOVIET MUSLIMS AND THE MUSLIM WORLD

Alexandre Bennigsen

After an absence of almost half a century from the political scene of the Muslim world, the USSR became aggressively active in the politics of the *Dar ul-Islam* (world of Islam) in the 1970s. Being a great Muslim power, as well as the inheritor of the tsarist empire, the Soviets' 'Islamic strategy' is fundamentally different from the strategies of western states. There are some forty-five million Muslims in the Soviet Union, and this fact strongly influences Soviet policy towards the Muslim world. To decide, however, whether the presence of a large Muslim community in the southern regions of the USSR is an asset for Soviet expansion, it is necessary first to look at the Russian-Muslim relationship in an historical context.

The first contacts between Russians and Muslims go back to the tenth century when the Kingdom of Bulghar adopted Islam. In the 13th to the 14th centuries, Russian princes were vassals of the Tatar Khans, and in the 15th century, during a short period when Russian strength equalled Muslim, many Tatar feudal lords of the Chingissid dynasty served Russian rulers in Moscow.

In 1552, when the armies of Ivan the Terrible conquered the Khanate of Kazan, the Russian state acquired its first Muslim subjects. Since then the number and relative proportion of Muslims has been steadily growing in the Russian empire. Today the USSR is the fifth largest Muslim power in the world after Indonesia, Pakistan, India and Bangladesh. There are more Muslims in the USSR than in Egypt and more Turks in Central Asia than in Turkey.

From the first the rulers of the Russian state were obliged to pay great attention to the role of their Muslim subjects in the military and diplomatic affairs of the empire, and this role has always been ambiguous. Already at the time of Ivan the Terrible, numerous uprisings of the newly conquered Tatars and the effects of the Ottoman Turk and Crimean military campaigns on Russia's Muslims offset the advantages which might have existed for using Muslim feudal lords as military commanders of Moscovite armies, ambassadors, middlemen in trade, interpreters, and propagandists. Such was the situation four hundred years ago, and it remains much the same today. Soviet Islam is still a tremendous asset for the Soviets but, potentially, a deadly liability.

To understand the current relations between Soviet Muslims, the Soviet government, and the Muslim world, we must keep in mind that the Kremlin's Islamic strategy is conditioned by a double heritage: the centuries-long tsarist tradition of treatment of its Muslim subjects and the short but violent legacy of the October Revolution and Civil War, when the Muslims behaved not only as rebellious citizens of the Russian Empire but as claimants to full independence.

Muslims in Tsarist Strategy

Seen in a global historical perspective, the existence of an important Muslim community in the tsarist empire has certainly been a handicap for Russian expansion in the Muslim world. It was only in the 15th and 16th centuries that the Moscow tsars trusted their Muslim vassals enough to use them as military commanders of purely Russian armies.

The Chingisside prince, Nurdevlet, former Khan of Crimea, led Ivan the Third's army against his Muslim cousins of the Golden Horde in 1480. Another Chingisside Khan, Shah Ali Khan of Kasimov, was several times commander-in-chief of the armies of Ivan the Terrible against the Poles, Swedes, and the Livonian Knights.[1]

After the death of Ivan the Terrible, the only Russian ruler who treated his Muslim subjects as equals to Christians, only converted Christians were accepted in the Tsar's service, Muslims being specifically excluded. This exclusion lasted until the reign of Nicholas II when a Muslim general, the Khan of Nakhichevan, commanded the Guard Cavalry Corps in 1914, and only etymology allows us to discover a Muslim ancestor (probably a Tatar) of, say, a Suvorov (Suvar oglu) or a Kutuzov (Qutuz oglu). Among the Muslims of the empire, the Tatars alone were drafted into the Russian army, incorporated directly into Russian regiments; they did not form special, homogeneous Muslim units. In the 19th century, the Bashkirs were included in conscription and for a short while formed special Bashkir regiments.[2] All other Muslims of the empire, Caucasians, Azerbaijanis, Kazakhs, Turkestanis, were not legal citizens but were aliens (*inorodtsy*) and were excluded from military service. During the reign of Nicholas II, Muslim volunteers formed the so-called Wild Division (*Dikaia Diviziia*) composed

Soviet Muslims and the Muslim World

of cavalry regiments of Daghestanis, Ossetians, Kabardians and Tekke Turkmens; however, the officers were almost entirely Russians. As a rule, Muslim soldiers of the tsarist army were never engaged against their fellow coreligionists, Turks, or Persians. In 1916 the attempt to mobilize the Kazakhs into labour battalions was the main reason for the great uprising of the nomadic tribes of Central Asia.

It seems that the tsarist military authorities' distrust of the Muslims was justified. In 1914 to 1917 the numerous Tatar prisoners of war in Germany became the target of very active anti-Russian propaganda by Muslim nationalist refugees in Germany and Turkey.[3] In 1917, an embryonic 'Tatar Legion' was formed, and a periodical, *Jihad-i Islam*, was published in Berlin.[4] For the first time, a foreign power at war with Russia was trying to turn its Muslim subjects against Russia. This short-lived experience was to be remembered during World War II by the German High Command and by Muslim émigrés.

Similarly, after the death of Ivan the Terrible who used his Muslim subjects — especially the Kasimov Tatars — as messengers to the Muslim world,[5] Muslims were systematically excluded from the Russian diplomatic service. Between 1583 and the October Revolution there was not a single Muslim ambassador, provincial governor, nor high-ranking civil servant in Russia. Russian authorities did not even dare to send their Muslims as intelligence agents to other Muslim countries. The British in India, employing local Muslims as secret service experts in Afghanistan and Central Asia, and the French, who formed African Muslim regiments of Tirailleurs Algeriens, Moroccans, and Senegalais, were in that respect much more astute. It was only during a relatively short period of some eighty years, between the conquest of the Crimea in 1783 and the conquest of Central Asia in the 1860s, that cooperation flourished between the Russian industrialists in the St Petersburg government and Volga Tatar merchants. The latter served as middlemen between Russian capitalism and the closed markets of Central Asia. This fruitful collaboration, paid for by important favours and concessions to the Tatars, ended when Russian armies conquered Turkestan and opened this immense territory to Russian entrepreneurs. The Tatar and Russian bourgeoisies, formerly partners, became competitors; once again the Russian state reverted to treating its Muslims not as true citizens but as potential enemies.

One may wonder whether the Russians' distrust was the result of an inherent visceral feeling of religious hostility toward the hated *busurman*, not unlike the traditional hostility toward the Jews for having 'sold Jesus Christ' (*Khristoprodavtsy*) or the belief that the real loyalties of

Russian Muslims were to the Turkish Sultan-Khalife rather than to the tsar.

The history of Russian-Muslim relations during the last four hundred years has been marked by an almost uninterrupted succession of bloody revolts, all of which were crushed ruthlessly, beginning in the Tatar territory of the Middle Volga and the Bashkir lands of the Urals, and spreading, in the 19th century, to the North Caucasus, the Kazakh steppes, and Turkestan. Muslims played a major role in the two most dramatic civil wars in Eastern Russia: the revolt of Stepan Razin in the 17th century and Pugachev's movement during the reign of Catherine II. The last major Muslim revolt, the uprising of the Central Asian nomadic tribes, took place in 1916, one year before the downfall of the Romanov monarchy.

Contrasted with the refusal of Russian authorities to initiate any dialogue with the Muslims of the empire, a refusal springing from ignorance and fear of the *busurman*, Muslim leaders, especially the Volga Tatars, demonstrated a much greater flexibility when dealing with the Russians. This flexibility came from a profound understanding of the politics of empire: a premature confrontation with the overwhelming might of the Russians could bring only disaster to the Muslim community.

The first Muslim political leader to advance the idea of a Russian-Muslim partnership for the conquest of the entire 'colonial' world, against Western (British and French) imperialism, was the Crimean Tatar Ismail bey Gaspraly (in Russian, Ismail Gasprinski).[6] Gaspraly made his overtures to the tsarist government, but, not surprisingly, no one paid the slightest attention to his bold plan. Other Muslim politicians tried their luck with various Russian political parties: the Muslim liberals with the Constitutional Democrats (K.D.),[7] the moderate revolutionaries with the Mensheviks and the Socialist-Revolutionaries,[8] and the more radical Muslims with the Bolsheviks.[9] Until, 1917 their hopes were frustrated; all Russian political parties, including the Bolsheviks (in spite of Soviet historians' efforts to prove the opposite), were uninterested. At best, the 'national question' in their view encompassed Finland, Poland, and, to a lesser degree, the Ukraine, Caucasian Christians, Georgians and Armenians. The Muslims were simply ignored, and not one Russian political party ever devised a 'Muslim strategy.'

Thus, until the October Revolution, the Muslim factor was a handicap rather than an asset for the expansion of the tsarist empire southward to the warm seas. Russian leaders had lost the religious tolerance which was at the heart of the visionary imperial policy of the Rurikid

Soviet Muslims and the Muslim World

Tsars, Ivan the Third and Ivan the Terrible, who behaved as heirs to the religiously tolerant Mongol emperors and were recognised as such by their Muslim neighbours. This loss resulted in large measure from the state of quasi-permanent war against the Ottoman Turks in the 18th century, which exacerbated religious antagonism, giving rise in the late 19th century to a perfect symbiosis between the notion of Russian and Orthodoxy under the influence of the Russian slavophiles. Under such conditions, there could be no cooperation with Islam; Russian Muslims could be treated only as potential traitors, members of a fifth column. Moreover, the century-long fierce resistance of the North Caucasian mountaineers (from the first Holy War in 1783 of the Naqshbandi Sheikh Mansur in Chechnia to the last great Daghestani uprising in 1877-78) ruined the tsarist empire economically and morally and undoubtedly saved the decadent Ottoman Empire and Iran, ruled even as it was by the weak Qajar dynasty. It also postponed the conquest of Afghanistan for a century.

The Legacy of the Revolutionary Years

The October Revolution opened a new chapter in the history of Russian Islam. It began with a short-lived and half-hearted attempt by the Bolshevik leaders to treat their Muslim comrades as equal partners and ended in 1923 with the Muslim national Communists opposing Stalin in a dramatic crisis. The crisis culminated in the liquidation of the Muslim Communist leaders some years later, which prefaced a new period of deep distrust between Russians and Muslims of the Soviet Empire which lasted until the mid 1970s.

In 1918, however, Moscow was the Mecca of the entire colonial world. Thousands of young radicals from Muslim territories of Russia, Africa and Asia flocked to Moscow. Although they may not have been very competent in Marxist doctrine, they were eager to accept Bolshevik leadership, organising in the colonies revolutionary anti-Western movements under Russian aegis. Among the Third World revolutionaries who were active in the USSR during this period we find such strange bedfellows as the leaders of the Indian Khalifatist movement and Enver Pasha. We also find a number of future leaders of Communist movements in the colonial world: Ho Chi-Minh, Liu Shao-Shi, the Indonesian Tan Malaka, the Japanese Sen Katayama, the Indian Manabendra-Nath Roy, and many others. A great number of Russian Muslim radical nationalists were accepted, sometimes as entire political

Alexandre Bennigsen

groups, into the Russian Communist Party. Their ignorance of the fundamentals of socialism was abysmal: they had never read Marx, and few of them had ever heard of Lenin, Plekhanov or Marx before October 1917. Moreover, their social background, almost without exception, was neither proletarian nor peasant. The majority belonged to the wealthy merchant bourgeoisie, the landlord class, or to the nomadic aristocracy; some of them, like the Kazakh Ali-Khan Bukeykhanov, were descendants of Ghengis Khan. In spite of their dubious social and national origins and lack of doctrinal preparedness, Russian Muslim leaders were not only accepted as full Party members but were promoted to the decision-making echelons of the Party — at least in domestic affairs.

Two main reasons explain why the Bolshevik leaders, usually so strict on doctrinal matters, had associated themselves unconditionally with these badly prepared fellow-travelling Muslim nationalists. The first reason is that the Muslim Communists were useful as 'scarecrows' to frighten the Western imperialists and the Muslim states of the Middle East, obliging them to break the 'capitalist encirclement' on the southern borders of Soviet Russia and easing the economic pressure exerted by capitalist Europe against the new revolutionary Russia. The threat to unleash against Europe a *jihad* (Muslim 'Holy War') led by Soviet Muslims was repeatedly brandished by the Bolsheviks during the Civil War years.[10]

Secondly, Soviet Muslims were even more precious as allies during the Civil War. For various reasons, particularly because of the ignorant indifference and, in some cases, the open hostility of the White generals, because of Lenin's vague promises, and also because it was simply impossible to remain neutral in the revolution's tragedy, the majority of the European Russian Muslims (Tatars and Bashkirs) sided with the Red Army. The few who sided with the Whites, such as the Bashkir leader Ahmed Zeki Validov (Zeki Velidi Togan) and the leaders of the Kazakh *Alash Orda*, soon discovered that a cooperation with White generals, especially with the Admiral Kolchak, fighting for a Russia 'united and indivisible' was an impossible dream. In 1919 they decided to switch allegiances to the Bolsheviks who, in spite of their atrocities and blunders, appeared more promising. The description of the role played by the Muslims in the civil war would be too long for this short chapter; it is enough to say that it had great impact upon the final outcome. Tatar and Bashkir soldiers and officers formed more than forty percent of the Fifth Red Army, led by Marshal Frunze who defeated Kolchak and invaded Central Asia. Other Muslim units were engaged on the southern front against Denikin, and many Bashkir soldiers were in the Red units which crushed the revolt of the Kronstadt sailors.

As a reward for the help provided during these crucial years (1918-1920), Muslims worked at the highest levels of the People's Commisariat for Nationalities (Narkomnats), chaired by Stalin, and were active in the Party and Soviet apparati in their national republics. It is not an exaggeration that during the first six or seven years of the Soviet regime, from 1918 to about 1925, the political and cultural life of the Muslim republics of the Middle Volga, Caucasus, and Central Asia was dominated by nationalist intellectuals who supported the Soviet regime without really becoming Marxist-Leninists.[11]

However, Muslim leaders asked for more than Party work. Above all, they clamoured for a decision-making position in the political and military strategy of the Komintern and of the Soviet government in the Muslim world; these demands were systematically rejected by the Bolshevik leadership. In 1920, a Muslim Communist writing under a pseudonym denounced the Russian orientation of the world Communist movement:

> Appearing in the East under the sole flag of the Russian Communist Party, we condemn ourselves to failure because our enemies will denounce us as simple successors to former Russian imperialism. The revolution must be carried into the East by Oriental and Muslim Communists.[12]

Instead of following this wise advice, the Bolshevik leaders excluded Soviet Muslims from the apparatus of the Komintern,[13] from the People's Commissariat for Foreign Affairs (Narkomindel), and from any political work in the outside Muslim world. There were almost no Muslims in the Red Army division which was sent to Ghilan in the spring of 1921 to help the Jengelis fight 'British imperialism' in Iran.[14] Contacts between the Russian Communist Party and local Communist organisations in Turkey, Iran, and the Arab world were maintained by Russian or European Communists.[15]

As early as 1919, one of the leading Tatar Communists, Mir Said Sultan Galiev, drew the necessary conclusions from this anti-Muslim behaviour of the Bolshevik leadership when he wrote:

> The process of development of the revolution was directed incorrectly ... almost all the attention of the leaders was turned to the West ...

the East with its one and half billion population enslaved by the West European bourgeoisie was forgotten ... Because of the ignorance of the East and because of the fear which it inspired, the idea of the participation of the East in the international revolution was systematically rejected.[16]

What were the reasons for Stalin's systematic refusal to allow his Muslim comrades to be part of the decision-making process in foreign strategy? They were many, and while it is impossible to enumerate all here, two reasons were certainly determinant: Muslim nationalism and anti-Soviet movements in Muslim territories.

Muslim intellectuals, former militants of pan-Islamic and pan-Turkic movements who joined the Russian Communist Party, did not discard their nationalism when they became superficially Marxist-Leninist. For them, the Russian Revolution was essentially the beginning of the colonial world's great revenge against European industrial governments, Soviet Russia included. It is easy to understand why neither Stalin nor any other Bolshevik leader could accept Muslim theories concerning the transfer of revolutionary energies from Europe (the 'dead hearth of revolution,' according to Sultan Galiev) to Asia; such a transfer would have deprived the Russians of their role as sole leaders of the Communist movement and would have made Kazan, Tashkent or Samarkand — not Moscow — the world capital of revolution.

For Stalin, the efforts of his Muslim comrades, such as Sultan Galiev, Turar Ryskulov, Fayzullah Khojaev, and Najmuddin Efendiev-Samurskii (who some years later were liquidated as 'traitors to the revolution'), to divert the spearhead of the world Communist movement toward Muslim Asia was proof that their loyalties were divided between Marxism and Islam; perhaps the appeal of Islam could easily become the stronger.

In the spring of 1921, at the Tenth Congress of the RCP(b), the first official attack against the 'Pan Turkic deviationists' within the Communist Party was launched:

Native Communists ... not entirely liberated from the ghosts of the past ... tend to neglect the class interests of the Toilers and to confuse them with the so-called national interest ... This situation explains the emergence of the bourgeois-nationalism which, in the East, sometimes takes the form of pan-Islamism and pan-Turkism.[17]

The second reason for Stalin's distrust was even more serious. In 1920, Moscow had to face two major anti-Soviet movements. In North Daghestan and Chechnia, the revolt of mountaineers led by the Naqshbandi sheikhs Najmuddin of Gotzo and Uzun Haji of|Salty was crushed in 1921 only after fierce resistance. In Central Asia, the Basmachi uprising, which erupted in the Ferghana valley as early as 1918, lasted with varying degrees of intensity until 1928; in some areas, southern Uzbekistan and the Turkmen steppes, the fighting continued until the mid 1930s. Both movements demonstrated the refusal of the Muslim masses to accept the Russian presence and Godless Communism. In the North Caucasus the revolt took the character of a *jihad* or holy war against the infidels and the evil Muslims who served them.

The psychological impact of these popular revolts upon the Muslim intellectuals who had joined the Communist Party is important. In the writings of Turkestani and Caucasian Communist leaders Turar Ryskulov, Najmuddin Efendiev-Samurskii, and Takho Godi,[18] it is easy to detect a badly-hidden admiration of their adversaries: Basmachi or Sufi adepts, although 'reactionary' and 'fanatical', represented an authentic heroic tradition of pure unadulterated Islam. Stalin was not far from the truth when he accused his Muslim comrades, Turar Ryskulov, Akmal Ikramov, Sultan Galiev and several others of disguised pro-Basmachi sympathies.[19]

With two major popular revolts just beyond Soviet southern frontiers, there was no question of any military or political adventure in the Muslim world. Consequently, Soviet Muslims lost their importance to Soviet leaders; formerly allies, they now appeared as possible enemies. In late 1920, following the Congress of the Toilers of the East in Baku and its bogus appeals to the 'Muslim Holy War against imperialist Europe,' Soviet Russia began its retreat from the Middle East. In September, Soviet-armed units evacuated Ghilan; in January 1921, the entire Central Committee of the newly-formed Turkish Communist Party was slaughtered in Trabzon. At the same time, the Jengeli movement collapsed, and all of northern Iran was reoccupied by the Iranian army. Three years later, in 1923, the purge of the Muslim National Communists began, lasting fifteen years and nearly destroying the pre-revolutionary Muslim intelligentsia. Thus, after a short period of cooperation, the revolution and civil war ended in a tragic conflict between Soviet leadership and the Muslim elite. It is certain that after 1923 Soviet leaders considered Central Asian and Caucasian Islam a severe handicap for their strategy abroad.

Alexandre Bennigsen

The Years of Isolation (1923-1964)

In 1923, a tight Iron Curtain descended, completely isolating Soviet Muslim republics from the outside Muslim world; all contacts between Soviet Muslims and their brethren beyond the borders were cut. Pilgrimages to the holy places in Saudi Arabia and Shia holy cities in Iran (Qom, Mashhad) and Iraq (Najaf, Karbala) were forbidden; Central Asia and the Caucasus were closed to foreign Muslims, and almost no Soviet Muslim was allowed to travel abroad. This isolation from the rest of Dar ul-Islam was heightened by the change of script: the Arabic alphabet was discarded in 1929 for Latin, and later, on the eve of World War II, it was replaced by the cyrillic.

In the Soviet Union, attempts to destroy Islam began in 1928 and lasted for ten years. Mosques and Koranic schools were closed,[20] *waqf* properties nationalised, Shariy'at courts suppressed, and Muslim clerics arrested, deported, or executed as 'parasites', 'saboteurs', and German or Japanese 'spies.' Stalin believed that this extermination campaign had to be concealed from the Muslim world, but who in the Middle East cared then about the fate of Central Asians? It is logical that during this period there were no Muslims, with a few exceptions, in the Soviet diplomatic service.[21]

The war against Germany increased Soviet distrust of its own Muslims. In 1941 a popular uprising erupted in the Chechen-Ingush republic — when the German armies were still thousands of miles away. It was led jointly by former members of the Communist Party and sheikhs of the Sufi brotherhoods. We do not know exactly what happened during the short German occupation of the Caucasus and Crimea, but in 1943, when the Wehrmacht was expelled from the North Caucasus, more than a million Muslims, accused of 'collaboration' with the Germans, were deported to Siberia and Kazakhstan.[22] The accusation of universal treason is obviously absurd, and, after Stalin's death, the Muslims were rehabilitated and allowed — with the exception of the Crimean Tatars and the Meskhetian Turks — to return to their homelands. It is undeniable that, in spite of Soviet historians' efforts to prove the opposite, Muslim people did not display an ardent Soviet patriotism and were not eager to die for their Russian 'elder brother.'[23]

After World War II, the USSR reappeared with flying colours on the political stage of the Middle East. It was haloed by the prestige of victory and had wide access to all Middle Eastern countries, formerly closed to Soviet influences, as the ally of Great Britain. But it is remarkable that it was under its Russian, rather than its Islamic, flag that the

Soviet Muslims and the Muslim World

Soviet Union emerged after a long eclipse in the Arab world. It was Monseigneur Alexis, Patriarch of Moscow, and not the *mufit* of Ufa who was the first Soviet religious dignitary to visit the Middle East (Syria, Lebanon, Palestine and Egypt). It is also curious that there were very few Soviet Muslim Azeri or Kurds in the Soviet divisions which occupied northern Iran during the war; there were even fewer Muslims among the political advisors and *agitprop* experts who helped create the two pro-Soviet republics of Azerbaijan and Kurdistan in 1945 and 1946. It is highly significant that in the 1950s, when Moscow was promoting Georgian and Armenian claims to their 'historical lands', covering all of Eastern Anatolia, no irredentist claims were formulated in connection with the Azeris, Turkmen, Tajiks, or Uzbeks living in Turkey, Iran or Afghanistan.[24] Soviet propaganda ignored them, and their ethnic or religious kinship with elements of the USSR's Muslim population was never mentioned.

Until the downfall of Nikita Khrushchev, a solid Iron Curtain protected Central Asia and the Caucasus from contamination by the rest of the Muslim world, and when foreign Muslims visited the Soviet Union they went to Moscow, Kiev, or Leningrad — seldom to Baku or Tashkent. During this entire period Soviet leaders avoided using their Muslims abroad. They needed neither the assistance of religious leaders nor Muslim Communists, and when Central Asians or Muslim Caucasians were employed in Soviet embassies in the Middle East it was, as a rule, at the lowest technical level, as drivers or interpreters but never as experts.

The post-World War II period in the Muslim republics was marked by a violent campaign against 'bourgeois nationalism' under Stalin and a new and equally violent offensive against Islam under Khrushchev. Under these conditions it was impossible for Soviet authorities to trust their Muslim Communist Party members and to use them abroad. It is not a paradox to say that, during this period of forty years (1923-1964), Islam was neither an asset nor a liability for Soviet rulers. It simply had no place in the Soviet strategy in the Middle East, where the USSR appeared as a bicephalous eagle either with its Russian profile (under Stalin) or its Communist face (under Khrushchev).

Soviet Muslims in the Brezhnev Era (1964-1980)

The downfall of Nikita Khrushchev marked a dramatic change in the triangular relations between Moscow, Soviet Muslims, and the Muslim world. Although the position of the Soviet government, that of the Russian 'elder brother' who alone bears the final responsibility for revolutionary strategy in the Third World and especially in the Muslim world, remained basically unchanged, for the first time since the revolution Soviet Muslims were involved in Soviet diplomatic, political, and even military activity in Muslim affairs beyond the borders of the USSR. What may be called the Islamic strategy or the Kremlin plan presents the USSR to the Muslim world not only as Islam's 'best friend', but as a great Muslim power with Muslim citizens numbering 45 million. Its Muslim territories are presented as showcases of socialist models of development supposedly more rapid and efficient than the Western capitalist models.

The new strategy has a triple aspect. First, Central Asian and Caucasian republics have been opened to foreign Muslims. Central Asia in particular has become an important training centre for political and military cadres from abroad, visited by thousands of revolutionary radicals from abroad, visited by thousands of revolutionary radicals from friendly Muslim countries: Syria, Libya, Algeria, Afghanistan and South Yemen.

Secondly, Tatars, Caucasians and Central Asians have been used as experts, interpreters, propagandists, political, administrative and technical cadres in Middle Eastern countries, particularly in Afghanistan between April 1978 and February 1980. In Afghanistan they appeared as 'us' (Muslims) as opposed to 'them' (European and American Christians and Jews). Contrary to previous regimes, Muslim cadres have been employed under Brezhnev at all levels, including ambassador; a Tatar Muslim currently is the Soviet ambassador in Kabul.

The third aspect of the new Islamic strategy is cooperation between the Soviet government and the Islamic religious leadership, represented by the chairmen of the four Muslim Spiritual Directoriates in Tashkent, Ufa, Makhach-Qala and Baku. For the first time in Soviet history, Moscow has delegated real authority to its own religious leaders within the Muslim republics of the USSR in order to preserve the loyalty of Muslim believers. Religious leaders are also the USSR's itinerant ambassadors abroad, particularly in the conservative pro-Western Muslim countries of Saudi Arabia, Egypt, Morocco, Tunisia and Jordan.

During the last fifteen years, numerous international conferences have been organised by *mufti* Ziautdin Babakhanov, the late chairman of the Muslim Spiritual Directorate of Tashkent, and were attended by delegations from all Muslim countries. Countless Muslim delegations, including those from countries that have no diplomatic relations with the USSR, have been invited to the Soviet Union, and Muslim religious leaders from Central Asia have been touring Muslim countries abroad. As propagandists they are certainly more effective than the official Soviet Russian propagandists. Even if the message they convey to the Muslim world is not very different from that of official Soviet propaganda, it is accepted more readily because it is presented by authentic Muslim scholars.[25]

Cooperation with its Muslim religious leaders has been, no doubt, very fruitful for Moscow. It was through the channel of its *muftis* that Soviet influence, in the 1970s, penetrated and gained a solid position in various international Islamic institutions. As a result of the *muftis'* intense activity, doors to conservative Muslim countries have opened slowly but steadily. Soviet religious leaders were certainly partly responsible for the projection into all of the Muslim countries of the image of the USSR as 'friend of Islam', mobilising public opinion in the Middle Eastern countries against the USA and China and in support of Soviet diplomatic and military strategy. Their role has been neglected by the Western countries, who have been for the most part ignorant and indifferent observers of this dramatic evolution.

Nevertheless, the Islamic strategy has not been without dangers. Religious leaders' cooperation was paid for by immediate and important concessions at home, such as a decrease in the anti-religious campaign, the reopening and building of mosques, and the limited publication of religious literature. It is obvious that Soviet authorities are not happy to promote a process of religious revival in their Muslim republics. Moreover, the dropping of the Iron Curtain and the flow of foreign Muslims into Central Asia also presented an unexpected but serious danger. Middle Eastern radicals who visit the USSR may be great admirers of the Soviet Union, but they are dubious Marxists. More nationalist than socialist, their political creed is closer to the national Communism of a Sultan Galiev, eradicated years ago by Stalin, than to the orthodox Marxism-Leninism. Through these contacts radical, heretical subversive ideas can and do penetrate into the Muslim republics of the USSR. However, in spite of the potential dangers of the Islamic strategy pursued by Brezhnev's administration, Islam, for the first time since the revolution, was a brilliant asset to Soviet foreign policy in the 1960s and 1970s.

Alexandre Bennigsen

Soviet Muslims after Kabul (1980 to ?)

It is possible that the invasion of Afghanistan marked a new era in the evolution of Soviet Islam. In December 1979, Soviet troops invading Afghanistan included a relatively high proportion (about 40 percent) of Central Asian soldiers. One may wonder whether their presence was a deliberate attempt to give an 'inter-Muslim' profile to the Afghan adventure or a sign that the Soviet military command did not expect to engage its Tajiks and Uzbeks in military operations against their Afghan cousins. Or was it, more simply, proof of the Soviets' ignorance of the real conditions in Afghanistan? In any case, the experience proved to be a failure: Soviet Muslims fraternized with their Afghan co-religionaries and, instead of teaching them the beauties of Marxism-Leninism, were taught Islam.

In October of 1980 Soviet Islamic strategy had another setback. The great international conference to celebrate the 15th century *Hijri*, convened in Tashkent by the late *mufti* Ziautdin Babakhanov and promoted months in advance by all Soviet media as the main post-war Muslim political meeting, ended in failure. Half of the invited countries, including the most important, refused to attend,[26] and some of the delegations in Tashkent adopted a spectacularly anti-Soviet attitude. No comments were published, and Soviet press and radio had difficulty hiding this failure.

Since then, few Soviet Muslim dignitaries have been sent abroad,[27] and few foreign religious delegations except from occupied Afghanistan have visited Central Asia. It seems that for the present Soviet leaders are less eager to use their official Muslim establishment for propaganda and contacts with the outside Muslim world. At the same time, the anti-Islamic campaign, not as pronounced since the downfall of Khrushchev, received a new and unexpected impetus. In 1980, out of the 154 antireligious books and pamphlets published in the USSR, twenty-seven (17.5 percent) were specifically devoted to Islam. In 1982, 37 out of 161 antireligious publications concerned Islam (23%). In 1983 the proportion was 45 out of 209 (21.5%).[28]

It is significant that the harsh and brutal character of the new anti-Islamic campaign is quite different from the 'scientific' and relatively moderate atheistic literature of the post-Khrushchev period. References to the subversive activity of 'parallel' (Sufi) Islam are more numerous than ever. In December 1980 the chairman of Azerbaijan' KGB, Major General Zia Yusif-Zade, published in the *Bakinskii Rabochi* of Baku an important article denouncing 'imperialist activity along the southern borders of the USSR.' He mentioned specifically the 'anti-social and harmful activity of the sectarian underground and the reactionary Muslim clergy,' two expressions frequently used by Soviet sources to designate the clandestine Sufi orders.[29] In March of 1981 it was the First Secretary of the Central Committee of the Communist Party of Turkmenistan, Mohammed-Nazar Gapurov, who attacked 'the religious extremists and fanatics,'[30] other terms synonymous with Sufi adepts.

Official religious authorities participated in the campaign against Sufism. In the spring of 1981 the *mufti* of Tashkent, Ziautdin Babakhanov, published a *fetwa* (legal pronouncement) in *Muslims of the Soviet East*, the official mouthpiece of his Spiritual Board. The piece condemned as contrary to the spirit of orthodox Islam the pilgrimages to holy places (tombs of saints, or *ziarat*) which are in Central Asia the main activities of Sufi brotherhoods.[31]

Parallel to the anti-religious drive, the authorities of the Muslim republics unleashed a new campaign against the dangers of 'imperialist subversion' spilling over the southern frontiers of the USSR. This campaign has been accompanied by appeals for a greater vigilance against the dangers of religious fanaticism and imperialist propaganda. A typical example is the ideologically important article by O.S. Rejepova in *Izvestia Akademii Nauk Turkmenskoi SSR*. After revealing several Western 'falsifiers of Soviet nationalities policy'[32] and praising some others, Rejepova makes the following unexpected statement about the vulnerability of Soviet Muslim intellectuals to foreign propaganda:

> Important armies of ideological saboteurs well-trained and equipped with the most modern technique, have been thrown on the propaganda front of the 'Cold War' waged by American imperialists against the USSR. We must never underestimate this reactionary force and its ability to influence the brains and hearts. A special responsibility for the struggle against the ideology and the propaganda of our enemies lies on our intelligentsia, not only because its direct task vis-a-vis the People and the Party is to unmask the false and slanderous character of bourgeois propaganda, but also because our intelligentsia is one of the main objects of the ideological manoeuvres of the imperialists. It is actively looking for potential dissidents.[33]

It is too early to speculate on the reasons for and the meaning of various measures undertaken by the Soviet government to protect Central Asia and the Caucasus from dangerous influences from abroad.

Alexandre Bennigsen

Is it the beginning of a new era of isolation for Soviet Islam? Or is it simply a long period of readjustment before a new offensive in the Middle East is conducted under a Muslim flag, at the very least using Islam as a trump card? It may be that Soviet authorities have decided that the price paid for help from the Muslim religious establishment was too dear and that its consequences, the religious revival among Muslim masses and intellectuals, is too dangerous. Or perhaps the Soviets have abandoned, for the time being, cooperation with Muslim religious leaders because they failed to project abroad the image of the USSR as the 'best friend of Islam,' as demonstrated by the failure of the conference in Tashkent.

The reason for the recent changes in Soviet Muslim strategy may also be more serious. It may be that Soviet leaders perceive the danger of a spillover of Iranian fundamentalism into the Soviet republics, especially into the Caucasus, where there still remain memories of the short-lived theocratical state of Uzun Haji in 1919-1920, which was amazingly similar to the present-day Iranian Islamic Republic. Or it may be the first backlash of the Afghan war which, among other things, has demonstrated proof that the Russian 'elder brother' is not invincible.[34] It is also possible that Soviet authorities are eager to limit contacts between their Muslim intellectuals and the Muslim world. After decades of enforced conformity to the Russian Marxism-Leninism, Soviet Muslims live in an ideological void and are likely to be influenced by ideas and ideologies from abroad — from the most conservative religious fundamentalism of a Khomeini or a Gulbuddin to the revolutionary radicalism of an 'Ali Shariyati, whose philosophy inspired the Iranian Mojahidin-i Khalq, or the doctrine of the Egyptian Ikhwan al-Muslimin ('the Muslim brothers') or even the Islamic socialism of Khaddafi. Seen from Moscow, all of these theories share one common characteristic: they possess the potential power to destabilise Soviet Islam and are therefore equally subversive and dangerous.

Conclusion

Soviet authorities, Russian dissidents and many Western observers agree on one issue: the USSR's nationalities problem represents one of the weakest points in the Soviet system, potentially the most dangerous and the only one capable of destroying the Soviet Empire from within.

Among all of the Soviet nationalities, Muslim people are the most different from the Russians by their historical and cultural background, by their social customs and the strength of their religious traditions: all are incompatible with the official materialism. Soviet Muslims have not been assimilated by their Russian conquerors; even the Volga Tatars, in spite of more than a hundred years of cohabitation, have remained apart.

The demographic explosion of the Muslim people of the USSR — 44 million today and around 70 million predicted in the year 2,000 — can only aggravate the already tense relations between Russians and Muslims. The general climate of xenophobia and demographic pressures are already pushing Russians and other Europeans out of the Caucasus; the same process has also begun in Central Asia. Population trends give the Muslims a feeling of security, of 'time is on our side.'

Since 1917, except for the period of Brezhnev's regime, Islam has been a liability and a handicap for Moscow's strategy in the Muslim world. In 1964, under Brezhnev, it became an asset as the Soviet government cooperated successfully with the Islamic establishment. It was during this period that the USSR made the most spectacular advances in the Middle East: Afghanistan, Ethiopia and South Yemen have Communist regimes; Syria and Libya are allies. It may be possible that because of Soviet problems in Afghanistan Islam has ceased to be an asset and is becoming again a liability. The cooperation between the Soviet government and Muslim religious leaders seems to have been temporarily, perhaps definitely, suspended since the fall of 1980.

The USSR is (or was) the only great power in the world to have a Muslim strategy, using Muslim religious leaders both within the USSR and abroad. This strategy is certainly not very sophisticated and is often primitive, but it is efficient and provides results. The Western powers, indifferent or ignorant, have never tried to use the Islamic card against Moscow; in the West, too often, not only public opinion but, alas, also scholars and policy-makers still consider the USSR and Russia to be synonymous terms, ignoring the minorities. Now more than ever, attention should be given especially to the Muslims who form 18 percent of the Soviet population. There is ample evidence that Soviet Muslims desire contact with the Western world, bypassing Russia and Russians. Such contacts could be the beginning of a Western 'Islamic strategy.'

Alexandre Bennigsen

Notes

1. For instance, in 1534, 1539-40, and 1547-48, the Khan of Shah Ali led an army of Kasimov Tatars against the Khanate of Kazan. In 1555, the Chingisside Prince Abdullah of Astrakhan commanded the vanguard campaign. In 1557-58, Shah Ali Khan of Kasimov was commander-in-chief of the great Moscovite army which invaded Livonia. Several other Muslim princes served under his command, including Prince Sibok of Kabarda and the Crimean Prince Tohtamysh who commanded the vanguard of the Moscovite force.

2. Bashkir horsemen, armed with bows and arrows, appeared at the battle of Leipzig in 1813. The French called them 'Les Amours.'

3. A group of radical nationalists, led by the Siberian Tatar, the *Kadi* Abdurrashid Ibrahimov, and the Volga Tatar Galimjan Idrissi, was responsible for this attempt to organise Muslim prisoners of war.

4. *Jihad-i Islam* ('The Holy War of Islam') was published twice a month in Kazan Tatar by Abdurrashid Kadi Ibrahimov for the use of Muslim prisoners of war. It was violently anti-Russian, and its ideology was close to the radical pan-Islamism of Jemaleddin al-Afghani.

5. The Muslim 'experts' served usually as 'deputy messengers' accompanying Russian ambassadors to various Muslim rulers. For instance, the Kasimov Tatar Jan Bulat accompanied ambassador Danilo Gubin to the Great Nogay Horde in 1535.

6. Ismail bey Gasprali (in Russian, Gasprinski) 1851-1914, a Crimean Tatar reformer and publicist, expressed his ideas on the Muslim-Russian partnership in his *Russkoe Musul'manstvo* (Russian Islam), published in Simferopol' in 1881. He expanded his ideas in a second pamphlet: *Russko-Musul'manskoe Soglashenie* (Russian-Muslim Agreement) (Simferopol', 1897), and in numerous editorials of his famous journal *Terjuman*, published between 1883 and 1914 in Baghchesaray.

7. For instance, Yusuf Akchura oglu (1876-1933), the Volga Tatar political leader who joined the K.D. Party and became in 1905-06 a member of its Central Committee. In 1908, completely disgusted with his Russian comrades' lack of understanding, he left Russia for Turkey and became one of the most outspoken enemies of Russia.

8. For instance, the Tatar writers and political leaders Ayaz Iskhaki (1878-1954) and Fuad Tuktar (?-1938) who joined in 1905 the Russian Party of Socialist Revolutionaries but left it soon afterwards. They founded their own purely Muslim socialist group of *Tangchylar*, which was dispersed by the police in September, 1906, and its members arrested.

9. For instance, the Tatar writers Husein Yamashev (1882-1912) and Ghafur Kulahmetov (1881-1918) joined the Bolshevik wing of the Russian Social Democrat Workers Party around 1905 and founded in 1907 a Marxist Tatar political group, *Uralchylar*. Muslims were more numerous in the Bolshevik Party in the Caucasus where a purely Muslim Marxist party, *Hummet*, had existed since 1904.

10. In particular by Zinoviev at the Congress of the Toilers of the East in Baku, September, 1920. It was, however, obvious that the Bolshevik leaders were unable and unwilling to provoke or even support a general uprising of Islam against Europe. Such a movement would have backlashed against the Soviets.

11. Already in 1922 a Bolshevik expert in national affairs, S. Dimanstein, noted the danger of this situation when he remarked that 'in the East [Soviet Muslim republics] nationalism is making more rapid progress than class consciousness *Zhizn'Natsional'nostei*, number 8 (14), 26 April 1922.

12. Al-Harizi (pseudonym) in *Zhizn'Natsional'nostei*, number 1 (58),

4 January, 1920.

13. Only foreign Muslims were employed at high levels in the Komintern, for instance, the Indonesian Tan Malaka. Soviet Muslim cadres had no access to the numerous organisations of the Komintern.

14. The Red Division sent to Ghilan was composed entirely of Russians, both officers and men, mostly from the northern province of Yaroslavl'. The division left Ghilan in September 1920, without firing a shot.

15. It is believed that the only exception was an obscure Bashkir Communist, Sherif Manatov, who in 1919 was sent to Turkey, where he helped found the Turkish Communist Party in Ankara. Some months later he was expelled by Kemal.

16. M.S. Sultan Galiev, 'The Social Revolution and the East,' in *Zhizn' Natsional'nostei*, number 42 (50), 1919; English translation in Alexandre Bennigsen and S. Enders Wimbush, *Muslim National Communism in the Soviet Union — A Revolutionary Strategy for the Colonial World* (Chicago, 1979), pp. 131-137.

17. Cf. R. Nafigov, 'Deiatel'nost' Tsentral'nogo Musul'manskogo Kommisariata pri Narodnom Kommissariate po delam Natsional'nostei v 1918 godu,' *Sovetskoe Vostokovedenie* (Moscow, 1958), p. 105.

18. Especially T. Ryskulov, *Revoliutsiia i Korennoe naselenie Turkestana*, Tashkent 1925; N. Samurskii (Efendiev), *Dagestan* (Moscow, 1925); and A.A. Takho-Godi, Makhach-Qala 1927. Of course, all three authors were later liquidated by Stalin for 'nationalist-bourgeois deviation.'

19. Cf. the speech of J.V. Stalin at the Fourth Conference of the Central Committee of the RCP(b) with the responsible workers of the national republics and regions, 10 June 1923, in J.V. Stalin, *Works*, Vol. 5, 1921-23, (Moscow, 1953), pp. 308-319. English translation in A.A. Bennigsen and S. Enders Wimbush, *Muslim National Communism in the Soviet Union*, op. cit., pp. 158-165.

20. All religious schools were closed in 1928, and, out of 25,000 mosques in the tsarist empire in 1913 (plus several thousands in the Emirat of Bukhara and the Khanate of Khiva) only 1,200 were in operation in 1943.

21. A Volga Tatar, Hakimov headed a Soviet mission to the Imam Yahya of Yemen in the early 1930s, and in the 1960s the former first secretary of the Communist Party of Uzbekistan, Muhitdinov was the Soviet ambassador to Syria.

22. Crimean Tatars, Karachais, Balkars, Chechens and Ingush. It seems that to these nationalities, submitted to genocide and deported (including the soldiers and officers who had served on the front), were added an unknown number of Muslim Ossetians (Digors) and Avars from northern Daghestan. After the end of the war an important group of Muslims from southwestern Georgia (the so-called Meskhetian Turks) were also deported to Siberia and Kazakhstan.

23. It is true, however, that the behaviour of other Soviet nationalities during the war was equally ambiguous and their will to defend the Socialist fatherlands questionable.

24. 1979 figures: Azeris, 5,500,000 in the USSR with five to six million in Iran; Tajiks, 3,000,000 in the USSR and four to five million in Afghanistan; Turkmen, 2,000,000 in the USSR and 1,000,000 in Iran, Afghanistan and Turkey; Uzbeks, 12,500,000 in the USSR and 1,500,000 in Afghanistan.

25. On this subject, see my article on 'Soviet Muslims and the World of Islam', *Problems of Communism*, March-April 1980, pp. 38-51.

26. Among those who refused to attend were Saudi Arabia, Iran, Gulf Emirates, Egypt, Indonesia, India, Morocco, Mauritania, Iraq, Bahrein, Somalia, Oman, Nigeria, Cameroon, Comorres, Djibuti, Gabon, Gambia, Guinea-Bissau, Haute-Volta, Malaysia, Qatar, Chad, Yugoslavia and Albania. Represented by journalists were Pakistan, Bangladesh, Lebanon, Algeria, Benin, and Tanzania.

27. In December, 1980, a small Soviet delegation headed by Mahmud Gekkiev, the *mufti* of the North Caucasus, visited North Yemen.

28. According to *Knizhnaia Letopis'*.

29. Major General Zia Yusif Zade, 'Protecting the Security of the State and of the People,' *Bakinskii Rabochii*, Baku, 19 December 1980.

30. *Turkmenskaia Iskra*, Ashkhabad, 18 March 1981; analysed in *Radio Liberty Research Papers* 161/81, 13 April 1981, 'Turkmen Party Chief sees danger of subversion in scientific and cultural contacts.'

31. *Les Musulmans de l'Orient Soviétique* (French version), Tashkent, number 2, 1981, pp. 18-19.

32. H. Seton-Watson, E. Allworth, T. Rakowska-Harmstone, L. Shyder, G. Simon, S.E. Wimbush, and A. Bennigsen.

33. Q.S. Rejepova, 'Nationalism — an Instrument of Ideological Diversion of Imperialism,' *Izvestia Akademii Nauk Turkmenskoi SSR, Seria Obshchestvennykh Nauk*, number 4, 1981, Ashkhabad, p. 15.

34. See Alexandre Bennigsen, 'Mullahs, Mujahidin and Soviet Muslims,' *Problems of Communism*, November-December 1984.

NATIONALITIES IN THE SOVIET ARMED FORCES

S. Enders Wimbush

Perhaps no other institution in Soviet life illustrates better than the Soviet armed forces the inherent problems of multinationalism for Soviet policy. Operating under the principle of universal conscription, in theory all young Soviet men are required to serve in some branch of the armed forces, usually when they are between the ages of 17 and 25. In practice this means that Soviet authorities are charged with the task of welding together into a cohesive and effective fighting force representatives of more than one hundred different nationalities of diverse cultural backgrounds speaking nearly as many distinct languages. Cultural diversity is especially pronounced among conscripts, who represent the following religio-cultural traditions, among others: Eastern Orthodox, Eastern Catholic, Catholic, Lutheran, Sunnite and Shiite Islam, Judaic, Ismaili (Nazarit), Armenian Gregorian, Buddhist, Buddhist-Lamaite, Nestorian Christian, and animist.

By any reckoning, creating a fighting force from this melange of different peoples, many with conflicting national pasts and enduring traditions, is a daunting assignment. Soviet planners, however, are not without a substantial body of evidence, much of which can be garnered from the experience of the pre-Soviet military establishment of the Russian Empire, to which they can turn for advice and policy guidance. As will be noted briefly below, the leaders of the Russian Empire before 1917 faced most of the same problems regarding the ethnic factor in the armed forces as today's Soviet Russian leaders. To this one could add the experience of other multinational empires — the Austro-Hungarian and Ottoman Empires come immediately to mind — which also found it necessary to construct armed forces of highly diverse ethnic material. (Comparisons with the former will be made occasionally in this analysis.) Both of these empires ultimately foundered in large part because of their inability to reconcile competing national interests within their state boundaries in times of crisis, but it is noteworthy that, with some exceptions, the ethnically diverse armed forces of both the Austro-Hungarians and of the Ottomans remained for the most part more ethnically stable and reliable than the state as a whole. While it is impossible in this analysis to complete a detailed comparison of the importance of the ethnic factor in the Austro-Hungarian, Ottoman, and Russian/Soviet armed forces, such a study is indeed necessary, and it is hoped that this treatment will suggest some analytical areas in which comparative analysis might be conducted profitably.

Western policy makers, too, would benefit from an examination of the historical record, from which they would certainly gain a healthy appreciation of the task facing the Soviets today, as well as an insight into the opportunities and vulnerabilities that are inherent in the Soviet position and which are determined to a large extent by current Soviet policy and practice. What is more, in the next few decades the ethnic factor in the Soviet armed forces will assume greater importance and take on new meaning for reasons which are described in part below. This awareness should stimulate a more thorough examination of the ethnic factor in the Soviet armed forces and its strategic implications than is now the case.

The Demographic Factor

As in so many areas of Soviet life, the factor auguring the most far-reaching and dramatic change in the Soviet armed forces is demographic evolution. Because of reduced birthrates among Slavs (Russians, Ukrainians, and Belorussians) — the peoples on which the Soviet military has always depended most heavily to comprise the bulk of its officers and men, especially those entrusted with responsibility to operate technologically advanced systems, to man front-line combat units, and to conduct operations in regions of political sensitivity — and heightened birthrates among non-Slavs, especially among Soviet Muslims in Central Asia and the Caucasus, the face of the pool of conscript-eligible young men for armed service is changing rapidly. Slavic populations are becoming 'older', while Soviet Asian populations are becoming 'younger', in the sense that an increasingly smaller proportion of the former and an increasingly larger share of the latter now fall into the conscript-eligible ages. The implications of this shift in the Soviet age structure for the draftable manpower cohort can be summed up as follows, according to a recent report by Edmund Brunner:

1. In 1980, ethnic Russians now appear to comprise less than half of the 18-year-old male conscript-eligible cohort and by 1995 will comprise

only 46 percent of the total.

2. The percentage of the major Slavic groups (Russians, Ukrainians, Belorussians) taken together will fall from 67 percent of the cohort in 1980 to 62 percent in 1995.

3. The Muslim-Turkic peoples comprise the only group for which the percentage of 18-year-old males in the Soviet total will increase — from 23.5 percent in 1980 to 28.7 percent in 1995.

4. The Muslim-Turkic group is also the only one that will gain in its share of the total population of the Soviet Union in this period, as all other groups will lose in relative strength.

5. The number of 18-year-old males will reach a low point of 2.15 million in 1985 but will increase thereafter to 2.32 million in 1995. The number of Russian draft-age males will also increase slightly from 1985 to 1995 but their percentage of the Soviet total will continue to decline.

6. Although the number of Muslim-Turkic draft-age males will increase steadily from 1980 to 1985, their percentage of the Soviet total will reach a peak of 28.9 percent in 1990 and will remain at this figure in 1995.[1]

One may conclude from these projections that by 1995 between one-third and one-fourth of the conscript-eligible cohort for the Soviet armed forces will come from a Muslim region of the USSR, while until that date the Russian/Slavic percentage of the cohort will steadily decrease. What this means for Soviet recruitment policies cannot now be foreseen. It is worth stressing, however, that Soviet Muslims will constitute a larger and larger percentage of the Soviet armed forces *only* if Soviet planners acquiesce to these developments. There are costly but probably effective ways in which Soviet planners can avoid having to translate demographic shifts in Soviet society as a whole into corresponding alterations in ethnic force structure. These will be discussed below.

Most institutions in which ethnicity plays a key role probably would find demographic change of this magnitude and speed hard to assimilate. It is likely that Soviet planners are finding the spectre particularly ominous if for no other reason than because there is almost no precedent in Soviet and pre-Soviet Russian history for employing non-Slavs systematically as full partners to Slavs in Russian military establishments. 'Even when the Russian regime instituted a modern conscription policy in 1699-1700,' note Curran and Ponomareff, 'most non-Russians in military service continued to serve as volunteers outside the framework of the regular army in units designated as "troops of different nationalities." The draft was only applied in Russian areas, apparently to restrict the number of minorities in the army and thus ensure Russian control.'[2] Conscription was made universal as part of the military reforms of 1874, but discrimination continued: those non-Russians considered of questionable loyalty (Caucasians, North Caucasians, and Central Asians) were excluded from service in practice, with the exception of some volunteer units raised among the North Caucasians and some conscripted Caucasians, but Central Asians were excluded from service until 1916.[3] An interesting comparison can be made here with recruitment policy in the Austro-Hungarian army. According to Norman Stone, in 1910 the percentage of the various nationalities that made up the Empire broadly approximated their percentage in the population as a whole. Recruitment seems to have been carried out evenly without regard to nationality.[4] Thus, as one empire was broadening the ethnic base of its armed forces the Russian Empire was acting to keep the ethnic base of its armed forces as narrow as possible. It is this legacy which the Bolsheviks inherited and which for similar reasons and some special ones of their own making chose to perpetuate.

An unsuccessful attempt was made to conscript Central Asians in 1916, which was a distinct departure from previous policy. The Russian government also encouraged the formation of some limited national units, especially among those nationalities with historical antagonisms toward the Central Powers. Many national units continued to exist well into the revolutionary period after 1917, and the Bolsheviks took advantage of these formations — usually through promises of self-determination to the peoples involved — in their fights against White Russian forces. As Chantal Lemercier-Quelquejay points out elsewhere in this volume, the importance of many of these isolated but highly effective national units should not be underestimated. Once Lenin, then Stalin, was firmly in power, however, the national units were demobilized, after a serious attempt to make them an integral part of the Red Army in 1924-1925, and they were officially abolished in March 1938. Some were brought back during World War II, but it is probably the case that even in nominally ethnic units one could find large concentrations, perhaps even majorities, of Slavic soldiers. Ethnic units were thought to be a symbolic asset but a strategic liability; hence they were held up for public view when this kind of symbolism was needed, but they appear to have had an unimportant military function and probably existed in name only. Other military units in theory were ethnically integrated, but after January 1943 as a result of the Soviet victory at the battle of Kursk the number of non-Slavs in the combined Soviet forces dropped dramatically. A former high-ranking Soviet staff officer explained the general focus of Soviet policy in this regard:

> In late 1941, or at the beginning of 1942, there was a top-secret decree of the Council of Labour and Defence about service by non-Russians, which was formulated by a special directive of the Supreme Soviet. It was entitled 'Concerning the Principle of Staffing in the Soviet Armed Forces,' and the decree went something like this: 'The war that has just begun has demonstrated that not all Soviet nations have similar fighting abilities. Certain units have been defeated, due to the fact that the nations forming the majority in them have poor fighting abilities.' The last item in the directive noted that Central Asians have proved 'completely unreliable' as far as their fighting abilities were concerned and were not very useful in any military respect.[5]

Yet another directive called for Slavic majorities in all units.[6] Political reliability of non-Russian soldiers appears to have been a primary concern of the Soviet leadership at that time, and German forces took advantage of this Soviet vulnerability on some occasions (see the chapter by Alex Alexiev in this volume).

Soviet policy regarding nationalities in the armed forces in many ways would appear to be an extension, even an exaggeration, of pre-Soviet Russian imperial policy. There have of course been occasional specific exceptions to this generalization, but for the most part Soviet policy by the end of World War II can be characterized as one of gradually excluding non-Slavic minorities of the Soviet empire from positions of military responsibility and political sensitivity.

Since 1945, we have had access until recently to little information about the ethnic factor in the Soviet armed forces. In the last few years, however, a series of Rand Corporation studies appeared in which the analysts, including the author, drew heavily on the first-hand testimony of former Soviet soldiers and officers now in emigration, most of whom had served within the last ten years. Their findings are included below and, where appropriate, compared to the experiences of other states.

Recruitment Policy in the Soviet Armed Forces

As already noted, it would appear that there are clear guidelines for recruiting different nationalities into the Soviet armed forces, despite

Soviet claims of equality and fairness in the process. At the lowest level, that of the military draft board (*voenkomat*), incoming recruits are categorized on the basis of many criteria of which ethnic background is one of the most important. These recruits are then 'bought' by a military buyer (*pokupatel'*) from an individual unit or from a military district, who is instructed to obtain a specific number of recruits of a specific ethnic profile. It is probably the case that the General Staff, which is in possession of all of the profiles from the different *voenkomats*, is responsible for directing buyers. By sending a buyer to a *voenkomat* in Moscow and then to a *voenkomat* in Uzbekistan, for example, it is possible for central military authorities to control the ethnic mix of specific units.

While there are some interesting and perhaps unforeseen malfunctions in this elaborate system, as the Rand studies point out, it is clear that there is no 'pot luck' factor at work here: Soviet military recruitment is a directed system which uses ethnicity as one of its fundamental criteria for assigning new recruits to service branch and functional speciality. This becomes clearer still when one considers the ethnic composition of various branches of the Soviet armed forces and of specific functional units.

Ethnic Composition of the Soviet Armed Forces

With some exceptions, the high technology services are heavily weighted toward Slavic recruits. Thus, one can find a large majority of Slavs, perhaps as much as 95 percent, in the Air Force, Navy, and Strategic Rocket Forces. Even within the Slavic group there is a very large Russian majority in these branches. The KGB Border Forces also contain a large majority of Russians and other Slavs due to the political reliability required for service in this branch.

The Ground Forces contains the great majority of non-Slavs that one finds in the Soviet armed forces. Non-Slavs can comprise as much as 20 percent of regimental-size units and perhaps even more than this in smaller units. The typical composition of a Ground Forces unit — infantry, for example — will be approximately 75-80 percent Slavs, 10 percent Central Asians, 5 percent Balts, and 5 percent Caucasians, with a scattering of other nationalities.

Despite this more favourable representation in Ground Forces units, non-Slavs are vastly underrepresented in front-line combat formations. Large numbers of them, probably a majority, serve in construction battalions (*stroibat*). Even in cases where non-Slavic minorities can be found in combat units they frequently are in a non-combatant role, such as in support and kitchen units.

Construction battalions frequently have from 80-90 percent non-Slavic minorities and a sprinkling of undesirable Slavs. They are commanded nearly always by Slavic officers. These units have identical internal structures as regular army units, and they draw recruits according to established criteria from the semi-annual conscript call-up. The conscripts they draw come almost exclusively from those thought to be of questionable reliability. Some Russian dissidents do serve here, for they are suspected of being disloyal individuals. But most *stroibats* are full of Central Asians, Balts, western Ukrainians (who because of their well-known quests for independence and their undisguised enthusiasm for the Germans in the early days of World War II are treated entirely differently from eastern Ukrainians), Jews, and Soviet Germans, among others: that is, groups who are collectively suspect.

One major exception to the prevailing pattern of ethnic selectivity in critical military units is the Internal Security Forces (MVD). A large percentage of these troops are in fact minorities, often coming from Central Asia. This anomaly is due to the Soviet regime's desire to meet internal dissent with forces from another part of the USSR, that is by soldiers who are unlikely to hesitate to eliminate the dissent, as local soldiers from the same ethnic group might be. Thus one finds Central Asian MVD forces in Smolensk and Russian, or even Baltic, MVD forces in Dushanbe.

Non-commissioned officers are of two types: professional and one-term. Both categories show a predominance of Slavic personnel, although it is possible for non-Slavic soldiers to become junior sergeants to fill immediate requirements of a specific military unit. Professional sergeants are mostly Slavs, but surprisingly not overwhelmingly Russian. In fact many, perhaps even a majority, are from the eastern Ukraine.

The Soviet officer corps is overwhelmingly Slavic and Russian. The Russian share of the total probably exceeds 80 percent, with the remainder coming from reliable Ukrainians and Belorussians. In all likelihood this disproportionate share of Russians is a matter of policy, but in any case the military educational system, which produces the majority of Soviet officers, is strongly biased in favour of Russian and Slavic candidates. Only a handful of non-Slavs become Soviet officers.

By comparison the national composition of the Austro-Hungarian officer corps showed a significant bias in favour of Germans, who made up 75 percent of its total in 1868.[7] The introduction of conscription in

1868 did little to alter these proportions. In 1910, Germans constituted approximately 79 percent of the professional officer corps and 60 percent of the reserve officers; yet they totalled a mere 25 percent across the ranks. This discrepancy, while consistent, was not deliberate Imperial policy as it almost certainly is in the Soviet case today. As far as the army was supposed to be a supra-national force, any overt support of a *Herrenvolk* was discouraged.[8] The advantages for Germans, nonetheless, were strikingly similar to those for Russians today: the way into the officer corps was through one of the military Hochschulen (pre-1868), the Military Academy in Vienna, or the Cadet training schools in Ollmutz, Graz, or Milan. Dominated by German culture and patronised by scions of wealthy German families, these schools naturally gave a cultural-linguistic advantage to Germans. After 1868, however, the army nominally opened up to talent, a concession that offered an advantage only to those nationalities with a middle class.[9]

Stationing Practices

Before World War II the Soviet military was deployed and manned on a territorial basis. Today the guiding principle is extraterritoriality: stationing recruits at considerable distance from their native territories. In part, this shift of emphasis can be said to derive from the Soviet regime's fear of ethnic disturbances in borderland territories and the possibility that ethnically similar soldiers might contribute to local causes at the expense of Moscow's control. Soldiers from afar are thus thought to represent more reliable instruments for internal policing and control if the need arises. So it is that soldiers from the Baltic states are likely to be found in Central Asia, the Caucasus, or Russia proper, while Central Asians most likely will see service (in construction battalions) in Russia or the Ukraine. Soviet forces abroad, as in the Warsaw Pact countries, are usually Slavs.

The Austro-Hungarians, like the Soviets, appear to have practised a kind of extraterritorial stationing, although experts differ on how much and why. Gunther Rothenberg, the accredited authority on the Austrian army, concludes that the policy of restationing was practised out of consideration for national diversities and was the major factor which saved the army in 1848.[10] Sked, who examines and questions Rothenberg's statistics, puts forward the view that 'moving most of the army about from time to time' was an historic practice designed to keep the army an integrated whole rather than an attempt at a nationalities policy. If the statistics were properly analyzed, he concludes, they would show that many soldiers were stationed on their own ethnic territory under commanding officers of their own nationality and that there was no consistent policy for restationing.[11]

For the most part, Soviet military units are stationed away from population centres, and measures are taken to isolate servicemen from the local population. This is particularly the case in Central Asia and the Caucasus. The practice probably results at least in part from hostile contact between soldiers and populations of different ethnic backgrounds.

Training and Education of Minorities

Non-Slavs without a sound knowledge of the Russian language (see below) are unlikely to receive advanced technical training of any kind. For the same reason, most are excluded from advanced infantry, artillery, and communications training. It probably is not the case across the board that quotas *per se* keep minorities from entering military academies and schools, however. Rather the opposite appears to be the case in fact: in recent years Soviet authorities have encouraged minorities to enter the military career path via an attractive list of 'affirmative' incentives, which include lower examination requirements for some academies, active recruitment by military authorities, and the location of some academies in minority regions rather than in Russia proper. On the other hand, some prestigious military schools, such as the naval academies, are Slavic preserves which minorities have virtually no chance to enter.

For most non-Slavs adopting a military career requires a conscious decision to undergo considerable russification. Most minorities appear to be unwilling to make this sacrifice.

For prospective recruits, access to pre-induction training facilities, such as those provided by DOSAAF (Voluntary Organization for Cooperation with the Army, Air Force, and Navy), is uneven, with the Slavic regions of the country enjoying by far the greater share and variety. Moreover, many minorities see DOSAAF activities as something purely Russian and decline to participate.

In-service military training for minorities is also uneven. Some minorities, especially those with command of the Russian language and an otherwise unblemished political record, can be found in the front line combat units, having completed exactly the same course of basic training as their Slavic counterparts. Most Caucasians and Central Asians, on the other hand, especially those in construction troops, frequently receive no or marginal combat or weapons training. Many construction troops never have access to weapons of any kind, including machine guns and rifles, and many have undergone only the most rudimentary military training, perhaps no more than a few hours drilling with a rifle. Thus, a substantial portion of the Soviet armed forces — up to 20 percent by some estimates — are simply intended to be workers without weapons.

The Language Problem

Like most modern armed forces, the Soviets employ one language of command, Russian. As noted above, national military formations no longer exist in the Soviet armed forces, formations which logically would employ the language of the nominal nationality. The difficulty for Soviet military authorities is that the peoples of the Soviet Union use nearly one hundred languages in everyday life, and while Soviet planners have managed to inculcate Russian as a second language in many parts of the USSR, entire segments of the conscript-eligible population — usually minority rural youth, especially those from Central Asia and the Caucasus — still often arrive for service with little or no Russian language capability.

It is language ability in Russian, probably more than any other criterion — but not forgetting historical perceptions of the political disloyalty of some minorities — that forces the Soviet military to continue its policy of Slavic overrepresentation. Simply, if more non-Russians could function adequately in the Russian language they could be used in more militarily advanced and challenging positions. But it bears repeating that a better understanding of Russian would mean only that minorities *could* be used in this way, not that Soviet authorities automatically would choose to so employ them; the political questions regarding the use of minority troops would remain. Better Russian would not by itself eliminate hostility between Russians and minorities; to speak Russian is not to love them, any more than for an Algerian to speak French or a Tibetan to speak Chinese is an indication of anything other than the acquisition of a useful skill. This being said, one can point to the presence in high-technology units of a few minorities — even Central Asians and Caucasians — who speak good Russian as evidence that the Soviet leadership probably would consider the addition of many more linguistically qualified minority troops to its militarily usable manpower pool to be a distinct plus.

It is paradoxical, then, that so little official effort has been devoted by Soviet military planners to preparing non-Russian-speakers in Russian language use. Until only recently, Soviet policy in this regard was characterized by a distinct lack of effort to provide pre-induction or even post-induction language courses. Now, however, apparently with their eyes firmly on the demographic shifts that promise to change the ethnic face of the conscript-eligible manpower pool in the next two or three decades, Soviet military and non-military experts have begun to devote considerable attention to this issue.[12]

Historically the Soviet armed forces have relied on an intensive Russian language environment to give minority conscripts the level of language ability deemed necessary. This approach appears to be partly successful: by the end of their conscription term, recruits with no or poor Russian usually progress to a level of functional 'kitchen' Russian, that is to an understanding of some basic commands and instructions.

Although similar in some particulars, this procedure is essentially different from that used in the Austro-Hungarian army.[13] From its formation, with the exception of Hungarian units after 1868 the Austro-Hungarian army used German as the language of command (*Kommando-Sprache*). In practice, this consisted of some eighty words of command used mainly on parade. The language of service (*Dienst-Sprache*) was employed for the thousand or so technical terms used to describe parts of the equipment and armoury. These two languages remained in German throughout the nineteenth century. 'Kitchen' Russian in today's Soviet armed forces probably falls somewhere between the *Kommando-Sprache* and the *Dienst-Sprache* of the Austro-Hungarians; common sense suggests that it is less than adequate to convey complex and rapid commands in a chaotic combat environment. Certainly Austro-Hungarian authorities understood the limitations of the *Dienst-Sprache*, and it is probably for this reason that all young officers were required to learn the majority language of their units within three years of posting or face dismissal. No such requirement exists in the Soviet armed forces today, and no evidence suggests that the acquisition of a minority language by young officers is even a high Soviet priority.

The language of command in the Austro-Hungarian army not surprisingly came to be seen as a symbol of German dominance, and repeated efforts to change this principle were always thwarted in the end by the personal insistence of the Emperor. Toward the beginning of World War I, protests against a single language of command became more frequent, such as when Czechs insisted on answering *zde* instead of *hier* at roll call, even though they could be court-martialed for this offence. The language problem was a continual irritant, but one which the Austro-Hungarians mitigated through the use of national or quasi-national units. This was illustrated graphically in 1914 when mobilization posters had to be printed in fifteen languages.[14]

One can speculate with confidence that Russian is viewed in much the same way by recruits in the Soviet armed forces. With virtually no institutional base from which to launch protests and severe punishments for disciplinary transgressions being certain, Soviet minority soldiers resort to other forms of protest, such as dissimulation: refusing to acknowledge that they understand Russian commands as a way of avoiding unwanted assignments and of irritating their Russian officers.

The cornerstone of anyone's military education is the ability to communicate; hence, the 'Russian-only' rule in the Soviet armed forces has clear military advantages but only if it can be enforced widely and if non-Russian speakers can be brought to a level of some fluency. Soldiers who are known to be deficient in the language of command or who are known to pretend not to know it are of limited military utility, the latter perhaps being even less reliable than the former. Complex commands involving modern technological systems and complex military operations require better educated soldiers, not the opposite as is sometimes thought. Where good communications is lacking, as it is in a significant part of the Soviet conscript-eligible manpower pool, human reliability is necessarily diminished, and the more innovative plans of military tacticians are subject to critical restraints. On balance, the problem is one that the Soviets are unlikely to solve after a linguistically deficient recruit has been inducted. Rather, it is a task for the non-military sector. Currently Soviet efforts in this regard are inadequate. New programmes, while indisputably necessary, will be expensive and require a substantial period of planning and implementation.

In practice, 'Russian only' is hard to enforce among minorities, and in construction units, where the majority usually comes from various minorities, the 'Russian-only' rule usually gives way to local languages.

Relations Between Minorities and Slavs

According to Soviet propaganda, the armed forces of the state are an important vehicle for bringing the diverse nationalities of the USSR together in an atmosphere of friendship and harmony. From this experience young men from minority nationalities are intended to return to the non-military world with a heightened sense of fraternal brotherhood with the Russian people and a commitment to the concept of the 'New Soviet Man.' In practice, the Soviet armed forces do not appear to function in this way at all; indeed, they may stimulate exactly opposite tendencies, namely the intensification of ethnic self-awareness and self-assertiveness and a strong antipathy toward Russians in particular.

Many conflicts appear to be racially motivated: light-skinned 'Europeans' versus dark-skinned 'Asians.' The attitude of Slavic soldiers toward their Central Asian or Caucasian counterparts is one of undisguised racial superiority, a fact poignantly underscored by the routine use of racial epithets.[15] Violent conflict is not a rare occurrence and may even be commonplace. Soldiers of the same or related nationalities tend to band together in the performance of daily tasks and for social activities after hours.

It is difficult to see how this picture of widespread ethnic antagonism, which can usually, but not always, be described in terms of a Slav-non-Slav dichotomy, could be different. None of the other policies or practices described could on the face of it be said to conduce to greater ethnic harmony or, more specifically, to contribute toward a climate of greater understanding and tolerance of Slavs for minorities and vice versa. Nearly all the main features of the Soviet military system would appear to promote precisely the opposite outcome.[16]

Soviet Alternatives

Soviet planners have a number of available alternatives to offset the demographic shortfalls in the Slavic component of the conscript-eligible manpower pool for the next few decades. There are some measures, or combinations of measures, that provide a safety valve for maintaining Russian-Slavic dominance as it is currently constituted. However, no single option or combination is without some costs of its own. No matter how the Soviets choose to solve their difficulties they must be prepared to pay a price.

The most obvious remedy would be simply to extend the conscription time of the recruit. Only recently, however, conscription time was reduced across the board as a means of freeing up more prime employment-age youth for non-military labour in the chronically labour-short European regions of the USSR. To reinstate a longer conscription period now would have the immediate effect of aggravating the non-military labour situation.

Another possibility is to conscript minorities — especially Central Asians, from whom the largest proportional incremental increases to the conscript-eligible pool will come — more completely into construction battalions and other support positions and then engage these units more fully in the non-military economy. This could have the doubly beneficial effect of easing the non-military labour problem while simultaneously freeing more Slavs for military service. Construction battalions currently are used in this way, as nearly anyone who has visited Moscow or other larger Russian cities can attest. It is questionable, however, if the average military construction battalion could meet technological levels of competence that Soviet industry increasingly requires.

Yet a third alternative would be to reduce the size of the armed forces altogether. A solution of this kind would have obvious appeal to publicly cost-conscious Western governments, whose military establishments fall under well-defined statutory authorities and public scrutiny. On the other hand it is somehow more difficult to imagine Soviet military leaders, who probably exercise more real political power in the Kremlin than do their Western counterparts in Washington, Bonn, or London, accepting this remedy without a damaging political fight. In view of current Soviet military commitments — Afghanistan, Poland, Warsaw Pact forces, Sino-Soviet border — the USSR's armed forces already look to be stretched a bit thin, with little room to react to an unanticipated crisis or opportunity (in Iran or Pakistan, for example). Soviet military leaders doubtlessly will fight to maintain their forces' strength, even perhaps to increase it.

The Soviet armed forces might look to labour saving high technology to ward off the demographic threat. This would be an expensive solution, requiring Soviet leaders to invest large sums to upgrade industries that currently lag behind the West's capabilities (computers, for example) or to buy abroad. The latter possibility underlines the Soviet Union's limited hard currency reserves and Western policies designed to prevent the transfer of military-relevant technology.

Another potential solution to the problem, *ceteris paribus*, would be to reinstitute national military units in which the language of command would be something other than Russian and only a few Russian speakers would be required to operate the command and control mechanisms between the national units and the larger Russian-speaking forces. All other things are not equal, of course. National units represent a particularly ominous political danger to the Soviet Russian leadership, which is almost certainly why they were abolished in the first place. Still, if units consisting almost entirely of minorities, with the exception of some Russian officers, could be made politically safe, this solution would certainly be an attractive one.

Finally, Soviet leaders could choose simply to enlist larger numbers of minorities in units which traditionally have had strong Russian/Slavic majorities. From the preceeding discussion, the economic, political and military costs and benefits of such a strategy are clear.

It may not be necessary for Soviet leaders to adopt one or more of these alternatives in its entirety: some of each or moderate doses of several might solve the problem at what the Soviets consider to be an acceptable cost. Those solutions which embody the concept of Slavic preeminence in the armed forces probably are the most logical, but also the most costly, choices. Those which will enhance the role of minorities in the military establishment are probably less likely to be chosen, if for no other reason than the difficulties inherent in reversing historical patterns. While one would be foolish to assert that the Soviets could never accept a solution that reduced Russian representation in the armed forces — and by implication watered down Russian authority — such a decision does have at least three hundred years of history pitted against it. Moreover, this decision could not be taken in isolation from an entire constellation of other issues affecting minorities in the Soviet state. If such a wide-ranging reassessment is currently being undertaken in Moscow evidence of it is lacking.

Operational Concerns

Until late 1979, no Soviet army had been engaged in sustained combat since 1945, although there have been limited engagements in Hungary (1956) and Czechoslovakia (1968) and an occasional skirmish along the Sino-Soviet border. The legacy of World War II regarding the use of minority soldiers is presumably critical in Soviet decision making today. This legacy, as noted earlier, revolves less around the technical competence of non-Russian troops than around their political reliability. No Soviet leader can ignore either the historical wounds caused by the Bolsheviks' reincorporation of the Russian Empire by force, local resistance to the extensive human and material misery Soviet Russian policies caused at one time or another in virtually every minority region, or the sizable desertions of non-Russian soldiers and civilians to Germany during the war years and their active resistance in large numbers to defeat the Soviets. Because some of these wounds remain open and running even today and others, while partially healed are not forgotten, Soviet planners who consider the problems and opportunities associated with the ethnic factor in the armed forces today must repeatedly address the fundamental question: What has changed since 1945 to eliminate the threat of minority unreliability?

Recent Soviet experience in Afghanistan has lent this question new urgency. Although the original Soviet invasion force contained many Central Asians, these were rapidly withdrawn from the combat arena beginning in late February 1980 and replaced mainly with Slavs. While hard evidence is sketchy, reports from Afghan resistance figures, from correspondents, from Muslims with access to Afghanistan, and, increasingly, from Soviet deserters,[17] describe what appears to be a fairly widespread pattern of fraternization between Soviet Central Asian troops and the Afghans, many of whom are ethnically related and who, like the Soviet Central Asians, are Muslims.

The Soviet decision to send Central Asians to Afghanistan in the first place was probably taken for purely practical reasons. Most of the divisions utilized during the invasion came initially from the Central Asian and Turkestan Military Districts but were not fully combat-ready divisions at the time of call-up. As is Soviet practice in situations of this kind, the divisions were filled with personnel from the local reserve units, in this case with large numbers of Central Asians. Among other things, we can conclude from this that Soviet leaders anticipated little resistance from the Afghans, for they were certainly fully aware that the large majority of the Central Asian reservists had had little or no combat and weapons training during their obligatory service terms, which for most was probably spent in construction battalions.[18]

Ethnic difficulties in the Soviet armed forces during the Afghan adventure are of particular interest at this time because they underline the dilemma posed by demographic shifts: there will be more and more Soviet Muslims of conscriptable age, but how are they to be used, if at all? Thus demography and history could coalesce to influence, perhaps restrict, Soviet military operational choice. If Soviet Central Asian troops proved to be less than satisfactory in Afghanistan, will they be any more so in other potential theatres of operations, say in Iran, Pakistan, Baluchistan, Turkey, Sinkiang, or for that matter anywhere in the Muslim Middle East? Can Baltic or Ukrainian troops be counted on in the event of a Soviet surgical invasion of Poland? With the supply of military-age Slavs dwindling, questions of this kind must cause Soviet leaders real concern.

The ethnic dimension to recruitment, stationing, and manning practices as they currently exist in the Soviet armed forces suggest the possibility of both preparatory and combat-related weaknesses and vulnerabilities. For example, unit training weaknesses could become a real possibility, and judging from the Soviet experience in Afghanistan some weaknesses are already apparent. The ethnic structuring of the forces also raises the spectre of substantial 'second battle' weaknesses in the event of a protracted military conflict, for example against the Chinese: the need to replace first-round Russian/Slavic soldiers with lesser trained and less politically reliable non-Slavs.

Some recent evidence suggests that Soviet planners might be moving to ease the demographic pinch somewhat while simultaneously strengthening the potential reliability of their non-Russian contingent. With an interesting shift of emphasis, Soviet authorities in Uzbekistan have begun to take serious steps to enroll more young Uzbeks in officer training schools.[19] It is still much too early to know if these plans will succeed, although the initial response is not encouraging. Because the Uzbeks are the largest group of Central Asians they are the logical focus for such a campaign among these particular non-Russians. Moreover, if through a combination of real incentives and the clever manipulation of symbols Soviet military leaders were able to convince one non-Slavic nationality that the military is a rewarding career and one in which real authority and perquisites are shared with the dominant Russians, it would be a valuable advertisement for future recruiting. Yet even if potential officer candidates are able to overcome their justifiable cynicism of these new prospects, it will be a long time before such a programme is widely accepted among non-Russians, even if the opportunities are real ones.

Conclusions

There is always a danger that someone will take an analysis like this one as evidence to argue that the Soviet armed forces are internally weak, that their military capabilities are vastly overestimated by cynical and greedy politicians and generals in search of ever greater expenditure on military equipment and armies, and, implicitly, that the Soviet threat can be discounted. One recent study takes exactly this approach and even uses the Rand studies cited here as proof that the ethnic factor in the Soviet armed forces is a primary cause for this internal military disintegration.[20] It must be said that the Rand analysts, including the author, do not support this conclusion; indeed, it cannot be supported on the basis of the research evidence available to them. Rather, they came to a completely opposite conclusion: namely that the Soviet armed forces, in spite of some ethnicity-caused internal weaknesses, is one of the most formidable military machines the world has ever seen, if in fact it is not the foremost. Specific weaknesses — including ethnic weaknesses — must be seen in context. Thus, while many Soviet minorities deserted and fought against the Soviets in World War II, many others fought long and well for the Soviet state. Historically, military machines on the offensive tend to radiate centripetal forces which can affect all manner of soldiers, including discontented ethnic minorities. For this reason, whatever ethnic vulnerabilities are present in today's Soviet armed forces are most immediately interesting to strategic analysts for their possible manifestations in those distinctive theatres where Soviet forward momentum cannot be sustained and where the ethnic tensions within the Soviet military come under intense local pressure unique to the operational environment. The Soviet invasion of Afghanistan comes immediately to mind in this regard, but other scenarios, noted above, merit consideration. In this more selective sense, Soviet ethnicity-related military vulnerabilities must be an important part of any Soviet strategic cost-benefit calculation; moreover, such vulnerabilities might suggest opportunities for Western policy. Nevertheless, no one should conclude on the basis of current evidence that the Soviet military is other than a mighty and dangerous force, regardless of the nagging ethnic factor.

The leaders of all military establishments must deal with problems from non-military society that overflow into their realm and frequently are exaggerated by the intensive micro-environment of military service. From this viewpoint, we should be alerted, perhaps, that Soviet multinational society generally is fraught with more latent ethnic conflicts than meet the eye of the analyst embarked on standard content examination of the Soviet media.

It is significant that at a time when the Soviet military structure is under considerable pressure to adjust itself to forces — such as demographic shifts and the lessons of the war in Afghanistan — which would seem to make some adjustment necessary if not inevitable, Soviet authorities appear to be doing very little to make the military a rewarding and attractive career to Soviet minorities. To do so would mean, at least implicitly, the reduction of the overbearing Russianness of the terms of service, if not of Russian authority.

Compared to the Austro-Hungarian multinational armed forces, today's Soviet forces are both similar in some respects and distinct in others. Where the former conscientiously eschewed attempts to make the military an instrument for Germanifying the minorities of the empire, the Soviet armed forces are based firmly on the one-language, one-culture principle. While this policy has obvious military benefits if it is successful, it has social costs in any case which could translate to military liabilities and post-service resentments. The Austro-Hungarian officer corps had a distinctive internationalist cast, very unlike the 'internationalism' that pervades Soviet dogma today, which is really a thin disguise for Russian culture under new conditions. Most importantly, the Austro-Hungarian army was a real avenue of upward mobility for minorities of all kinds. Soviet armed forces appear very different by comparison: few enjoy the opportunity to rise beyond a certain level, while those who are required to serve seldom remain in the military beyond the obligatory service period.

Before 1848, there were no significant manifestations of national disaffection in the Austro-Hungarian army, apart from occasional Hungarian demands that Hungarian soldiers should be commanded by Hungarian officers. In part, this can be explained by the incompletely developed sense of cultural-political self-definition on the part of the Croats, Czechs, Slovaks, and Slovenes. Those nationalities whose territories lay mostly outside Austria — Serbs, Rumanians, Poles, Ukrainians, and Italians — remained relatively tranquil until irredentist claims from their co-nationals across the border began to disturb the peace. Moreover, soldiers were recruited for relatively long periods of time, which encouraged the creation of a body of professionally trained men who had developed feelings of loyalty and obedience over the years. Even during the uprisings of 1848, when various nationalisms stimulated strong centrifugal forces among the ethnically diverse citizens of the empire and the army experienced 70,000 desertions, ultimately it was the army which saved the dynasty.

Has the multinational Soviet army such resilience today? Can it control or accommodate the developing national consciousness of large groups of non-Russian recruits? Has it the proper spiritual and psychological defences to withstand those influences from abroad — from Afghanistan, Iran, Poland, even China — which likely will find some resonance among minority servicemen? Can it provide its minorities not only real participation but also a sense of being part of an historic institution in which loyalty, integrity, and service are meaningful concepts which bind them to the goals and leadership of the Soviet state? Will the multinational Soviet armed forces pull together under fire?

One would have to conclude from the historical record and from current Soviet policies and practices that the answers to these questions are currently distinctly mixed. As conditions change, Soviet leaders will be encouraged to ask themselves how long policies and practices which emphasize control and exclusion of minorities in the armed forces rather than participation and incentive can be effective, how long the Soviet armed forces can succeed without a military tradition that embraces minorities in more than a token manner. Military traditions are not created overnight. As far as most Soviet minorities are concerned no Soviet military tradition which features them in anything other than a subordinate, even subservient role exists. For many, such as the men of many nationalities who were removed from the front lines in 1943 or for the Soviet Central Asians who were removed from Afghanistan rather more recently, it might even be described as an anti-tradition. Medal bedecked minority veterans are occasionally trotted out before the adoring cameras of the Soviet mass media to be seen and to tell of their exploits during the last war. This is good theatre, but it is not the stuff of which traditions are made. Nor is it likely to have a positive impact on the young non-Russian recruit who knows perfectly well that his conscription time vistas may well include not weapons, and training, and comradeship but a shovel, two years of construction battalion duty, and discrimination. Without a tradition, whatever incentives are eventually offered to minorities to participate more fully in Soviet military life will have less appeal. These are formidable problems with no easy solutions.

Notes

I wish to thank Nadia Diuk of St. Antony's College, Oxford University, for timely research assistance and suggestions, especially on the comparative aspects of this chapter.

1. Edmund Brunner, Jr., *Soviet Demographic Trends and the Ethnic Composition of Draft Age Males, 1980-1995*, The Rand Corporation, N-1654/1, February 1981, pp. 20-24.
2. Susan L. Curran and Dmitry Ponomareff, *Managing the Ethnic Factor in the Russian and Soviet Armed Forces: An Historical Overview*, The Rand Corporation, R-2640/1, July 1982, p. v.
3. *Ibid.*
4. Norman Stone, 'Army and Society in the Hapsburg Monarchy, 1900-1914,'

Past and Present, No. 33 (April, 1966), pp. 95-111. See also, Alan Sked, *The Survival of the Habsburg Empire* (London, 1979), p. 45.

5. S. Enders Wimbush and Alex Alexiev, *The Ethnic Factor in the Soviet Armed Forces*, The Rand Corporation, R-2787/1, March 1982, p. 7.

6. *Ibid*.

7. Rudolf Kiszling, 'Das ¡Nationalitätenproblem in Habsburgs Wehrmacht, 1848-1918,' *Der Donauraum*, No. 4, 1959, p. 85.

8. Stone, *passim*. See also, Oscar Jaszi, *The Dissolution of the Habsburg Monarchy* (Chicago, 1929), pp. 141-148.

9. Stone, p. 99. The reserve officer corps especially became rapidly ethnically diversified. In 1910, it contained approximately 24 percent Magyars (who constituted only 9 percent of the professional officer corps against 23 percent of the army as a whole; 16 percent Jews (who were a mere 5 percent of the population of Austria-Hungary); 10 percent Czechs (against 5 percent in the professional officer corps and 13 percent in the army as a whole); and Poles and Serbo-Croats 3 percent and 2 percent respectively (against 2.5 and 2.4 percent in the professional corps and 8 percent and 9 percent in the army as a whole). Ukrainians and Rumanians failed to reach a whole percent between them in either corps, although they represented 8 percent and 7 percent respectively of the army as a whole.

10. See, Gunther Rothenberg, 'The Habsburg Army and the Nationality Problem in the Nineteenth Century, 1815-1914,' *Austrian History Yearbook*, III, 1967, pp. 70-87.

11. Sked has done a thorough analysis and has included material on national composition of regiments. By tracking the itinerary of several, he is able to address the question of whether restationing was deliberate or unsystematic.

12. See, for example, Ann Sheehy, 'Efforts Stepped Up to Improve Russian-Language Proficiency of Draft-age Uzbeks,' *Radio Liberty Research Bulletin*, RL 256/83, July 5, 1983.

13. Sked, p. 53. In some respects the Austro-Hungarian problem was more difficult than the Russian problem today. In the former empire, recruitment was carried out by district, not by nationality, so that levies in Bohemia turned up many Germans, and Hungarian units included Croats and Rumanians. Very few were of one nationality exclusively, unlike today's Soviet front-line units which are intended to be dominated by Russians and other Slavs. In 1888, for example, of the forty-seven regiments raised in Hungary only five were purely Magyar and of the remaining thirty-seven, Magyar was the language of the majority in only sixteen. Although the everyday language of these units (*Regiments-Sprache*) was usually the language of the largest nationality, the Austro-Hungarian units were themselves notable ethnic conglomerations: hence the need for a lingua franca, as when two soldiers of different nationality were handling the same gun. See, Rothenberg, who appears to have taken his figures from Oscar Jaszi. Jaszi in turn may have taken his figures from Theodor von Sosnosky, *Die Politik im Habsburgerreiche* (Berlin, 1913).

14. Stone, p. 100. Even so, according to Rothenberg, when troops were finally sent into combat, only German, Magyar, and Bosnian regiments could be committed anywhere.

15. Wimbush and Alexiev, *The Ethnic Factor in the Soviet Armed Forces*, pp. xiii-xiv.

16. Ibid., p. 49. See also the analysis by a former Soviet political officer, Sergei Zamascikov, 'The Role of the Military in the Social Integration of Ethnic Muslims in the USSR,' Radio Liberty Research Bulletin, RL 477/83, December 23, 1983, pp. 20-21.

17. Jim Ghallagher, '2 Soviets tell of Aghan horror,' *Chicago Tribune*, December 4, 1983, p. 1.

S. Enders Wimbush

18. S. Enders Wimbush and Alex Alexiev, *Soviet Central Asian Soldiers in Afghanistan*, The Rand Corporation, N-1634/1, January 1981, *passim*.
19. Bess Brown, 'Further Efforts to Enroll Uzbeks in the Soviet Officer Corps,' Radio Liberty Research Bulletin, RL 31/84, January 18, 1984.
20. Andrew Cockburn, *The Threat: Inside the Soviet Military Machine* (London: Hutchinson and Co.: 1983).

INDEX

Afghanistan, xii, 9, 23, 30, 31, 52, 55, 56, 75, 88; Soviet invasion of, Afghan *mujahidin* resistance, 52, 56, 91-94, 192-193, 198, 217, 218, 220, 223, 242, 243, 244
Albanians, 10
Aliyev, Geidar, 78
Alptekin, Isa Yusuf, 137
Andropov, Yuri, xiv, 160, 161, 162, 163
Anenkov, General, 111
Animists, 227
Arabs: in the US, 3, 8, 10, 11, 31; advance into Central Asia, 105
Armenia, Armenians, viii, 8, 10, 11, 12, 16, 17, 18, 20, 21, 22, 23, 28, 29; Armenian Dashnaks, 49, 58, 64, 67, 71; in US, 3, 42, 58; Armenian separatist movement, 44
Armenian-Gregorian church, 166, 187, 188, 190, 210, 217, 227
Armenian militia of the Dashmaktsutun Nationalist and Socialist Party, 41
Austro-Hungarian Empire, 227; army, 230, 233-234, 237-238, 245
Avars, 225
Azerbaijan, 166, 217, 192, 208; Azerbaijan Republic, 57; Mussawatists, 49
Azerbaijanis, 8, 12, 13, 18, 19, 27, 36, 217

Baku, 8, 12, 16, 42, 45, 67, 215, 218
Balkan Christians, 10, 11
Balkars, 225
Baltic region, Baltic republics, Balts, viii, xii, 7, 12, 16, 18, 20, 23, 26, 27, 29, 30, 36, 61, 62, 63, 64, 65, 66, 67, 68, 69, 76, 83-84; indigenous armed units in WW II, 70; national combat units under German supervision, 71, 173, 191, 232, 233, 234
Baptists, 194, 197
Bashkiria, 47, 48; Revolutionary Committee (Bashreskom), 48
Bashkirs, 18, 36, 38, 39, 48; All-Bashkir Congress, 1917, 38; Bashkir Council, 1917, (Shura), 40, 41; Bashkir Army, 41, 46, 59, 208, 210, 212, 213, 224
Basmachis, 41, 42, 43, 46, 49, 52-54, 55, 56, 59; uprising, 192, 215
Baytursun, Ahmed, 43, 48, 57
Belorussia, 61, 64, 84-85, 165, 168, 169, 174, 184, 185, 189, 191; Uniate Church of Belorussi, 184
Belorussian, 18, 28, 29, 65, 70, 80, 158, 182, 186, 228, 229, 233
Bialer, Seweryn, 79
Bolsheviks, 13, 36, 37, 39, 40, 41, 42, 47, 48, 49, 54, 62, 77, 78, 210, 211, 212, 213
Border politics; Afghanistan, 91-92; China, 95-96, 101-157; Eastern Europe, 82-87; European-Russian agreements, 103; Iran, 90-91; Turkey, 88-90
Brezhnev, Leonid, xiv, 160, 165, 181, 217-219, 223
Buddhists, 77, 227
Buddhist-Lamaite, 227
Buffer states, 87-88
Bukeykhanov, Ali, 40, 57, 212
Bulgarians, 11
Burkhan, 129
Burma, 102

Catholicism, Catholics, 17, 77, 159, 171, 172, 194; Eastern Catholics, 227
Caucasians, 71, 191, 208, 213, 216, 217, 218, 221, 228, 230, 232, 235, 236, 239

249

Index

Caucasus, x, 8, 26, 28; North Caucasus; 36, 61, 62, 63, 64, 67-69, 72, 192, 210, 216, 230
Central Asia, x, xi, 7, 8, 9, 13, 15, 26, 28, 40, 49, 52, 75; establishment of republics in, 81; labour surpluses, 94; People's Council, 40
Central Asians, 71, 182, 192, 207, 209, 210, 213, 215, 216, 217, 218, 219, 220, 221, 223, 228, 230, 231, 232, 233, 234, 236, 239, 240, 242; Elites, 79; Interest in Turkey, 90
Chang Chi-chung, 129-130
Chechnia, 50, 51, 52, 54, 211, 215; Chechen-Ingush Republic, 216; Chechens, 225
Chernenko, Konstantin, xiv, 76, 160, 165
Ch'in Shita Huang-ti, 107
Chiang Kai-shek, 124, 126-127
China, People's Republic of, xii, 16, 28; New nationality policies, 95, 145-148
Chinese Islamic Association, 146
Crimea, 47, 63, 64
Crimean Tatars, 7, 12, 15, 18, 36, 216, 225
Cultural Revolution (PRC), 139-143, 146, 147

Daghestan, 42, 49, 50, 51, 52, 54, 60, 211, 215; Daghestani Bolsheviks, 50; Daghestani ghazis, 56
Daghestanis, 209
Dekanosov, 123-124
Denikin, 44, 46, 47, 49, 50, 213
Djan, Akhmed, 127
Dos Mohammedov, 40, 57

Enver Pasha, 11, 52, 53, 211
Estonia, Estonians, viii, 18, 66; Estonian military units under German supervision in WW II, 160, 169, 170, 174
Estonian Party, 167, 171
Evangelical Christians, 194

Fainsod, Merle, 78
Finland, 83, 210
Finns, 36
Fireworshippers, 77

Georgia, Georgians, viii, 8, 12, 16, 17, 18, 19, 22, 23, 27, 42, 58; Georgian separarist movement, 44; Georgian Mensheviks, 49, 51, 64, 67, 71, 166, 188, 210, 217; Georgian Orthodox Church; 186, 187, 188
Germans, viii, 8, 18, 190, 233
German policy towards soviet union in WW II, 62, 63-65, 86-87
'Great Game', 87-88
Greeks, viii, 3, 10, 11
Gypsies, 8

Hami revolt, 112-113
Hispanics, 3, 5, 22
Hitler, 15, 28, 63, 66, 69, 70, 71
Hummet Party, 41

Ibrahim Beg, 52, 54
Imam Shamil, 12, 50
India; Soviet-Indian Friendship Treaty, 102
Ingush, 225
Iran, xii, 16, 17, 55, 90-91, 217
Islam, 9, 12, 17, 18, 31, 45, 55; arrival in Central Asia, 104-107; in China, 131-133, 145-147; influence in USSR from abroad, 92-94; jihad, 52, 106-107, 212, 215; overlap with nationality, 104-107; renaissance in USSR, 96-97, 101
Ismail bey Gaspraly, 209, 224
Ismaili (Nazarit), 227

Jehovah's Witnesses, 195, 197, 198
Jews, viii, 8, 18, 21, 77; Russian, in the US, 3; Jewish autonomous region of Birobidzhan, 14, 233
John Paul II (Pope), 171, 172, 173
Judaism, 193, 197
Junayd Khan, 52, 54

Kabardians, 209
Karachais, 225
Karakalpaks, 52
Kasimov Tatars, 209, 224
Kazakhs, 12, 21, 36; *Alash Orda*, 40, 41, 43, 47, 48, 57, 208, 209, 212; in China, 111, 112, 126-128, 135-136, 138-143; Kazakh steppes, 210
Kazakhstan, 192, 216
Kazan, 38, 40, 214
Kemal Ataturk, Mustafa, 11, 13, 89
Khorezm, 103
Khrushchev, Nikita, 187, 194, 217, 220

Index

Kiev, 8, 38, 158, 166, 171, 172
Kirghiz, 43, 52, 66; Second Pan-Kirghiz Congress, 40
Kokand, 103
Kolchak, Admiral, 43, 44, 46, 47, 48, 53, 212
Koreans, viii; in the US, 3
Kornilov, General, 42
Krym, Salomon, 44, 47
Kuban Cossacks, 44
Kuldja Group, 129-130
Kunayev, Dinmukhamed, 78
Kuomintang, 127, 129
Kurds, 217; Kurdish question, 89; Kurdistan, 217

Latvia, Latvians, viii, 18, 38; Catholic Church in, 172; Latvian army under German supervision, 74, 160, 163, 166, 170, 171, 174; Latvian Party, 167; Latvian Rifle Regiment, 38, 42, 62, 66
Lenin, Leninism, viii, ix, 1, 11, 33, 45, 48, 53, 62, 77, 212, 230
Lithuania, Lithuanians, viii, 8, 17, 62, 66, 163, 166, 168, 170, 171, 173; Catholic Church in, 172, 187, 188; Lithuanian Party, 158, 167, 169
Lutherans, 227; of Latvia, 190; of Estonia, 190
Lvov, 8, 65, 197

Ma Ch'ung-ying, 113-117
Ma Shao-wu, 114
Mao Tse-tung, 101, 130
Marx, 1, 212
Marxism-Leninism, 24, 142, 144-145, 181, 219, 220, 222; Marxist-Leninist parties, 167; Marxist-Leninists, 213, 214
Meskhetian Turks, 216, 225
Minsk, 8
Moldavia, Moldavians, 85, 182, 191; Moldavian Church, 185
Mongolia, Mongols, 107, 108, 110, 126, 128
Muslims; All-Russian Muslim Military Congress, 1917, 38; 'East Legion' military units under German supervision, 72; Muslim separatist movement, 44, 68, 71, 72; Soviet, xiii, 8, 9, 12, 16, 17, 18, 19, 22, 23, 25, 27, 28, 30, 36-60, 77
Mustafa Chokay, 40

Nariman Narimanov, 44
Narkomnats (People's Commissariat of Nationalities), 45, 213
National Communists, 45, 211-212
Nationalism, ix, x, 10, 11, 12, 13, 16, 42, 81; Armenian, 12; Lithuanian, 187; Muslim, 54, 214, 229, 242, 207-226; Russian, xiii, 24-25, 181-182, 185; Tatar nationalists, 41; Ukrainian, 66, 187; Ukrainian nationalist groups in 1941, 65
Nationalism; and religion, 171-174, 181-199
Nepal, 102
Nestorian Christians, 227
North Manchurian Army, 114
Novikov, General, 111

Odessa, 8
Old Believers, 190-191
Orenburg Cossacks, 40, 44, 46, 47, 48, 53, 58
Orthodox Christianity, Christian Orthodox (Eastern), viii, 8, 77, 185, 227
Ossetians, 209, 225
Ottoman Empire, x, 1, 2, 8, 10, 30-31, 33, 88, 108; millet system, 10

Pakistan, 102
Pan-Turkism, 11, 55, 89, 214; Turkic renaissance in USSR, 96-97
'Peitachan Affair', 128-129
Penitents (*pokutnyky*), 195
Pentecostals, 194, 197
Persian empire, 88
Persian Gulf, 88
Pogodin, General, 117
Poland, xi, 17, 30, 31, 158
Poles, viii, 8, 12, 32, 36, 158, 210, 245; Polish minority in Eastern Galicia, 189
Protestants, 77

Radio Liberty, 28, 176
Rashidov, Saraf, 78
Romania, Romanians, 11, 66, 245
Roosevelt, Franklin D., 126-127
Rosenberg, Alfred, 64, 65
RSFSR, Russian Republic, 21, 26
Russian Catacomb Church, 196
Russian émigré church, 198
Russian Empire, xii, 1, 2, 8, 10, 12, 13, 62, 77, 184, 241; Expansion into Central Asia, 102-104, 108

251

Index

Russian language, 80
Russian Orthodoxy, 181, 182, 193; Russian Orthodox church, 184, 185, 186, 189, 197
Russian Revolution (1917), 36, 37, 75, 76, 210, 211-215
Russians, xiii, 8, 13, 16, 17, 18, 19, 20, 22, 24, 26, 27, 31, 32, 36, 42, 61, 66; 'Great Russia', 64, 73, 207, 209, 228, 229, 233
Russification, viii, 18, 80, 182, 184
Ryskulov, Turar, 44, 55, 214, 215

Sabri, Masud, 129
Saifuddin (Saif ad-Din), 130-131, 134
Sakharov, Andrei, 76
Samizdat, 25, 158, 169, 170, 188, 194
Sarts, 34
Sblizhenie, 5, 6, 162
Self-determination, 28, 45
Semirechie Cossacks, 44, 48, 53
Serbia, Serbs, 10, 11, 245
Seventh Day Adventists, 194, 197
Shang Pei-yuan, 115
Sheng Shi-chi, 124
Sheng Shih-ts'ai, 115, 118, 121, 124-127
Shiite Islam, 207, 211, 214, 215, 216, 217, 218, 219, 220, 221, 222, 223, 227
Siberia, 7, 15, 18, 19, 28, 192, 216
Simferopol, 40, 45; massacre, 46
Sino-Soviet relations, 101-157; Chuguchak Protocol, 102; Soviet use of separatist movements, 109; Treaty of Friendship and Alliance, 127; Treaty of Kiatkha, 107; Treaty of Nerchinski, 107; Treaty of Peking, 102; Treaty of St. Petersburg, 102
Sliianie, 5, 6, 162
Solidarity (movement in Poland), 158, 166, 167, 168, 169, 170, 171
Solzhenitsyn, Aleksandr, 76
Soviet armed forces, 22, 35, 79-80, 227-248; Russian language in, 236-238
Soviet Union; Census, viii, xii, 20, 225; Communist Party of, vii-viii, xiii, xiv; Democratic National Front of, 170; Gulag system, 14; leaders, 27, 28; military structure, 14; nationality question, viii, ix, 7, 28, 159-163, 185, 210; New Soviet Man, ix, 6, 25, 27, 96, 239; 'Soviet people', 186; trade unions, 164, 167

Stalin, 15, 28, 48, 54, 55, 56, 62, 73, 185, 187, 211, 213, 214, 215, 216, 217, 219, 230; nationalities policy, 185
Sufi brotherhoods, 54; Naqshbandiya, 42, 43, 46, 49, 50, 51, 54, 57, 211, 215; Qadiriya, 54; *Vaisov Boznii Polk* ('God's Own Regiment'), 39, 41, 54, 57, 215-216, 221
Sultan Galiev, 15, 43, 45, 46, 55, 213, 214, 219
Sunnite Islam, 227
Suslov, Mikhail, 84

Taipov, Zunun, 138
Tajiks, xii, 52, 217, 220
Tamizdat, 25
Tashkent, 16, 20, 39, 41, 53, 214, 218, 220, 222
Tatars, 38, 39, 46, 59; Harbi Shura (Tatar military Committee) 1917, 38, 39, 40, 41, 46; khanates, 76, 207, 208, 209, 210, 212, 218; Milli Firka (Nationalist Party), 40, 46, 47; National Assembly (Millet Mijlisi) 1917, 40, 41; National Tatar Directory (Milli Idare) 1917, 40, 41, 47; Tatar Legion (1917), 209
Tbilisi, 8
Tekke Turkmens, 209
Terek Cossacks, 44, 49, 50
Tibet, 88
Tsalikov, Ahmed, 40
Tsin Shu-yen, 112-115, 118
Turkestan, Turkestanis, 34, 36, 39, 41, 43, 48, 53, 56, 59; destruction of unity, 102-104; East Turkestan, 101-157; Republic of East Turkestan, 127, 129; Turkestan Commission, 53, 64, 72, 208, 209, 210
Turkey, xii, 11, 28, 55, 67, 71, 88-90, 217
Turkmens, 217
Turkmenistan, 21, 54
Turks, 9, 12, 31, 49

Ukraine, 7, 18, 26, 30, 46, 61, 63, 64, 65, 67, 68, 69, 83, 85-87; geopolitical position of, 86-87; Western Ukraine, 62, 63, 77, 160, 164, 165, 167, 168, 171, 172, 173, 175, 184, 185, 187, 189, 190, 195, 196, 197, 233; Western Ukrainian Republic,

Index

189; Ukrainian Autocephalous Church, 185, 197; Ukrainian Greek Catholic (Uniate) Church, 172-173, 185, 187, 188-190, 195, 197; Ukrainian Orthodox Church, 184
Ukrainians, viii, x, xi, 8, 12, 18, 23, 27, 28, 29, 80; Eastern Ukrainians, 233; in the US, 3; military unit, 'Bohdan Khmelnitski', 38; nationalism, 66; nationalist military organisation (UPA), 70; nationalist organisation, 167; separatist movement, 44, 65, 70; Ukrainian cossacks, 76, 228, 229, 245, 158, 174, 175, 182, 186, 190; Ukrainian Helsinki Group, 170
'Unequal treaties' (Sino-Soviet), 101-102, 107
United Nations, 29; Human Rights Commission, 170
United States, x, 1, 2, 3, 7, 18, 19, 20, 21, 25, 33
Ural Cossacks, 44, 48, 53, 58
Usman Batur, 126-129
Uzbeks, xii, 12, 16, 20, 23, 27, 52, 243, 217, 220

Uzbekistan, 215
Uzun Haji, 50, 51, 215, 222

Veli Ibrahimov, 47
Vilno, Vilnius, 8, 174
Volga Germans, 15
Volga Tatars, 7, 12, 18, 36, 40; Central National Council (*Milli Stuna*), 40, 41, 209, 210, 223

Walesa, Lech, 169, 170
Wallace, Henry A., 126-127
Wang En-mao, 134
World War I, 15, 33
World War II, x, 6, 15, 16, 18, 23, 61-74, 209, 216, 230, 231, 241, 244
Wrangel, General, 44, 47

Xinjiang, 88; border dynamics, 94-96, 101-157; Soviet economic interest in 111, 113, 118-129

Yang Tseng-hsin, 110-113, 118
Ya'qub Beg, 108-109

Zeki Validov, Ahmed, 38, 40, 41, 47, 48, 212
Zionists, 193

253